SECOND EDITION

FUNDAMENTAL STATISTICS FOR PSYCHOLOGY

SECOND EDITION

FUNDAMENTAL STATISTICS FOR PSYCHOLOGY

Robert B. McCall
The Fels Research Institute and Antioch College

Under the General Editorship of
JEROME KAGAN
Harvard University

HARCOURT BRACE JOVANOVICH, INC.
New York   Chicago   San Francisco   Atlanta

ISBN: 0–15–529413–X

Library of Congress Catalog Card Number: 74–34524

Printed in the United States of America

PREFACE

This book is designed for undergraduates in the behavioral sciences who are taking a first course in applied statistics. Although most of the examples are from psychology and education, the topics are taken from basic descriptive and inferential statistics and are therefore appropriate to a variety of disciplines. In order to give students a thorough understanding of the fundamentals, I have emphasized concepts and presented relatively few specific techniques.

The material can be thoroughly understood with no more mathematical background than high school algebra and geometry. Those students needing a review of these concepts should read through Appendix I and check themselves with the accompanying exercises.

My goal has been to help the student develop an understanding of the rationale, application, and interpretation of each concept. I have tried to discuss the logic of each formula, with frequent reference to graphic illustrations. Occasionally I have presented contrasting sets of data to enable the student to observe the "behavior" of the statistic under different circumstances; some sections are devoted to specific circumstances that alter the interpretation of a statistical result. The problems and questions at the end of each chapter are designed to test not only the student's command of the correct use and computation of a statistic but also, more important, the student's conceptual understanding of its logic and purpose.

Consequently, several special features have been included to facilitate learning: (1) Important definitions are set off in distinctive type. (2) Mathematical derivations and proofs have been kept to a minimum and are presented in Optional Tables, which the student may skip altogether or may refer to without losing the train of thought of the text proper. (3) No steps are omitted in algebraic proofs or derivations, and the reason for each step is given. (4) The use of statistical tables is explained at each table as well as in the text. (5) Symbols are accompanied by their verbal name several times, so that the reader has more than one opportunity to associate the meaning with the symbol. (6) Concepts and formulas are briefly reviewed as needed.

Instructors who have used the first edition of the book will find several major modifications in this edition. The optional chapter on probability has been shortened and placed at the beginning of the discussion of statistical inference. The introduction to hypothesis testing is now presented in two short chapters rather than one long one. The text has been simplified where possible by rewriting major sections, eliminating peripheral topics (e.g., *F*-test for two independent variances, *t*-test for two groups having heterogeneous variances, the second regression line, and advanced topics in probability), and expanding for greater clarity (e.g., the sections on confidence limits and power-efficiency).

The principles guiding the text are also evident in the *Study Guide,* a new learning aid that accompanies this edition of the book. The *Study Guide* is not simply a collection of fill-in-the-blanks or extra computational problems. Rather, it reviews the major concepts presented in the text in a simple, straightforward style. Concepts are presented and discussed in terms of simple numerical examples. Moreover, the *Study Guide* requires the student to observe what a statistic means by computing several contrasting examples in which data are changed to illustrate how the statistic is affected. The *Study Guide* also contains a Self-Test for each chapter and additional computational problems with solutions. Finally, structured tables provide an outline of the form and sequence that computational procedures should follow.

The book has been organized so that the instructor may emphasize descriptive and correlational methods, inferential statistics, or both. Chapters 1 through 6 cover basic descriptive and correlational techniques. Chapter 7 presents a thorough introduction to probability, which can be omitted without loss of continuity. Chapters 8 and 9 introduce hypothesis testing and include the concepts of sampling distribution and sampling error, a brief statement of the role of probability, and the terminology, rationale, and strategy of statistical inference. The most common elementary statistical tests are described and illustrated in Chapter 10; presentations of simple and two-factor analysis of variance follow in Chapters 11 and 12. A final chapter contains a selection of nonparametric techniques. Thus, the core chapters are 1 through 4 and 8 and 9, to which instructors will add at their option material on correlation and regression (Chapters 5 and 6), probability (Chapter 7), simple techniques of statistical inference (Chapter 10), the analysis of variance (Chapters 11 and 12), and nonparametric procedures (Chapter 13).

Many people shared their time and knowledge with me as I prepared successive drafts of the manuscript. The incisive comments of Mark Appelbaum of the Psychometric Laboratory of the University of North Carolina at Chapel Hill were invaluable as I tried to blend my personal approach to teaching the subject matter with the demands of formal theory. Edward Hoffman of Kenyon College, John E. Milholland of the University of Michigan, and Julian C. Stanley of The Johns Hopkins University criticized the entire manuscript for the first edition, and many of their technical suggestions have been retained in this revision. Jerome Kagan of Harvard University has been a source of great encouragement since the inception of the book. I thank Cindy Bellows, who graciously assisted me in preparing exercises, and Debbie Anderson, Bob Engstrom, Bob Rappaport, Ann Weisler, and Becky Zwick, who painstakingly student-tested every word and exercise. I am also grateful to the many users of the text who communicated with me directly.

The book could not have been written without the help and patience of my own teachers—Ray Frankmann, Lloyd Humphreys, William Kappauf, Ledyard Tucker, and Donald Burkholder.

I am grateful to the Literary Executor of the late Sir Ronald A. Fisher, F.R.S., to Dr. Frank Yates, F.R.S., to Longman Group Ltd., London, for permission to reprint Tables III, IV, VII, and XXXIII from their book *Statistical Tables for Biological, Agricultural and Medical Research* (6th edition, 1974), and to the Samuel S. Fels Fund and The Fels Research Institute for their support of this project.

In many respects, a statistics book represents an uncommonly frustrating production. Therefore, I am very grateful to Joanne Steinhilber who organized and typed the entire manuscript, to Cindy Bellows and Carol Dodds who assisted me in proofreading, and to Mary Garvey, Judy Greissman, and Ellen Okin of Harcourt Brace Jovanovich, Inc., who translated the manuscript into book form.

Special thanks go to my wife, Rozanne, for her encouragement and for the absence of complaints while she was temporarily widowed for this cause.

ROBERT B. McCALL

CONTENTS

THE STUDY OF STATISTICS

1

measurement and the statistical method

One can find measurement everywhere in our society. It exists from the measurement of flight times between major cities to the intricate calibration of manned rockets. **Measurement** is the systematic assignment of numbers to objects or events, and it forms the very basis of science. If an event or attribute cannot be measured, it does not find its way into the domain of science.

The result of scientific observation is usually a collection of measurements. These measurements are called **data. Statistics** is the study of methods of handling such quantitative information, including techniques for organizing and summarizing as well as for making generalizations and inferences from data. These methods can be grouped into two broad classes. First, the term **descriptive statistics** refers to procedures for organizing, summarizing, and describing quantitative information or data. Most people are partially familiar with this aspect of statistics. The baseball fan is accustomed to checking over a favorite player's batting average, the sales manager relies on charts showing the sales distribution and cost-efficiency of an enterprise, the head of a household may consult articles describing the average domestic expenditures of families of comparable size and income, and the actuary possesses charts outlining the life expectancy of people in various professions. These are relatively simple statistical tools which facilitate the description of data, but additional techniques also are available to describe such things as the extent to which measured values deviate from one another and the relationship between performance of one kind and that of another. For example, what is the degree of relationship between scores on a college entrance examination and later performance in college?

The second major aspect of statistics, known as **inferential statistics**, concerns the methods by which inferences are made to a larger group on the basis of observations made on a smaller subgroup. For example, suppose a social psychologist wished to compare two approaches to changing people's attitudes about a given political issue. Specifically, are attitudes changed more easily if the persuader adopts a position just slightly different from the original attitude of the people being converted or if the persuader presents a very extreme stand? To study this question, two groups of people might be given an attitude questionnaire. Then each group is exposed to a persuader who attempts to change their attitude about a given political issue. For one group, the persuader presents a statement that is slightly more positive than the original opinion of the people, whereas for the other group the statement is considerably more positive than their initial feelings. Later, a similar attitude questionnaire is again given to the people to determine whether one group shifted their attitude about the issue more than the other.

Suppose this experiment is performed and the first group averages an 8-point change in attitude while the second group averages a 5-point change. These data show that for the subjects studied, a small discrepancy between original attitude and the tenor of the persuasion produces more attitude change than a large discrepancy. However, a more interesting question is whether this would be true for every set of two groups tested. That is, is this observation of an average difference of 8 versus 5 only a "chance" finding, one to be expected simply because people differ from one another, or is this difference sufficiently large that it cannot be attributed to more or less random differences among people or groups of people?

One feels some uncertainty about answering this question. People do differ from one another in their attitudes, and though the group exposed to only a slightly more positive political stand changed their attitudes more *on the average* than the other group, not all individuals in the slight-discrepancy group changed more than even the majority of people in the extreme group. We are faced with the question of how much difference in average attitude change between groups is enough to warrant the conclusion that the observed group difference is not simply a result of chance differences known to occur among people and groups of people?

What is needed is some way to quantify the uncertainty that one feels about this decision so that it would be possible to say that in n of every 100 such experiments one should expect a difference of this magnitude or greater between the groups purely by "chance" factors associated with the particular subjects selected to be in the observations. If the likelihood is high that the observed difference is just "lucky" or due to chance, then one might conclude that the two persuasion strategies probably do not differentially affect the degree of attitude change. Conversely, if the likelihood is quite small that the observed difference is due to chance, then perhaps the two strategies do, in fact, determine the differing amounts of attitude change. This quantification of uncertainty is done with **probability**, and the task of statistical inference is to attach a probability value to the validity of certain statements, often for the purpose of making inferential decisions.

One common kind of decision that scientists are often required to make occurs when a theory is tested. A scientific theory attempts to explain certain phenomena. Deductions are made from the theory which predict what will happen in a special experimental situation. The experiment is executed and the data are evaluated to decide whether or not they are in accord with the theory. Usually, one cannot tell simply by looking at the numbers generated by an experiment in social science whether the data are consistent with the theoretical predictions or not. People do not score the same, even when each is measured under identical circumstances, and scientists need a method to conveniently deal with this kind of uncertainty and enable them to decide for or against the theory. Statistical procedures are often used to make this decision.

Thus, statistics is the study of methods of handling data. Descriptive statistics organizes, summarizes, and describes data, while making inferences from small to larger groups of subjects or events is the province of inferential statistics.

the study of statistics

WHY IS STATISTICS NECESSARY?

A knowledge of statistics is important, both to be able to conduct and analyze data from social science experiments and to read, understand, and interpret research results published in textbooks and journals. Statistics is required primarily because almost all data in the social sciences contains **variability**. Variability refers to the fact that the scores or measurement values differ from one another, even when the people were all assessed under the same circumstances. If you administered an IQ test to all the people in your statistics class, they would not all obtain the same IQ or value. Similarly, all rats tested in a multiple-T maze do not make the same number of errors. Recall that in the preceding persuasion example it was this same notion of variability that made it difficult to decide whether one technique of persuasion was better than another.

There is variability in social science data for at least three reasons. First, social scientists are not always able to agree on how to measure a concept, even one as apparently straightforward as "learning." If a rat is to learn to solve a T-maze problem, shall we assess its learning by the number of errors it makes, the length of time it takes to get to the end of the maze, the number of trials required before it makes an errorless trial (or two trials), etc.? These different scores (and others) have all been used to measure learning in psychological experiments, but they do not all reflect the same behavioral attribute and they do not all yield the same results. Thus, any single type of measurement is often incomplete and inaccurate in reflecting the concept we really wish to study.

Second, the units (e.g., people, animals, etc.) which social scientists measure are rarely identical to one another. A chemist or a physicist measures the behavior of molecules, atoms, electrons, etc. and assumes that each of the units is identical in its composition and behavior to every other unit of its kind. But the social scientist is not so fortunate. The assumption cannot be made that all people will respond similarly in a given situation. In fact, the social scientist can count on the fact that they will not respond the same. This constitutes variability attributable to **individual differences** in the behavior of different subjects.

Third, even a single unit (e.g., person, animal) does not respond the same way on two different occasions. If you have a person step on a sensitive scale 10 times in succession, the scale will probably record the same weight each time. But if you give a person several opportunities to rate the attractiveness of advertising displays or the degree of aggressiveness in filmed episodes of each of 15 nursery school children, you will not be likely to get the same scores on each occasion. This type of variability is called **unreliability**.

Variability means that less faith can be placed in a single score. Therefore, it may be necessary either to measure a single subject several times or to assess many different subjects or events in order to have confidence that the data faithfully reflect the characteristics being studied.

The fact that measurement is crude, that a variety of factors other than those being studied frequently govern the behavior of interest, and that one subject is not the same as the next, all conspire to make it difficult to draw conclusive decisions about the results of controlled observations. It is the task of statistics to quantify the variability in a set of measurements, to describe the data for a group of subjects despite the variability inherent in the measurements, and to derive precisely stated and consistent decisions about the results by quantifying the uncertainty produced by such variability.

WHY STUDY STATISTICS?

There are good reasons for studying statistics. First, if a person ever expects to intelligently read and evaluate social science literature, a knowledge of statistics is almost essential. Obviously, to design and carry out experiments, one will have to describe the results and make inferences from data, which will require a knowledge of statistical techniques. It is for this reason that statistics is usually required of undergraduate and graduate students in many of the social sciences.

However, even those who will never be researchers themselves will want to maintain an acquaintance with certain topics, perhaps because many professions require application of research literature (e.g., a clinical psychologist, a special education teacher, etc.). They will be expected to comprehend and evaluate detailed research literature, much of which is couched in statistical terms. For example, it is of considerable interest to a psychologist, an educator, a teacher, and a parent, to know the relative contributions of heredity and environment to intelligence. Although the question is not really an either-or problem, it is often conceived in that manner. For example, a correlation (degree of relationship) of .35 was found between the intelligence of adopted children and the intelligence of their biological mothers, but child IQ correlated only .09 with the intelligence of the mothers who reared those children.[1] Yet, the average IQ of the children was approximately equal to the average IQ of their rearing mothers and much higher than that of their biological mothers. The correlations seem to support heredity while the averages appear to favor environment as the more powerful determinant of intelligence. How is this possible? What does it mean to have a correlation or a difference between means? How shall this collection of information be interpreted? A knowledge of statistics—even the basic introduction that this book will hopefully provide—would answer these questions (e.g., see pp. 227–29).

Therefore, it should be clear that if the individual is going to produce research or evaluate the reports of others, some knowledge of statistical principles is necessary. Consequently, if the student expects to attend graduate school in any of a variety of disciplines, this course will but foreshadow a far deeper and broader encounter with such quantitative procedures.

But what about the student who does not expect to attend graduate school and who will probably not read professional scientific literature? Of what benefit can a study of statistics be? First, rudimentary statistics finds its way into the communications media. For example, the **average** (mean) family income in the United States is higher than the **median** income, yet both are used as measures of typical incomes. Why are they different, and which is more appropriate as an expression of typical income? Consider another set of facts once reported in newspapers and magazines[2] across the country and not atypical of presentations that may prompt unreasoned conclusions. Ordinarily, at conception each person is given 23 pairs of chromosomes, and these determine much of the individual's development. One such pair of chromosomes determines the sex of the individual. If this pair is XX a female results, whereas if the pair is XY a male results. Occasionally, in the course of the generation of sex cells, an extra chromosome is contributed to a cell such that the result is XYY. This person is a male, tends to be approximately six inches taller than the average, and has other distinguishing characteristics. Interestingly, among male

---

[1] M. Skodak and H. M. Skeels, "A final follow-up study of one-hundred adopted children," *Journal of Genetic Psychology*, 1949, LXXV, 85–125.
[2] *Time*, May 3, 1968, 41.

prisoners the incidence of an XYY condition has been estimated to be 60 times more common than in the general population. What does such a statistic imply? Does this argue for giving each male individual a chromosomal analysis and keeping track of the XYY people or even restricting their freedom? Does this observation mean that the XYY grouping causes hyperaggressiveness or criminal behavior? Again a knowledge of statistics might help in interpreting these data.

Lastly, a course in statistics, like a course in logic, generally breeds a healthy skepticism in its participants for the way they approach issues and problems, statistical or otherwise. Consider the preceding information on genetic combinations and criminals.[3] Suppose that an XYY combination occurs once in every 2000 male births. For convenience, assume there are 100,000,000 males in the United States and 120,000 men in prisons. Therefore, in the general population there are approximately 50,000 men in the country with an XYY combination, only 3600 of which (7.2%) are in prison. Is one then to set up a program to observe or even restrict the liberty of 50,000 men when 46,400 of them are not likely to cause any trouble? The point here is that a person experienced with statistics would be more likely to treat these issues with skepticism than one not acquainted with statistics.

measurement

One of the major functions of statistics is to describe efficiently the nature of (1) experimental results, (2) observations on large groups of subjects, and (3) relationships between two different types of measurement. The next chapter presents a basic method of describing the nature of a group of measurements—the frequency distribution. However, the description depends in part on how the measurements were made, so it is necessary first to discuss some terminology and characteristics of the measurement process.

SCALES OF MEASUREMENT

properties of scales   A major concern about a measurement technique is that it faithfully reflect the attribute being measured. For example, if one wants to measure the heights of people in the class, it is necessary to have a number scale that indeed reflects the "tallness" of the class members. Although this proposition appears trivial at first, it happens that in many sciences the concepts of interest to the scientist can only be measured in relatively rudimentary ways. For example, suppose a researcher wanted a single number that would represent the aggressiveness of children in a given nursery

---

[3] The incidence and implication of an XYY configuration are still being debated.

school. One method might be to have a clinical psychologist interview and then rate the subjects from 1 through 10 according to the extent of their aggressiveness. The important question for the present discussion is what are the general mathematical attributes of the scale of aggressiveness created by rating the children from 1 to 10?

What attributes can a measurement scale possibly have? For this discussion there are three: **magnitude, equal intervals**, and an **absolute zero point.**

> When a scale has **magnitude,** one instance of the attribute can be judged greater than, less than, or equal to another instance of the attribute.

If the clinical psychologist in the preceding example assigns a score of 8 to John and a score of 5 to Harry, this scale of measurement reflects the difference in magnitude of aggressiveness in the two boys—John is more aggressive than Harry.

Another attribute a scale may possess is equal intervals.

> **Equal intervals** denotes that the magnitude of the attribute represented by a unit of measurement on the scale is equal regardless of where on the scale the unit falls.

Take the measurement of height in inches as an example. One is confident that the difference in height between someone measuring 61 inches versus someone measuring 60 inches is the same magnitude as the difference in height that exists between someone measuring 75 inches versus someone measuring 74 inches. In short, an inch reflects a certain amount of height regardless of where that inch falls on the scale. However, consider the year-end baseball standings in the National League. This simple ordering of teams is a crude scale of the baseball prowess of these teams. But, if Cincinnati edges out Atlanta by a half game for first place while third place goes to San Francisco which is eight games behind the two leaders, we somehow feel that the difference between Cincinnati and Atlanta is less than between Atlanta and San Francisco despite the fact that the standings place them equally apart—1, 2, 3. Thus, as a scale of team quality, the baseball standings do not possess the attribute of equal intervals because the difference in quality between two teams adjacent in the standings is not necessarily equal to the difference in quality of two other adjacent teams.

A third possible attribute of a scale is an absolute zero point.

> An **absolute zero point** is a value that indicates that nothing at all of the attribute being measured exists.

Thus, "0 inches" of height is a scale value that implies no height whatsoever—absolute zero. However, in the case of rating aggressiveness, the lowest score that the psychologist can assign (i.e., "1"), does not indicate "no aggressive tendencies whatsoever." A child receiving a score of "1" may still hit other children or verbally abuse them on occasion. The child displays little aggression only in a *relative* sense, and even if the value "0" were a part of the scale, it would not necessarily imply *absolutely* no aggressive behavior. Thus, the rating scale for aggressiveness does not possess an absolute zero point.

types of scales   It is clear from the previous discussion that if the attribute of height is measured in inches then the resulting scale has magnitude, equal intervals, and an absolute zero. Many of the measurements one makes in everyday life possess all three of these attributes.

> Any scale of measurement possessing magnitude, equal intervals, and an absolute zero point is called a **ratio scale.**

This scale is termed "ratio" because the collection of properties that it possesses allows ratio statements to be made about the attribute being measured. If an adult is 70 inches tall and a child is 35 inches, it is correct to infer that the adult is twice as tall as the child. Such ratio statements may be made only if the scale possesses all three of these characteristics.

Not all scales used in research in psychology, education, sociology, etc. are ratio scales. That is, many attributes cannot be measured with scales that reflect all three of these properties.

> An **interval scale** possesses the attributes of magnitude and equal intervals but not an absolute zero point.

The most common example of an interval scale is the scale for measurement of temperature in degrees Fahrenheit. Although from the standpoint of physics or chemistry the absolute zero point is reached when all molecular movement ceases, for all practical purposes there is no point at which one says that there is no temperature whatsoever.[4] Note that neither 0° Fahrenheit nor 0° centigrade denotes the point at which there is no temperature at all, i.e., absolute zero. Further, if the temperature today is 30° and yesterday it was 15° one does not proclaim that it is "twice as hot" today as yesterday. Ratio statements cannot be made without an absolute zero point. In contrast, the temperature scale does possess the properties of magnitude and equal intervals. For example, 25° is a greater temperature than 19°, and the difference between 50° and 40° represents the same difference in temperature as the difference between 90° and 100°. Hence, the temperature scale has the attributes of magnitude and equal intervals,

---

[4] The Kelvin scale of temperature does have an absolute zero and therefore is a type of ratio scale.

but not absolute zero. Therefore, it is an interval scale.

Some scales have only one of the three attributes discussed previously.

An **ordinal scale** reflects only magnitude and does not possess the attributes of equal intervals or an absolute zero point.

For example, take the people in the class and line them up according to height, and then rather than measuring them with a tape measure merely rank them according to their height, the shortest receiving a rank of "1," the next tallest "2," etc. The result is an ordinal scale of height.

Clearly the scale has the attribute of magnitude but does it possess equal intervals? In order to assess this, one must be aware of the distinction between the scale and the aspect of nature which the scale is supposed to measure. The rank order constitutes the scale, but the scale is being used to assess the height of people in the class. Consider the graphic example below:

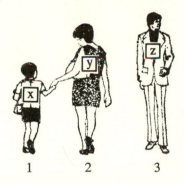

1   2   3

Although the ranking places these people at equally spaced locations on the scale (i.e., 1, 2, 3), the difference in height between persons X and Y is not the same as between Y and Z. Thus, the ranking scale of height does not possess equal intervals. Recall that the same was true for the baseball standings. Neither is there an absolute zero point since there is no ranking that always expresses "no height at all." Hence, the ranking of height produces an ordinal scale because it possesses the attribute of magnitude but not equal intervals or an absolute zero.

It is possible to have a "scale" which has none of the three attributes discussed in the preceding material, but one would hardly think of it as a "scale," a term usually reserved for measurements which at least imply differences in magnitude.

A **nominal "scale"** refers to the classification of items into discrete groups which do not bear any magnitude relationships to one another.

For example, if a person were to stand on a busy street corner and name cars, some classifications might be Ford, Chevrolet, Plymouth, etc. The dimension of classification is "make of car." However, one would not say that Ford is more or less of a "make of car" than is Chevrolet. It may be more or less expensive or appealing to the eye, but not more or less a make of car. Hence, grouping cars according to make represents a nominal scale, which does not possess the properties of magnitude, equal intervals, or an absolute zero point.

VARIABLES

variables versus constants   Most data consist of values of a variable. A **variable** is a type of quantity that may take on more than one value. If the quantity is the height in inches of members of a class, then height is a variable because the heights of members of the class may differ from one to another.

In contrast, a **constant** is a quantity which does not change its value within a given context. The mathematical symbol, π, is a constant because it always equals approximately 3.1416. Its value does not change. Thus, if one obtains the heights of people in a class in terms of inches and wishes to report these measurements in terms of feet, height would be considered a variable but the 12:1 conversion factor of inches to feet is a constant.

discrete versus continuous variables   Variables may be either **discrete** or **continuous**.

> A **discrete** variable is one for which there is a finite number of potential values that the variable can assume between any two points on the scale.

For example, a family can have only 1, or 2, or 3, etc. children. One does not think of a family having $1\frac{1}{2}$ children. Thus between the possible values of 1 and 3, there is only one other possible value, 2.

> A **continuous** variable is one which theoretically can assume an infinite number of values between any two points on the scale.

Consider, for example, weight measured in pounds. Even between 100 and 101 pounds there is an unlimited number of values possible. Time in seconds is another example of a continuous variable.

The discrete-continuous distinction is really a theoretical one, because in practice most variables are measured in such a way that one obtains only discrete scores. For example, IQ is a continuous variable but only whole numbers are actually obtained—no one speaks of a person having an IQ of $113\frac{1}{4}$.

Thus, regardless of how one goes about measuring a variable, it is continuous if *theoretically* there is an underlying dimension for the trait or behavior which permits an infinite number of values to be obtained if one had an ultimately sensitive instrument for measuring them. Therefore, just because a variable is measured only in whole numbers or because all numbers are rounded to the nearest tenth's digit, does not necessarily make that variable discrete.

Notice that the discrete-continuous distinction is applied to variables not to the type of scale used to measure them. A continuous variable and some discrete variables may be measured with ratio, interval, or ordinal scales. For example, IQ is a continuous variable because given a sufficiently fine instrument, theoretically there could be an infinite number of values between any two points. Yet, the current measurement of IQ is relatively crude and probably constitutes an ordinal scale if the extremes of the dimension are included.

REAL LIMITS

Since a continuous variable is one for which an infinite number of values exist between any two points on the scale, the actual measurements are rounded off and are therefore approximate. For example, the continuous variable of time may be measured in years, months, days, hours, minutes, seconds, milliseconds, etc. If one measured to the nearest second, it is clear that more refined approximations could be made with more sophisticated timers. Consequently, if a child is asked to solve a given mathematics problem and does so in "33 seconds," the value 33 probably does not mean "*exactly* 33 seconds" but "*approximately* 33 seconds." More precisely, it means between 32.5 and 33.5 seconds, which values are called the **real limits** of 33 seconds. The **lower real limit** is 32.5 because any number lower than this (e.g., 32.4) would be rounded to a whole number other than 33 seconds (i.e., 32), and the **upper real limit** is 33.5 because any number greater than this also would be rounded to a whole number other than 33 (i.e., 34).

> The **real limits** of a number are those points falling one-half a measurement unit above and one-half a measurement unit below that number.

To illustrate, if measurement is being made in whole seconds, the unit of measurement is one second and thus the real limits of 33 seconds are 32.5 seconds and 33.5 seconds, one-half unit (.5 second) below and one-half unit above 33 seconds, respectively.[5]

However, note that the definition states that the limits fall one-half *unit* above and below the number. Therefore, the real limits of 33 seconds are different for

---

[5] Technically, the upper real limit of 33 is not 33.5 but 33.49999 . . . . This degree of accuracy will not be necessary here.

measurements made in units other than whole seconds. Suppose that a stop watch is available and that the length of time to solve a problem is recorded in tenths of a second. In this case, the unit of measurement is .1 second and one-half unit is .05 second. Consequently, when measuring in tenths of a second the real limits of 33.0 are 32.95 and 33.05. Similarly, if measurement is made in hundredths of a second, the real limits of 33.00 are 32.995 and 33.005. These points are presented graphically in Figure 1–1.

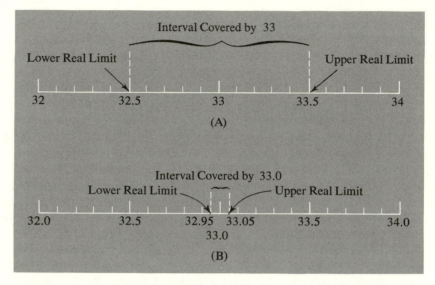

Fig. 1–1.   The real limits of 33 when the measurement unit is whole seconds (top) and when it is tenths of seconds (bottom).

ROUNDING

If measurements are taken in tenths of a second but are to be reported in terms of whole seconds, they are said to be **rounded** to the nearest whole second.

Numbers are **rounded** according to the following convention:
(a) If the remaining decimal fraction is less than .5 unit, drop the remaining decimal fraction.
(b) If the remaining decimal fraction is greater than .5 unit, increase the preceding digit by one.
(c) If the remaining decimal fraction is exactly .5 unit, add 1 to the preceding digit if that digit is an odd number but drop the remaining decimal fraction if the preceding digit is an even number.

For example, if the unit of measurement is a whole second and the value 33.4 is obtained, round this to 33 seconds in accordance with convention (a) above.

If the obtained value is 32.6, round to 33 in accordance with (b). If the obtained value is 34.5, convention (c) dictates to round to 34 because the preceding digit (i.e., 4) is even; but if 37.5 is to be rounded the result is 38 because the preceding digit (e.g., 7) is odd. Note, however, that 34.51 is rounded to 35 because the remaining decimal fraction is more than .5 unit (i.e., .51 is more than .50).

The reason that some numbers whose remaining decimal fractions are exactly .5 are rounded up and some are rounded down is so that over many instances of rounding numbers approximately half will be rounded up and half rounded down. In contrast, if a simple rule of always rounding .5 up were invoked, more numbers would be rounded up than down. By rounding some of these cases up and some down according to the convention outlined in (c), this "bias" is eliminated.

summation sign

Statistics are measures computed on a group of scores, and when formulas are given for statistics it is convenient to have some symbolic terminology to represent groups of scores and operations on groups rather than on single scores. Consider the group of five scores below:

Subject	Score Symbol	Score Value
1	X_1	2
2	X_2	3
3	X_3	8
4	X_4	4
5	X_5	7

Suppose we denote by the capital letter X the variable reflected by these scores. In actuality, it could be any kind of measurement—response time, number correct, eye movements per minute, etc. But since formulas can apply to any variable, it is convenient to symbolize the variable by some capital Roman letter (e.g., X, Y, V, etc.). (In contrast, when the value of a constant is unknown it is symbolized by a lower case letter, usually c or k.) There are five scores in the above group and each score represents a specific example of an X. In order to be able to distinguish one specific score from another, each X symbol is given a subscript corresponding to the number of the subject who made that score. Customarily, in a group of five scores, these subscripts would be 1, 2, 3, 4, 5. In general, if there are N scores, the subscripts would run from 1 to N. Frequently, it is useful to be able to refer to a single score, but not necessarily any particular one—just any single score in the distribution of X's. This single score is referred to as the ith score in the distribution and it is written X_i. Thus, in this example the distribution of all the X_i has five scores, and if one refers to X_i where $i = 3$ one refers to X_3 which has a score value of 8.

In later chapters of this book it will be necessary to consider more than one group of scores of the same type of measurement. In this case, in order to specify a particular score it is necessary to indicate both the group and the subject within that group. Two subscripts are used to accomplish this type of score designation. For example, any particular score would be written X_{ij}, where i indicates the subject number and j specifies the group number. The score for the fourth subject in the third group would be designated as X_{43}. This topic will be considered again in the sections on the analysis of variance.

One of the most frequent operations performed in statistics consists of summing all or a portion of the scores in a group. For example, in computing the average of a group of measurements, one sums all the scores and divides by the number of scores. However, when writing the formula for the average it is cumbersome to use

$$\text{Average} = \frac{\text{sum of all the scores}}{\text{the number of scores}}$$

Usually, N is used to symbolize the number of scores in the distribution, but the operation of summing all the scores also requires a symbolic abbreviation because it occurs in so many formulas.

The Greek capital letter sigma, $\sum$, is employed to indicate the operation of summing. This summation sign is often used in the symbolic phrase

$$\sum_{i=1}^{N} X_i$$

The small notations under and over the $\sum$ are called the "limits of the summation." The entire symbol is read, "sum of the X_i from $i = 1$ to N." It means to add X_1 plus X_2 plus . . . plus X_N. In symbols,

$$\sum_{i=1}^{N} X_i = X_1 + X_2 + X_3 + \cdots + X_N$$

Thus, $\sum_{i=1}^{5} X_i$ signifies the sum of the first five X scores and $\sum_{i=2}^{4} X_i$ means the sum of the second through the fourth X_i scores, inclusive. In terms of the above data,

$$\sum_{i=1}^{5} X_i = 2 + 3 + 8 + 4 + 7 = 24$$

and

$$\sum_{i=2}^{4} X_i = 3 + 8 + 4 = 15$$

Often, when all the scores in a distribution are to be summed, the limits of the summation are not written and the subscript i is omitted:

$$\Sigma \, X \text{ implies } \sum_{i=1}^{N} X_i$$

There are three short cuts for using the summation sign in algebraic operations which will help the student in working with the summation sign.

1. **The sum of a constant times a variable equals the constant times the sum of the variable.** If c is a constant and X_i a variable,

$$\sum_{i=1}^{N} cX_i = c \sum_{i=1}^{N} X_i$$

To understand why this is true, consider what the expression $\sum_{i=1}^{N} cX_i$ means:

$$\sum_{i=1}^{N} cX_i = cX_1 + cX_2 + cX_3 + \cdots + cX_N$$

But, this series of terms may be factored in the same manner as

$$ca + cb = c(a + b)$$

with the following results:

$$\sum_{i=1}^{N} cX_i = c\underbrace{(X_1 + X_2 + X_3 + \cdots + X_N)}_{c\left(\sum_{i=1}^{N} X_i\right)}$$

Since the expression within the parentheses is what has been defined to be the $\sum_{i=1}^{N} X_i$, the sum of a constant times a variable is the constant times the sum of the variable:

$$\sum_{i=1}^{N} cX_i = c \sum_{i=1}^{N} X_i$$

2. **The sum of a constant taken N times is N times the constant.** If c is a constant,

$$\sum_{i=1}^{N} c = Nc$$

This fact can be seen by writing out the expression being considered.

$$\sum_{i=1}^{N} c = \underbrace{c + c + c + \cdots + c}_{N \text{ terms}}$$

The symbol $\sum\limits_{i=1}^{N} c$ implies adding N c's together. However, the operation of multiplication is precisely this repetitive addition, so that adding N c's is identical to multiplying c by N. Therefore, the sum of a constant c taken N times is Nc.

3. **The summation of a sum of variables is the sum of each of these variable sums.** If X and Y are variables,

$$\sum_{i=1}^{N} (X_i + Y_i) = \sum_{i=1}^{N} X_i + \sum_{i=1}^{N} Y_i$$

Again, writing out the expression,

$$\sum_{i=1}^{N} (X_i + Y_i) = (X_1 + Y_1) + (X_2 + Y_2) + \cdots + (X_N + Y_N)$$

removing parentheses,

$$= X_1 + Y_1 + X_2 + Y_2 + \cdots + X_N + Y_N$$

and regrouping produces

$$= \underbrace{X_1 + X_2 + \cdots + X_N}_{\sum\limits_{i=1}^{N} X_i} + \underbrace{Y_1 + Y_2 + \cdots + Y_N}_{\sum\limits_{i=1}^{N} Y_i}$$

$$\sum_{i=1}^{N} (X_i + Y_i) = \sum_{i=1}^{N} X_i + \sum_{i=1}^{N} Y_i$$

This result may be generalized to any number of terms. For example,

$$\sum(X_i + Y_i + W_i) = \sum X_i + \sum Y_i + \sum W_i$$

Understanding and being facile in the use of the summation sign is imperative in order to follow the mathematics presented in the rest of this text. The student is advised to practice the exercises for mastery in the use of the summation sign. In compensation, no new mathematics other than elementary algebra and geometry will be required to understand the material presented in this text. Moreover, most mathematical material will be presented in optional tables which may be skipped. If the reader feels a bit shaky about basic algebra, consulting Appendix I which presents a brief review and the appendix of the *Student Guide* which accompanies this text will help.

EXERCISES

1. Indicate the scale of measurement presented for each of the following concepts and justify your choice:
   (a) A social psychologist obtains a measure of leadership for 20 people in a group discussion by having an observer assign points (1 through 10) to each member of the group in accordance with the observer's judgment of leadership potential.

(b) A physiological psychologist weighs a rat before and three months after removing a portion of the animal's brain. The difference between the weights
(in grams) is used as a measure of weight gain in response to the operation.

(c) After making a response to a Rorschach inkblot the person is asked to report
the characteristics of the figure that prompted the stated interpretation. A
clinical psychologist determines whether the responses focused on the form,
color, or shading of the figure.

(d) Discuss the difference in the scales of temperature produced by the centigrade
versus the Kelvin methods. (The Kelvin method uses $-273\,^{\circ}C$ as its zero
point. This is the point at which all molecular movement ceases.)

2. Below is a set of scores for seven students on an examination as well as the rank
ordering of these students on the basis of their performance. Using students d, e,
and f, illustrate the nature of the information lost when one resorts to ordinal
scales rather than interval (or ratio) scales of measurement.

Student	Rank	Score
a	7	79
b	6	52
c	5	46
d	4	41
e	3	25
f	2	24
g	1	21

3. Which of the following variables are discrete and which are continuous?
(a) IQ
(b) number of responses made by a rat in a bar-pressing situation
(c) the rate of bar-pressing (responses/time)
(d) biological sex

4. What are the real limits for the following numbers?
(a) 1	(d) 1.1	(g) 3.84
(b) 18	(e) 24.3	(h) 12.61
(c) 77	(f) 1002.4	(i) 129.80

5. Round the following numbers to tenths.
(a) 2.74	(d) 8.55
(b) 9.46	(e) 6.050
(c) 4.0502	

6. Given the following data, determine the numerical value of each of the following expressions.

Subject (*i*)	X_i	Y_i
1	4	5
2	1	6
3	6	3
4	7	4
5	3	2

(a) $\displaystyle\sum_{i=1}^{5} X_i$ (e) $\displaystyle\sum_{i=1}^{5} (X_i + Y_i)$

(b) $\displaystyle\sum_{i=1}^{3} Y_i$ (f) $\displaystyle\sum_{i=1}^{5} X_i Y_i$

(c) $\displaystyle\sum_{i=3}^{5} X_i$ (g) $\displaystyle\sum_{i=1}^{5} X_i^2$

(d) $\sum Y$ (h) $\displaystyle\left(\sum_{i=1}^{5} X_i\right)^2$

7. Given the data from Exercise 6 for X and Y and that c, a constant, equals 5, determine the numerical value of each of the following expressions.

(a) $\sum c X_i$ (d) $\displaystyle\sum_{i=1}^{5} c$

(b) $\sum c X Y$ (e) $\displaystyle\sum_{i=1}^{3} (X + c)$

(c) $\sum c(X + Y)$

8. Simplify the following expressions (W and Z are variables, k is a constant).

(a) $\dfrac{\sum(kW + W)}{\sum W}$

(b) $\dfrac{\sum(W + k) + \sum(Z - k)}{\sum(W + Z)}$

(c) $\dfrac{\sum(k - W) + \sum(Z + W) + (\sum k)(\sum Z)}{N\left(\sum kZ + \dfrac{\sum k}{N}\right)}$

FREQUENCY DISTRIBUTIONS AND GRAPHING

2

frequency distributions

Given that a variable and a scale of measurement have been selected and a group of scores has been obtained, how can one efficiently describe this collection of observations? It is often desirable to be able to characterize the entire group of scores rather than to denote any single value. For example, one might want to know the range of score values included in the group, the value about which most of the scores seem to cluster, the dispersion of the scores over the measurement scale, etc. It would be highly cumbersome and inefficient to enumerate each score every time these questions were posed, and furthermore such a listing would not provide an obvious picture of the characteristics of the group.

A **frequency distribution** is a tallying of the number of times each score value (or interval of score values) occurs in a group of scores.

Suppose a short history quiz was given to a class of 10 students, and the essay was graded on a 10-point scale. The scores are presented in Part A of Table 2–1. The first thing to do in order to obtain a clearer picture of this small group of scores is to list them in descending order as in Part B of Table 2–1. Next, observe that there was one score of 10, two of 9, three of both 8 and 7, and one of 6. If a score value is symbolized by "X" and a tally is made next to the X for each occurrence of that value, the result is the frequency distribution presented in Part C of Table 2–1 in which f indicates the frequency for any given value of the variable X.

2–1 The Development of a Frequency Distribution.	
A. Scores on a History Quiz	**B. Scores on a History Quiz presented in Decreasing Order**
8	10
10	9
9	9
7	8
9	8
8	8
7	7
6	7
8	7
7	6

C. Frequency Distribution of Scores on a History Quiz

X	Tally	f
10	/	1
9	/ /	2
8	/ / /	3
7	/ / /	3
6	/	1
		$N = 10$

A second example of a frequency distribution might involve an opinion researcher who gives a questionnaire that asks a sample of people to what extent they approve of the way the President of the United States is carrying out his duties. The researcher provides five possible responses and arbitrarily attaches a number to each level of response:

1. disapprove to a great extent,
2. generally disapprove but do agree with some policies,
3. disapprove of about half of his actions and approve of half,
4. generally approve but disapprove of some policies,
5. approve to a great extent.

Suppose 80 people were questioned and asked to indicate one of these five opinions. The frequency of their responses is presented in Table 2–2. It is clear from this frequency distribution that people seem to be somewhat split on their opinion about the President's actions. A sizable group generally disapproves while another sizable group approves of his actions. Few people seem either ambivalent ($X = 3$) or adamantly positive or negative. Such descriptive conclusions would be difficult to arrive at if all 80 scores were written down without the assistance of the frequency distribution. Hence, not only does a frequency distribution save time in displaying data, it also organizes the numbers in a way in which the data may be summarized more easily than a complete listing of each score would allow.

A distribution that indicates the proportion of the total number of cases which were observed at each score value (or interval of score values) is called a **relative frequency distribution.**

An example of a relative frequency distribution (*Rel. f*) is given in the last column of Table 2–2. The advantage of a relative frequency distribution is that it expresses the pattern of scores in a manner which is not so dependent on the specific number of cases involved. Thus, an opinion pollster would not say that 9 people emphatically approved of the President's actions, but rather that 11% did. Of course, it is always informative to know the total number of people polled.

2–2   Frequency Distribution of Opinions on Presidential Policy.

	X	*f*	*Rel. f*
Approve Greatly	5	9	.11
Approve	4	30	.38
Ambivalent	3	10	.12
Disapprove	2	25	.31
Disapprove Greatly	1	6	.08
		$N = 80$	1.00

These two examples of frequency distributions have had either a small number of cases or they have involved only a few score values. While arranging data in the form of a frequency distribution in these cases demonstrated two assets of this technique, the frequency distribution is used to its greatest advantage when there are a large number of scores and a wide range of score values.

To illustrate, suppose 150 eighth-grade students were given a mathematics ability test prior to taking an algebra course. The scores for these students are presented in Table 2–3. This display emphasizes the fact that enumerating all the scores does not provide much immediate information about the nature of the group of scores. A frequency distribution is necessary.

2–3	Mathematics Ability Test Scores for 150 Eighth-Grade Students.								
79	51	67	50	78	71	77	75	55	65
62	89	83	73	80	67	74	63	32	88
88	48	60	71	79	79	47	55	70	34
89	63	55	93	71	81	72	68	75	93
41	81	46	50	61	72	86	66	54	58
59	50	90	75	61	82	73	57	87	41
75	98	53	79	80	64	67	51	36	52
70	37	42	72	74	78	91	69	95	76
67	73	79	67	85	74	70	62	76	69
91	73	77	36	77	45	39	59	63	57
53	67	85	74	77	78	73	61	47	43
71	43	42	96	83	83	84	67	81	75
70	92	59	86	53	71	49	68	42	46
32	67	67	71	71	59	80	66	39	49
82	68	30	72	57	92	50	38	73	56

If a frequency distribution were constructed from these scores in the previous manner, namely stating each possible score value between 0 and 100 and its corresponding frequency, there would be almost no gain in the efficiency of characterizing this data. In order to obtain the advantage of concise presentation, several score values must be grouped together forming a **class interval**. For example, how many frequencies were there for the set of score values (30, 31, 32, 33, and 34)?

Table 2–4 was constructed by ordering the scores and grouping them into clusters. From this table, one can see that there were only three cases of a score between 95 and 99 inclusive (namely, 95, 96, and 98), seven cases within the interval of 90 to 94 inclusive, nine between 85 and 89 inclusive, etc. A summary of this accounting is presented in the frequency distribution shown in the two leftmost columns of Table 2–5. The only difference between this frequency distribution and previous ones is that rather than having frequencies stated for each possible score value, sets of frequencies comprise certain class intervals, e.g., 30–34, 35–39, 40–44, etc. When scores are presented in this manner, they are sometimes referred to as **grouped data.**

In addition to the frequency distribution of raw scores, the relative frequency distribution provides another method of examining grouped data. An example of it is presented in the third column of Table 2–5. Two other distributions are

2–4	Ordering of Mathematics Ability Test Scores.	
—	74, 74, 74, 74	49, 49
98	73, 73, 73, 73, 73, 73	48
—	72, 72, 72, 72	47, 47
96	71, 71, 71, 71, 71	46, 46
95	70, 70, 70, 70	45
—	69, 69	—
93, 93	68, 68, 68	43, 43
92, 92	67, 67, 67, 67, 67, 67, 67, 67, 67	42, 42, 42
91, 91	66, 66	41, 41
90	65	—
89, 89	64	39, 39
88, 88	63, 63, 63	38
87	62, 62	37
86, 86	61, 61, 61	36, 36
85, 85	60	—
84	59, 59, 59, 59	34
83, 83, 83	58	—
82, 82	57, 57, 57	32, 32
81, 81, 81	56	—
80, 80, 80, 80	55, 55, 55	30
79, 79, 79, 79, 79	54	
78, 78, 78	53, 53, 53	
77, 77, 77, 77	52	
76, 76, 76	51, 51	
75, 75, 75, 75, 75	50, 50, 50, 50	

also displayed. They are the **cumulative frequency** and **cumulative relative frequency** distributions.

A **cumulative frequency distribution** is one in which the entry for any class interval is the sum of the frequencies in that interval plus all class intervals below. A **cumulative relative frequency distribution** is one in which the entry for any class interval is the proportion of the total number of cases corresponding to that interval's cumulative frequency.

2–5 Distributions for 150 Math Ability Scores.				
Class Interval	**f**	**Rel. f**	**Cum. f**	**Cum. Rel. f**
95–99	3	.02	150	1.00
90–94	7	.05	147	.98
85–89	9	.06	140	.93
80–84	13	.09	131	.87
75–79	20	.13	118	.79
70–74	23	.15	98	.65
65–69	17	.11	75	.50
60–64	10	.07	58	.39
55–59	12	.08	48	.32
50–54	11	.07	36	.24
45–49	8	.05	25	.17
40–44	7	.05	17	.11
35–39	6	.04	10	.07
30–34	4	.03	4	.03
	N = 150	1.00		

Quite simply, these are respective modifications of the frequency and relative frequency distributions in which the entries are progressively accumulated starting from the lowest class interval. Cumulative distributions provide a means for rapidly ascertaining the number or proportion of scores that fall below the upper limit of a given class interval.

Suppose for this mathematics test, Johnny had a score of 64. The cumulative percentage (i.e., *Cum. Rel. f.*) for scores in the interval 60–64 in Table 2–5 is .39 which says that 39% of the scores were equal to or below the score of 64. Johnny is sometimes said to be at the 39th percentile. Percentiles will be discussed in more detail in Chapter 4.

A distribution of scores, then, may be displayed as a frequency, relative frequency, cumulative frequency, or cumulative relative frequency distribution. The advantage of such distributions is that they provide an efficient method of organizing and presenting a large group of scores in such a fashion that certain characteristics of the group as a whole become apparent.

CONSTRUCTING FREQUENCY DISTRIBUTIONS FOR GROUPED DATA

number of class intervals It is somewhat easier to read and understand a frequency distribution involving grouped data than it is to actually organize a set of scores into that form because certain decisions must be made about the nature of the class interval to be used. In the above case, an interval such as 30–34 was selected, but would 30–32 or 30–47 have done just as well? Table 2–6 illustrates these two alternatives.

2–6 Two Distributions with Class Intervals of Different Sizes.			
Class Interval	f	Class Interval	f
96–98	2	84–101	20
93–95	3	66–83	71
90–92	5	48–65	37
87–89	5	30–47	22
84–86	5		$N = 150$
81–83	8		
78–80	12		
75–77	12		
72–74	14		
69–71	11		
66–68	14		
63–65	5		
60–62	6		
57–59	8		
54–56	5		
51–53	6		
48–50	7		
45–47	5		
42–44	5		
39–41	4		
36–38	4		
33–35	1		
30–32	3		
	$N = 150$		

Consider these examples from the standpoint of the general goal of frequency distributions which is to **summarize** data into a form which **accurately depicts** the group as a whole. In the first instance (left-hand distribution in Table 2–6) with 23 different class intervals the summarization advantage of the frequency distribution is lost. Taking the proliferation of class intervals to a ridiculous extreme, one could enumerate each possible score value just as in Table 2–4. Several scores would have no frequencies and there would be little advantage in making a frequency distribution at all. Further, the frequencies at the left of

Table 2–6 do not provide a smooth picture or description of the pattern of frequencies in relation to the score values. This distribution is too spread out or diffuse to accomplish the goal of summarization.

Conversely, the right-hand distribution in Table 2–6 has too few class intervals. It is clear that most of the scores fall between 66–83, but this interval is so big that considerable accuracy and detail have been lost in grouping the data into only four classes. For example, it is not known if the 22 cases between 30–47 fell rather near the value of 47, nearer to 30, or were relatively evenly spaced within the interval. The lowest score in the group could be anywhere between 47 and 30 given only the information provided by this distribution.

From these examples it should be clear that too many class intervals do not provide adequate summarization or description of the group of scores, whereas too few intervals reduce the accuracy of the description. One must select a number of class intervals that represents a compromise between these extremes.

It is usually suggested that between 10 and 20 class intervals be chosen, but there can be a great difference between the picture one obtains of a distribution if it is displayed with 10 or with 20 intervals. Hence, although this is a good rule of thumb to employ, one has to make an intelligent decision depending upon the nature of the data. In the example illustrated in Table 2–5, 14 intervals were chosen. In general, if the total number of frequencies is small (e.g., 20–50) one would tend to pick fewer intervals than if there were 100 or 200 cases. If the distribution had only 10 scores one would want even fewer intervals than 10, perhaps 4 or 5; but if there were 2000 cases as many as 20 or more intervals might be contemplated. Hence, although the guideline of 10 to 20 intervals is one which is usually appropriate, it merely reflects the concern for an accurate summarization and display of a group of scores.

the size of the class interval   Once a tentative decision on the approximate number of class intervals has been made, the size of the interval must be determined. A good approach is to subtract the smallest score from the largest. This provides a crude measure of the span of values covered by the group of scores which must be broken into intervals. If this result is divided by the approximate number of intervals, an estimate of the size of the intervals is obtained. For example, if approximately 15 intervals would be appropriate for the data in Table 2–4 and the difference between the largest and smallest scores is $98 - 30 = 68$, then

$$
\begin{array}{r}
4.5 \\
15\overline{)68.} \\
60 \\
\hline
80 \\
75 \\
\hline
5
\end{array}
$$

yields an approximate interval size. However, it is usually inconvenient to use intervals involving fractions like 4.5. Hence, one might use an interval of 5, thus covering a range of 68 with 14 intervals.

To determine the size of a class interval from a distribution already constructed, subtract the lower **real limit** from the upper **real limit** of any interval. For the interval 30–34 (30 and 34 are called the **stated limits**), the lower real limit is 29.5 and the upper real limit is 34.5 which yields an interval size of 5:

$$34.5 - 29.5 = 5$$

It may seem a bit puzzling that the size of the interval 30–34 is 5 and not 4 as it might initially appear, but if the various scores which are contained within the range of 30–34 are listed (30, 31, 32, 33, 34) there are clearly 5 not 4 of them. This notion is further illustrated in Figure 2–1 in which the linear scale of measurement is drawn and the real limits for each score in the interval are shown.

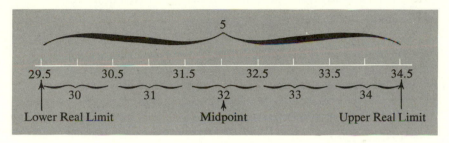

Fig. 2–1.   Illustration of the fact that the size of the interval 30–34 is 5.

the lowest interval   Now that the number and size of the class intervals have been established, all that remains is to specify the first interval and the scale will be completely determined. There is a custom that the first **stated** limit (not the lower **real** limit) be evenly divisible by the size of the interval. Thus, the size of the lowest interval 30–34 is 5 and the lowest **stated** limit is 30. Since 30 divided by 5 is an even 6, this meets the requirement. If the lowest score in a distribution is 49 and an interval of size 4 is selected, the first interval would be 48–51, because 48, (but not 49), is evenly divisible by 4.

midpoint of an interval   The **midpoint** of a class interval is the precise center of that interval or half-way between the endpoints. It can be determined by adding one-half of the size of the interval to its lower real limit.

For the interval 30–34 whose size is five (half of which is 2.5) and whose lower real limit is 29.5, the midpoint is

$$29.5 + 2.5 = 32$$

For the interval 45.6–48.3 whose size is 2.8 and lower real limit is 45.55, the midpoint is

$$45.55 + 1.4 = 46.95$$

The important thing to remember is to take the lower **real** limit (e.g., 45.55) not the **stated** limit (e.g., 45.6).[1]

summary illustration As a final presentation of some of these topics, Table 2–7 provides a summary of the guidelines for constructing a frequency distribution using class intervals, and Table 2–8 displays the resulting distribution for the sample data presented in Table 2–5 including the real limits, interval size, and midpoints.

2–7 Summary of Guidelines for Constructing Frequency Distributions with Grouped Data.

---

1. Estimate the number of class intervals. This usually should be 10 to 20, but it may be less if the total number of cases is small or it may be more if the total is very large.

2. Estimate the size of the class interval by dividing the difference between the largest and smallest score in the distribution by the number of intervals selected in Step 1. Round this result up to the nearest whole number (or convenient fraction if a whole number is not appropriate).

3. Select the lowest class interval such that its lowest **stated** limit is evenly divisible by the size of the interval.

4. Place the lowest interval at the bottom of the table which contains the class intervals and their respective frequencies.

GRAPHS OF FREQUENCY DISTRIBUTIONS

frequency histogram Describing a group of scores can be done by drawing a graph of the frequency distribution. One type of graph is a frequency histogram, and it is presented in Figure 2–2 for the data in the example of the math ability scores of 150 eighth-grade students (Table 2–8).

When constructing this histogram, a horizontal scale was drawn corresponding to the scale of math ability scores. The horizontal dimension of such a plot

---

[1] Since the midpoint of a class interval is the point falling in the center of the interval, it may also be computed by taking half the distance between the **stated** limits and adding that result to the lower **stated** limit. Thus, in the case of the interval 30–34, $(34 - 30)/2 + 30 = 32$ yields the same result as above. Since other procedures require use of the real limits and since the size of the interval is usually known (note that the difference between **stated** limits is **not** the size of the interval), the text uses the form involving real limits and interval size.

2–8	Frequency Distribution with Real Limits, Interval Size, and Midpoint.			
Class Interval	Real Limits	Interval Size	Midpoint	Frequency
95–99	94.5–99.5	5	97	3
90–94	89.5–94.5	5	92	7
85–89	84.5–89.5	5	87	9
80–84	79.5–84.5	5	82	13
75–79	74.5–79.5	5	77	20
70–74	69.5–74.5	5	72	23
65–69	64.5–69.5	5	67	17
60–64	59.5–64.5	5	62	10
55–59	54.5–59.5	5	57	12
50–54	49.5–54.5	5	52	11
45–49	44.5–49.5	5	47	8
40–44	39.5–44.5	5	42	7
35–39	34.5–39.5	5	37	6
30–34	29.5–34.5	5	32	4
				$N = 150$

is called the **abscissa.** Notice that the numbers along the abscissa are the midpoints of the intervals as found in Table 2–8. The vertical dimension is called the **ordinate,** and in the case of frequency distributions it will correspond to "Frequency." The abscissa and ordinate are collectively called **axes.** Note that the axes are clearly marked with the numbers of their respective scales and then labeled. The width of the "bar" of the histogram covers the entire range of its respective class interval, from lower to upper **real** limits. Therefore, they exactly straddle the midpoint of their interval as designated along the abscissa. The height of a bar corresponds to the number of frequencies for that interval as indicated on the ordinate. A summary of the steps in constructing a frequency histogram as well as the other graphs described below is presented in Table 2–9.

frequency polygon An example of a **frequency polygon** is presented in Figure 2–3. The graph is constructed by placing a point above the midpoint of each class interval corresponding to the frequency within that interval. The adjacent points are connected by straight lines. Note also that the line formed by connecting the points intersects the abscissa at points corresponding to what would be the midpoint of the next interval were it constructed. This closing of the line with the abscissa completes the formation of a polygon from which this graph derives its name.

2–9   Summary of Steps in Constructing Histograms and Polygons.

Frequency Histogram

1. Mark off the abscissa with values corresponding to the midpoints of the class intervals and mark off the ordinate in frequencies. Label the axes appropriately.

2. Construct the bars of the histogram over each class interval so that their width equals the size of the class interval covering from lower to upper real limits (not from midpoint to midpoint), and the height corresponds to the frequency of scores in that interval. There should be no space between bars.

Frequency Polygon

1. Mark off and label axes as for a frequency histogram but add one interval below the lowest and one above the highest class interval, and assign them 0 frequencies.

2. Place points corresponding to the frequencies of each interval (including the two 0 frequency intervals) directly over the midpoints of each

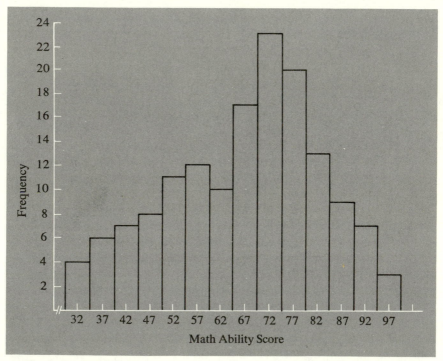

Fig. 2–2.   Frequency histogram for the math ability scores of 150 eighth-grade students as presented in Table 2–5.

2–9 continued

class interval. Connect all adjacent points (including the 0's) with straight lines.

Relative Frequency Histogram or Polygon

1. These are plotted in the same way as above but the ordinate (and the height of the bars or points) consists of relative frequency not frequency.

Cumulative Frequency Histogram or Polygon

1. Follow the steps for constructing a frequency histogram or polygon, except:
   a. Mark off and label the ordinate for cumulative frequency rather than frequency.
   b. In the case of a cumulative frequency polygon, the points are placed over the upper real limit of each class interval, including the lowest interval of 0 accumulated frequencies (note there is no upper 0 frequency interval).

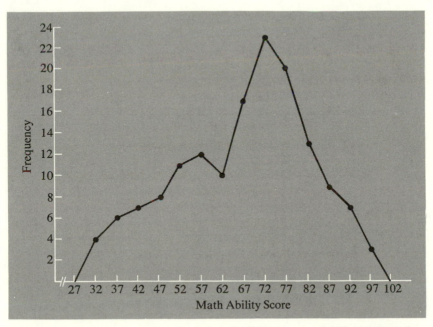

Fig. 2–3.　Frequency polygon for the math ability scores of 150 eighth-grade students as presented in Table 2–5.

relative frequency histogram and polygon   Figure 2–4 presents a relative frequency histogram and polygon for these same data. Note that these plots are graphically similar to the previously illustrated plots except that the ordinate is relative frequency and the values are taken from the column labeled "Rel. f" in Table 2–5.

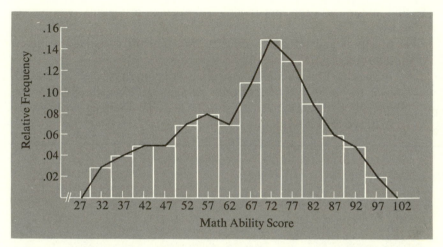

Fig. 2–4.   A relative frequency polygon and histogram for the data on mathematics ability presented in Table 2–5.

cumulative frequency histogram and polygon   Just as frequency and relative frequency distributions have been plotted in the form of histograms and polygons, the two cumulative distributions in Table 2–5 can also be graphed in these ways. For example, Figure 2–5 presents a cumulative frequency polygon.

One difference between the graph of a frequency distribution and a cumulative frequency distribution is that the ordinate changes from frequency to cumulative frequency. A second difference is that the point on the graph is now placed over the upper real limit of each interval rather than over its midpoint. This is because this point must indicate that up to the *end* of that interval, a certain number or percentage of cases have occurred. Since the scores that fall within a given interval may be located anywhere within that interval, the point representing the accumulation of all frequencies within and below this interval is placed at the upper real limit of the interval.

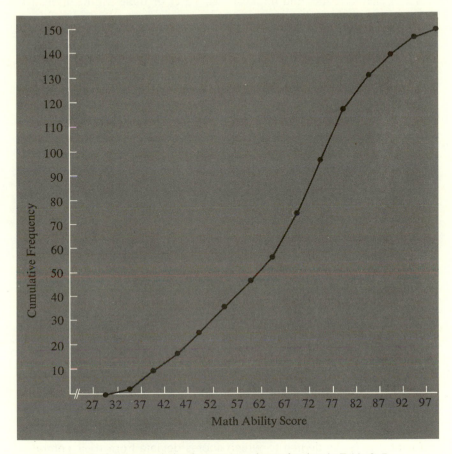

Fig. 2–5.   A cumulative frequency polygon for data in Table 2–5.

HOW DISTRIBUTIONS DIFFER

Some of the most important ways distributions differ one to another are with respect to (1) **central tendency,** (2) **variability,** (3) **skewness,** and (4) **kurtosis.** The next chapter will take up numerical expressions of some of these characteristics. It will be profitable to preface this material with an overview of the general meaning of these concepts.

The **central tendency** of a distribution is a point on the scale corresponding to a typical, representative, or central score.

There are several more specific definitions of central tendency, each with its own set of characteristics and implications. Three of these will be discussed in Chapter 3: the **mean, median,** and **mode.**

To illustrate the concept of central tendency, consider the two curves (smoothed frequency polygons) in Figure 2–6. They differ only with respect to central tendency. They have the same shape, but occupy different places on the scale of measurement.

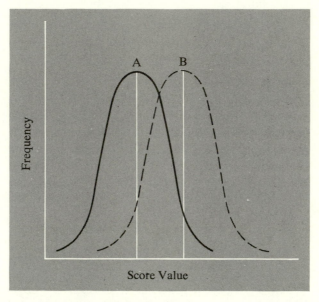

Fig. 2–6.   Two distributions which differ only with respect to central tendency.

Variability is the degree to which scores deviate from their central tendency.

Figure 2–7 shows two curves with similar central tendencies but different amounts of variability. The scores in Distribution A tend to cluster more closely about the central tendency of the distribution which is indicated by the vertical line. In contrast, there is a disproportionate number of cases in Distribution B that do not fall as closely around that central value as do the cases in the A curve. There is more variability in B than in A. The concept of variability is probably the most central idea in statistics.

Skewness refers to the bunching of scores on one side of the central tendency or to the trailing out of scores in one (as opposed to the other) direction from the central tendency.

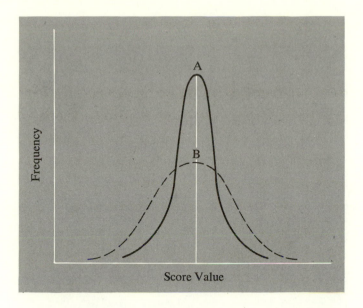

Fig. 2–7. Distributions with similar central tendency but with different variability.

These traits are reflected in the lack of symmetry of some distributions. Figure 2–8 presents two skewed distributions. Both lack symmetry, and B is more skewed than is A because there is a greater tendency for the scores to bunch at one end and trail off to the other end.

Skewness has direction as well as magnitude. In Distribution A the scores tend to trail off to the right or positive end of the scale. It is said to be **positively skewed** or **skewed to the right.** Distribution B, conversely, trails off to the left or to the negative end of the scale (recall that the first integer to the left of 0 is −1, i.e., negative). Distribution B is said to be **negatively skewed** or **skewed to the left.**

The **kurtosis** of a distribution is the "curvedness" or "peakedness" of the graph.

Figure 2–9 depicts two curves with similar central tendencies but different kurtoses. Curve A is more peaked than B, and the changes in the height of the curve as the score value increases are more marked for A than for B. Kurtosis is frequently used in a relative sense. Distribution A is more **leptokurtic** than B. The Greek *lepto* means "thin," so leptokurtic implies a thin distribution which seems appropriate to describe curve A relative to B. On the other hand, B is said to be more **platykurtic** than A. *Platy* means "flat" (e.g., *platy*helminthes—flatworms, *platy*pus—a flat-billed mammal). Hence, B is flatter than A.

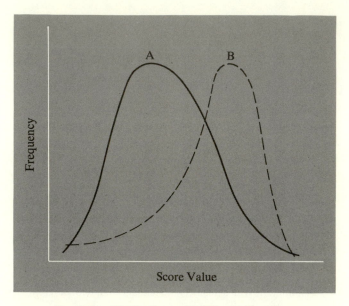

Fig. 2–8.   Distributions with different skewness.

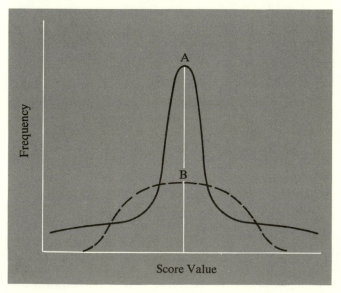

Fig. 2–9.   Distributions with similar central tendency but different kurtosis.

These terms may be used to describe the general form of a distribution. Thus, one might say that a distribution is positively skewed and rather platykurtic. This verbal description gives one some idea of the form of the curve of this distribution. However, one might wish to be more precise than merely to use these relative terms. For purposes of comparing distributions it would be helpful if mathematical indices were available that reflect these characteristics. Although measures of skewness and kurtosis are available[2] they are not often used. Therefore, only indices of central tendency and variability will be taken up in the next chapter.

EXERCISES

1. Below is a set of scores on a mathematics exam. Construct a frequency distribution appropriate for these data. Present the distribution in the manner of Table 2–8, with real limits, midpoint, interval size, and frequency indicated. Then compose a relative frequency distribution, cumulative frequency distribution, and cumulative relative frequency distribution for these data.

54	81	18	44	24
63	67	60	34	39
91	47	75	72	36
87	49	86	57	74
26	41	90	59	14
13	31	68	13	29
29	70	22	63	35
50	42	27	95	77
42	31	69	73	11
31	45	51	56	40

2. Construct polygons and histograms for the frequency and relative frequency distributions above. Make a polygon for the cumulative frequency distribution.

3. Perform the tasks required in Exercises 1 and 2 with the following data:

40	41	38	43	35	42
41	37	36	34	38	34
34	31	35	41	45	39
30	38	40	36	32	32
46	38	30	29	38	41
36	34	36	44	42	41
32	43	38	35	36	37
50	35	33	38	31	46
37	36	41	39	44	35
42	37	44	39	39	38

[2] See, for example: G. A. Ferguson, *Statistical Analysis in Psychology and Education.* New York: McGraw-Hill, 1966, (76).

4. The procedures for constructing a frequency distribution were described for data composed of whole numbers. Obviously, many of the measurements made by scientists are in decimal form. The guidelines for constructing frequency distributions listed in Table 2–7 also apply to decimal data. Perform the tasks required in Exercises 1 and 2 with the numbers below.

1.8	1.5	2.3	2.7
2.5	1.9	1.3	1.5
2.0	3.1	2.4	1.1
2.1	2.2	1.6	2.0
1.6	2.2	.4	2.0
1.3	1.4	2.2	1.2
2.8	.8	.9	2.3

CHARACTERISTICS OF DISTRIBUTIONS

3

The purpose of this chapter is to introduce numerical indices of some characteristics of frequency distributions. For example, it is often convenient to talk about the central tendency of a distribution, the point on the measurement scale that represents a typical score. To make the meaning of central tendency more precise, a numerical index of this attribute is needed. One such central point is the mean or average score. Other indices of central tendency are the median and the mode. However, central tendency is not the only characteristic of a distribution that requires numerical description. Another attribute of a group of scores is their variability, the extent to which the scores differ from one another. Variability is reflected in the range, variance, and standard deviation. In conjunction with the presentation of these concepts, a discussion of statistical estimation will show how measures obtained from a limited number of observations may be used to estimate characteristics of much larger groups of subjects.

measures of central tendency

THE MEAN

definition The most common measure of the central tendency of a group of scores is the average or mean.

The **mean**, symbolized by $\bar{X}$ (read "X bar"), is given by the formula

$$\bar{X} = \frac{\sum\limits_{i=1}^{N} X_i}{N}$$

in which X_i is the ith score in the distribution, N is the number of scores, and $\sum\limits_{i=1}^{N}$ instructs one to add all the scores. Usually, the limits of the summation and the subscript on X are not written since it is always understood that the summation is over all N scores. Therefore, the most common expression for the mean is simply

$$\bar{X} = \frac{\sum X}{N}$$

The mean is also called the arithmetic average of the scores.[1]

   computational example   The mean is calculated in the following manner if the values of X are 8, 3, 4, 10, 7, and 1.

$$
\begin{array}{c}
X \\
\hline
8 \\
3 \\
4 \\
10 \\
7 \\
1 \\
\hline
\sum X = 33 \\
N = 6
\end{array}
\qquad
\bar{X} = \frac{\sum X}{N} = \frac{33}{6} = 5.5
$$

   deviations about the mean   The mean possesses several properties that make it very useful. First,

If the mean is subtracted from each score in the distribution, the sum of such differences is zero. Symbolically,

$$\sum_{i=1}^{N} (X_i - \bar{X}) = 0$$

which is often stated: The sum of the deviations about the mean is zero. The phrase "deviation about the mean" signifies the difference between a score and the mean, $X_i - \bar{X}$.

----

[1] Texts differ in the symbols given to different statistical concepts. Although this text will use the notation $\bar{X}$ to denote the sample mean, other books use M.

Consider the following numerical example:

X_i	$\overline{X}$	$(X_i - \overline{X})$
3	5	$3 - 5 = -2$
6	5	$6 - 5 = 1$
5	5	$5 - 5 = 0$
1	5	$1 - 5 = -4$
10	5	$10 - 5 = 5$

$$\Sigma X_i = 25$$
$$N = 5$$
$$\overline{X} = 5$$

$$\sum_{i=1}^{N} (X_i - \overline{X}) = 0$$

This fact can be proven true of all distributions. The proof, presented in optional Table 3–1, uses two of the summation rules discussed in Chapter 2 plus the fact that the mean $(\overline{X})$ of any distribution is a constant—it does not change value with respect to that distribution. The value of a score (X_i) can change depending upon which score is selected; but the mean remains constant for a particular distribution. This proof may be omitted.

It is important to notice that while the sum of the deviations of all the scores about the mean is always zero, the sum of the **squared** deviations about the mean usually is not zero.

That is, while

$$\sum_{i=1}^{N} (X_i - \overline{X}) = 0$$

the expression

$$\sum_{i=1}^{N} (X_i - \overline{X})^2 \text{ is } not \text{ usually equal to } (\neq)\ 0$$

To illustrate, consider the numerical illustration given at the top of the page. If one squares the difference between each score and the mean [square $(X_i - \overline{X})$ in the third column at the right], and then sums these squared deviations, one obtains

$$(-2)^2 + (1)^2 + (0)^2 + (-4)^2 + (5)^2 = 46$$

which is obviously not zero. This will always be true (if the scores are not all the same value) because squared numbers can never be negative, and thus positive values will not be balanced out by negative ones. Although this distinction between the sum of squared and unsquared deviations about the mean may seem trivial at this point, there will be many situations which will require the fact that the sum of the unsquared (but not the squared) deviations about the mean is zero.

minimum variability of scores about the mean A second property of the mean concerns the squared deviations of scores about their mean value.

OPTIONAL TABLE

3–1 Proof that the Sum of the Deviations about the Mean Equals Zero.	
Operation	**Explanation**
1. $\sum(X_i - \bar{X}) = \sum X_i - \sum \bar{X}$	1. The sum of the differences between two quantities equals the difference between their sums.
2. $ = \sum X_i - N\bar{X}$	2. The sum of a constant added to itself N times (i.e., $\sum \bar{X}$) is N times the constant.
3. $ = \sum X_i - N\left(\dfrac{\sum X_i}{N}\right)$	3. Substitution of $\dfrac{\sum X_i}{N}$ for $\bar{X}$
4. $\sum(X_i - \bar{X}) = \sum X_i - \sum X_i = 0$	4. Cancellation of N's in second term.

The sum of the squared deviations of all the scores about their mean is less than the sum of the squared deviations of those scores about any other value.

This is a fundamental principle and will be invoked in the explanation of many subsequent concepts. The proposition states that although the sum of the **squared** deviations about the mean usually does not equal zero, this sum is nevertheless smaller than if the squared deviations of those same scores were taken about any value other than the mean of their distribution. For example, in the above illustration the sum of the squared deviations about the mean equaled 46. The mean of that distribution was 5.0. The sum of the squared deviations about the number 6.0 equals 51, about the number 4.0 it equals 51, and about the number 7.0 it equals 66. The sum taken about the mean (46) is less than any other of these examples, and it can be shown (see the following) that it always will be less than about any other value. It is in this sense that the mean is a measure of central tendency: The mean is "closer" (in terms of squared deviations) to the individual scores over the entire group than is any other single value.

The proof that the sum of the squared deviations about the mean is less than about any alternative value is presented in optional Table 3–2. The logic of the proof is that "any other value" may be expressed in terms of the mean, $\overline{X}$, plus some value, call it c. Thus, the alternative value is $(\overline{X} + c)$, where it is understood that the value of c may be positive or negative. The procedure in proving that the sum of the squared deviations about the mean is a minimum involves determining the sum of squared deviations about any other value (i.e., the value $\overline{X} + c$), and then demonstrating that this sum will always be greater than if the deviations were taken about $\overline{X}$. Again, as with all optional tables, Table 3–2 may be omitted without loss of continuity.

THE MEDIAN

Another measure of central tendency is the median.

> The **median**, symbolized by M_d, is the point that divides the distribution into two parts such that an equal number of scores fall above and below that point.

computational examples   The computation of the median depends on whether there is an odd or an even number of scores in the distribution and whether there is a duplication of score values near where the median point is located. The phrase "duplication of score values" implies that more than one score of the same value exists in the distribution. The distribution (3, 4, 5, 5, 7) has a duplication of score value while the distribution (2, 3, 5, 6, 8) does not. Duplication of score values is important only when it occurs near the point where the median is located. Otherwise, score duplication can be ignored.

(a) **No duplication near the median; odd number of scores.** When there is an odd number of scores and no duplication of scores near the median, the median is the middle score. Consider the distribution (3, 5, 6, 7, 10). In this case, the point that divides the distribution into two equal parts is 6, since two scores fall below and two scores fall above this value.

(b) **No duplication near the median; even number of scores.** By convention, when there is an even number of scores in the distribution and no duplication exists near the median, the average of the middle two scores is taken as the median. Suppose the distribution was (3, 5, 6, 7, 10, 14). The point that divides the distribution in half lies between 6 and 7. The average of these points (6.5) is taken as the median. Another example illustrates the convention that is followed when the scores near the median are not adjacent values. If the distribution is (3, 4, 8, 14), the median is 6, since $(4 + 8) \div 2 = 6$.

(c) **Duplication of scores near the median.** When more than one instance of a score value falls near the median, the median is obtained by interpolation which proceeds basically in the same way regardless of whether there is an odd

3-2 Proof that the Sum of the Squared Deviations about the Mean is a Minimum.

Operation	Explanation
1. $(\bar{X} + c)$, $c \neq 0$, is a value other than $\bar{X}$.	1. Assumption
2. The sum of the squared deviations about $\bar{X}$ equals $$\sum (X_i - \bar{X})^2$$ and about $(\bar{X} + c)$ it equals $$\sum [X_i - (\bar{X} + c)]^2$$	2. Definition
3. To prove $$\sum (X_i - \bar{X})^2 < \sum [X_i - (\bar{X} + c)]^2$$	3. To prove
4. $\sum [X_i - (\bar{X} + c)]^2 = \sum [(X_i - \bar{X}) - c]^2$	4. Working with the right side of the inequality and regrouping
5. $\quad = \sum [(X_i - \bar{X})^2 - 2c(X_i - \bar{X}) + c^2]$	5. Binomial expansion of the form: $(a - b)^2 = a^2 - 2ab + b^2$
6. $\quad = \sum (X_i - \bar{X})^2 - 2c\underbrace{\sum (X_i - \bar{X})}_{\longrightarrow \ 0} + \underbrace{\sum c^2}_{\longrightarrow \ Nc^2}$	6. The sum (or difference) of several variables is the sum (or difference) of their sums, and the sum of a constant times a variable is the constant times the sum of the variable.
7. $\quad = \sum (X_i - \bar{X})^2 - \quad 0 \quad + Nc^2$	7. $\sum (X_i - \bar{X}) = 0$ and the sum of N c^2's equals N times c^2.
8. $\sum (X_i - \bar{X})^2 < \sum (X_i - \bar{X})^2 + Nc^2$	8. Substituting for the right-hand term in No. 3 above. The expression is true because Nc^2 will always be greater than zero.

or an even number of scores in the distribution. For example, suppose the distribution is (3, 4, 5, 5, 5, 6, 6, 7). Since the median is the point dividing the distribution such that an equal number of scores fall below and above it, such a point for this example lies between the second and third instance of the score 5. In such a case, presumably the scores 3, 4, 5, 5 would fall below the median point and 5, 6, 6, 7 would lie above it. However, stating that the median is "between the second and third instance of the score 5" is a bit clumsy; a single numerical value that expresses this situation would be preferred.

Consider Figure 3–1 which presents this example in graphic form. Here, each score is represented by a rectangular block located on the measurement scale over the real limits of its score value. Since there are eight scores, half of them, or four, must be below the median point. The scores 3 and 4 must be below the median, as well as two of the three scores of 5—that is, two-thirds of the 5's,

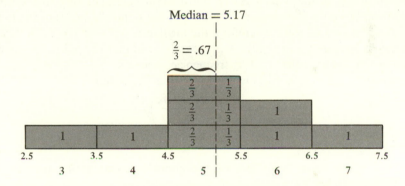

Fig. 3–1. Computing the median when there is duplication of scores.

or two-thirds of the score interval corresponding to the score value 5. Since scores are in whole numbers, two-thirds of a score interval equals .67, which should be added to the lower real limit of 4.5 to produce the point which is two-thirds through this interval. Thus, 4.5 + .67 = 5.17 is the median. If the frequencies in Figure 3–1 are added above and below the median, one can see that a total of 4 of the 8 frequencies lie above and 4 lie below the median of 5.17. In short, the median divides the shaded area of Figure 3–1 into two equal portions.

The logic is the same if an odd number of frequencies are in the distribution. Suppose the distribution consisted of (3, 4, 5, 5, 5, 6, 6, 7, 7), which case is presented in Figure 3–2. There are 9 scores, and thus the median must be the point such that $4\frac{1}{2}$ frequencies fall below and $4\frac{1}{2}$ fall above it. Counting from the low end upward, it is clear that the scores 3 and 4 will be below the median, plus $2\frac{1}{2}$ of the three scores of 5. But, $2\frac{1}{2}$ of three equals

$$\frac{2\frac{1}{2}}{3} = \frac{\frac{5}{2}}{3} = \frac{5}{6} = .83$$

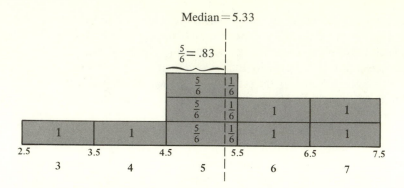

Fig. 3–2.   Computing the median when there is duplication of scores.

Thus, the scores 3 and 4 plus .83 of the interval corresponding to the score value 5 will be below the median. This will be the point .83 up from the lower limit of 4.5 of that interval. Therefore, the median is $4.5 + .83 = 5.33$. Again, if frequencies are added in Figure 3–2, it can be seen that the point 5.33 indeed places $4\frac{1}{2}$ frequencies below and $4\frac{1}{2}$ frequencies above it.

Fortunately, a formula exists which formalizes these steps:

$$M_d = L + \left(\frac{N/2 - n_b}{n_w}\right) i$$

in which

M_d = the median

L = the lower real limit of the score interval containing the median

N = the number of scores in the total distribution

n_b = the number of scores falling below the lower real limit of the score interval containing the median

n_w = the number of cases within the score interval containing the median

i = the size of the score interval ($i = 1$ if the data are in whole numbers)[2]

In terms of the last example,

$$L = 4.5 \qquad\qquad M_d = L + \left[\frac{N/2 - n_b}{n_w}\right] i$$
$$N = 9$$
$$n_b = 2 \qquad\qquad\quad = 4.5 + \left[\frac{\frac{9}{2} - 2}{3}\right] 1$$
$$n_w = 3$$
$$i = 1 \qquad\qquad\qquad = 4.5 + \frac{\frac{5}{2}}{3}$$
$$= 4.5 + .83$$
$$M_d = 5.33$$

[2] If the scores are 5.1, 5.3, 5.3, 5.8, the score interval is .1.

THE MODE

A third measure of central tendency is the mode.

The **mode**, symbolized M_o, is the most frequently occurring score.

If the distribution is (3, 4, 4, 5, 5, 5, 6, 8), the mode is 5. Sometimes a distribution will have two modes, such as the distribution (3, 4, 4, 4, 5, 6, 6, 7, 7, 7, 8). In this case, the modes are 4 and 7 and this distribution is called **bimodal**.

COMPARISON OF THE MEAN, MEDIAN, AND MODE

The essential difference between the mean and the median is that the mean reflects the values of each score in the distribution whereas the median is based largely on where the midpoint of the distribution falls without regard for the particular value of many of the scores. For example, consider the following illustration:

Scores	Mean	Median
1, 2, 3, 4, 5	3	3
1, 2, 3, 4, 50	12	3
1, 2, 3, 4, 100	22	3

Only the last number differs from one distribution to the other. The mean reflects these differences but the median does not. This is because the median is the midpoint of the distribution such that an equal *number* of scores fall above and below it. The particular value of the extreme scores does not matter, only the fact that those scores exist and are above the midpoint is considered. In contrast, the mean takes into account the value of every score. This fact can be seen by inspecting the numerator of the formula for $\overline{X}$, $\sum X_i$. Thus, changing a score value will change the value of the mean.

The mode is a simple measure of central tendency and reflects only the most frequently occurring score. It is not used much in the social sciences.

Because the three different measures of central tendency are sensitive to different aspects of the group of scores, they are usually not the same value in a given distribution. If the distribution is symmetrical and unimodal (one mode), then the mean, median, and mode are indeed identical. This condition is graphed in Part A of Figure 3–3. If the distribution is symmetrical but has two modes, such as in Part B, the mean and median are the same but the modes are different (the distribution is **bimodal**). In Chapter 2, a skewed distribution was defined to be one that was not symmetrical, having scores bunched on one end.

Parts C and D of Figure 3–3 illustrate two skewed distributions and the relative positions of the three measures of central tendency. The distribution in Part C is fairly common and illustrates a condition in which most scores have moderate values but a few are very high. In this case, the mean, being sensitive to those extreme values, is somewhat higher than the median which divides the area under the curve (i.e., the total number of cases) into two equal parts. A common illustration of this situation occurs in the reporting of typical family income. In a given year mean family income in the United States is usually higher than the median income because the relatively few really high incomes will push the mean upward but not influence the median. Part D of Figure 3–3 illustrates the relative positions of the measures of central tendency when the skewness of the distribution is in the other direction.

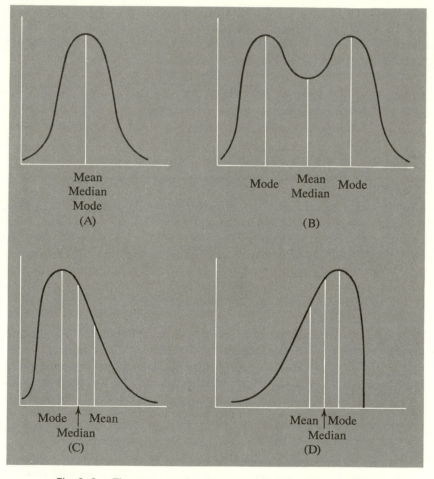

Fig. 3–3. The mean, median, and mode in different distributions.

Ordinarily, the mean is selected as the measure of central tendency. There are several reasons for preferring the mean, but one of the major considerations is that the mean is required by so many other statistical procedures. For example, later in this text techniques for comparing the central tendency of one group with that of another group of scores will be described, and these calculations require that the means of the groups be used. Consequently, in most situations the mean is the preferred measure of central tendency.

However, sometimes the circumstances are such that the median would reflect the central tendency of the distribution more accurately than would the mean. When the distribution is very skewed, the mean may not yield a value that coincides with one's intuitive impression of what the "typical score" should be. For example, the distribution (1, 2, 3, 4, 100) has a mean of 22 and a median of 3. In this case the median seems to characterize the central tendency of the group more faithfully than does the mean of 22 which is not close in value to any score in the distribution. Thus, in the case of a markedly skewed distribution the median demonstrates a distinct advantage in characterizing the central tendency. The mode is used most often as a supplement to the mean or median especially in the case of a bimodal distribution.

estimation

POPULATION AND SAMPLE

Frequently, a scientist performs an experiment on a relatively small group of subjects. At the conclusion of the research, however, the results are generalized to a much larger group of subjects of which the sample is a small part. For example, an experiment might be performed using a group of 40 students at State University, but the results are discussed in terms of "all college students." The small group actually used as subjects in the experiment is known as a **sample** whereas the larger group of subjects to which the researcher wishes to generalize the results is called the **population**. Succinctly stated:

A **population** is a collection of subjects or events that have some common characteristic.[3]
A **sample** is a subgroup of a population.

It is important to note that sample and population are relative terms. "All students enrolled at State University" might be the population from which a sample of 50 students is drawn for a given experiment, but it might also function as a sample of the larger population of "all college students."

[3] Very frequently, although not always, a population is considered to be composed of an infinite number of cases. While such a conception of the population has certain advantages, particularly for theoretical mathematical statistics, the definition presented here will be used for certain pedagogical reasons.

One obvious reason why samples rather than populations are used in research is that the populations are usually too large to be studied efficiently. However, it is usually of trivial interest for the scientist to consider the results as being appropriate only to the specific subjects experimented upon. Therefore, the scientist designs the experiment so that generalizations may be drawn from the sample to the population. One aspect of this process is to **estimate** characteristics in the population by computing various measures on the sample.

Characteristics of a population are called **parameters**, while those of a sample are termed **statistics**. Therefore, the research scientist attempts to estimate parameters with statistics.

CHARACTERISTICS OF A "GOOD" ESTIMATOR

Frequently, a researcher wants to estimate the mean of the population. For example, suppose a research program was being established to investigate procedures for teaching mynah birds to talk. It would be important to know how much vocalization an untrained mynah bird emits in the course of a 12-hour day before special procedures are attempted to mold that natural vocalization into something resembling human speech. Consequently, the mean time spent vocalizing in a 12-hour period for all mynah birds would be desired, but it will be estimated from a small sample of 20 birds. Suppose the mean time in this sample is 88 minutes, the median is 83, the mode is 92, and the longest single time was 112. Which sample statistic should be used to estimate the population mean, and on what grounds should this choice be made?

There are several criteria for a good estimator. The one that will be of major concern in this book is the quality of **unbiasedness**.

> An **unbiased estimator** of a population parameter is one whose average over all possible random samples of a given size equals the value of the parameter.

Suppose that the sample mean is to be used to estimate the population mean time spent vocalizing by mynah birds in a 12-hour period. If the sample mean is an unbiased estimator of the population mean the following would be true: If many, many samples of 20 mynah birds were selected and the mean were computed for each sample, then as the number of such samples becomes very large the average of the sample means would tend to equal the population mean. For example, suppose somehow we knew that the population mean vocalization time was in fact 90 minutes. If we obtained one sample of 20 birds and timed their vocalizations, the mean might be 83 minutes. Now suppose that we obtained five samples of 20 birds, each sample selected independently of the others, and the mean vocalization times were calculated separately for each sample. Assume the average of these five means was 96 minutes. Table 3–3 lists these results plus those for 10, 50, 100, 1000, and an infinite number of samples (assuming that were possible).

3–3 Average of Sample Means for Different Numbers of Samples.		
Number of Samples	Average of Sample Means	Difference between Average Mean and Population Mean (90)
1	83	−7
5	96	+6
10	93	+3
50	86	−4
100	88	−2
1000	91	+1
∞	90	0

Recall that an estimator is considered unbiased if there is a tendency for the value of the estimator to converge exactly on the population value as the number of samples increases. In this contrived example, the average mean does tend to converge on the population value of 90 as the number of samples increases, a fact which can be seen most clearly by the diminishing size of the difference between the average mean and the population value given in the third column.

Actually, of course, mathematical statisticians do not determine whether a sample statistic is an unbiased estimator of a given population value by obtaining hundreds of samples and averaging the observed values of the statistics as implied in the above illustration. There are sophisticated theoretical mathematical procedures (derived from "expectation theory") which can be used. Moreover, there are more attributes of a good estimator than just unbiasedness. However, these topics are beyond the scope of this text.[4]

The fact that this course is usually called "statistics" and not "parameters" indicates that the focus is on computing measures on samples and not on populations. Consequently, for some statistics presented in this volume, the relationship between sample value and corresponding parameter will be discussed (e.g., the variance—see following), whereas in other cases only the sample statistic will be considered (e.g., median, mode). To facilitate distinguishing between statistics and parameters, statistics are usually abbreviated with Roman letters while parameters often have Greek designations. This custom will be illustrated in the following statement on sample and population means.

[4] For more details on the characteristics of good estimators, see: W. L. Hays, *Statistics for the Social Sciences, Second Edition* (New York: Holt, Rinehart, & Winston, 1973).

SAMPLE AND POPULATION MEANS

The sample mean was symbolized by $\bar{X}$ and was computed with the formula

$$\bar{X} = \frac{\Sigma X}{N}$$

The **population mean** is symbolized by the Greek letter μ (read "mew"). $\bar{X}$ is frequently used as an estimator of the population mean, μ.

EXERCISES

A	B	C	D
1	1	1	1
3	3	2	3
5	4	2	4
6	6	2	5
7	7	3	6
7	8	5	6
8	8	6	6
	9	6	9
	9	6	25
	9	8	
		9	

1. Compute the mean, median, and mode for each of the above distributions.

2. Which measure of central tendency is most appropriate for each distribution and why?

3. Indicate for each of the following distributions which measure of central tendency would be preferred and explain why.
   (a) family incomes in the U.S.A.
   (b) heights of seniors in a public high school
   (c) IQ scores in the third grade of a public school

4. Find the median for the following distributions.
   (a) 1, 4, 6, 7, 10
   (b) 1, 3, 4, 7, 8, 11
   (c) 1, 2, 3, 3, 3, 3
   (d) 1, 2, 3, 3, 3, 3, 5
   (e) 5, 10, 11, 11, 15
   (f) 3.2, 3.3, 3.3, 3.4, 3.6 (Note the score interval is .1.)

5. Draw the distributions such that the following are true.
   (a) The mean, median, and mode are identical.
   (b) The mean and median are identical but the mode is different.
   (c) The mean is greater than the median.
   (d) The median is greater than the mean.

6. Show that the sum of the deviations about the mean of Distribution A is zero. Compute the sum of the deviations about the median of Distribution A. Which is less, the sum of the deviations about the mean or about the median?

7. In what way are the terms "population" and "sample" relative?

8. Why is this course called "statistics" and not "parameters"?

9. Define the concept of an unbiased estimator.

measures of variability

In order to characterize a distribution more fully, a measure of variability is needed in addition to an index of central tendency.

Variability refers to the extent to which the scores differ from each other.

For example, suppose two groups of scores, A and B, are defined to be

$$A = (5, 7, 9)$$
$$B = (3, 7, 11)$$

Although they both have the same mean of 7, set B has more variability than A. The purpose of this section is to discuss measures that provide a numerical index of the extent of the variability of scores in a distribution.

THE RANGE

One measure of variability is the range. The range may be estimated by taking the largest score minus the smallest score in the distribution.[5] In the distribution (3, 5, 6, 6, 8, 9), the range is 6.

However, the range is limited in its ability to reflect the variability of a distribution. While it is certainly true that as the variability increases in a distribu-

---

[5] Technically, the range should probably be defined as the difference between the upper real limit of the largest score minus the lower real limit of the smallest score. Since the range is an approximate index of variability at best, it does not seem appropriate to insist upon this level of "accuracy."

tion, the range of scores is also likely to increase, the range is not sensitive to the variability of all the scores, only the two most extreme values. Further, the range itself is a statistic with a great deal of variability from sample to sample. When a statistic is said to have a great deal of variability, its value is not very consistent from one sample to the next, and thus not very much confidence can be placed in the accuracy of that statistic when it is calculated on only one sample of scores. Therefore, although the range is easily computed, it is usually employed only as a crude approximation of variability.

THE VARIANCE AND STANDARD DEVIATION

An index that reflects the degree of variability in a group of scores but which does not have the limitations of the range is the **variance**.

The **sample variance**, symbolized by s^2, is defined to be

$$s^2 = \frac{\sum_{i=1}^{N} (X_i - \bar{X})^2}{N - 1}$$

In words, the variance is the sum of the squared deviations of the scores from their mean, $\sum(X_i - \bar{X})^2$, divided by the number of scores minus one ($N - 1$). Conceptually, it is very much like the average squared deviation of the scores about their mean except that the squared deviations are divided by $N - 1$ rather than N. The reason for having $N - 1$ as the denominator is that this "correction" makes s^2 an unbiased estimator of the population variance. If N were used in the denominator, the value of the variance based on a sample of scores would not converge on the population variance as the number of such samples became larger and larger. Such a biased estimator tends to be just a little bit smaller than the population value on the average. However, the mathematics of expectation has determined that if $N - 1$ rather than simply N is used in the denominator, such a statistic would then indeed be an unbiased estimator of the **population variance** which is symbolized by σ^2 (read "SIG-mah squared"). Since in practice one almost always uses the variance s^2 based upon a sample of cases to estimate the population variance σ^2, this text will always use the formula for s^2 which contains $N - 1$ as the denominator.

computational example   One method for calculating the variance simply uses the definitional formula given above. (Another method of computation more suitable for using hand calculators is explained on pages 57–60).

X_i	$\overline{X}$	$(X_i - \overline{X})$	$(X_i - \overline{X})^2$
5	7	-2	4
7	7	0	0
9	7	$+2$	4

$$\sum_{i=1}^{N} X_i = 21 \qquad\qquad 0 \qquad\qquad \sum_{i=1}^{N} (X_i - \overline{X})^2 = 8$$

$$N = 3$$
$$\overline{X} = 7$$

$$s^2 = \frac{\sum_{i=1}^{N} (X_i - \overline{X})^2}{N - 1}$$

$$s^2 = \tfrac{8}{2}$$

$$s^2 = 4.00$$

Notice that the mean is computed first ($\overline{X} = 7.0$). Then the mean is subtracted from each score ($X_i - \overline{X}$) and this difference is squared [$(X_i - \overline{X})^2$]. The sum of the squared deviations from the mean is divided by $N - 1$ to obtain the variance.

The variance is difficult to "explain" because it cannot be diagrammed or "pointed at." Rather, the variance is an abstract numerical index that increases with the amount of variability in the group of scores. Despite the fact that the variance escapes being pictured, it does have a certain logic to it. The mean is the central value of the distribution and it seems natural to base a measure of variability upon the extent to which the scores deviate from their central tendency [i.e., $(X_i - \overline{X})^2$]. In addition one may recall from the discussion of the mean that the sum of the squared deviations about the mean is less than the sum about any other value. This fact adds to the logic of selecting squared deviations about the mean (as opposed to some other value) as an index of variability.

Consider the implications of squaring the deviations $(X_i - \overline{X})^2$. First, all of the deviations make a positive contribution to the total because squaring a negative number results in a positive value. If the deviations were not squared then the negative deviations would cancel out the positive and their sum would be zero because

$$\sum_{i=1}^{N} (X_i - \overline{X}) = 0$$

Second, large deviations, when squared, contribute disproportionately to the total (e.g., a deviation of 4 units becomes 16 when squared, but a deviation of twice that size, that is of 8 units, contributes 64 to the total sum of squared deviations). Thus, the final index is especially sensitive to extreme departures from the mean because of the squaring procedure.

Third, the fact that the squared deviations are divided by $N - 1$, makes the variance a sort of "average squared deviation," and thus the variance of distributions having different numbers of scores may be compared just as means from distributions having different N's may be compared.

A last point to be made about the variance as a measure of variability is this: Recall that the definition of variability is "the extent to which the scores deviate from one another." One way to measure such variability would be to sum the squared deviations between each score and every other score in the distribution and divide this total by the number of such pairs $[N(N-1)/2]$. This procedure for obtaining a measure of variability follows the definition of variability quite closely, and it is important to note that the variance is directly proportional to this alternative index. Therefore, the variance is indeed closely associated with the concept of variability which it measures.

the standard deviation, s   The variance measures variability in squared units. If the researcher recorded how long it took animals to find their way to a goal box at the end of a maze, the mean time would be in seconds but the variance would be in "squared seconds." This results from the fact that the formula for the mean uses the scores as they are (e.g., $\sum X$) but the formula for the variance squares the deviations (e.g., $\sum (X - \overline{X})^2$) thus changing them from seconds to "squared seconds." However, it will be convenient to have a measure of variability in terms of the original units of measurement, not squared units.

The **standard deviation** (symbolized by s) is defined to be the positive square root of the variance:

$$s = \sqrt{s^2}$$

or (without subscripts)

$$s = \sqrt{\frac{\sum (X - \overline{X})^2}{N - 1}}$$

Since the variance was in squared units, by taking its square root, a return is made to the original units of measurement.[6] The **population standard deviation** is symbolized by σ (read "SIG-mah").

SPECIAL COMPUTATIONAL PROCEDURES
FOR s^2 AND s

The formulas given above are called "definitional formulas" because they define and usually provide the most logical explanation of the concept. However,

[6] The notation SD is used in some other texts to symbolize the standard deviation.

when sufficient amounts of data are collected, the definitional formulas are frequently not very convenient to use in making the calculations. An expression for a statistic that is mathematically equivalent to the definitional formula but more convenient for calculating is called a "computational formula." In the case of the variance and standard deviation, it is tedious to first compute the mean and then subtract it from each score, particularly if the mean is a lengthy decimal. Not only is the decimal subtraction laborious, but the squaring of these decimal remainders is even more cumbersome. Therefore, an expression more appropriate for calculation is desirable.

The computational formula for the variance is (summations of X are from $i = 1, N$)

$$s^2 = \frac{N\sum X^2 - (\sum X)^2}{N(N-1)}$$

The computational formula for the standard deviation is

$$s = \sqrt{\frac{N\sum X^2 - (\sum X)^2}{N(N-1)}} \quad \text{or} \quad s = \sqrt{s^2}$$

It is important to realize that these computational formulas yield results which are equivalent (within rounding error) to those calculated by the definitional formulas. Optional Table 3–4 demonstrates the algebraic equivalence of the two formulas.

The computational formula has the advantage of having only one division, not requiring that the mean be calculated first, and facility in computing on a standard hand calculator. Only three quantities are needed: $\sum X^2$, $\sum X$, and N. Consider the variance and standard deviation of the following distribution:

X	X^2
3	9
4	16
7	49
8	64
8	64
9	81
10	100
$\sum X = 49$	$\sum X^2 = 383$
$N = 7$	

3-4   The Algebraic Equivalence of the Definitional and Computational Formulas for the Variance.

Operation	Explanation
To prove	
$$s^2 = \frac{\sum(X_i - \bar{X})^2}{N-1} = \frac{N\sum X_i^2 - (\sum X_i)^2}{N(N-1)}$$	
1. $\quad s^2 = \dfrac{\sum(X_i - \bar{X})^2}{N-1}$	1. Definition
2. $\quad = \dfrac{\sum(X_i^2 - 2X_i\bar{X} + \bar{X}^2)}{N-1}$	2. Expanding $\sum(X_i - \bar{X})^2$ in the manner: $(a-b)^2 = (a^2 - 2ab + b^2)$
3. $\quad = \dfrac{\sum X_i^2 - \sum 2X_i\bar{X} + \sum \bar{X}^2}{N-1}$	3. The sum of several terms is the sum of the separate terms: $\sum(X + Y + Z) = \sum X + \sum Y + \sum Z$
4. $\quad = \dfrac{\sum X_i^2 - 2\bar{X}\sum X_i + \sum \bar{X}^2}{N-1}$	4. The sum of a constant times a variable equals the constant times the sum of the variable ($\bar{X}$ is a constant): $\sum kX = k\sum X$
5. $\quad = \dfrac{\sum X_i^2 - 2\bar{X}\sum X_i + N\bar{X}^2}{N-1}$	5. The sum of a constant taken N times is N times the constant: $\sum_{i=1}^{N} k = Nk$

6.
$$= \frac{\sum X_i^2 - 2\left(\frac{\sum X_i}{N}\right)\sum X_i + N\left(\frac{\sum X_i}{N}\right)\left(\frac{\sum X_i}{N}\right)}{N-1}$$

6. Substitution: $\bar{X} = \dfrac{\sum X_i}{N}$

7.
$$= \frac{\sum X_i^2 - 2\left(\frac{\sum X_i}{N}\right)\sum X_i + (\sum X_i)\left(\frac{\sum X_i}{N}\right)}{N-1}$$

7. Cancellation in the third term.

8.
$$= \frac{\sum X_i^2 - \left(\frac{\sum X_i}{N}\right)\sum X_i}{N-1}$$

8. Subtraction involving the last two terms of the numerator.

9.
$$= \frac{N\sum X_i^2 - N\left(\frac{\sum X_i}{N}\right)\sum X_i}{N(N-1)}$$

9. Multiplying numerator and denominator by N.

10.
$$s^2 = \frac{N\sum X_i^2 - (\sum X_i)^2}{N(N-1)}$$

10. Cancellation

variance	standard deviation

$$s^2 = \frac{N\sum X^2 - (\sum X)^2}{N(N-1)}$$

$$s = \sqrt{s^2}$$

$$s = \sqrt{6.67}$$

$$s = 2.58$$

$$s^2 = \frac{7(383) - (49)^2}{7(7-1)} = \frac{2681 - 2401}{42}$$

$$s^2 = \frac{280}{42}$$

$$s^2 = 6.67$$

It is very important to distinguish between two quantities used in the formula: $\sum X^2$ and $(\sum X)^2$. The first, $\sum X^2$, means the sum of all the squared scores—square each score then add. The second, $(\sum X)^2$, means the square of the sum of the scores—add all the scores and then square this sum. Confusion between these two quantities is often the source of computational error.

PROPERTIES OF s^2 AND s AS MEASURES OF VARIABILITY

The first property of the variance as a measure of variability is that it is proportional to the average squared deviation of each score from every other score. As previously noted, the intuitive concept of variability embodies the extent to which each of the scores deviates from every other score. Since the variance is proportional to the average squared deviation of each score from every other score, it follows that the variance indeed reflects the variability of the scores.

Second, as the variability of the scores increases, the statistical variance also increases. This can be seen in the few examples listed below:

Scores	s^2
10, 10, 10	0
8, 10, 12	4
6, 10, 14	16
4, 10, 16	36
2, 10, 18	64

As the scores show more and more variability, the value of s^2 increases, faithfully reflecting the extent to which the scores deviate from one another. Similar arguments can be made for the standard deviation.

Third, consider the definitional formula for the variance:

$$s^2 = \frac{\Sigma(X_i - \bar{X})^2}{N - 1}$$

Since all quantities involving X are squared, the variance will always be positive.

Fourth, if there is no variability among the scores, that is, all the scores in the distribution are identical to one another, then each quantity $(X_i - \bar{X})^2$ and their sum will be zero because X_i and $\bar{X}$ will always be identical. Therefore, when there is no variability among the scores of a distribution (all scores are the same value), $s^2 = 0$.

Fifth, s^2 and s are more sensitive to variability in a group of scores and they are less variable in themselves (different samples tend to yield more similar values) than the range. The range is neither a precise nor a very stable measure of variability, and s^2 and s are much preferred in this regard.

Sixth, the variance frequently is used in other statistical manipulations, and therefore its computation as a measure of variability also finds application in the calculation of other formulas.

Seventh, under certain conditions the variance may be partitioned into various parts which can be attributed to different sources. This capability of being partitioned permits statisticians to ask the following types of questions: A group of scores possesses a certain amount of variability. What portion of that variability can be attributed to cause A as opposed to cause B? This aspect of the variance will be taken up in more detail later in the chapters on the analysis of variance.

FORMULAS

1. Mean

$$\bar{X} = \frac{\Sigma X_i}{N}$$

Population mean symbolized by μ.

2. Median

(a) **No duplication near the median, odd number of scores:**
M_d is the middle score.
(b) **No duplication near the median, even number of scores:**
M_d is the average of the two middle scores.

(c) **Duplication of scores near the median:**

$$M_d = L + \left[\frac{N/2 - n_b}{n_w}\right] i$$

where L = lower real limit of the score interval containing the median
N = number of scores in the distribution
n_b = number of scores falling below the lower real limit of the interval containing the median
n_w = number of cases within the score interval containing the median
i = the size of the score interval ($i = 1$ if the data are in whole numbers)

3. Mode

The mode, M_o, is the most frequent score.

4. Range

The range is estimated by taking the largest minus the smallest score.

5. Variance

$$s^2 = \frac{\sum(X_i - \bar{X})^2}{N - 1} \qquad \text{(definitional)}$$

$$s^2 = \frac{N\sum X_i^2 - (\sum X_i)^2}{N(N - 1)} \qquad \text{(computational)}$$

Population variance symbolized by σ^2

6. Standard Deviation

$$s = \sqrt{s^2} = \sqrt{\frac{\sum(X_i - \bar{X})^2}{N - 1}} \qquad \text{(definitional)}$$

$$s = \sqrt{\frac{N\sum X_i^2 - (\sum X_i)^2}{N(N - 1)}} \qquad \text{(computational)}$$

Population standard deviation symbolized by σ

EXERCISES

1. Define the concept of variability and compose three distributions which differ in their amount of variability.

2. Discuss the limitations of the range as a measure of variability and whenever possible present some numerical examples to illustrate your points.

3. Compute with both the definitional and computational formulas the variance and standard deviation for each of the following distributions. Also compare the means of these distributions.

   (a) 6, 7, 7, 8
   (b) 4, 5, 9, 10
   (c) 0, 1, 3, 4, 7, 7, 8, 8, 9, 9, 9, 10, 10, 10, 10

4. Why does the formula for the variance have $N - 1$ in the denominator and not N?

5. Discuss the properties, characteristics, and advantages of s^2 as a measure of variability. Does s have any potential advantages over s^2?

MEASURES
OF
RELATIVE
STANDING

4

Although the characteristics of a distribution discussed in the previous chapter help to describe that distribution, they do not provide direct assistance in interpreting individual scores. For example, suppose you received a grade of 88 on a statistics examination. Just knowing your numerical score without any knowledge of the nature of the distribution of scores does not offer much information. Your score of 88 might be the highest or the lowest in the class—one simply cannot tell without more information. Knowing that the mean was 81 tells you that you were above the mean but very little else. What is needed in order to interpret a score of 88 is some index of your relative standing within the total distribution. Percentiles and standard scores perform this function.

percentiles

One of the most common measures of relative standing is the percentile.

> The **Pth percentile** is that value on the scale of measurement below which *P* percent of the cases in the distribution fall. The value on the scale of measurement is called a **percentile point**, while its corresponding percentage is known as its **percentile rank**.

Thus, if a score of 88 was at the 92nd **percentile rank**, 92% of the people in the group scored less than the **percentile point** of 88. The **upper quartile** is determined by the score value separating the top 25% from the remainder of the distribution while the **lower quartile** is determined by the score value separating the bottom 25% of the distribution. The **interquartile range** is determined by the score values that separate the middle 50% of the distribution from the remainder—that is, the percentile points corresponding to $P_{.25}$ and $P_{.75}$ where $P_{.25}$, for example, signifies the 25th percentile. Notice that a percentile rank corresponds to the cumulative relative frequency of its corresponding score value.

COMPUTATION OF PERCENTILE POINTS

Computing percentile points is very similar to computing the median. Indeed, the median is $P_{.50}$. First, consider how to determine the score value corresponding to a given percentile rank.

For example, what is the score value corresponding to the 30th percentile in the distribution of 40 scores on a statistics examination presented in Table 4–1? First, recall the definition of a percentile point: It is that score value below which P percent of the cases in the distribution fall. In this problem, P is .30 and the number of cases in the distribution is $N = 40$. Therefore,

$$P(N) = .30(40) = 12$$

cases must fall below the required score value. Looking at the data in Table 4–1, the 12th student from the bottom of the distribution had a score of 59. Therefore, 12 students scored below the upper real limit of the score of 59, and consequently the percentile point corresponding to $P_{.30}$ is 59.5.

This logic is expressed in a formula which will also determine percentile points in more complicated situations involving duplication of scores near the required score value.

The percentile point corresponding to the Pth rank is given by

$$\text{Percentile Point} = L + \left[\frac{P(N) - n_b}{n_w} \right] i$$

in which

$P =$ the percentile rank of the required point (P ranges between 0 and 1.00)

$N =$ the number of scores in the distribution

$L =$ the lower real limit of the score value containing the required percentile point

$n_b =$ the number of cases falling below L

$n_w =$ the number of cases falling within the score value containing the required percentile point

$i =$ the size of the score interval ($i = 1$ if the data are whole numbers)

In the current problem, one would first determine $P(N)$ as above. P is .30 and $N = 40$, so

$$P(N) = .30(40) = 12$$

students must score lower than the required score value. One then looks up the 12th student from the bottom of the distribution and observes that his score was 59, which has a lower real limit of 58.5. Therefore, $L = 58.5$. There are 11 scores below this lower real limit (i.e., $n_b = 11$), only one person scored 59 (i.e., $n_w = 1$), and $i = 1$. Therefore,

$$L + \left[\frac{P(N) - n_b}{n_w} \right] i$$

$$58.5 + \left[\frac{12 - 11}{1} \right] 1 = 59.5$$

The formula also determines percentile points when there is duplication of scores near the desired point. For example, consider determining the percentile point corresponding to the 20th percentile rank (i.e., $P_{.20}$). In this case, $P = .20$ and $N = 40$ so $P(N) = .20(40) = 8$ cases must fall below the desired score value. The eighth lowest subject scored 55 but so did three others. Therefore, the lower real limit of the score of 55 is $L = 54.5$, there were five people who scored below 55 (i.e., $n_b = 5$), and four people scored 55 (i.e., $n_w = 4$). The 20th percentile point is given by

$$L + \left[\frac{P(N) - n_b}{n_w} \right] i$$

$$54.4 + \left[\frac{.20(40) - 5}{4} \right] 1 = 55.25$$

The two illustrations just given show how one computes the score (i.e., percentile point) corresponding to a given percentile rank. However, the question can be reversed. What is the percentile rank corresponding to a given score?

What is the percentile rank of a score of 83? Looking at Table 4–1 one can see that the score of 83 was 32nd in the distribution. This implies that 32 people scored lower than 83.5 which is the upper real limit of 83. Similarly, 31 people scored below 82.5 which is the lower real limit of 83. Therefore, 31.5 of 40 people or $31.5/40 = 78.75\%$ of the cases recorded a score below exactly 83.0. Therefore, the score of 83 is at the 78.75th percentile rank, or more conventionally at the 79th percentile. Thus, 83 corresponds to $P_{.79}$.

Again a formula exists which will produce this result as well as percentile ranks when duplication of scores is a problem.

4–1	Distribution of Scores on a Statistics Examination for a Class of 40 Students.						
Student No.	Score	Student No.	Score	Student No.	Score	Student No.	Score
40	97	30	80	20	72	10	56
39	93	29	79	19	72	9	55
38	92	28	78	18	72	8	55
37	91	27	78	17	71	7	55
36	88	26	78	16	70	6	55
35	85	25	78	15	65	5	51
34	85	24	76	14	61	4	49
33	84	23	75	13	60	3	49
32	83	22	75	12	59	2	48
31	82	21	74	11	58	1	46

The percentile rank corresponding to a given score is determined by

$$P = \frac{n_w(X - L) + in_b}{Ni}$$

in which

P = the desired percentile rank (P ranges between 0 and 1.00)
X = the score value corresponding to the desired percentile rank
L = the lower real limit of X
n_w = the number of cases having a score of X
n_b = the number of cases having a score lower than X
N = the total number of cases in the distribution
i = the size of the score interval (i = 1 if the data are in whole numbers)

To determine the percentile rank for a score of 83, let $X = 83$, with the lower real limit $L = 82.5$. There is only one score of 83 in the distribution (i.e., $n_w = 1$); 31 scores are below L (i.e., $n_b = 31$), $i = 1$; and there are $N = 40$ scores in the entire distribution. Therefore,

$$P = \frac{n_w(X - L) + in_b}{Ni}$$

$$= \frac{1(83 - 82.5) + 1(31)}{40(1)} = \frac{31.5}{40}$$

$$P = .7875$$

Therefore, $X = 83$ is at the 78.75th or 79th percentile rank (i.e., $P_{.79}$).

Suppose one had to determine the percentile rank corresponding to a score of 72. In this case, $X = 72$ with a lower real limit of $L = 71.5$, three people scored exactly 72 (i.e., $n_w = 3$), and 17 people scored lower than 72 (i.e., $n_b = 17$). Consequently,

$$P = \frac{n_w(X - L) + in_b}{Ni}$$

$$P = \frac{3(72 - 71.5) + 1(17)}{40(1)} = \frac{18.5}{40}$$

$$P = .4625$$

Thus, $X = 72$ is at the 46.25th or 46th percentile rank (i.e., $P_{.46}$).

EXERCISES

1. Using the frequency distribution presented in Table 4–1, determine the score values corresponding to the following percentile ranks.

(a) $P_{.30}$	(c) $P_{.10}$	(e) $P_{.45}$	(g) $P_{.675}$
(b) $P_{.65}$	(d) $P_{.85}$	(f) $P_{.475}$	(h) $P_{.50}$

2. Using Table 4–1, determine the percentile ranks corresponding to the following score values.

(a) 51	(c) 82	(e) 55	(g) 85
(b) 75	(d) 78	(f) 60	(h) 49

changing the properties of scales

Centigrade and Fahrenheit are two different scales of temperature. They differ in that they do not have the same origins (not to be confused with absolute zero) or the same sized units. The transformation formula for converting degrees centigrade to degrees Fahrenheit is given by

$$°F = °C(1.8) + 32°$$

The 1.8 is the factor used to convert the size of the centigrade degree to the size of the Fahrenheit degree. Consider the freezing and boiling points of water on the two scales. For the Fahrenheit scale, these points are 32° and 212°, respectively, whereas for the centigrade scale they are 0° and 100°, respectively. Thus, between the freezing and boiling point of water on the Fahrenheit scale there are 180 Fahrenhiet degrees. Between the freezing and boiling point of water on the centigrade scale there are only 100 centigrade degrees. Therefore the centigrade degree is larger, and it takes 1.8 Fahrenheit degrees to equal 1 centigrade degree. This is the reason why the 1.8 appears in the conversion formula; it changes the centigrade unit into a Fahrenheit unit.

However, the two scales are not yet equivalent. Even if the centigrade degree is transformed to the Fahrenheit degree, the freezing point is still at 0° and the boiling point is at $(1.8)(100) = 180°$, both values 32° short of their corresponding Fahrenheit values. That is, the origins of the scales are different. One is 32°F away from the other. To change the origin to match the Fahrenheit origin, 32° must be added. Thus, the conversion formula is

$$°F = °C(1.8) + 32°$$

in which the 1.8 converts the centigrade unit to the Fahrenheit unit and the 32 adjusts the origin of the centigrade scale to match that of the Fahrenheit scale.

To formalize these rules:

> To change the size of the unit of measurement, multiply or divide the old values by the proper constant (conversion factor). To change the origin of a scale, add or subtract the appropriate number of units.

Most transformations common to everyday life are ones in which only the size of the unit is converted. For example:

$$\text{feet} = \frac{\text{inches}}{12} \longleftarrow \text{conversion factor}$$

$$\text{kilometers} = (.6)\ \text{miles} \qquad \text{conversion factor}$$

However, in research in the social sciences, transformations are frequently made from one scale to another which do involve changing both the unit size and the origin of the scale. Since these transformations are common, it will be instructive to consider what happens to the mean and variance of a distribution as a function of altering the unit size and origin.

EFFECTS OF SCALE CHANGES ON THE MEAN

The origin of a scale is changed by adding or subtracting a constant from every score. If a constant is added to (or subtracted from) every score in the distribution, the mean of the new distribution is the mean of the old plus (or minus) that constant. If $X' = X + c$, then

$$\overline{X}' = \overline{X} + c$$

Therefore, if the mean of a distribution is 15 and 3 is added to every score, the new mean would be $15 + 3 = 18$. If 3 were subtracted from every score, the new mean would be $15 - 3 = 12$. Optional Table 4–2 presents a formal proof of this statement.

4–2 Change in the Mean with a Change in Origin.	
Operation	**Explanation**
1. $\overline{X}' = \dfrac{\sum(X + c)}{N}$	1. Definition of the mean for a distribution in which c has been added to each X.
2. $= \dfrac{\sum X + \sum c}{N}$	2. The sum of several terms is the sum of the separate terms.
3. $= \dfrac{\sum X + Nc}{N}$	3. The sum (from 1 to N) of a constant is N times that constant.
4. $= \dfrac{\sum X}{N} + \dfrac{\not{N}c}{\not{N}}$	4. Simplification.
5. $\overline{X}' = \overline{X} + c$	5. Substitution: $\dfrac{\sum X}{N} = \overline{X}$

OPTIONAL TABLE

The unit of a scale is changed by multiplying or dividing every score by a constant. If every score in a distribution is multiplied (or divided) by a constant, the mean of the new distribution is the mean of the old distribution multiplied (or divided) by that constant. In symbols, if $X' = cX$, then

$$\overline{X}' = c\overline{X}$$

Therefore, if the mean of a distribution is 15 and if every score is multiplied by 3, the new mean will be multiplied by 3 ($15 \times 3 = 45$). Since dividing each score by c is the same as multiplying each score by $1/c$, if every score is divided by 3, the mean will be divided by 3 ($15 \div 3 = 5$). Optional Table 4–3 gives a general proof of this fact.

4–3 Change in the Mean with a Change in Unit.	
Operation	**Explanation**
1. $\overline{X}' = \dfrac{\sum cX}{N}$	1. Definition.
2. $= \dfrac{c\sum X}{N}$	2. The sum of a constant times a variable is the constant times the sum of that variable.
3. $\overline{X}' = c\overline{X}$	3. Substitution: $\dfrac{\sum X}{N} = \overline{X}$

OPTIONAL TABLE

In summary, if the scale of measurement is altered, the mean will also change in the same manner and to the same extent as the scale. This makes sense because the mean can be conceived to be a "typical score," and thus if every score is incremented or multiplied by a constant, it should follow that the mean, as a typical score, should also undergo the same change.

EFFECTS OF SCALE CHANGES ON THE VARIANCE AND STANDARD DEVIATION

Consider now the effects of these same transformations of scale on the variance and standard deviation of a distribution.

If the origin of a scale is changed by adding (or subtracting) a constant from every score in the distribution, the variance and standard deviation are not changed. If $X' = X + c$ and s_x^2 symbolizes the variance of the original variable X_i, then

$$s_{x'}^2 = s_x^2$$

and

$$s_{x'} = s_x$$

Thus, if the variance of a distribution is 16 and the standard deviation is 4, then when 5 is added to every score these statistics will remain unchanged and $s^2 = 16$ and $s = 4$. This makes intuitive sense if one considers that s^2 and s are really functions of the distance between the various points of the distribution, not the distance those points are from the origin. For example, consider the distance between points in the following distribution before and after a change of origin (5 is added to each score):

	X			$X' = X + 5$	
3	7	11	8	12	16

$(X - \overline{X})$: 4 4 $(X' - \overline{X}')$: 4 4

Since s^2 and s are based upon the distances between the points and the mean $(X - \overline{X})$ and since these distances do not change when the origin is changed, adding a constant to each score does not alter s^2 and s. The formal proof that such a change in origin leaves s^2 and s unaffected is presented in Optional Table 4–4.

If the unit of measurement is changed by multiplying (or dividing) every score in the distribution by a positive constant, the new variance will equal the old variance multiplied (or divided) by the square of that constant and the new standard deviation will equal the old

4-4 No Change in the Variance (and Standard Deviation) with a Change in Origin.	
Operation	**Explanation**
1. $s_{x'}^2 = \dfrac{\sum[(X+c)-(\overline{X}+c)]^2}{N-1}$	1. Definition and if a constant is added to every score, the mean will also be incremented by that constant.
2. $= \dfrac{\sum[X+c-\overline{X}-c]^2}{N-1}$	2. Removing parentheses.
3. $s_{x'}^2 = \dfrac{\sum(X-\overline{X})^2}{N-1} = s_x^2$	3. Subtraction.

standard deviation multiplied (or divided) by that constant. If $X' = cX$, and s_x^2 symbolizes the variance of the original variable X_i, then

$$s_{x'}^2 = c^2 s_x^2$$

and

$$s_{x'} = c s_x$$

Thus, if the variance of a distribution is 16 and the standard deviation is 4 and each score in the distribution is multiplied by 2, the variance of the new distribution will be $(2^2)(16) = 64$ and the new standard deviation will be $(2)(4) = 8$. Notice that while adding and subtracting a constant does not affect s^2 and s, multiplying or dividing by a constant does influence these statistics. This distinction can be seen more clearly by considering the deviations and squared deviations which are part of the variance when the scale undergoes a change in unit (every score is multiplied by 2):

	X				$X' = 2X$		
	3	7	11		6	14	22
$(X - \overline{X})$:		4	4	$(X' - \overline{X}')$:		8	8
$(X - \overline{X})^2$:		16	16	$(X' - \overline{X}')^2$:		64	64

Two important points are to be gained from this example. First, when the unit of measurement is changed by multiplying every score by 2, the distances between points are also multiplied by 2. Second, when these deviations are squared, the differences in the size of the squared deviations between the two scales increases by $2^2 = 4$ (in general, c^2). Since the variance uses these squared deviations in its formula, the size of the variance will be multiplied by c^2 if each score is multiplied by c. On the other hand, the formula for the stan-

4–5 Changes in Variance and Standard Deviation with a Change in Unit.

Operation	Explanation
Variance	
1. $s_{x'}^2 = \dfrac{\sum(cX - c\bar{X})^2}{N - 1}$	1. Definition and if each score is multiplied by a constant the mean is multiplied by that same constant.
2. $= \dfrac{\sum[c(X - \bar{X})]^2}{N - 1}$	2. Factoring in the manner of $ca - cb = c(a - b)$.
3. $= \dfrac{\sum[c^2(X - \bar{X})^2]}{N - 1}$	3. Simplification in the manner of $(ab)^2 = a^2 b^2$.
4. $= \dfrac{c^2\sum(X - \bar{X})^2}{N - 1}$	4. The sum of a constant times a variable is that constant times the sum of the variable.
5. $s_{x'}^2 = c^2 s_x^2$	5. Substitution.
Standard Deviation	
1. $s_{x'} = \sqrt{s_{x'}^2}$	1. Definition.
2. $= \sqrt{c^2 s_x^2}$	2. Substitution.
3. $s_{x'} = c s_x$	3. Simplification in the manner of $\sqrt{a^2 b^2} = ab$ in which c is a positive constant.

OPTIONAL TABLE

dard deviation takes the positive square root of these squared deviations, and thus it will be changed by a factor of c (assuming c is a positive constant).[1]

The formal proof of this proposition can be found in Optional Table 4–5.

A numerical example illustrating all of these principles is given in Table 4–6.

EXERCISES

1. If the mean of a distribution was 50, and the standard deviation was 8, what would be the mean, variance, and standard deviation if each of the following operations was done?

(a) 10 was added to each score.
(b) 12 was subtracted from each score.
(c) Each score was multiplied by 10.
(d) Each score was divided by 5.
(e) Each score was divided by 8 and then 50 was subtracted from it.

[1] If c is negative, $s_{x'} = |c| s_x$.

4-6 Numerical Example of the Effects of Changing the Origin and Unit of the Scale of Measurement.

X		Y = X + 5		W = 3X	
X	X^2	Y	Y^2	W	W^2
3	9	8	64	9	81
5	25	10	100	15	225
6	36	11	121	18	324
10	100	15	225	30	900
$\sum X = 24$ $\sum X^2 = 170$		$\sum Y = 44$ $\sum Y^2 = 510$		$\sum W = 72$ $\sum W^2 = 1530$	

$N = 4$

$$\bar{X} = \frac{\sum X}{N} = \frac{24}{4} = 6$$

$$s_x^{\,2} = \frac{N\sum X^2 - (\sum X)^2}{N(N-1)}$$

$$= \frac{4(170) - (24)^2}{4(4-1)} = 8.67$$

$$s_x = \sqrt{8.67} = 2.94$$

$N = 4$

$$\bar{Y} = \frac{\sum Y}{N} = \frac{44}{4} = 11$$

$$s_y^{\,2} = \frac{N\sum Y^2 - (\sum Y)^2}{N(N-1)}$$

$$= \frac{4(510) - (44)^2}{4(4-1)} = 8.67$$

$$s_y = \sqrt{8.67} = 2.94$$

$N = 4$

$$\bar{W} = \frac{\sum W}{N} = \frac{72}{4} = 18$$

$$s_w^{\,2} = \frac{N\sum W^2 - (\sum W)^2}{N(N-1)}$$

$$= \frac{4(1530) - (72)^2}{4(4-1)} = 78.00$$

$$s_w = \sqrt{78.0} = 8.82$$

Summary		Change the Zero Point	Change the Unit
	X	$Y = X + 5$	$W = 3X$
Mean	6	11	18
Variance	8.67	8.67	78.00
Standard Deviation	2.94	2.94	8.82

2. If an original set of measurements was made in inches and had a mean of 24 and a variance of 36, what would be the mean, variance, and standard deviation if the unit was changed to feet? If 16 inches had to be added to each measurement to correct an error? If the measures were converted to centimeters (2.5 centimeters = 1 inch) and then 15 centimeters were subtracted from each score?

standard scores and the normal distribution

STANDARD SCORES

One reason for introducing changes in the origin and unit of measurement was to describe how the transformation from one scale of measurement to another may take place. Within this context it would be of great importance if two very different scales could somehow be made comparable. For example, suppose a teacher gave two exams to a class. A score of 88 on each exam might mean quite different things. It could be an extremely high score on the first test but quite a low score on the second. While percentiles provide some idea of relative standing, they only represent an ordinal expression of position within a distribution. That is, percentiles reveal only the proportion of people scoring below a given score, but they do not indicate how *much* below that score the remainder of the distribution was. For example, the results of two tests might be

$$A = (78, 81, 87, 88)$$
$$B = (59, 61, 63, 88)$$

The person who scored 88 would have the same percentile value within each distribution, but the 88 on Test *B* represents a considerably greater relative achievement than it did on Test *A* because it stands so far apart from the remaining scores. Therefore, it would be desirable to be able to characterize the position of a score within a distribution in a more refined manner than merely by indicating its ordinal position.

The interpretation of a score within a distribution is based upon both (a) its relative standing with respect to the mean and (b) the variability of the scores within the distribution. Consider the following example:

$$A = (10, 36, 38, 40, 42, 44, 70)$$
$$B = (10, 12, 14, 40, 66, 68, 70)$$

In both distributions, the mean is 40, but the variability is much greater in the *B* distribution. A score of 70 deviated $+30$ points from the mean in both distributions, but the variability was greater in the second distribution. Thus, somewhat less importance is placed on a score of 70 in Group *B* than in Group *A* since other scores were also more likely to deviate a great deal from the mean in *B* than in *A*. Therefore, the interpretation of a score is relative not only to the mean of the distribution but also to the variability of the scores in the distribution.

If a single scale of measurement was adopted as being "standard," then all distributions being considered, regardless of their origin and unit, could be transformed to that single scale for mutual comparison by changing their origins and units with appropriate constants. This is essentially what is done when measures are converted into standard scores. By this "standardization" process the relative standing of persons in one distribution may be compared with their relative standing in another distribution even though the two distributions represent different measurement scales.

A **standard score** is defined to be

$$z_i = \frac{X_i - \overline{X}}{s_x}$$

To transform a score (X_i) into standard score form (z_i) subtract the sample mean of the scores $(\overline{X})$ from X_i and divide the result by the sample standard deviation (e.g., s_x). (The subscript x indicates the variance of the X_i.)

Consider what this formula does to the mean and standard deviation of the X_i. First, the transformation subtracts the mean $(\overline{X})$ from the score (X_i). Since the mean is a constant and this subtraction could be performed for all scores, the mean of the new distribution of all

$$X_i - \overline{X}$$

will be zero because if a constant (the mean) is subtracted from each score in a distribution, the new mean will be the old mean minus that constant:

$$\text{New Mean} = \overline{X} - c$$
$$c = \overline{X}$$
$$\text{New Mean} = \overline{X} - \overline{X}$$
$$\text{New Mean} = 0$$

Therefore, subtracting the mean from every score makes the mean of the new distribution zero (i.e., $\overline{z} = 0$).

But, subtracting a constant does not alter the standard deviation of a distribution. Therefore, the distribution of the scores $(X_i - \overline{X})$ has a mean of zero but a standard deviation of s_x. Suppose, however, that every score in this distribution of $(X_i - \overline{X})$ were divided by s_x. If every score in a distribution is divided by a constant (and s_x is a constant), the standard deviation of the new distribution will equal the original standard deviation divided by that constant:

$$\text{New Standard Deviation} = s_x/c$$
$$c = s_x$$
$$\text{New Standard Deviation} = s_x/s_x$$
$$\text{New Standard Deviation} = 1$$

Note that dividing by s_x does not change the mean in this case because the mean is zero and $0/s_x = 0$. Therefore, if every score in the distribution of X_i has the mean of that distribution subtracted from it and this result divided by the standard deviation of that distribution, the new distribution will have a mean of 0 and a standard deviation of 1.

The task of interpreting the relative position of a score by considering the mean and variability (standard deviation) of the distribution is accomplished by changing the measures into standard scores which possess a mean of 0 and a standard deviation of 1. For example, if you had a score of 88 on an examination, the class mean was 79, and the standard deviation was 6, the standard score, z, corresponding to $X = 88$ is given by

$$z = \frac{X - \overline{X}}{s_x} = \frac{88 - 79}{6} = \frac{9}{6} = 1.50$$

This standard score is in standard deviation units. For example, in the above case, the standard deviation of the X_i was 6. The z score represents the number of standard deviations the score X is from its mean, $\overline{X}$. Since $(X_i - \overline{X})$ was 9, X_i is $\frac{9}{6} = 1.5$ standard deviations from the mean. It is in this sense that the units of the z scale are "standard deviation units."

Standard scores become useful when one wishes to compare performance on several measures, each of which has a different mean and standard deviation. Suppose a teacher gave three examinations and wanted to combine the scores into a single score for the purpose of grading at the end of the course. Merely adding the scores on the three tests could give a biased picture of a student's relative performance. Table 4–7 compares adding raw scores across tests with adding standard scores for the same data. Notice that the rank order of the students is not the same using standard scores as when raw scores are employed. This is particularly striking when Students 2 and 3 are compared. They had identical raw score totals (245), but Student 2 had a total z score of $-.29$ compared to 1.50 for Student 3. This difference was primarily a result of Student 3 scoring 90 on the third test. The 90 was an extremely high score in a distribution that otherwise did not have much variability. Therefore, that performance was weighted more in terms of standard deviation units than in terms of raw scores. A comparison of Students 2 and 5 shows the case in which two students scored quite differently in terms of raw score but had the same standard score total. In general, adding scores in standard score form provides a fairer, truer index of performance than does adding raw scores because the means and variances of the individual distributions are equated. This means that standard scores take into account not only how much a student's performance deviates from the average of the group on that test but also how likely it was that other individuals in the group would score as high (or low) as that student did.

4–7   The Effect of Computing Standard Scores and Adding across Distributions.

Student	Raw Scores			Total
	Test 1	Test 2	Test 3	
1	93	80	85	258
2	81	80	84	245
3	70	85	90	245
4	76	81	85	242
5	65	89	82	236
6	65	90	81	236
7	69	86	79	234
	$\overline{X} = 74.14$	$\overline{X} = 84.43$	$\overline{X} = 83.71$	
	$s = 10.14$	$s = 4.20$	$s = 3.55$	

Student	Standard Scores			Total
	Test 1	Test 2	Test 3	
1	1.86	-1.05	.36	1.17
2	.68	-1.05	.08	$-$ .29
3	$-$ .41	.14	1.77	1.50
4	.18	$-$ .82	.36	$-$ .28
5	$-$ .90	1.09	$-$ .48	$-$ .29
6	$-$ .90	1.32	$-$ .76	$-$ .34
7	$-$ .51	.37	-1.33	-1.47

THE NORMAL DISTRIBUTION

Standard scores take on greater meaning when they are placed in relationship to the normal distribution.

The **normal distribution** is defined by

$$Y = \frac{1}{\sqrt{2\pi\sigma^2}} \, e^{-(X-\mu)^2/2\sigma^2}$$

in which
 Y = the height of the curve at point X
 X = any point along the X-axis
 μ = mean of the distribution
 σ^2 = variance of the distribution
 π = a constant, 3.1416 . . .
 e = the base of Napierian logarithms, 2.71828 . . .

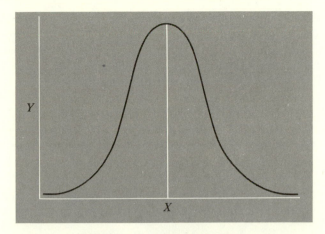

Fig. 4–1.   A normal distribution.

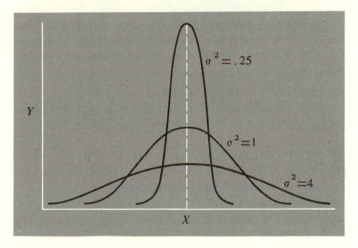

Fig. 4–2.   Three normal distributions with the same mean but different variances.

The normal distribution is different from the distributions described in the last chapter. It is a **theoretical distribution**.[2] The fact that it is "theoretical" implies that it is based upon a population of an infinite number of cases. Therefore, it is a hypothetical or "idealized" distribution. Further, since the formula given above refers to a population, not a sample, the mean and variance used in its formula are population parameters (e.g., μ and σ^2) not statistics based upon only a sample of cases (e.g., not $\overline{X}$ and s^2).

Typically, the normal distribution is characterized as being bell-shaped like the one pictured in Figure 4–1. However, because the formula includes the population mean and variance, a different normal distribution can be drawn for each combination of μ and σ^2. For example, Figure 4–2 displays three nor-

---

[2] This is also called a probability distribution.

mal distributions that have the same mean but different variances. Although the extent to which the normal distribution looks bell-shaped depends upon the values of its parameters, certain attributes are present in every normal distribution. For example, the mean, median, and mode are all the same value and they divide the distribution into two equal sized parts. Moreover, the normal distribution is symmetrical about this central point such that if the distribution were folded over at the mean, the right and left sides would fall exactly on top of one another. Finally, the "tails" of the distribution get closer and closer to the x-axis as they get further from the mean, but they never touch it. These tails are said to be **asymptotic** to the x-axis, and thus the normal distribution actually stretches from minus infinity $(-\infty)$ to plus infinity $(+\infty)$ along the x-axis. However, the most important characteristics of the normal distribution can best be understood by considering the normal distribution after transforming it into a standardized form.

standard normal distribution   In the sections above, we saw how any distribution of X_i could be transformed or "standardized" into a distribution of z_i such that the mean of the z_i is zero and the standard deviation equals 1.00. Suppose the original distribution of X_i was a population distribution with a mean μ_x and a standard deviation σ_x, and further that the X_i followed the normal distribution. Then, the formula

$$z_i = \frac{X_i - \mu_x}{\sigma_x}$$

would convert this normal population distribution of X_i into a normal population distribution with a mean of zero and a standard deviation of one. This special normal distribution with parameters $\mu_z = 0$ and $\sigma_z = 1.00$ is called the **standard normal distribution**.

The real importance of the standard normal distribution derives from the fact that it is a theoretical distribution with special characteristics which will allow us to determine percentile ranks and points very easily. Moreover, since normal distributions are common in nature (e.g., height, weight, intelligence, etc.) and since any normal distribution can be transformed into the standard normal distribution by employing the conversion formula above, the standard normal distribution can be used as the single reference distribution for statistically comparing a wide variety of otherwise incomparable phenomena. Notice that when different normal distributions are converted to the standard normal, the several transformed distributions each have the same mean (i.e., $\mu_z = 0$) and variance ($\sigma_z^2 = 1.00$), and thus the percentiles determined for one measure can be directly compared with those for another. Thus, for example, if percentiles were determined by using the standard normal, a student could be at the 87th percentile in math and the 87th percentile in English, and this would imply that the student was at precisely the same relative position in the math and

English distributions. There would be no need to worry about the fact that the original untransformed math and English distributions had different means and variances because these contrasting distributions would have been converted into a single distribution, the standard normal distribution.

It is important to notice that one must be able to assume that the original distributions of untransformed scores are normal in form. *Converting scores of a non-normal distribution to standard score form does not make the standardized distribution normal.* Standardization only changes the numerical values of the mean and variance of that distribution—it does not change the distribution's form or "normalize" it. Therefore, one must always ask if the original distribution is normal in form before converting it to the standard normal.

Some of the special characteristics of the standard normal distribution can be seen by examining Figure 4–3. One can determine percentiles of the standard

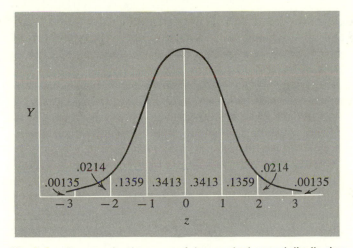

Fig. 4–3.   Areas under the curve of the standard normal distribution.

normal distribution by observing that the area under the distribution curve represents the proportion of frequencies which occur between various values of z. Thus, the proportion of the total area under the curve which is located between two points along that axis equals the proportion of frequencies falling between those two z values. For example, in the standard normal distribution the mean, median, and mode are all located at $z = 0$. The area under the curve between $z = 0$ and $+\infty$ is one-half the total area and thus one would expect that 50% of the cases should fall above $z = 0$. Similarly, 50% of the cases should also fall below $z = 0$, because the standard normal is symmetrical about $z = 0$. The important point to remember is that *the area under the standard normal curve implies relative frequency (or proportion of cases).*

With this in mind, certain points can be selected along the z-axis and the proportions of the total area under the curve between these points can be determined as has been done in Figure 4–3. Here it can be seen that 34.13% of the cases are between $z = 0$ and $+1$ and another 34.13% are between $z = 0$ and -1. Further, almost all the cases in a normal distribution (all but .27%) will be included between $z = -3$ and $z = +3$. This means that in any normal distribution, almost all the cases will be within three standard deviations above the mean and three standard deviations below the mean, because the z scale is in standard deviation units. If the mean of a normal distribution is 55 and the standard deviation is 10, then almost all of the scores are likely to fall between

$$\mu \pm 3(\sigma)$$
$$55 \pm 3(10)$$
$$55 \pm 30$$
$$25 \text{ and } 85$$

Indeed, the fact that the z scale is in standard deviation units is why z scores from normal distributions are sometimes called **standard normal deviates**, because they indicate how many standard deviations a score deviates from the mean.

The few points along the z-axis which were selected for Figure 4–3 were chosen for convenience. Actually, many points along the z-axis are listed in Table A of Appendix II in the back of this book. Turn to this table now. The first column is labeled z and corresponds to values along the z-axis which have been transformed from a normal distribution of X_i by

$$z_i = \frac{(X_i - \mu)}{\sigma}$$

The second column gives the proportion of area under the curve (i.e., proportion of frequencies) falling between the mean ($z = 0$) and the z value for that row. The third column provides the area beyond z (i.e., between the z value and $+\infty$). Thus, for $z = .35$, the proportion of area falling between the mean ($z = 0$) and $z = .35$ is .1368, and the proportion of area falling between $z = .35$ and $z = +\infty$ is .3632. Notice also that although the standard normal distribution contains negative z values to the left of the mean and positive values to the right of it, the table presents only positive z values. Since the standard normal distribution is perfectly symmetrical, the area relating to each positive z value is equally appropriate for each negative z value. Thus, for example, the third column of the table implies area to the right of a positive z value or area to the left of a negative z value.

application of the standard normal distribution   Several types of questions can be answered by using the percentiles of the standard normal distribution.

(1) In a normal distribution with mean $\mu = 45$ and standard deviation $\sigma = 10$, at what percentile rank does a score of 58 fall?

(a) Determine the z score corresponding to $X = 58$:

$$z = \frac{X - \mu}{\sigma} = \frac{58 - 45}{10} = 1.30$$

(b) Draw a picture similar to Figure 4–4. Look in Table A, Appendix II for the area between the mean ($z = 0$) and a $z = 1.30$. This area constitutes .4032 of the total. Since all of the distribution to the left of the mean also falls below a z of 1.30, .5000 should be added to .4032 to obtain

$$.4032 + .5000 = .9032$$

Thus, an $X = 58$ corresponds to the 90th percentile rank.

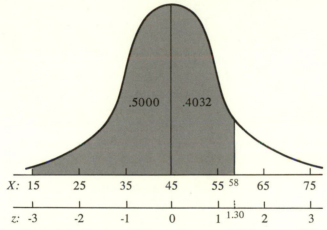

Fig. 4–4. Determining the percentile rank of a score of 58 in a normal distribution with $\mu = 45$, $\sigma = 10$.

(2) In the normal distribution described above, what score is at the 23rd percentile? This is the same type of problem as before only it is solved in the reverse direction.

(a) Draw a picture of the normal distribution such as Figure 4–5. The question asks for the X score corresponding to the 23rd percentile. In the standard normal distribution, the z score corresponding to $P_{.23}$ will have 23% of the cases below it. The third column of the table gives the proportion of cases between z and $+\infty$. However, since the distribution is symmetrical, it also gives the relative frequency between $-z$ and $-\infty$. Therefore, look down the third column until you find .23. The closest figure is .2296, and the z corresponding to that area is .74. Since

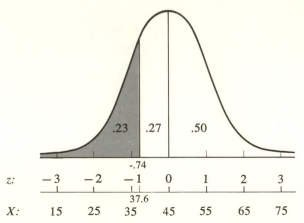

.23   .27   .50

-.74

z: -3   -2   -1   0   1   2   3

37.6

X: 15   25   35   45   55   65   75

Fig. 4–5.   Finding the X score at the 23rd percentile of a normal distribution.

the left side of the distribution is being worked with, the z value for the 23rd percentile is −.74.

(b) Since 23% of the area falls below $z = -.74$, the problem may be solved by converting $z = -.74$ into its corresponding X value:

$$z = \frac{X - \mu}{\sigma}$$

$$-.74 = \frac{X - 45}{10}$$

$$X = 45 - 7.4$$

$$X = 37.6$$

Therefore, $X = 37.6$ represents the 23rd percentile.

(3) What percent of the cases in a normal frequency distribution will fall between $z = -1.00$ and $z = 1.00$?

(a) The problem is solved by determining the area between the mean and $z = 1.00$ and between the mean and $z = -1.00$, and then adding these together. The table shows that the area between the mean and $z = 1.00$ is .3413 of the total. Therefore,

$$.3413 + .3413 = .6826$$

gives the right answer.

(4) What proportion of the frequencies fall between $X = 88$ and $X = 95$ if the normal distribution of X_i has a mean of 85 and a standard deviation of 5?

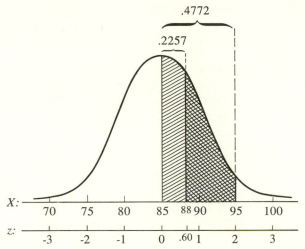

Fig. 4–6. Determining the proportion of cases falling between $X = 88$ and $X = 95$.

(a) Draw a picture similar to that presented in Figure 4–6 describing the problem. This diagrams the X distribution and indicates that the desired area falls between 88 and 95.

(b) Convert 88 and 95 to z values:

$$z = \frac{X - \mu}{\sigma} = \frac{88 - 85}{5} = .60$$

$$z = \frac{X - \mu}{\sigma} = \frac{95 - 85}{5} = 2.00$$

(c) Look in the table under $z = 2.00$ (corresponding to $X = 95$). The area between the mean and this point is .4772. However, the area between the mean and $z = .60$ (corresponding to $X = 88$) is not to be included in the desired answer. Therefore, since this area amounts to .2257, subtract it from the proportion of area between the mean and $z = 2.00$,

$$.4772 - .2257 = .2515$$

to obtain the required proportion.[3]

standard scores and standard normal distribution

Because the standard normal distribution is a theoretical distribution, conversions between other normal distributions and the standard normal require

[3] The solution presented for this type of problem assumes that the values of 88 and 95 are exactly 88.000 ... and 95.000 .... . If not, then their real limits would be 87.5 to 88.5 and 94.5 to 95.5, respectively, in which case the interval of concern would be (87.5–95.5) rather than (88–95).

μ and σ rather than their corresponding sample statistics, $\overline{X}$ and s. However, the standard normal distribution may be used even if only sample estimates of these population parameters are at hand as long as two conditions are met:

(1) **The population distribution from which the sample is drawn must be normal in form.** One way to examine the tenability of this assumption is to plot the sample distribution and casually observe its general form. If the sample distribution does not depart severely from a normal pattern and there is no reason that it should not be normal, then this condition is satisfied.

(2) **There must be enough measurements in the sample.** A reasonable number of cases is needed in order to determine if the sample is normal in form and in order for $\overline{X}$ and s to be accurate estimators of μ and σ. For samples of approximately 30 or more, $\overline{X}$ and s^2 are sufficiently good estimators of their respective parameters, but it must be remembered that they are still only estimates or approximations to μ and σ.

If these two conditions are met, then one can relate the sample distribution to the theoretical standard normal distribution in the same manner as has been illustrated for normal populations by using the usual formula but with μ replaced by $\overline{X}$ and σ_x replaced by s_x:

$$z_i = \frac{X_i - \overline{X}}{s_x}$$

Although the accuracy of this procedure depends directly on the extent to which the assumptions stated above are met, using a theoretical relative frequency distribution to estimate percentiles in a sample in this manner is a very common procedure. In fact, most of elementary statistical inference uses essentially this same strategy, as we will see beginning in Chapter 7.

The logic of this procedure is that $\overline{X}$ and s_x are estimators of μ and σ, and therefore may be used to estimate these parameters when only sample data are available. However, the accuracy of the results of using sample data and this procedure depends upon the normality of the distribution and the sample size which in turn determines the accuracy of $\overline{X}$ and s_x as estimators of their corresponding parameters. Therefore, this practice may be employed only with the knowledge that it will yield approximate results.

OTHER "STANDARDIZED" DISTRIBUTIONS

The standard normal distribution discussed in the preceding section had a mean of zero and a standard deviation of one because the mean was subtracted from each score and the result divided by the standard deviation. However, these parameter values are arbitrarily designated. It could just as easily be made to have a mean of 100 and a standard deviation of 20 by the transformation

$$\text{standard score} = 20 \left[\frac{X_i - \overline{X}}{s_x} \right] + 100$$

or a mean of 500 and a standard deviation of 100 by the transformation

$$\text{standard score} = 100 \left[\frac{X_i - \overline{X}}{s_x} \right] + 500$$

The Army General Classification Test of World War II used the former standard score and the Graduate Record Exam has employed the latter. Thus, it is obvious that the concept of standard scores is perfectly general, and that the selection of a mean of zero and a standard deviation of one is convenient but arbitrary.

EXERCISES

1. What are the limitations of percentiles as measures of relative position and how do standard scores overcome these limitations?

2. Explain and illustrate why it is necessary to consider the variance of a distribution in order to accurately reflect the relative position of a score.

3. Compute the standard score for each of the members of the following distribution. Then calculate the mean and the standard deviation of the z_i. Would you have predicted these last two values? Why?

$$X_i = (5, 7, 7, 8, 9, 12)$$

4. What does the area under a theoretical distribution signify?

5. What proportion of the cases of a normal distribution will fall to the left of $z = 0$? To the right of $z = 0$? To the right of $z = 1.00$? To the right of $z = -1.00$?

6. Determine the proportion of cases falling under the normal curve in the following circumstances.
   (a) Between $z = -1$ and $z = +1$.
   (b) Between $z = 1.0$ and $z = 2.0$.
   (c) To the right of $z = 1.5$.
   (d) To the left of $z = -1.96$ plus the cases to the right of $z = 1.96$.
   (e) To the left of $z = -2.575$ and to the right of $z = 2.575$.

7. If the mean of a normal distribution is 43 and the standard deviation is 2, within how many standard deviations of the mean would you expect almost all of the cases to fall? What score values correspond to these points?

8. In a normal distribution with mean of 31 and standard deviation 12, at what percentile is a score of 40 likely to fall? $X_i = 19$? $X_i = 27$?

9. In a normal distribution with mean 50 and standard deviation 8, what score is likely to fall at the 95th percentile? 25th? 1st?

10. What percent of the cases are likely to fall between the values of 42 and 61 in a normal distribution with mean 50 and standard deviation 10? Between 56 and 65? Between 31 and 36?

11. If your score on a statistics test was 90, and the professor determined grades separately for each of four sections, which section would you prefer? Why?

    (a) $\bar{X} = 65$, $s = 13$
    (b) $\bar{X} = 75$, $s = 10$
    (c) $\bar{X} = 80$, $s = 8$
    (d) $\bar{X} = 85$, $s = 2$

REGRESSION

5

Thus far the discussion has focused upon the several ways to characterize or describe a frequency distribution: the central tendency, variability, and relative position of the scores.

In addition to characterizing the properties of a distribution one also might want to consider how scores in one distribution relate to those in another. For example, it may be of interest to determine if there is a relationship between scores on college entrance tests, such as the Scholastic Aptitude Test (SAT), and college grades so that this relationship could be used to predict how applicants will fare in college. Further, one may wish to describe the magnitude or degree of this relationship. Is there quite a close correspondence between SAT scores and grades or is there only a very imprecise relationship between these two variables? These questions fall under the topics of regression and correlation.

linear relationships

Relationships between two variables can be plotted and the resulting graph often approximates a straight line that relates specific values of one variable to values of the other. Since a very precise description of such graphic displays is needed, it will be beneficial first to consider the geometric and algebraic characteristics of straight lines and then to show how these concepts can be used to describe approximate relationships between variables.

THE EQUATION FOR A STRAIGHT LINE

Suppose a young baby sitter charges $1.00 per hour for services. Consider the relationship between money earned (call it Y) and hours worked (labeled X). If the baby sitter does not work at all ($X = 0$), then no money is earned ($Y = 0$). If the baby sitter works two hours ($X = 2$), $2.00 is made ($Y = 2$). For four hours, $4.00 is made. A table displays these values:

X	Y
0	0
2	2
4	4

The basis of this table is the relationship: an hour worked is a dollar earned. Using the symbols Y for dollars earned and X for hours worked, this statement reduces to:

$$Y = X$$

This is a simple mathematical equation to describe the relationship between hours worked and money earned, and it will indicate the earnings for any amount of time worked. For example, if the baby sitter worked $3\frac{1}{2}$ hours ($X = 3.5$), then the amount earned would be $3.50.

$$X = 3.5 \text{ (hours)}$$
$$Y = X$$
$$Y = 3.5 = \$3.50$$

The same information may be expressed by graphing this equation, letting specific pairs of values for X and Y be the coordinates of a set of points. Figure 5–1 shows the X and Y axes and the three points from the preceding table [(0, 0), (2, 2), (4, 4)]. The line passing through them is described by the equation, $Y = X$. The line really represents an infinite number of points which indicate the amount of money earned for a given amount of time worked; therefore, if the baby sitter worked $3\frac{1}{2}$ hours, a vertical line could be drawn at $X = 3.5$ which would intersect the graphed line of the relationship at $Y = \$3.50$. This fact is indicated in the figure. Hence, the equation ($Y = X$) and the graph of that equation in Figure 5–1 both describe the relationship between money earned and hours worked and provide a method of predicting one (Y) from the other (X).

The previous example illustrates a linear relationship.

A **linear relationship** is an association between two variables which may be accurately represented on a graph by a straight line.

In this case, the association was between money earned and hours worked, and the equation $Y = X$ describes the graph in Figure 5–1 which is indeed a straight line. However, relationships are not always linear. If they are not, they are called **non-linear** or **curvilinear relationships**. Their graphs will not be straight lines.

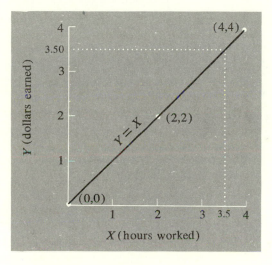

Fig. 5–1.   Graph of the line, $Y = X$.

The above example of a linear relationship is one of the simplest kind. Suppose the baby sitter was paid only $.75 an hour. Once again for zero hours worked ($X = 0$), pay would be 0 ($Y = 0$); for 1 hour ($X = 1$), earnings would be 75¢ ($Y = .75$); and for 3 hours, earnings would be $2.25. Putting these values into a table, one obtains

X	Y
0	0
1	.75
3	2.25

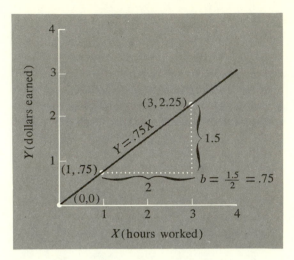

Fig. 5–2.   Graph of the line, $Y = .75X$, indicating the slope of the line, b, to equal .75.

The table uses the relationship: dollars earned equals $.75 times the number of hours worked, which symbolically stated is

$$Y = .75X$$

Figure 5–2 graphically describes this relationship. Note that the two lines, $Y = X$ (Figure 5–1) and $Y = .75X$ (Figure 5–2), are quite similar, differing only in terms of the tilt or slope of the line.

The **slope**[1] of a line is defined to be the vertical distance divided by the horizontal distance between any two points on the line. In symbols, given the two points (x_1, y_1) and (x_2, y_2), the slope b of the line is

$$\text{slope} = b = \frac{\text{vertical distance}}{\text{horizontal distance}} = \frac{y_2 - y_1}{x_2 - x_1}$$

For example, two points found for the line above were $(1, .75)$ and $(3, 2.25)$. Putting them in the formula one obtains

$$b = \frac{y_2 - y_1}{x_2 - x_1} = \frac{2.25 - .75}{3 - 1} = \frac{1.5}{2}$$

$$b = .75$$

Graphically, this fact can be seen in Figure 5–2. Recalling that the slope equals

---

[1] Some students define the slope to be slope = rise/run, remembering that alphabetically "rise" precedes ("is over") "run."

the vertical distance between any two points on the line divided by the horizontal distance between the same two points, one can see that this ratio of distances is always equal to .75 for this line. In particular, this fact is illustrated in Figure 5–2 for the points (1, .75) and (3, 2.25).

It is not just coincidence that the slope of this line equals .75 and the equation of the line is $Y = .75X$. The coefficient of X in an equation of this sort is identical to the slope of the line that the equation describes. In the first illustration, $Y = X$, the coefficient of X is 1 [e.g., $Y = (1)X$]. An examination of Figure 5–1 reveals that two points on the graph are (2, 2) and (4, 4), yielding a slope of 1:

$$b = \frac{4 - 2}{4 - 2} = \frac{2}{2} = 1$$

The slope of a line may be negative as well as positive. Consider the line in Figure 5–3. Two points on that line are (2, 3) and (4, 2), which substituted into the formula for the slope, b, yield

$$b = \frac{y_2 - y_1}{x_2 - x_1} = \frac{2 - 3}{4 - 2} = \frac{-1}{2}$$

$$b = -.50$$

In terms of the graph, to get from the point (2, 3) to (4, 2) one must go down a unit, equivalent to going -1 vertical units, and to the right two units ($+2$), giving a slope of

$$b = \frac{-1}{2} = -.50$$

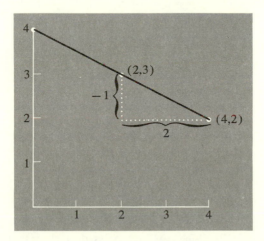

Fig. 5–3. An illustration of a line with negative slope, $b = -\frac{1}{2} = -.50$. Note that low values of X are associated with high values of Y, an inverse or negative relationship.

The slope of the line determines whether the relationship is positive or negative.

A line with a positive slope indicates a **positive** or **direct** relationship and a line with a negative slope represents a **negative** or **inverse** relationship.

Notice that lines with positive slope tend to run upward from left to right across the graph, indicating that low values on one variable are associated with low values on the other, and high values on one go with high values on the other. In terms of the baby-sitting example, few hours worked returned few dollars and many hours worked earned many dollars. Since the slope in such a situation is positive the relationship is called positive, or it may be referred to as being direct because of the direct correspondence of values on the two dimensions. In contrast, if the slope is negative the line tends to run down from left to right on the graph, indicating that low values on one dimension go with high values on the other. Because the slope is negative in these instances, the relationship is called negative, or it also might be called inverse because high values are associated with low values (rather than high with high and low with low as in direct relationships).

As a final example of a linear relationship, suppose the baby sitter works for an agency. The agency operates in the following manner: Once parents contact and arrange for a baby sitter there is a $1.00 charge which is made regardless of whether or not the engagement is fulfilled. Baby-sitting is paid at the rate of $.75 an hour in addition to the $1.00 service charge. Thus, if parents make an appointment and then have to cancel it, in terms of the number of hours worked ($X = 0$), the cost to the parents is $1.00. If the date is completed and the sitter was occupied for three hours ($X = 3$), the charge is 3 hours at $.75 an hour plus $1.00 service charge for a total of $3.25. A five-hour evening would cost 5 × $.75 plus $1.00 or $4.75. In tabular form:

X	Y
0	1.00
3	3.25
5	4.75

These values were arrived at by multiplying .75 times the number of hours worked and adding 1.00 which can be expressed by the general equation

$$Y = .75X + 1.00$$

The plot of these points together with the previously discussed lines are presented in Figure 5–4. Observe first that the line $Y = X$ has a slope of 1 while the other two lines both have a slope of .75 ($Y = .75X$ and $Y = .75X + 1$). On the graph, the line for ($Y = X$) definitely has a different tilt or slope, while the two lines which have identical slopes are parallel. But these two parallel lines differ in another way. One is always one unit above the other. If the Y-axis is arbitrarily selected as the place to measure this separation, the line $Y = .75X + 1$ goes through the Y-axis at 1 whereas the line $Y = .75X$ goes through the Y-axis at 0.

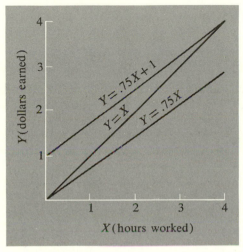

Fig. 5–4. A plot of the three lines discussed in the text having different slopes and intercepts.

The point at which a line intersects the Y-axis is called the **y-intercept** and its value is symbolized by **a**.

Note that the value of the y-intercept, or a, equals the constant which is added to the equation:

Equation	y-intercept
$Y = .75X + 1$	$a = 1$
$Y = .75X \quad\Rightarrow Y = .75X + 0$	$a = 0$

The y-intercept can be found from the equation of the line by setting $X = 0$, which is, in fact, the point on the X scale where the Y-axis is located. Thus, to compute the y-intercept:

$$Y = .75X + 1$$
$$Y = .75(0) + 1$$
$$Y = +1 = y\text{-intercept}$$

In summary, one needs to know two values to determine the equation of a straight line: the *y*-intercept (*a*) and the slope (*b*). Further, since *a* provides one point and *b* tells one how to arrive at some other point on the line, *a* and *b* completely specify a particular line.

Therefore, any straight line will have the general equation of

$$Y = bX + a$$

If $a = 1$ and $b = .75$, then the equation

$$Y = .75X + 1$$

describes the line with slope .75 and *y*-intercept at 1.

The usefulness of the equation of a linear relationship lies in determining a *Y* value given any *X* score. Suppose the appropriate equation is $Y = .75X + 1$, and one wishes to know the *Y* score corresponding to an *X* of 2, then, substituting $X = 2$,

$$Y = .75X + 1$$
$$Y = .75(2) + 1$$
$$Y = 1.5 + 1$$
$$Y = 2.5$$

Thus, in the baby sitting example, if the parents are to be gone for 2 hours, they could plan on spending $2.50 for a baby sitter through the agency.

The baby sitting examples illustrate that graphs of linear relationships have a slope and a *y*-intercept and that they can provide the basis for predicting a *Y* value given a certain *X* value. However, all of these cases have dealt with perfect linear relationships. That is, all of the points have fallen precisely on the line. None has deviated from it. Regrettably, most of the relationships observed in social science are not so precise. A plot of an approximate linear relationship is presented in Figure 5–5. Note first that the relationship does have a positive linear trend as indicated by the straight line drawn through it, but this line is certainly only an approximation. Yet it still might be useful to have its equation in order to make approximate predictions of *Y* given *X*. This plot represents a hypothetical relationship between Scholastic Aptitude Test (SAT) scores and freshman college grades in a certain year. If the equation of the line were known, educated guesses of the scholastic performance for next year's applicants could be made on the basis of their SAT scores, assuming the relationship would be much the same from year to year. Such information could be used to determine admission policy. Previously in this chapter the determination of the equation of the line has been rather obvious, but this task is no longer so intuitive when the relationship is not perfect. In fact, it may not be

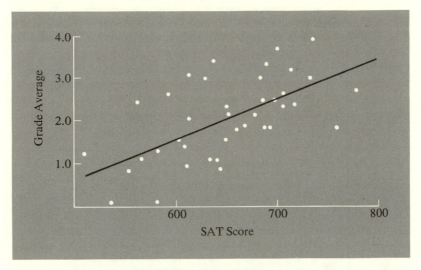

Fig. 5–5. An approximate linear relationship between SAT scores and freshman grades (Table 5–1).

immediately obvious that the data do indeed follow a linear trend. The first step is to check on the linear trend by constructing a scatterplot.

SCATTERPLOTS

One way to obtain some information on the precision and linearity of a relationship is to construct a graph of it. Suppose that a college admissions officer had a group of 40 students with both SAT score and first year college grades ($A = 4.0$) as presented in Table 5–1. This collection of pairs of scores may be treated in the same manner as the small tables of values described in the previous section, and a point may be placed on a graph corresponding to each pair of values.

A **scatterplot** is a graph of a collection of pairs of scores.

Figure 5–5 is an example of a scatterplot. It was constructed simply by recording a point corresponding to each pair of scores. The variable about which predictions are to be made (predicted variable) is always placed on the ordinate. Thus, to plot the first pair of scores in Table 5–1, a point is placed directly over 510 on the SAT scale and precisely to the right of a grade average of 1.3.

Although precise techniques exist which help in making a decision about linearity, for our purposes an observation of the total scatterplot is usually sufficient to determine if the trend in the data is approximately linear or if it is curvilinear.

5–1 SAT Scores and Grades for a Sample of 40 College Students.			
SAT	**Freshman Grades**	**SAT**	**Freshman Grades**
510	1.3	659	2.1
533	0.1	663	1.7
558	0.8	670	1.8
565	2.4	678	2.1
569	1.1	679	2.9
580	0.1	680	2.3
581	1.3	687	1.8
590	2.6	688	3.2
603	1.5	693	1.8
610	1.3	698	2.4
612	0.9	700	3.6
615	2.0	710	2.5
618	3.0	710	2.2
630	2.9	718	3.1
633	1.1	724	2.3
639	3.3	734	2.9
643	1.1	739	3.8
645	0.9	750	3.9
651	1.5	767	1.7
654	2.2	778	2.6

regression constants

Obviously, if the scatterplot tends to be curvilinear, trying to describe it with a straight line would hardly be appropriate. If, however, it is approximately linear, the next task is to determine the equation of the line which best describes the linear relationship between the two observed variables.

The line describing the relationship between two variables is known as the **regression line** and is expressed in the form, $\hat{Y} = bX + a$. The variable $\hat{Y}$ is called **predicted Y**, and the values a and b are known as **regression constants**.

The task, then, is to specify the regression constants for the regression line that best describes the relationship. In order to do this with some degree of precision, a criterion is needed to determine which line of the many possible lines is "best." The criterion selected is called the **least squares criterion**.

In order to examine the meaning of this concept it is necessary to observe a scatterplot in more detail. For purposes of illustration the following few subjects have been selected from the original sample of 40 students. Their SAT scores (i.e., X_i) and grade averages (i.e., Y_i) are as shown.

X_i	Y_i
510	1.3
533	0.1
603	1.5
670	1.8
750	3.9

A scatterplot of just these five points is presented in Figure 5–6.

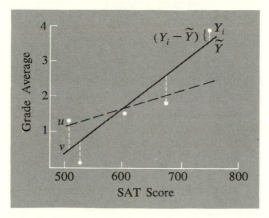

Fig. 5–6. A plot of a selected group of points with two possible regression lines, *u* and *v*.

For the purpose of explaining the least squares criterion for fitting a regression line, several definitional points will be reviewed, using Figure 5–6 as a graphic example. First, note that when a linear relationship is not perfect, the points do not all fall directly on the line. Second, the vertical distance between the abscissa and any point on the graph is simply its Y_i value (that person's grade average). Since every Y_i value is associated with some X_i value, what would the regression line predict the Y_i value to be on the basis of the subject's X_i score? The predicted value of Y_i would be the vertical height of the regression line at that particular X_i value. More specifically, one would predict $\tilde{Y}$ (read "Y predicted" or "Y TIL-dah"). However, $\tilde{Y}$ will probably not precisely equal the subject's actual Y_i score. That is, there will be some error in predicting his actual grade average (Y_i) simply by knowing his SAT score (X_i) and the regression line. The quantity ($Y_i - \tilde{Y}$) represents the amount of this error. This is the difference between the actual and the predicted value of the subject's grade average.

Now consider the two lines in Figure 5–6. Notice that in the upper right-hand corner of the graph the distance between Y_i and $\tilde{Y}$ is shown by a solid white line. Observe that this distance is a vertical rather than a perpendicular distance between the point Y_i and the line $\tilde{Y}$. The error in prediction should be measured in terms of Y units. If the error is measured along the perpendicular from the point Y_i to the line $\tilde{Y}$, the measurement would not be in Y units since such a measurement scale would not be parallel to the Y-axis. Therefore, the error is measured in the vertical dimension in order to state these deviations in Y units.

The distances between the actual points (Y_i) and their respective predicted values ($\tilde{Y}_i$) represent the **error** in prediction ($Y_i - \tilde{Y}$). This difference is commonly called a **residual**, since it represents variability remaining after predicting Y_i with the regression line, $\tilde{Y}$. It would be advantageous to select regression lines which make such error as small as possible. For example, using the vertical distance between each point and the line as a criterion in Figure 5–6, it is obvious that the points cluster more closely about line v than about line u. These distances between the points and the line might give a convenient measure of how closely the points group about the line and thus be a criterion for which line "best" fits the data. However, notice that if the simple distances ($Y_i - \tilde{Y}$) are used, some of these deviations are positive and some are negative. Thus, points could deviate markedly from the line but if the positive deviations were balanced by equally large negative deviations, the sum $\sum(Y_i - \tilde{Y})$ of these positive and negative errors sum to zero for many lines, leaving unresolved the choice of which line is best. This same situation occurred in the case of the variance, s^2, because the sum of the deviations of scores about the mean is always zero. In that instance, the *squared* deviations about the mean were used which resulted in summing only positive values. The same solution is used in the case of regression. Just as $\sum(X_i - \bar{X})^2$ yields a measure of the extent to which points deviate about their mean,

$$\sum(Y_i - \tilde{Y})^2$$

provides an index of how much the points deviate from the regression line. It would be desirable to have this total sum of squared errors as small as possible. Therefore, one picks the regression line so that

$$\sum(Y_i - \tilde{Y})^2$$

is a minimum.

> The **least squares criterion** states that the best regression line is one which makes the sum of the squared deviations between points and the regression line, $\sum(Y_i - \tilde{Y})^2$, a minimum.

Since the regression line is completely determined if a and b are known, the task reduces to the selection of these regression constants in accordance with the least squares criterion.

OBTAINING THE REGRESSION LINE

The formulas for a and b which can be found by the calculus are

$$b = \frac{N(\sum XY) - (\sum X)(\sum Y)}{N\sum X^2 - (\sum X)^2}$$

$$a = \bar{Y} - b\bar{X}$$

These expressions provide a means for computing a and b from the original scores such that when these constants are placed into the regression equation ($\bar{Y} = bX + a$) it will describe precisely the line which best fits the data in the sense of having minimized the squared deviations between the data points and the line [i.e., $\sum(Y_i - \tilde{Y})^2$ will be minimum].

The use of these formulas will be illustrated with the data provided by the five subjects selected previously. Of course, the admissions director mentioned in the original illustration would use the data from as many college students as possible. The more subjects involved in a regression analysis, the more confidence one can have in generalizing its results. However, using just these few subjects will provide the reader with a simple example of the computational routine required. These procedures are presented in Table 5–2. An examination of the formulas reveals that five quantities are needed:

$$N, \sum X, \sum X^2, \sum Y, \text{ and } \sum XY$$

The N is the number of *pairs* of scores or the number of subjects, *not* the number of X and Y scores together. Note also that XY is X_i multiplied by Y_i (sometimes called a "cross product") and $\sum XY$ is the sum of these cross products over all pairs of scores. The values of b and a are arrived at by substituting into the formulas given above and reducing. The last step is to substitute the resulting constants into the regression equation which yields

$$\tilde{Y} = .012X - 5.638$$

With the regression equation obtained, one may pose the problem the admissions director is constantly faced with. If applicant John Greenley's SAT score is 718, what would one predict his freshman grade average to be? The

5–2	The Computation of the Regression Equation.			
Subject	**X**	**Y**	**X^2**	**XY**
1	510	1.3	260100	663.0
2	533	.1	284089	53.3
3	603	1.5	363609	904.5
4	670	1.8	448900	1206.0
5	750	3.9	562500	2925.0

$$\sum X = 3066 \quad \sum Y = 8.6 \quad \sum X^2 = 1919198 \quad \sum XY = 5751.8$$
$$(\sum X)^2 = 9400356$$
$$\overline{X} = 613.20 \quad \overline{Y} = 1.72$$
$$N = 5$$
$$b = \frac{N(\sum XY) - (\sum X)(\sum Y)}{N\sum X^2 - (\sum X)^2} = \frac{5(5751.8) - (3066)(8.6)}{5(1919198) - 9400356}$$
$$= \frac{2391.4}{195634} = .012$$
$$a = \overline{Y} - b\overline{X} = 1.72 - (.012)(613.20) = -5.638$$
$$\tilde{Y} = bX + a$$
$$\tilde{Y} = .012X - 5.638$$

question is answered by substituting $X = 718$ into the regression equation and computing $\tilde{Y}$:
$$\tilde{Y} = .012(718) - 5.638$$
$$\tilde{Y} = 2.978$$

Geometrically this amounts to drawing a vertical line through $X = 718$ parallel to the Y-axis and asking for the Y value at the point of intersection of that vertical line and the regression line.

It is sometimes necessary to plot a regression line once you have obtained its algebraic equation. Since two points determine a straight line, the regression constants, a and b, will provide those two points. First, mark off a set of axes. Remember, the variable doing the predicting goes on the horizontal axis (i.e., variable X), and the variable being predicted goes on the vertical axis (i.e., variable Y). Since the value of a is the y-intercept, simply place a point on the Y-axis at the point corresponding to the value calculated for a. Now the task is to determine any second point on the line. Recall that the slope represents the amount of vertical distance relative to horizontal distance between any two points. Thus, start with the point you just made on the Y-axis and move horizontally one X unit to the right and then move vertically b units. That is, if the slope is .75, move up .75 units on the Y-axis for every unit you move horizontally. If the slope is $-.75$, move down .75 units on the Y-axis.

THE SECOND REGRESSION LINE

All of the discussion has been directed at predicting Y from X. It would appear that if two variables are measured on each person in a group the relationship between them should be the same regardless of whether one predicts Y from X or X from Y. It is true that the *degree* of relationship is the same regardless of the direction of prediction as will be demonstrated in the next chapter on correlation. However, the regression constants will be different depending upon which variable is being predicted. This fact becomes more obvious if one considers the SAT-grades example in terms of the y-intercept. When trying to predict grades from SAT scores, the y-intercept of the line was measured in the units of the predicted variable, namely, -5.638 grade points. If the direction of prediction is reversed making SAT scores the predicted dimension and placing it on the ordinate (Y-axis), then the y-intercept for the regression line should be in SAT-score points, not grade points. Obviously, the value of a will be different in these two cases because the measurement scale constituting the y-axis is different.

The fact that the regression constants are different depending upon which variable is being predicted may be understood further by examining the manner in which a and b were derived. When predicting grades from SAT scores, the criterion for selecting the regression constants is such that $\sum(\text{grade} - \text{pre-directed grade})^2$ is a minimum. In contrast, when SAT scores are being predicted, the $\sum(\text{SAT} - \text{predicted SAT})^2$ must be a minimum. It happens that making one of these sums a minimum does not guarantee that the other sum will also be minimized by the same line. From another perspective, if one considers a graph (Figure 5–7) with SAT scores on the abscissa and grades on the ordinate, when grades are predicted the squares of the vertical distances between the points and the line are minimized. But, if one uses the same axes and predicts SAT scores, the squares of the horizontal distances between points and regression line must be minimized. This is diagrammed in Figure 5–7. However, making one set of squared distances as small as possible does not simultaneously reduce the other squared distances to a minimum. If the relationship were perfectly linear and all the points fell on the regression line, the two regression lines would coincide. However, since perfect relationships are very rare in the social sciences, there are usually two regression lines.

The formulas which were given above for a and b were for the case in which Y was being predicted from X. This case is sometimes referred to as the **regression of Y on X**, and therefore the regression equation is frequently written

$$\tilde{Y} = b_{yx}X + a_{yx}$$

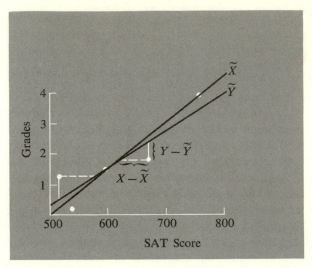

Fig. 5–7.   The two regression lines for the sample data, Y on X ($\tilde{Y}$) and X on Y ($\tilde{X}$). The lines connecting a few points to the regression lines indicate the squared distances minimized in determining $\tilde{Y}$ (solid lines) and $\tilde{X}$ (dashed lines).

with the subscript yx meaning the regression of Y on X (Y is predicted). In contrast, for the case in which one is predicting X from knowledge of Y, the regression equation is

$$\tilde{X} = b_{xy}Y + a_{xy}$$

and it is called the **regression of X on Y**. It is important for the reader to understand that ordinarily there are two regression lines and that b_{yx} is not equal to b_{xy} and a_{yx} is not equal to a_{xy}. Although different formulas exist for calculating the regression constants for the "second regression line," they are rarely used. All you need to remember is that for any computational situation the variable being predicted is designated Y while the variable doing the predicting is labeled X. Then, use the formulas as presented for the regression of Y on X.

factors in the use of the regression line

The discussion thus far has focused upon describing procedures that attempt to fit a straight line to a set of data points. These procedures may always be carried out regardless of the form of the scatterplot, but ordinarily in the application of regression techniques certain assumptions are made which permit more extensive interpretation of the results of linear regression.

LINEARITY

The procedures described in the preceding sections are appropriate for data having an underlying linear relationship in the population. A linear relationship probably exists in the population when the form of the scatterplot of the sample data is a straight line ($Y = bX + a$). Obviously, if it is doubtful that a linear relationship exists, it is foolish to attempt to fit a straight line to data which would be more appropriately described by some curvilinear trend.

RANGE OF X

One must be careful to restrict predictions to those X values that fall within the range of X values used in the process of determining the regression constants. It is this original set of data that one examines if the relationship appears to be linear. Therefore, since one's confidence in the assumption of linearity is based only upon the original range of X values, extending the scope of prediction to more extreme X_i exceeds the information on the linearity of regression. Consider an example in which rats were placed under food deprivation for from 0 to 48 hours prior to performing ten trials in a two-choice problem. The solid line in Figure 5–8 represents the hypothetical relationship

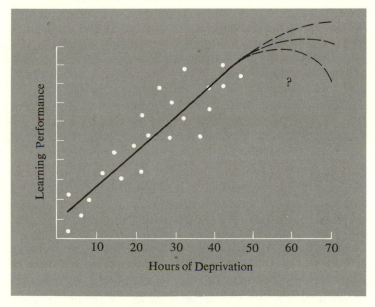

Fig. 5–8. A hypothetical relationship between hours of deprivation and learning performance (solid line) and the ambiguity of the form of the relationship for X values outside of the tested range (dashed lines).

between hours of deprivation and the percent of correct responses. The equation of this hypothetical line is

$$\tilde{Y} = .015X + .02$$

If one wanted to predict performance for 31 hours of deprivation, he would simply substitute $X = 31$ into the equation, obtaining a predicted figure of 48.5% correct responses. If $X = 72$, which is outside of the range of original X values, then the regression equation would predict that 110% of the trials would be correct! Clearly, the relationship between hours of deprivation and learning performance is not linear over such an extensive range of values. Obviously, performance cannot continue to improve with each extra hour of deprivation because ultimately the animal will die. Therefore, it is appropriate to predict only from X values falling within the range of the original values because information on the linearity of the relationship at more extreme values is not available.

STANDARD ERROR OF ESTIMATE

One of the purposes in considering regression and the attempt to predict one variable from another was to describe a linear relationship between two variables. Yet, although techniques have now been discussed that will yield the equation for a straight line which best fits the data, the data points only tend to cluster around rather than fall precisely on the line. Thus, although one would predict that John Greenley would make a 3.0 grade average his freshman year, John's actual performance will probably not be precisely 3.0. It is clear that this predicted value probably will be in error to some extent. It would be useful to have some sort of numerical index to indicate the extent of the error in prediction. What is required is a measure of the variability of points about the regression line that operates in the same manner as the variance of points about the mean. The greater the variability of the points about the line, the greater the error in prediction.

Although the nature of the distribution of the points in a scatterplot determines the slope of the regression line, it is possible to have scatterplots with regression lines of equal slope but with different amounts of variability of the points about this line. Figure 5–9 displays such a situation.

In Part A the sum of the squared distances, $\sum(Y_i - \tilde{Y})^2$, is quite a bit smaller than for Part B. For any specific prediction it is likely that the predicted Y would be closer to the person's actual Y score in Part A than in Part B, even though both lines are the best fitting lines for their data. The task in this section is to develop a quantitative index of the extent of this variability or error in estimating a person's Y score given X.

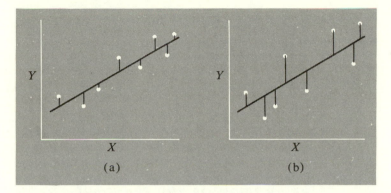

Fig. 5–9. Two regression lines with different amounts of error in prediction.
Graph B has larger errors than does Graph A.

The **standard error of estimate**, $s_{y \cdot x}$ read "s y dot x," is defined
to be the square root of the sum of squared deviations of Y_i about
the line ($\tilde{Y}$) divided by ($N - 2$). In symbols,

$$s_{y \cdot x} = \sqrt{\frac{\sum(Y_i - \tilde{Y})^2}{N - 2}}$$

The standard error of estimate is abbreviated $s_{y \cdot x}$ in order to distinguish it
from the standard deviation of the Y distribution which is written s_y (s_x for the
X distribution), and to indicate that it is appropriate for the regression of Y
on X. Consider the logic of this index.

First, recall the discussion of variability of points about the mean in Chapter 3.
In that case, an index of variability about a constant value, the mean, was
developed by taking the sum of the squared deviations about that mean and
dividing them by $N - 1$, to obtain the variance, or its square root, the standard
deviation:

$$s_y = \sqrt{\frac{\sum(Y_i - \overline{Y})^2}{N - 1}}$$

The present task is similar: to index the variability of the Y scores, not about
their mean, but about the regression line, $\tilde{Y}$. If the sum of these squared deviations, $\sum(Y - \tilde{Y})^2$, is divided by $N - 2$, one has

$$s_{y \cdot x} = \sqrt{\frac{\sum(Y_i - \tilde{Y})^2}{N - 2}}$$

Conceptually, this statistic is very similar to the standard deviation, except that
it reflects variation about the regression line ($\tilde{Y}$) rather than about the mean ($\overline{Y}$).

Note that while the denominator for the standard deviation was $N - 1$ in order to improve the estimation of σ, the denominator for the standard error of estimate is $N - 2$. This quantity is used to improve $s_{y.x}$ as an estimator of its corresponding population parameter, $\sigma_{y.x}$.

The formula for $s_{y.x}$ given above is a definitional formula. To use it for actual computation would be tedious since a $\tilde{Y}$ would have to be computed for every X. Therefore, an alternative formula is used which will give the identical result but which is easier to compute:

$$s_{y.x} = \sqrt{\left[\frac{1}{N(N-2)}\right]\left[N\sum Y^2 - (\sum Y)^2 - \frac{[N\sum XY - (\sum X)(\sum Y)]^2}{N\sum X^2 - (\sum X)^2}\right]}$$

APPLICATION OF THE STANDARD ERROR OF ESTIMATE

Suppose a student who has an SAT score of 620 applies to a college, and the relationship between SAT and grades predicts a grade average of 1.8. It might be of interest not only to predict a specific grade average of 1.8 but to determine an interval of values which is likely to contain the person's actual score. Further, suppose the interval were constructed such that in 95 of every 100 such cases the actual value would fall within the limits of the interval. This constitutes useful information. For example, suppose the predicted grade average for applicant Harriet Chandler is 1.8—roughly a C— on a 4-point grade scale. If the points clustered closely about the line, the measure of prediction error $s_{y.x}$ would be small and we would have confidence in our prediction. Consequently, in addition to saying that Chandler's probable grade average is 1.8, one could say that most of the people having an SAT score of 620 would have a freshman grade average between 1.6 and 2.0, for example. Therefore, since Chandler is very likely to sport a C or D average her freshman year, she might not be included in the new class. However, suppose the accuracy of prediction was poorer than this (i.e., the standard error of estimate is larger), and most applicants with such an SAT score are likely to obtain grade averages as far apart as 1.2 to 2.4. In this case, one might not eliminate Chandler quite so fast. Since it is possible that she could be a "C+ student", with some desirable non-academic assets, the admissions officer might consider accepting her. Thus, rather than simply predicting an average of 1.8 (a process called **point estimation**), predicting a range of values (called **interval estimation**) reflects the accuracy of prediction and provides additional useful information.

How would one determine an interval, within which the grade averages of 95% of those applicants having a given SAT score would be expected to fall? In this case, the task is to specify score points at the 2.5th percentile and at the 97.5th percentile of the distribution of grade averages (Y scores) for applicants having an SAT score of $X = 620$. That is, 95% of the applicants having an SAT score of 620 would have grade averages between the percentile points $P_{.025}$ and $P_{.975}$. One obvious route to determining these values is to go directly to the original data, select all those applicants having an SAT score of 620, and calculate $P_{.025}$ and $P_{.975}$ for the Y scores of just these subjects according to the procedures described on pages 65–66. Unfortunately, this procedure has at least two major liabilities. First, unless a very large sample is available, there will not be many people scoring exactly 620 on the SAT. Consequently, there will not be an adequate distribution of cases for determining the required percentiles. Moreover, even if an enormous sample was available, one would have to calculate $P_{.025}$ and $P_{.975}$ separately for each specific SAT score value in order to provide an interval estimate for every possible applicant.

As an alternative, consider the following strategy. Suppose it could be assumed that in a very large population of applicants, the separate distributions of grades at each value of the SAT were normal in form. Then, the percentiles associated with the standard normal distribution could be used. An example of this situation is presented in Figure 5–10. However, such a procedure requires that the mean and standard deviation of each of these distributions be available. Fortunately, we can be saved from making all those calculations by using the predicted grade average based upon the regression line ($\tilde{Y}$) as an estimate of the mean of each distribution and by using the standard error of estimate ($s_{y \cdot x}$) as an estimator of the standard deviation of each of these distributions. The next paragraphs detail this procedure and consider the assumptions it requires.

Some clarity of explanation will be gained if we shift to a simpler example,

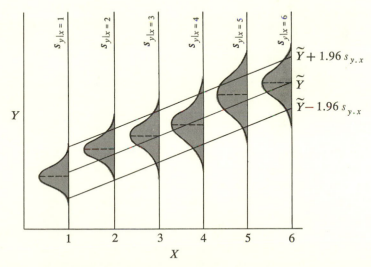

Fig. 5–10.   Graph showing the use of the line ($\tilde{Y}$) and the $s_{y \cdot x}$ to construct confidence intervals about the line. The graph also shows the subdistributions of Y_i at each X value.

such as the one depicted in Figure 5–10. The graph shows the regression line ($\tilde{Y}$) and the individual "subdistributions" of Y scores for each of the six values of X. The notation $s_{y|x=1}$ signifies the standard deviation of the Y scores for the subdistribution corresponding to $X = 1$.

Now, suppose you were to determine the $P_{.025}$ and $P_{.975}$ for just one of these subdistributions. If the subdistribution were normal in form, one could use the percentiles of the normal distribution. For example, Table A, Appendix II, shows that the value of z corresponding to $P_{.975}$ is 1.96, and since the standard normal distribution is symmetrical, the value for $P_{.025}$ will be $z = -1.96$. Recall that z values are really standard deviation units. This means that 95% of the cases should fall between -1.96 standard deviations and $+1.96$ standard deviations of the mean of a normal distribution. Therefore, the required percentile points can be found by first subtracting and then adding 1.96 times the standard deviation to the mean of that Y distribution.

However, suppose the relationship between X and Y were indeed quite linear. Then, the means of the separate Y subdistributions (indicated by dashed lines in Figure 5–10) would fall very close to the regression line, $\tilde{Y}$. In that case, $\tilde{Y}$ could be used to estimate the mean of each of the Y distributions. Moreover, suppose that the standard deviation of these subdistributions was the same value for each of them. In this case, the standard error of estimate would constitute a single number that would estimate the standard deviation of each of these separate distributions. Now, we have estimates of the mean (i.e., $\tilde{Y}$) and standard deviation ($s_{y.x}$) of *each* subdistribution, and if these distributions are normal in form, the standard normal distribution can be used to determine the required percentile points. Specifically, based upon the logic described in the preceding paragraph, $P_{.975}$ will be 1.96 times the standard deviation (to be estimated by $s_{y.x}$) above the mean (to be estimated by $\tilde{Y}$) and $P_{.025}$ will be -1.96 standard errors below the estimated mean. In symbols,

$$P_{.975} = \tilde{Y} + 1.96s_{y.x} \quad \text{and} \quad P_{.025} = \tilde{Y} - 1.96s_{y.x}$$

If $\tilde{Y} = 1.80$ and $s_{y.x} = .30$,

$$P_{.975} = 1.80 + 1.96(.30) = 2.39 \quad \text{and} \quad P_{.025} = 1.80 - 1.96(.30) = 1.21$$

Percentile points used in this way are called **confidence limits**, since they define an interval of score values associated with a given level of confidence (e.g., 95%) that an individual will in fact score between these limits. Of course, not all confidence limits need to be 95% confidence limits. One may desire to know the interval of scores within which 90%, 75%, or maybe 50% of such individuals are likely to score. The only change in procedure is to determine from Table A in Appendix II the number of standard error units (i.e., the z value) corresponding to these percentile ranks. For example, suppose one wanted to construct 90% confidence limits. The central 90% of a distribution falls between $P_{.05}$ and $P_{.95}$, and for the standard normal distribution the corresponding points are -1.645

and $+1.645$ (z values obtained from Table A, Appendix II). Therefore, 90% confidence limits will be defined by

$$P_{.95} = \tilde{Y} + 1.645s_{y.x} \quad \text{and} \quad P_{.05} = \tilde{Y} - 1.645s_{y.x}$$

The entire procedure is contingent upon certain assumptions: (1) linearity, (2) normality of the individual Y distributions at each X value, and (3) homoscedasticity or the property of each separate Y distribution having the same standard deviation. We now consider these three assumptions in more detail.

First, the **relationship must be linear**. If it is not linear but curvilinear, then a straight line will not approximate the central tendencies of all the groups. One can see in Figure 5–10 that the means of the individual Y distributions do not fall precisely on the line. The greater the linearity the more accurate will be the regression line estimate the subdistribution means.

Second, in order to use the proposition that 95% of the cases will fall within ± 1.96 standard deviation units from $\tilde{Y}$, it must be assumed that **each of the Y subdistributions is normal in form**. The value 1.96 is derived from the standard normal and will not mark off the correct percentiles in distributions that are not normal in form.

Third, the standard error of estimate is computed over all the Y subdistributions and is therefore a composite measure of their variability. If, however, the single value $s_{y.x}$ is to be an appropriate index of the variability of each of these separate distributions, then the actual standard deviations $s_{y|x=k}$ should be comparable from one subdistribution to the other. This comparability of variance is called either **homogeneity of Y-distribution variance** or **homoscedasticity**.

The effect of not having homogeneity of variance within each of the Y distributions at each value of X is displayed in Figure 5–11. In this diagram an irregular scatterplot is drawn with its regression line and lines indicating ± 1.96 standard errors of estimate. The confidence limits for the regression line are not appropriate for most Y distributions at specific values of X because there is not homogeneity of Y-distribution variance across these X values. If the confidence limits were used to indicate the values of Y within which a predicted score would likely fall, they would represent too narrow a range at $X = 3$ but too wide a range at $X = 10$. The use of the standard error of estimate in this manner is appropriate only if the variances of the individual Y distributions are comparable at each value of X.

In summary, to use the standard error of estimate to establish confidence intervals about the regression line one must assume that (1) there is a linear relationship between X and Y so that the regression line is an appropriate estimate of the subdistribution means, (2) the Y distributions at each X value are all normal so that the percentiles of the standard normal distribution may be applied, and (3) the variability of these separate Y distributions is relatively comparable one to another (homoscedasticity) so that a single measure of variability ($s_{y.x}$) will be appropriate for each one.

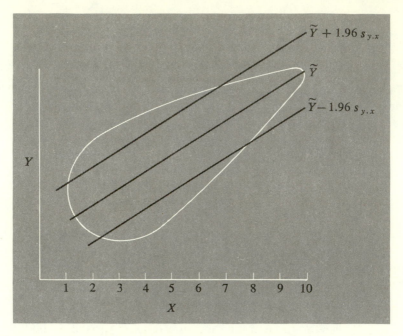

Fig. 5–11. A scatterplot that does not possess homogeneity of subdistribution Y variances (absence of homoscedasticity). Notice that the confidence interval underestimates the range of Y at X = 3 but overestimates it at X = 9.

Are these assumptions ever met? Although they appear to be very restrictive, they can be assumed occasionally, but a large number of scores usually is needed to provide enough cases in each Y distribution to determine if those distributions appear normal and of comparable variability.

FORMULAS

1. Geometry of a Straight Line

$$\text{Slope} = \frac{y_2 - y_1}{x_2 - x_1} \text{ for points } (x_1, y_1) \text{ and } (x_2, y_2) \text{ on the line}$$

y-intercept: Y value at $X = 0$

2. Regression of Y on X

a. Regression equation

$$\tilde{Y} = bX + a$$

b. Slope

$$b = \frac{N(\sum XY) - (\sum X)(\sum Y)}{N\sum X^2 - (\sum X)^2}$$

c. y-intercept

$$a = \bar{Y} - b\bar{X}$$

d. Standard error of estimate

$$S_{y.x} = \sqrt{\frac{\sum(Y_i - \tilde{Y})^2}{N - 2}}$$

(definitional formula)

$$S_{y.x} = \sqrt{\left[\frac{1}{N(N-2)}\right]\left[N\sum Y^2 - (\sum Y)^2 - \frac{[N(\sum XY) - (\sum X)(\sum Y)]^2}{N\sum X^2 - (\sum X)^2}\right]}$$

(computational formula)

EXERCISES

1. Compute the regression constants for the regressions of Y on X, W on X, and W on Y. Also write the regression equation for each of these relationships

X	Y	W
2	8	10
3	2	7
5	4	1
6	6	5
8	10	2
10	5	3

2. Using the equations from Exercise 1, what would you predict in the following cases?
   (a) $\tilde{Y}$ for $X = 6$
   (b) $\tilde{W}$ for $X = 3$
   (c) $\tilde{W}$ for $Y = 3$
   (d) $\tilde{Y}$ for $X = 12$

3. Construct 95% confidence intervals for your predictions in (a), (b), and (c) of the previous exercise. (Disregard assumptions. See Exercise 8.)

4. The squared deviations $\sum(Y_i - \tilde{Y})^2$ are called squared errors of prediction or residuals. Explain the logic of their use for this purpose, and their role in the least squares criterion. Why is the regression line the line of "best fit"?

5. If a salesperson receives a base pay of $350 per month and a 5% commission on sales, what is the regression equation relating sales and income for this person?

6. Compare the standard error of estimate with a simple standard deviation. In what way are they similar and in what way are they different?

7. Why are there usually two regression lines?

8. In order to use the standard error of estimate to construct confidence limits about the regression line, it is necessary to make three assumptions. Describe these assumptions and explain why these propositions are vital to this application of the $s_{y.x}$.

9. Indicate whether each of the following sets of facts could or could not exist simultaneously. If not, why not?
   (a) $a = 5$, $b = 1.00$, the regression line crosses the X-axis at 5.
   (b) $a = 10$, $b = .5$, $s_y = 4$
   (c) $b = -.4$, $s_y = 15$, $s_{y.x} = 20$

CORRELATION

6

In the previous chapter on regression, the problem of linear prediction was discussed. It was found that the equation for a straight line relating two variables could be obtained such that the sum of the squared distances between the line and the actual data points was a minimum. Further, the standard error of estimate provided a means of gauging the interval of Y values within which a subject with a given X score was likely to fall. But, since the standard error of estimate is always in the units of the predicted variable, it is not possible to compare the degree of linear relationship between two different pairs of variables (e.g., X and Y vs. W and Z). Consequently, it would be useful to have an index of the degree of relationship between two variables that is not expressed in the units of one of the variables and therefore is an index that will permit comparisons to be made between different sets of variables. Such an index of the degree of a linear relationship between two variables is the **correlation coefficient**.

derivation of the correlation coefficient

The approach to developing the formula for the correlation coefficient rests on the fact that the square of the correlation coefficient represents the amount of variability in the Y_i that is associated with differences in the variable X. For example, suppose a reading test were given to a group of children at the termination of first grade. Not every child obtains the same score on this reading test, and the extent to which the scores are dissimilar from child to child is reflected in the variability of the scores (e.g., their variance, s^2). Also suppose that an intelligence test was also administered at the end of first grade and thus the mental age of each child was also available. Since the children would not likely all have the same mental age, there would be variability in the distribution of mental ages as well. Now, to what extent are these individuals differing from the mean of the mental age distribution in the same manner and relative extent as they differed from the mean of the reading score distribution? For example, are individuals who score substantially above the mean reading score also near the top of the mental age distribution? What proportion of the difference in the reading scores of individuals (i.e., variability) is reflected in the variability of the mental ages of those same subjects? That percentage is the square of the correlation coefficient. We now consider the details underlying this statement.

Recall that the concept of variability expresses the extent to which individual scores differ from one another. We index the amount of variability with the variance, s^2, which statistic is based upon the squared differences between each score and the mean of the distribution. The strategy below breaks up this variability into two parts, one of which is associated with another variable and one part which is not. In the population, the total variability in reading score (i.e., in the Y_i) is symbolized by σ_y^2. The square of the standard error of estimate, $\sigma_{y.x}^2$, reflects the amount of variability in reading which is *not* related to mental age, since it is the variability in Y_i *after* one predicts Y from its relationship to mental age (X). Therefore, $\sigma_y^2 - \sigma_{y.x}^2$ represents the amount of variability in Y which is indeed associated with Y's relationship to X. When this quantity is taken as a proportion of the total variability, $(\sigma_y^2 - \sigma_{y.x}^2)/\sigma_y^2$, one has the square of the population correlation coefficient.

To examine this logic more concretely, consider Figure 6–1 which presents an imperfect relationship between mental age and reading score for five pupils. The score for one pupil (with mental age 100) and its deviations from the mean and regression line have been illustrated in detail. Call this pupil Johnny. Locate three points in Figure 6–1 for this pupil: Y_i, Johnny's actual observed reading score; $\bar{Y}$, the mean of all five reading scores; and $\tilde{Y}_i$, the reading score which would be predicted for Johnny on the basis of the relationship between reading and mental age (i.e., the regression line at $X = 100$). To begin, try to predict Johnny's score without any knowledge of the relationship between reading and mental age. In the absence of any additional information, a good estimate of Johnny's reading score would be the mean score for the entire group of children sampled since the squared deviations of scores about their mean is a minimum. In the case of the data presented in Figure 6–1, this prediction would be $\bar{Y} = 50$. However, suppose Johnny actually scored 100 on the reading test ($Y_i = 100$); then the prediction of 50 would be in error by

$$(Y_i - \bar{Y}) = 100 - 50 = 50$$

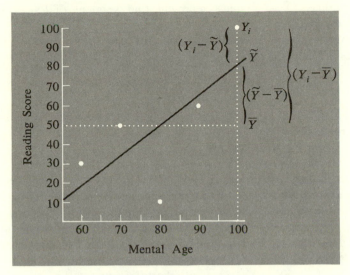

Fig. 6–1. Scatterplot showing three deviations:
$(Y_i - \bar{Y})$, $(Y_i - \tilde{Y})$, and $(\tilde{Y} - \bar{Y})$.

Now suppose that one knew that Johnny had a mental age of 100 and that one also knew the linear relationship between mental age and reading score. If one were now asked to predict Johnny's reading score, he would guess the point on the regression line at $X = 100$, namely, $\tilde{Y} = 80$. Again, there would be error in this estimation, in particular

$$(Y_i - \tilde{Y}) = 100 - 80 = 20$$

Notice in this case that although there is still an error, it is less than if $\bar{Y}$ were used to make the prediction. Specifically, the reduction in error is given by

$$(Y_i - \bar{Y}) - (Y_i - \tilde{Y}) = 50 - 20 = 30$$

If the left side of the above expression is simplified, one obtains

$$(Y_i - \bar{Y}) - (Y_i - \tilde{Y}) = Y_i - \bar{Y} - Y_i + \tilde{Y}$$
$$Y_i - \bar{Y} - Y_i + \tilde{Y} = (\tilde{Y} - \bar{Y})$$
$$(\tilde{Y} - \bar{Y}) = 80 - 50 = 30$$

It should be observed in Figure 6–1 that the distance between the point and the mean of the Y_i can be partitioned into two parts:

$$(Y_i - \bar{Y}) = (\tilde{Y} - \bar{Y}) + (Y_i - \tilde{Y})$$

Since $(Y_i - \tilde{Y})$ reflects error still remaining after the prediction with the regression line, $(\tilde{Y} - \overline{Y})$ must represent that segment of $(Y_i - \overline{Y})$ that is associated with X.

However, if one is to speak of variability and proportions of variability, measures of such concepts usually involve squared deviations. It happens that when

$$(Y_i - \overline{Y}) = (\tilde{Y} - \overline{Y}) + (Y_i - \tilde{Y})$$

is squared and summed, all the cross-product terms drop from the expression and the result is

$$\sum(Y_i - \overline{Y})^2 = \sum(\tilde{Y} - \overline{Y})^2 + \sum(Y_i - \tilde{Y})^2$$

This states that the total squared deviations of points about their mean may be partitioned into the sum of two parts. Notice that the quantity $\sum(Y_i - \tilde{Y})^2$ represents the squared deviations that still remain after prediction has been made with the regression line. Therefore, $\sum(\tilde{Y} - \overline{Y})^2$ must represent the segment of the total squared deviations in Y_i that indeed is associated with X. Consequently, if $\sum(\tilde{Y} - \overline{Y})^2$ represents the squared deviations in Y associated with X and if $\sum(Y_i - \overline{Y})^2$ represents the total squared deviations in Y, then their ratio

$$\frac{\sum(\tilde{Y} - \overline{Y})^2}{\sum(Y_i - \overline{Y})^2}$$

constitutes the proportion of squared deviations in Y associated with differences in X. Often this ratio is said to express the **proportion of variability**[1] in Y that is associated with differences in X. If the value of the ratio was .55 for the mental age-reading example described above, it would mean that 55% of the total variability in reading scores is associated with differences in mental age.

While this ratio indeed provides an index of the degree of relationship by indicating the proportion of variability in Y that is associated with differences in X, it does not reflect the direction of the relationship. Was it positive or negative? That is, were high scores on one variable associated with high scores on the other (positive or direct relationship), or did high scores on one measure relate to low scores on the other (negative or inverse relationship)? Regrettably, since this proportion is a ratio of two positive quantities, it will always be positive. However, consider the fact that although one ordinarily accepts the positive root when one extracts the square root of a number, technically the roots of a number include both a positive and a negative root. Hence, there are really two results in taking the square root of a^2, $+a$ and $-a$, because both $(+a)^2$ and $(-a)^2$ equal a^2. Therefore, one could take the square root of the proportion of variability, accepting the positive root if the relationship between X and Y is positive or the negative root if it is negative.

---

[1] If X is error free.

The **Pearson product moment correlation coefficient,** named after Karl Pearson and symbolized by **r,** is precisely this quantity:

$$r = \sqrt{\frac{\sum(\tilde{Y} - \bar{Y})^2}{\sum(Y_i - \bar{Y})^2}}$$

Once again the formula which defines a statistic is inconvenient to use in computational work. To use this expression requires that $\tilde{Y}$ be computed for every value of X. However, by substituting the equality ($\tilde{Y} = bX + a$) into the above formula and then substituting the raw-score formulas for both b and a, the above quantity becomes

$$r = \frac{N \sum XY - (\sum X)(\sum Y)}{\sqrt{[N \sum X^2 - (\sum X)^2][N \sum Y^2 - (\sum Y)^2]}}$$

The distinct advantage of this formula, in addition to its ease of computation when large numbers of subjects are involved, is that since the formula for b, the slope of the regression line, was used in its derivation one does not have to be concerned about selecting the positive or negative root to indicate the direction of the relationship. The slope is positive for positive relationships and negative for negative relationships; therefore, since this formula includes the slope, it provides the appropriate sign for r without further labor.

Table 6–1 presents a numerical example of both formulas which yield identical results. The regression line for these data is $\tilde{Y} = .75X + 1.25$. $\tilde{Y}$ has been computed for each pair of scores. Columns five through seven yield $\sum(Y_i - \bar{Y})^2$, $\sum(Y_i - \tilde{Y})^2$, and $\sum(\tilde{Y} - \bar{Y})^2$. The square of the correlation coefficient is defined as the proportion of the total variability in Y which is associated with differences in X. In this case $r^2 = .49$. The correlation coefficient, r, is the square root of this value, or .70. In the last three columns of Table 6–1 are the values X^2, Y^2, and XY for use in the computational formula. Again, N is the number of subjects or pairs of scores. These values are substituted into the computational formula, which gives a result of $r = .70$. The square of r is .49, which is the proportion of variance in Y that is associated with differences in X.

properties of the correlation coefficient

THE RANGE OF r

The correlation coefficient may assume values from -1 to $+1$. Consider first the case of a perfect linear relationship between X and Y in which the points all fall precisely on a line of non-zero slope (the line is not parallel to the X-axis).

6–1 Calculation of the Correlation Coefficient.

X	Y	$\bar{Y}$	$\tilde{Y}$	$(Y_i - \bar{Y})^2$	$(Y_i - \tilde{Y})^2$	$(\tilde{Y} - \bar{Y})^2$	X^2	Y^2	XY
9	10	5	8.0	25	4.00	9.00	81	100	90
7	6	5	6.5	1	.25	2.25	49	36	42
5	1	5	5.0	16	16.00	.00	25	1	5
3	5	5	3.5	0	2.25	2.25	9	25	15
1	3	5	2.0	4	1.00	9.00	1	9	3
25	25			46	23.50	22.50	165	171	155

$$r^2 = \frac{\text{Variability Associated with } X}{\text{Total Variability}} = \frac{\sum(\tilde{Y} - \bar{Y})^2}{\sum(Y_i - \bar{Y})^2} = \frac{22.50}{46} = .49$$

$$r = \sqrt{r^2} = \sqrt{.49} = .70$$

Computational Formula

$$r = \frac{N\sum XY - (\sum X)(\sum Y)}{\sqrt{[N\sum X^2 - (\sum X)^2][N\sum Y^2 - (\sum Y)^2]}}$$

$$= \frac{5(155) - (25)(25)}{\sqrt{[5(165) - (25)^2][5(171) - (25)^2]}}$$

$$r = \frac{150}{\sqrt{(200)(230)}} = \frac{150}{\sqrt{46000}} = \frac{150}{214.476} = .70$$

$$r^2 = \text{Proportion of Variance Associated with } X = (.70)^2 = .49$$

In this situation each point Y_i is also a point $\tilde{Y}$, therefore $\sum(\tilde{Y} - \bar{Y})^2$ and $\sum(Y_i - \bar{Y})^2$ are identical, and

$$r = \sqrt{\frac{\sum(\tilde{Y} - \bar{Y})^2}{\sum(Y_i - \bar{Y})^2}} = \sqrt{1} = \pm 1.00$$

Thus, in the case of a perfect relationship in which all points fall on the regression line ($b \neq 0$), the correlation coefficient will equal $+1.00$ or -1.00, depending upon whether the relationship is positive or negative.

Suppose now that there is no relationship between X and Y. The scatterplot may appear to be a rather circular clustering of points (for example, see Figure 6–3C). Here the regression line will be parallel to the X-axis and will be the same line as $\bar{Y}$. Since the two lines, $\tilde{Y}$ and $\bar{Y}$, are identical, then $\sum(\tilde{Y} - \bar{Y})^2$ must be equal to zero, leaving

$$r = \sqrt{\frac{\sum(\tilde{Y} - \bar{Y})^2}{\sum(Y_i - \bar{Y})^2}} = \sqrt{\frac{0}{\sum(Y_i - \bar{Y})^2}} = .00$$

Therefore, when there is no relationship, $r = .00$.

Can r ever be greater than 1.00 or less than -1.00? No, because it can be shown that $\sum(\tilde{Y} - \bar{Y})^2$ is always less than or equal to $\sum(Y_i - \bar{Y})^2$ which means that the fraction

$$\frac{\sum(\tilde{Y} - \bar{Y})^2}{\sum(Y_i - \bar{Y})^2}$$

will always be less than or equal to 1.00, and therefore so will r. Besides, proportions never exceed 1.00.

Hence, the correlation coefficient ranges in value between -1.00 and $+1.00$. It is ± 1.00 if all the points fall precisely on a line of nonzero slope, and it is .00 if there is no relationship at all. If there is no variability in Y_i (they are all the same value), r is not defined (See Figure 6–3D).

VARIANCE INTERPRETATION[2] OF r^2

Examine the preceding facts in terms of the proportion of variability of the Y_i that is attributable to X. Suppose there is a grade school composed of children from kindergarten to sixth grade. Consider the heights of these children. Obviously, although this distribution of heights has a mean, most of the scores are not precisely equal to the mean value. They deviate from the mean, and the extent to which they deviate constitutes the total variability in Y_i (in this case, heights). But, careful thought suggests that at least some of this variability in the heights of children is attributable to the fact that the children span a large age range, and there is certainly a relationship between the ages of the children and their heights. It might be of interest to ask what proportion of the variability in heights is associated with differences in ages. If the figures of the illustration in Table 6–1 were appropriate for this example, $r^2 = .49$ would suggest that 49% of the variability in the heights of the children in the school is attributable to the fact that the children were of different ages. The higher this proportion, the greater the degree of linear relationship between age and height.

Suppose the baby sitter in the example in Chapter 5 had recorded both the hours worked and the money earned on sitting jobs over the last year. Obviously, the baby sitter did not earn the same amount of money for each job. That is, there is variability in the per-job return on baby sitting. What proportion of that variability is attributable to the hours worked on each job? If the pairs

---

[2] Assumes X is measured without error.

of points (hours, earnings) were plotted, they would all fall on a straight line with slope equal to the hourly rate. Since the regression line perfectly predicts earnings (Y) from hours worked (X), there is no variability in Y_i which is not predictable from X. Therefore, 100% ($r^2 = 1.00$) of the variability in the Y_i is attributable to X.

Suppose one attempted to relate height and IQ. There is almost no relationship between these variables. The regression line would be horizontal to and $\overline{Y}$ units above the X-axis (i.e., $\tilde{Y} = \overline{Y}$). Of course there would be variability in the heights of the subjects, but none of this variability would be attributable to the fact that the subjects differed in IQ. The fact that 0% of the variability in height is associated with IQ is reflected in the correlation of .00 ($r^2 = .00$, $r = .00$).

THE RELATIONSHIP BETWEEN r AND r^2

It has been said that the square of the correlation coefficient (r^2) may be interpreted as the proportion of variance in Y_i attributable to differences in X. The correlation coefficient was taken to be the square root of this proportion with the algebraic sign indicating the direction of the relationship. Since r is obviously not the same as r^2, one must exercise caution in interpreting the size of the correlation between two measures. For example, consider the following table:

Correlation: r	Proportion of Variance: r^2
.10	.01
.20	.04
.30	.09
.40	.16
.50	.25
.60	.36
.70	.49
.80	.64
.90	.81
1.00	1.00

Note that a correlation of from .10 to .30 suggests that not very much variance in Y_i is associated with differences in $X(1\%-9\%)$. In fact, a correlation of .50, which is frequently considered high in psychological and educational research, implies that only 25% of the variance in Y_i is associated with X. That means that 75% of the variability in Y_i is associated with factors other than X. One needs a correlation of .71 before one can say that half of the variability in Y_i is attributable to X. The implication is that in terms of proportion of variance in Y, the *unsquared* correlation coefficient (i.e., r) gives the impression of indicating a higher degree of relationship with X than should be connoted.

THE EFFECT OF ORIGIN AND UNIT UPON r

In Chapter 4 it was shown how adding a constant to every score or multiplying every score by a constant affected the value of the mean and variance of that distribution. It was also demonstrated that adding or multiplying (or subtracting and dividing) really amounted to changing the origin and the unit of the measuring scale. An extension of that exercise is to ask what happens to the correlation coefficient if the unit and/or origin of either scale of measurement (X and/or Y) is altered.

> The correlation coefficient does not change if every score in either or both distributions is increased or multiplied by a constant ($c \neq 0$). Thus, r is not altered by changes in the origin and unit of the measurement scale.

The algebraic proof of this assertion is given in Optional Table 6–2. Therefore, adding or subtracting, multiplying or dividing, or both adding (or subtracting) and multiplying (or dividing) X and/or Y by the same or different nonzero constants does not alter the value of r. More succinctly, r is invariant under transformations of unit and/or origin.

This result has important implications for the use of the correlation coefficient. This fact means that it does not matter if the measurement is in feet or inches, minutes or seconds, units or dozens. The correlation between the variables will be the same. If r indexes the degree of relationship between two variables (e.g., age and height), it must be the case that the degree of association between age and height is the same regardless of whether age is measured in months or years and height is measured in inches or centimeters. Indeed, the immutability of r to changes in the origin and/or unit of measurement in either one or both of the variables gives this statistic a large range of applications.

THE RELATION BETWEEN CORRELATION AND REGRESSION

slope and correlation By certain algebraic manipulations it can be shown that

$$r = b_{yx} \left(\frac{s_x}{s_y} \right)$$

This expression shows that the correlation coefficient is a joint function of the

6–2 Proof that the Correlation Coefficient is Not Altered by Changing the Measurement Scale.

Operation	Explanation

Change in Origin (Adding a Constant)

1. $r = \dfrac{\sum(X - \bar{X})(Y - \bar{Y})}{\sqrt{\sum(X - \bar{X})^2 \sum(Y - \bar{Y})^2}}$

    1. Definition of r (see next section)

2. $r = \dfrac{\sum[(X + c) - (\bar{X} + c)][(Y + k) - (\bar{Y} + k)]}{\sqrt{\sum[(X + c) - (\bar{X} + c)]^2 \sum[(Y + k) - (\bar{Y} + k)]^2}}$

    2. Substituting $(X + c)$ for X and $(Y + k)$ for Y

3. $r = \dfrac{\sum(X + c - \bar{X} - c)(Y + k - \bar{Y} - k)}{\sqrt{\sum(X + c - \bar{X} - c)^2 \sum(Y + k - \bar{Y} - k)^2}}$

    3. Removing parentheses

4. $r = \dfrac{\sum(X - \bar{X})(Y - \bar{Y})}{\sqrt{\sum(X - \bar{X})^2 \sum(Y - \bar{Y})^2}}$

    4. Subtracting the c's and k's within parentheses leaves the formula for r unchanged.

continued

slope of the regression line (b_{yx}) and the standard deviations of the two variables (s_x and s_y). Consequently, the size of r is not simply reflected in the slope of the regression line alone. However, if the scores within the X and Y distributions are converted to standard scores which both have standard deviations of 1, then the formula for the correlation coefficient is

$$r = b_{z_y z_x}$$

In short, when both X and Y distributions are in standard score form (have the same standard deviation), the correlation coefficient is precisely the slope of the regression line. Note, however, that the slope of the line computed with raw

---

6–2   continued

Change in Unit (Multiplying by a Constant)

1. $r = \dfrac{\sum(cX - c\overline{X})(kY - k\overline{Y})}{\sqrt{\sum(cX - c\overline{X})^2 \sum(kY - k\overline{Y})^2}}$

   1. Definition of r with cX and kY substituted for X and Y. As a result, the means will be $c\overline{X}$ and $k\overline{Y}$.

2. $r = \dfrac{\sum c(X - \overline{X})k(Y - \overline{Y})}{\sqrt{\sum[c(X - \overline{X})]^2 \sum[k(Y - \overline{Y})]^2}}$

   2. Factoring in the manner of $ab - ac = a(b - c)$

3. $r = \dfrac{ck\sum(X - \overline{X})(Y - \overline{Y})}{\sqrt{c^2 k^2 \sum(X - \overline{X})^2 \sum(Y - \overline{Y})^2}}$

   3. In the numerator, $\sum cW = c\sum W$, and in the denominator $(ab)^2 = a^2 b^2$

4. $r = \dfrac{ck\sum(X - \overline{X})(Y - \overline{Y})}{ck\sqrt{\sum(X - \overline{X})^2 \sum(Y - \overline{Y})^2}}$

   4. $\sqrt{a^2 b^2 WZ} = ab\sqrt{WZ}$

5. $r = \dfrac{\sum(X - \overline{X})(Y - \overline{Y})}{\sqrt{\sum(X - \overline{X})^2 \sum(Y - \overline{Y})^2}}$

   5. Cancellation, thus leaving r unchanged

---

scores and the slope computed with standardized scores will not be the same value. That is, ordinarily $b_{yx} \neq b_{z_y z_x}$.

r_{xy} **and** r_{yx} Usually there will be two regression lines, one for the regression of Y on X and the other for X on Y. However, the correlation coefficient for these two cases is the same. That is, $r_{xy} = r_{yx}$. The truth of this can be readily seen by examining one form of the formula for r:

$$r = \frac{\sum(X - \overline{X})(Y - \overline{Y})}{\sqrt{[\sum(X - \overline{X})^2][\sum(Y - \overline{Y})^2]}}$$

If the positions of X and Y are reversed, the formula remains the same.

From an intuitive standpoint this is as it should be. If r is a measure of the degree of relationship between X and Y, the two variables should be related to the same extent regardless of the direction of prediction. Conversely however, the regression lines predict in score units, and if X and Y are not identical scales, then it is reasonable that the regression lines should be different for the two directions of prediction.

$s_{y \cdot x}$ **and** r At the beginning of this chapter, a conceptual derivation of the correlation coefficient of the following sort was presented: (1) σ_y^2 represents the total variability in Y; (2) $\sigma_{y \cdot x}^2$ reflects the variability in Y which is *not* associated with Y's relationship to X; (3) thus $\sigma_y^2 - \sigma_{y \cdot x}^2$ represents variability in Y which is associated with Y's relationship to X; and (4) $(\sigma_y^2 - \sigma_{y \cdot x}^2)/\sigma_y^2$ is the proportion of variability in Y which is associated with X, which is the square of the correlation coefficient:

$$r^2 = \frac{\sigma_y^2 - \sigma_{y \cdot x}^2}{\sigma_y^2} = 1 - \frac{\sigma_{y \cdot x}^2}{\sigma_y^2}$$

If the sample statistics s_y^2 and $s_{y \cdot x}^2$ are substituted for their corresponding parameters

$$r^2 = 1 - \frac{s_{y \cdot x}^2}{s_y^2}$$

These equations[3] state that the size of the relationship as reflected in the correlation coefficient is a function of the ratio of the variability of points about the line (as expressed by $s_{y \cdot x}^2$) to the total variability of the Y scores (s_y^2). More specifically, r will be higher if the fraction

$$\frac{s_{y \cdot x}^2}{s_y^2}$$

is relatively small. In words, the correlation will be high if the variability of the points about the line is small relative to their total variability.

Moreover, since the magnitudes of both $s_{y \cdot x}^2$ and s_y^2 are reflected in a scatterplot, it is possible to judge the relative size of different correlations by observing their graphs.

Consider the graphs in Figure 6–2. Plots A and B have approximately the same variability in Y_i but differ in the extent to which the points cluster about the line. Since the $s_{y \cdot x}$ in A is less than in B, the fraction

$$\frac{s_{y \cdot x}^2}{s_y^2}$$

---

[3] The expression above and the definitional and computational formulas for $s_{y \cdot x}$ given in the previous chapter on regression will yield similar but not identical results. The computational formulas on page 108 are preferred, though the difference between the two formulas is very small when N is large.

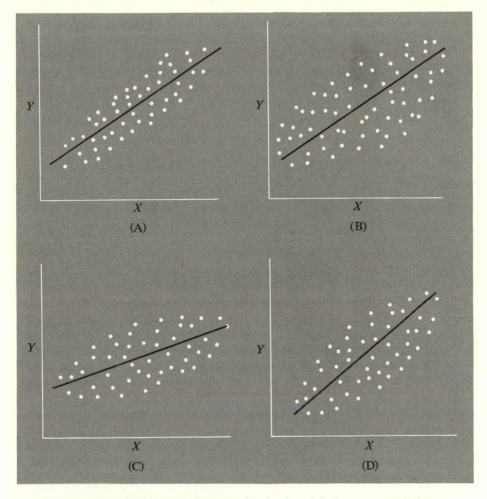

Fig. 6–2.   Hypothetical scatterplots. In Graphs A and B the s_y are equivalent but since the $s_{y.x}$ is less in A its correlation is higher. In Graphs C and D, the $s_{y.x}$ are comparable, but since the s_y is greater in D the correlation is higher.

is smaller and thus the correlation is larger for A than for B. The converse situation is presented in Graphs C and D. The variability of Y_i is greater in D than in C while the $s_{y.x}$ is approximately the same in each. Therefore, the ratio

$$\frac{s_{y.x}^2}{s_y^2}$$

is smaller in D than in C, and consequently the correlation is higher in D.

Figure 6–3 provides several examples of different scatterplots with their

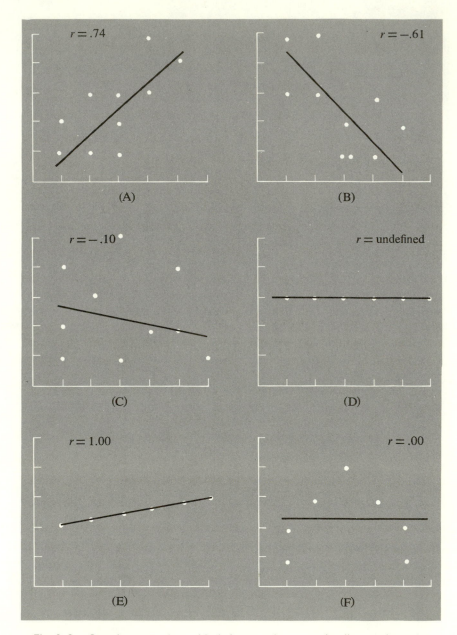

Fig. 6–3.   Sample scatterplots with their respective regression lines and correlations.

respective correlation coefficients. Scatterplots A, B, and C reflect the concepts just discussed. Scatterplots D, E, and F represent some interesting special cases. Plot D shows a perfect relationship in the sense of clustering, but one which is maximally imperfect with respect to the variability of Y_i. Here the deviations $\sum(\tilde{Y} - \overline{Y})^2$ and $\sum(Y_i - \overline{Y})^2$ are 0 making $r = \frac{0}{0}$ which is best left as **r is undefined**. This result makes intuitive sense also, because prediction of Y_i is not improved by knowing this relationship since regardless of the X value one always predicts Y_i to be $\overline{Y}$. Hence, knowledge of a person's X score does not assist prediction over using $\overline{Y}$, and the correlation is undefined. However, Plot E shows that if all points do fall precisely on a regression line which does not have a slope of 0 (not parallel to the X-axis), then the correlation is 1.00. Plot F depicts the case of a perfect but nonlinear relationship. Depending upon the nature of the curvilinearity, one can obtain r's of various sizes. Thus, it is not valid to conclude that if $r = .00$ there is "no relationship" between X and Y; rather, the conclusion should be that there is no **linear relationship** between X and Y. These facts punctuate the advice to examine the scatterplot before going on with procedures of linear relationship.

factors influencing the size of the correlation coefficient

The discussion of correlation up to this point has been concerned with developing a measure of the degree of linear relationship between two variables in a sample. However, in practice one usually wishes to use the sample correlation, r, to estimate the correlation which exists in the larger population whose parameter is symbolized by ρ (pronounced "rho"). The topics discussed in this section are concerned with practical problems that arise when one wants to estimate ρ with r. Obviously, the accuracy of any statistic as an estimate of a population value depends upon how representative the sample is of the population. The illustrations below describe in detail how r may be a distorted estimate of the population value when certain biases exist in the sample.

effect of the range As discussed in a previous section, the size of r is a function of the relative values of $s_{y.x}^2$ and s_y^2 such that r becomes large as s_y^2 becomes large relative to $s_{y.x}^2$. Therefore, if the degree of clustering about the regression line was fairly constant over all segments of the line, then as the range and thus the variance of the Y_i is reduced, the correlation is reduced.

Consider the following example. Suppose a new test of language skills is given to some pupils in grades 1 through 6. Further, the mental age (MA) from a standardized IQ test is also available for each youngster, and the correlation between MA and language skills is computed for the entire sample. A hypothetical plot of this relationship is presented in Figure 6–4. Suppose the cor-

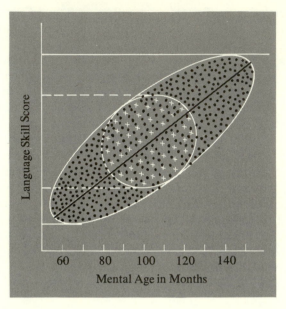

Fig. 6–4. Hypothetical scatterplot showing relatively equal clustering of points about the regression line for a group of pupils and for a subsample of third graders, but a marked reduction in the range of the Y_i for the third graders. The correlation is much larger for the total group than for the subsample.

relation is .76. This result says that for children in grades 1 through 6 the test of language skills is rather closely related to MA. However, now consider the degree of relationship between these two tests just for the third graders. The scores of the third graders are indicated in Figure 6–4 with little x's rather than dots. Notice that for this subsample the variability of the Y_i (amount of vertical dispersion of the scores) is markedly reduced relative to the entire sample. However, the general amount of dispersion about the regression line for the subsample is about equal to that of the entire group of pupils. Since

$$r = \sqrt{1 - \frac{s_{y.x}^2}{s_y^2}}$$

and restricting the range tends to reduce the size of s_y^2 relatively more than $s_{y.x}^2$, the fraction $s_{y.x}^2/s_y^2$ tends to become larger and thus r will become smaller. The correlation for just the third graders might be .28.

   Simply put, the size of a correlation is a function of the range (more precisely, the variability) of the Y_i relative to the standard error of estimate. Usually when the sample of scores is restricted, the correlation is less than it would be if the complete range were sampled. The safest course to follow is to limit the interpretation of a correlation to the population from which the sample was drawn. Thus, the correlation of .76 between the test of language skills and MA is appropriate for children in grades 1 through 6, but this figure may not reflect the degree of relationship for children in a portion of that sample (e.g., third graders).

An important application of this fact sometimes occurs when a given test is applied in a new context. Suppose that a test of reading ability is given to children in grades 1 through 6. These scores are correlated with some other criterion of reading competence. A high degree of relationship between the test and the criterion would suggest that the test is a valid indicator of reading ability. Suppose the correlation for the entire sample is .85. Now on the basis of this validity information a reading specialist proposes to use the test on all second graders to single out those students who need special reading instruction. However, when the sample is restricted to second graders, the test may not be nearly as valid as it was for the entire sample. Perhaps, the correlation is only .15 for this subgroup, a figure which would certainly discourage using the test for that particular purpose.

effect of extreme groups   The size of r is altered when researchers select extreme groups of subjects in order to compare these groups with respect to certain behaviors. For example, a researcher might select very good and very poor readers in an elementary school in order to evaluate personality factors that may distinguish the groups. In the course of the research an IQ test might be given and the researcher wishes to know the degree of relationship between IQ and reading achievement as measured by a standard reading test. Thus, he correlates the two tests, obtaining an $r = .84$. However, since the subjects were either very good or very poor readers, the scores tend to be in two groups as displayed by the dots in Figure 6–5. All the cases which would have fallen between these two groups (x's) were eliminated; but if they had been included in the computation of r, r would equal .66, not .84.

Why should selecting extreme groups on one variable increase the size of r over what would be obtained with more random sampling? This is seen more easily if the following formula for r is considered:

$$r = \frac{\sum(X - \bar{X})(Y - \bar{Y})}{\sqrt{\sum(X - \bar{X})^2 \sum(Y - \bar{Y})^2}}$$

The numerator is composed of the sum of products of the deviation of an X value from its mean and the deviation of a Y value from its mean. Therefore, r becomes large when there are many subjects whose X and Y scores both deviate markedly from their respective means. Consequently, by selecting

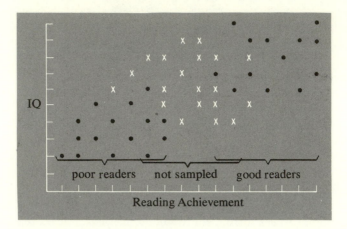

Fig. 6–5.   Illustration of a scatterplot for the case in which two extreme groups were selected, poor and good readers (dots). The $r = .84$. The x's indicate students of average reading ability who were not sampled. The r over all subjects is .66. Selection of extreme groups increases r.

extreme groups the subjects whose scores would be near the means (which would be located between the two extreme groups) are systematically eliminated, leaving those subjects who have large $(X_i - \overline{X})(Y_i - \overline{Y})$ values to predominate in the group. As a result, the correlation coefficient is likely to be larger than if random sampling had been employed.

combined groups   One must also be cautious when the correlation between two variables is computed for subjects who represent a combination of two groups of subjects which differ in their mean values on one or both of the variables. For example, suppose the relationship between mental age and the fear of dying is approximately .10 for a group of first graders but $-.40$ for sixth graders. However, when the two groups of children are combined into one, the correlation reverses to approximately $+.52$. How is this possible?

Figure 6–6 illustrates what could happen when groups that differ in mean values are combined for the purposes of correlation. The first graders have lower mental ages and are also less concerned with death, and therefore points for them cluster in the lower left corner of the scatterplot. The correlation between mental age and fear of death within that group is almost zero, $r = .10$. Conversely, the sixth graders have higher mental ages and show considerably more concern about death. Points for them therefore cluster in the upper right corner of the plot. Within this group there is a moderately negative association

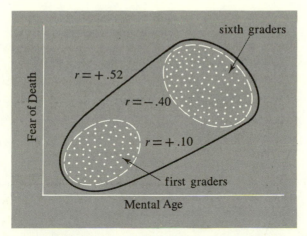

Fig. 6–6. An illustration of how the relationship between mental age and fear of death may be approximately $+.10$ for first graders, $-.40$ for sixth graders, but $+.52$ for these two groups combined.

between mental age and fear of death, $r = -.40$. Now if one considers the scatterplot for these two groups combined it takes on the form of a positive relationship extending from lower left to upper right with two extreme groups to enhance the correlation to $+.52$ which is a highly unrealistic representation of the true state of affairs.[4]

It is quite possible to have any combination of positive and negative correlations between disparate subgroups and the r of their combined group. Figure 6–7 presents some of these possibilities. If the group means are not very different, then combining these groups, while it may change the value of r somewhat, will not do so merely because of the combination itself. If, on the other hand, the group means are different, the r for the combined sample is not likely to faithfully represent the true situation.

effect of an extreme score Lastly, consider the problem of an extreme case in a sample by examining the scores in Figure 6–8. Most of the scores (dots) cluster in a circular array, but there is one extreme case, x. Without x the correlation is .05, but with it $r = .48$. It is interesting to note,

---

[4] Although the data on mental age and fear of death are fictitious, they reflect some general trends found in research reported in the following papers: F. C. Jeffers, C. R. Nichols, and C. Eisdorfer, "Attitudes of Older Persons to Death," *Journal of Gerontology*, 1961, XVI, 53–56. A. Mauer, "Adolescent Attitudes toward Death," *Journal of Genetic Psychology*, 1964, CV, 75–90. J. M. Natterson and A. G. Knudson, "Children and Their Mothers: Observations Concerning the Fear of Death in Fatally Ill Children," *Psychosomatic Medicine*, 1960, XXII, 456–465.

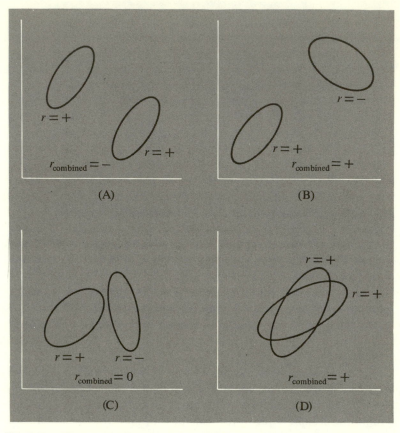

Fig. 6–7.   Three examples of what combining two groups of subjects having different means can do to *r*. Graph D shows that if the two groups have comparable means the *r* may change somewhat but not merely because of the regrouping.

however, that if one of the dots other than *x* were dropped, the correlation would not change a great deal. Thus, only cases which deviate markedly from the general cluster have such a big effect. This is true because the numerator of *r* contains the expression $\sum(X_i - \overline{X})(Y_i - \overline{Y})$. Therefore, an extreme case can alter the size of a correlation a great deal.

Ordinarily, if sufficient numbers of cases are sampled in a random manner it is unlikely that such a situation will occur. However, if the sample is small, extreme cases can play a significant role in determining the size of *r*. In this case some researchers use other types of correlation coefficients which are not so sensitive to an extreme score (see pp. 321–328).

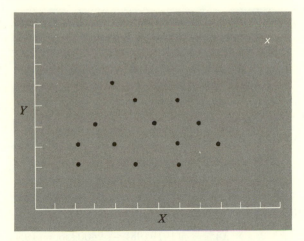

Fig. 6–8. An illustration of the effects of a single extreme case, *x*. Without *x* the correlation is .05, with it *r* = .48.

CAUSALITY AND CORRELATION

The correlation coefficient represents the degree of observed association between two variables, not the extent of their causal relationship. Although having a runny nose correlates with having a cold, one would hardly suggest that the runny nose *causes* the cold. We may say that the cold causes the runny nose, but the correlation between runny nose and cold is the same regardless of which way one states it. Because the sun comes up when we wake in the morning does not prompt the megalomaniacal delusion that our getting up causes the sun to rise.

If *A* correlates with *B*, three possible causal relationships exist:

> *A* causes *B*,
> *B* causes *A*, or
> *C* causes both *A* and *B*.

Of course, *C* may be quite remote with long causal chains interposed before *A* and *B* actually occur, but the point is that there is always the possibility that a third variable may produce an observed relationship between *A* and *B*. Consequently, one can never infer causality between two variables solely on the basis of their correlation.

This fact has loomed important in certain popular controversies. For example, in the early days of the smoking and cancer issue, it was reported that there was a correlation between the amount of smoking and the likelihood of lung cancer. These data do not compel the conclusion that smoking causes lung cancer. Smoking might do that, but some other factor could cause both the

---

6–3   Complete Computational Example for Several
Concepts in Chapters 2 to 6.

Raw Data

SAT		Grades	
$\sum X =$	3066	$\sum Y =$	8.60
$(\sum X)^2 =$	9400356	$(\sum Y)^2 =$	73.96
$\sum X^2 =$	1919198	$\sum Y^2 =$	22.40
$N =$	5	$N =$	5

$$\sum XY = 5751.8$$

Intermediate Quantities

(I) $N\sum X^2 - (\sum X)^2 = 5(1919198) - 9400356 = 195634$

(II) $N\sum Y^2 - (\sum Y)^2 = 5(22.40) - 73.96 = 38.04$

(III) $N\sum XY - (\sum X)(\sum Y) = 5(5751.8) - (3066)(8.6) = 2391.40$

Statistical Computations

$$\bar{X} = \frac{\sum X}{N} = \frac{3066}{5} = 613.20$$

$$s_x^2 = \frac{N\sum X^2 - (\sum X)^2}{N(N-1)} = \frac{(I)}{N(N-1)} = \frac{195634}{5(4)} = 9781.70$$

$$s_x = \sqrt{s_x^2} = \sqrt{9781.70} = 98.90$$

$$\bar{Y} = \frac{\sum Y}{N} = \frac{8.6}{5} = 1.72$$

$$s_y^2 = \frac{N\sum Y^2 - (\sum Y)^2}{N(N-1)} = \frac{(II)}{N(N-1)} = \frac{38.04}{5(4)} = 1.90$$

$$s_y = \sqrt{s_y^2} = \sqrt{1.90} = 1.38$$

---

tendency to smoke and the predisposition of the organism toward lung cancer. For example, it may be that relatively nervous people tend to smoke and the more nervous the person, the more he smokes. Further, it could be the case (at least for the purposes of illustration) that nervousness tends to produce a high level of a certain chemical in the person's physiological system that predisposes him toward lung cancer. Thus, it could be the case that nervousness leads both to heavy smoking and a predisposition to lung cancer, and that there is no causal relationship at all between smoking and cancer. Therefore, it

---

6–3 continued

Regression of Y on X

$$b = \frac{N(\sum XY) - (\sum X)(\sum Y)}{N\sum X^2 - (\sum X)^2} = \frac{(III)}{(I)} = \frac{2391.4}{195634} = .012$$

$$a = \bar{Y} - b\bar{X} = 1.72 - .012(613.20) = -5.638$$

$$\tilde{Y} = bX + a = .012X - 5.638$$

$$s_{y.x} = \sqrt{\left[\frac{1}{N(N-2)}\right]\left[N\sum Y^2 - (\sum Y)^2 - \frac{[N\sum XY - (\sum X)(\sum Y)]^2}{N\sum X^2 - (\sum X)^2}\right]}$$

$$= \sqrt{\left[\frac{1}{N(N-2)}\right]\left[(II) - \frac{(III)^2}{(I)}\right]}$$

$$= \sqrt{\frac{1}{5(3)}\left[38.04 - \frac{(2391.4)^2}{195634}\right]} = \sqrt{.5873}$$

$$s_{y.x} = .77$$

If $X = 620$, predicted Y:

$$\tilde{Y} = .012(620) - 5.638 = 1.80$$

95% of such cases would fall within the interval:

$$\tilde{Y} \pm 1.96 s_{y.x} = 1.80 \pm 1.96(.77) \text{ or } .29 \text{ to } 3.31$$

Correlation

$$r = \frac{N(\sum XY) - (\sum X)(\sum Y)}{\sqrt{[N\sum X^2 - (\sum X)^2][N\sum Y^2 - (\sum Y)^2]}} = \frac{(III)}{\sqrt{(I)(II)}}$$

$$= \frac{2391.40}{\sqrt{(195634)(38.04)}}$$

$$r = .88$$

---

must be remembered that a correlation suggests covariation but not necessarily causality.

COMPUTATIONAL PROCEDURES

Although this and previous chapters contain several computational examples, they have been presented as illustrations of isolated techniques. In practice, it is often the case that many of the statistics presented in the last several chapters are computed within the context of a single problem. When this is done, certain computational conveniences are available which facilitate this task. Therefore, Table 6–3 presents an integrated example that displays the calculation of several statistics and also illustrates a short cut for the computational labor. The task is facilitated if three subquantities are computed first:

$$\text{(I) } N\sum X^2 - (\sum X)^2$$
$$\text{(II) } N\sum Y^2 - (\sum Y)^2$$
$$\text{(III) } N\sum XY - (\sum X)(\sum Y)$$

The table demonstrates how these three subquantities can be used to simplify the computation of the variance, slope, standard error of estimate, and correlation coefficient.

FORMULAS

1. Pearson Product Moment Correlation

$$r = \sqrt{\frac{\sum(\tilde{Y} - \bar{Y})^2}{\sum(Y_i - \bar{Y})^2}}$$ (definitional formula)

$$r = \frac{N\sum X_i Y_i - (\sum X_i)(\sum Y_i)}{\sqrt{[N\sum X_i^2 - (\sum X_i)^2][N\sum Y_i^2 - (\sum Y_i)^2]}}$$ (computational formula)

r^2 = proportion of Y variance associated with differences in X.

2. Correlation and Regression

$$r = b_{yx}\left(\frac{s_x}{s_y}\right)$$ (r in terms of slope and variance)

$$r = b_{z_y z_x}$$ (standard score version of relationship between r and slope)

$$r = \sqrt{1 - \frac{s_{y.x}^2}{s_y^2}}$$ (r in terms of the variability about the line ($s_{y.x}^2$) relative to the total variability (s_y^2) in Y)

EXERCISES

1. On the next page are three scores for each of 9 subjects. Compute the correlation between A and B, A and C, and B and C. Add 5 to each score in Distribution A and then multiply each score by 2. Recompute the correlation between A and B. Explain the effect of changing scales on the correlation.

Subject	A	B	C
1	5	2	9
2	4	9	3
3	8	7	4
4	1	0	3
5	6	5	0
6	3	6	5
7	6	4	9
8	7	2	7
9	9	3	2

2. Compute the correlation for the following data. Then add the score pair (12, 8) and recompute. Why does adding one score change the correlation so much? Can you think of other pairs of scores which would alter the situation in a different direction? Illustrate.

X	Y
1	2
2	3
2	1
3	5
4	2
4	4
4	3

3. If children are divided into two groups containing just the top 50 and bottom 50 children on a First Grade Readiness Test in a school of 500 children, why might the relationship between IQ and leadership potential as determined by a specially designed test given to these two extreme groups be unreasonably high relative to that obtained on the complete group of 500?

4. What squared deviations are said to compose the "variability" associated with differences in X? Explain the logic of this reasoning.

5. Why are there usually two regression lines but only one correlation for a pair of variables, X and Y?

6. If the point $(\bar{X}, \bar{Y})$ is (15, 25), why will a pair of scores such as (50, 85), probably influence the regression and correlation between X and Y more than a pair of scores on the order of (10, 22)?

7. Explain why the correlation coefficient is identical to the slope of the regression line if the scores are in standard score form but that this is not the case if raw scores are used.

8. In what way is the ratio of the variability about the regression line relative to the total variability in the Y_t related to the value of r?

9. Discuss and explain whether or not the following combinations of values are possible or impossible:

(a) $N = 2$, $s_{y.x} = 2.5$, $r = .00$

(b) $N = 25$, $b = .80$, $s_{y.x} = 0$, $r = .65$

(c) $N = 30$, $b = -.80$, $a = 10$, $r = .70$

(d) $N = 30$, $r_{xy} = .0$, $r_{xw} = .90$, $r_{yw} = .15$

(e) $N = 30$, $\bar{X} = 0$, $s_x = 1$, $\bar{Y} = 0$, $s_y = 1$, $b = .60$, $r = .40$

(f) $r = .50$ for $N = 8$, but r would be $-.30$ if one more score were added

TOPICS IN PROBABILITY

7

The first six chapters of this book have been concerned with **descriptive statistics** —procedures that describe and summarize groups of measurements. Attention is now turned to **inferential statistics** which includes techniques for making inferential decisions when we have only partial information.

The basis of inferential statistics is probability, and this chapter presents an introduction to the traditional topics of probability. The next chapter focuses on the application of the concept of probability to the processes of statistical inference. While an introductory knowledge of formal probability will be helpful to those students who plan to attend graduate school in the social sciences or who will study statistics again at a more advanced level, the material in this chapter is not a prerequisite for understanding the remainder of this text. Therefore, this chapter may be considered optional in some courses.

set theory

SETS AND RELATIONS AMONG SETS

A discussion of probability is greatly facilitated if it can be couched in terms of set theory. Therefore, some very elementary definitions and operations of set theory will be presented first.

A **set** is a well-defined collection of things.

The ordinary concept of a set, such as a set of drinking glasses or a set of carving knives, is quite analogous to the mathematical notion of a set. The critical factor in the definition is that there is some rule or quality that the objects in the set possess which unequivocally determines whether or not they are contained in the specified set. For example, husbands are a set. Every human male, if he is married, is a member of the set of husbands. If he is not married, if he is a "she," if he is a giraffe, etc., then he is not a member of the set, husbands. In short, it can be determined unequivocally for any object whatsoever whether it is a member of the set, husbands. Thus, a set is a collection of objects or events that are distinguishable from all other objects on the basis of some particular characteristic or rule.

> An **element** of a set is any one of its members.

It is customary to arbitrarily label a set by some capital letter, such as, A, B, C, etc., and to denote an element of a set with a small letter, such as, a, b, c, etc.

There are two special sets that should be mentioned, the universal and the empty set.

> The **universal set** includes all objects to be considered in any one discussion. It is symbolized by S.

> The **empty** or **null set**, contains no elements. It is symbolized by $\emptyset$.

A very important concept for the study of probability is that of subset.

> If every element in set A is also an element of set B, then A is a **subset** of B.

Since the phrase "is a subset of" is rather long and cumbersome, it is customary to write it with the symbol $\subseteq$.

One of the primary applications to statistics of the concepts of set and subset is their analogy to the concepts of population and sample. A sample is a subset of the population. In Figure 7–1 one might consider the entire space, S (the universal set), as the population composed of all college students. Perhaps the sample is only composed of college students attending State University and is symbolized by A. Further, the researcher randomly selects only a few college students at State, symbolized by B. Thus, $A \subseteq S$, $B \subseteq S$, and $B \subseteq A$.

> If S is the entire space and A is a subset of S, then the symbol A', read "not A," denotes the set of all elements in S which are not in A. A' is called the **complement**[1] of A.

---

[1] Other symbols sometimes used for the complement of A include $\overline{A}$, $\tilde{A}$, A^c and $\sim A$.

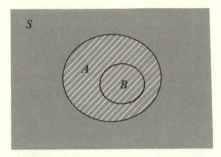

Fig. 7–1.   Set-subset relationship. *S* is the set of all college students, *A* is college
students at State, and *B* is a small sample of the students at State.

If *S* includes all the integers from 1 to 10, and *A* includes 1, 4, 5, 8, and 9, then
A' includes 2, 3, 6, 7, and 10. The complement relationship is displayed in
Figure 7–2. The shaded portion is *A'*.

If every element in *A* is also an element of *B* and if every element in
B is also an element of *A*, then *A* **equals** *B* (i.e., if $A \subseteq B$ and $B \subseteq A$,
then $A = B$).

If $A = \{1, 2, 5, 9\}$ and $B = \{5, 1, 9, 2\}$, then $A = B$. Note that the order in
which the elements of *A* and *B* are stated is irrelevant.

OPERATIONS

An important operation is the union of two sets.

Given two sets, *A* and *B*, the **union** of *A* and *B* is the set of all elements
which (1) are in *A*, **or** (2) are in *B*, **or** (3) are in both *A* and *B*.

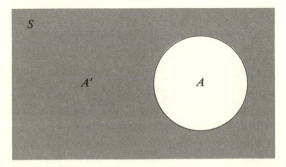

Fig. 7–2.   Complementation. *S* is the universal set, *A* is a subset of *S*, and *A'*
(not *A*) is the complement of *A* since it contains all the elements in
S which are not in *A*.

The word "union" is symbolized by ∪ so that *A* union *B* (the union of *A* and *B*) is written *A* ∪ *B*.

Figure 7–3 illustrates the concept of union in which the shaded area represents the union of *A* and *B*, symbolized *A* ∪ *B*. The crucial word to remember

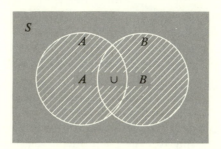

Fig. 7–3.   Union. *A* union *B* (*A* ∪ *B*) is represented by the shaded area. *A* ∪ *B* contains all elements in *A*, in *B*, or in both *A* and *B*.

about the concept of union is "or." The criterion for including any element in the union of *A* and *B* is whether that element is contained in either *A* **or** *B* **or** both *A* and *B*. For example, if *A* includes {1, 2, 3, 4, 5} and *B* includes {3, 4, 5, 6, 7, 8}, then *A* ∪ *B* = {1, 2, 3, 4, 5, 6, 7, 8}. Notice that numbers contained in both *A* and *B* are not represented twice in *A* ∪ *B*. That is, *A* ∪ *B* is *not* equal to {1, 2, 3, 4, 5, 3, 4, 5, 6, 7, 8}.

Given two sets, *A* and *B*, the **intersection** of *A* and *B* contains all elements which are in both *A* **and** *B*, but not *A* or *B* alone.

The symbol for "intersection" is ∩, and *A* intersection *B* is written *A* ∩ *B*. Figure 7–4 illustrates the intersection of *A* and *B* in which *A* ∩ *B* is the shaded portion of the diagram.

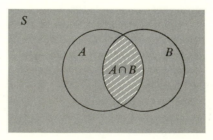

Fig. 7–4.   Intersection. *A* ∩ *B* is represented by the shaded area which includes all elements which are members of both set *A* and set *B*.

Thus, if

$$A = \{1, 2, 3, 4, 5\} \text{ and}$$
$$B = \{3, 4, 5, 6, 7, 8\}$$

then

$$A \cap B = \{3, 4, 5\}$$

Here the emphasis is on the word "and" because in order for an element to be a member of the intersection of A and B ($A \cap B$), it must be contained in both A **and** B. The intersection represents the common portion of two sets, or the elements shared by two sets.

It is useful to be more explicit about the distinction between union ($\cup$) and intersection ($\cap$). An element belongs to the **union** of A and B, if it qualifies under *any one* of the following criteria:

(1) If it is a member of A
(2) If it is a member of B
(3) If it is a member of both A and B

However, in order to determine if an element qualifies for inclusion in the **intersection** of A and B, (3) is the only criterion. An element must be a member of both A and B. The difference between the important words in the definitions also highlights the distinction between union and intersection. $A \cup B$ contains elements which are in A **or** B **or** in both A and B; whereas $A \cap B$ contains only those elements which are in both A **and** B simultaneously.

There is a special case of intersection which defines a particular relationship between two sets that should be pointed out. Suppose $A \cap B$ contains no elements, that is, $A \cap B = \emptyset$. Such a condition says that A and B share no common elements, no element in A is also in B and no element in B is also in A. If $A \cap B = \emptyset$, then A and B are called **disjoint sets**, because there is no common element to "join" them together. Figure 7–5 illustrates a pair of disjoint sets. Another example of disjoint sets is A and A'. Recall that A' contains all elements not in A and is called the complement of A. It is clear that for any set A, A and A' are disjoint.

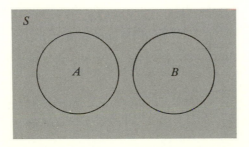

Fig. 7–5.   Two disjoint sets. $A \cap B = \emptyset$, that is, A and B share no common elements.

A summary of the terms and concepts discussed in this section is presented in Table 7–1.

7–1   Terminology of Set Theory.

1. **Set:** A well-defined collection of things.
2. **Element:** A member of a set.
3. **Universal Set,** S: The set of all objects under discussion.
4. **Empty Set,** $\emptyset$: The set containing no elements.
5. **Subset:** If every element in A is also in B, A is a subset of B (i.e., $A \subseteq B$).
6. **Complement:** Set A' is the complement of set A if it contains every element in S which is not also in A.
7. **Equality:** Set A equals set B if every element in A is also in B and every element in B is also in A (i.e., if $A \subseteq B$ and $B \subseteq A$, then $A = B$).
8. **Union:** The union of sets A and B, $A \cup B$, is the set of all elements which are (1) in A, (2) in B, or (3) in both A and B.
9. **Intersection:** The intersection of A and B, $A \cap B$, is the set of all elements which are in both A and B simultaneously.
10. **Disjoint Sets:** Two sets are disjoint if they share no common elements (i.e., $A \cap B = \emptyset$).

---

simple classical probability

Probability usually involves thinking about an **idealized experiment** in which a given phenomenon is repeatedly observed an indefinite number of times under "ideal" conditions. For example, when someone says the chance of flipping a coin and obtaining a head is $\frac{1}{2}$, this means that over an uncountable number of flips of that coin under fair and ideal conditions, heads will turn up $\frac{1}{2}$ the time. This concept of flipping a coin over and over again is the idealized experiment.

In probability, the collection of all the elements of an idealized experiment is called the **sample space**, symbolized by S. The elements of this set are known as **elementary events** or **outcomes**. An **event** is any subset of elements in S. Therefore, an "event" may be an elementary event, a subset of elementary events, or all elementary events (i.e., S). Thus, in the idealized experiment of rolling a single die, the sample space consists of the set of six elementary events (or outcomes): {1, 2, 3, 4, 5, 6}. Examples of an event in this idealized experiment include a roll of three or less {1, 2, 3}, a roll of a deuce {2}, or a roll of an even number {2, 4, 6}.

Simple classical probability involves making probabilistic statements on a sample space whose elementary events are all equally likely to occur. This is why discussions of probability frequently employ the flipping of coins, drawing of cards, rolling of dice, etc., because all these experiments have equally likely elementary events.

> In a sample space containing equally likely elementary events, the **probability** of a given event *A* is defined to be the number of outcomes in *A* divided by the total number of outcomes in the sample space, *S*. If $\#(A)$ signifies the number of outcomes in *A* and $\#(S)$ symbolizes the number of outcomes in *S*, then $P(A)$, the "probability of event *A*" is given by
>
> $$P(A) = \frac{\#(A)}{\#(S)}$$

In tossing a coin the sample space consists of the two equally likely outcomes, heads and tails, and the probability of a head is

$$P\,(\text{Head}) = \frac{\#\,(\text{Head})}{\#\,(\text{Possible Outcomes})} = \frac{1}{2}$$

In the idealized experiment of throwing a die, the sample space consists of the equally likely alternatives {1, 2, 3, 4, 5, 6}, and the probability of throwing a two is $\frac{1}{6}$. The probability of a five is also $\frac{1}{6}$. The probability of a four or less is $\frac{4}{6}$.

In any situation, the probability of an event cannot be any less than .00, nor can it be greater than 1.00. Therefore, a probability value is always between 0 and 1.00, inclusive.

some important definitions

conditional probability Conditional probability refers to a situation in which the probability of a given event is dependent upon the occurrence or non-occurrence of a previous event.

Consider the following situation. Suppose one took the 12 picture cards from a deck of playing cards (4 jacks, 4 queens, and 4 kings) and shuffled them. Define event *A* as drawing a king from this deck. Since there are four kings in the deck of 12 cards, the probability of event *A* is

$$P(A) = \frac{\#\,(A)}{\#\,(S)} = \frac{4}{12} = \frac{1}{3}$$

Suppose that whatever card is drawn on this trial is *not* put back into the deck before making a second draw. This kind of sampling is known as **sampling without replacement**, because cards are not replaced into the deck after their selection. Now consider the probability of event B, obtaining a king on the second draw. This probability depends upon the result of the first draw. If a king were drawn first and not replaced, then for the second draw there would be three kings left in the deck which now consists of 11 cards. Thus, $P(B) = \frac{3}{11}$. However, if a card other than a king were drawn on the first trial, all four kings would remain in the deck of 11. Then, $P(B) = \frac{4}{11}$.

This circumstance illustrates the concept of conditional probability.

Conditional probability is the probability that an event will occur given that some other event has already occurred. The probability that event B shall occur given that event A has already occurred is written

$$P(B \mid A)$$

which is read "the probability of B given A."

In the example above, the probability of B (drawing a king on the second draw without replacement) was "conditional" upon the occurrence of event A (selecting a king on the first draw). Given that A had indeed occurred, the probability of B is written

$$P(B \mid A) = \frac{3}{11}$$

since three kings were left in the deck of 11 remaining cards after one king had been selected on the first trial.

dependent events   The above example also illustrates the concept of dependent events.

Two events are said to be **dependent** if the occurrence of one event alters the probability of the occurrence of the other.

Since the probability of obtaining a king on the second draw (event B) was either $\frac{3}{11}$ if a king was drawn on the first trial (event A) or $\frac{4}{11}$ if a non-king was picked first, events A and B are said to be dependent because the probability of B "depends" on the occurrence or non-occurrence of event A.

independent events   As one might expect, independent events are such that the occurrence of one does not alter the probability of the other.

Two events are said to be **independent** if the occurrence of one event does not alter the probability that the other event will occur. This can be expressed in terms of conditional probability as

$$P(B \mid A) = P(B)$$

which implies that the probability of B is not affected by (i.e., is not conditional upon) the occurrence of A.

In the example given above for conditional probability, cards were drawn from a 12-card deck without replacement. But, suppose cards were replaced after a selection was made, a circumstance called **sampling with replacement**. Now consider the probability of event B, drawing a king on the second draw, as a function of the occurrence of event A, obtaining a king on the first draw. If a king is selected first and put back into the deck before the second draw, the probability of getting a king on the second draw is $\frac{4}{12}$ since there would be four kings in the complete deck of 12 cards. If a king is not found on the first draw and the card is replaced, there are again four kings in 12 cards. Thus, the probability of getting a king on the second draw is independent (i.e., not conditional upon) the outcome of the first event. In symbols,

$$P(B \mid A) = P(B) = \frac{4}{12}$$

which implies that the probability of B given that A has occurred is simply the probability of B ignoring what happened with respect to event A.

An interesting application (or lack of application) of the concept of independence is known as the **gambler's fallacy**. The gambler's fallacy is the failure to appreciate the independence of some sequential events, and it is epitomized when a gambler who has lost 10 straight times at cards feels that there is a better than average chance of winning the next game because of this long string of misfortune. Another example is the parent who feels that after five boys in a row, surely the probability of having a girl as a sixth child is greater than .50. Actually the theoretical probabilities of these events do not depend upon previous events as these people suppose. The probability of having a girl (or a boy) is approximately .50 for any given birth, and the sex of a forthcoming child is probably independent of the sex of the previous children. Therefore, the probability of having a girl is approximately .50 whether it is one's first child or whether the child will have 10 brothers (or sisters) upon its arrival. So, too, for the gambler, just because of a bad losing streak, it is no more likely that the next game will be a winner than if a fantastic winning streak were in progress.

Games of chance are very likely to be independent in actuality as well as theoretically. On the other hand, if a basketball team loses 10 games in a row and they come up against their rival school which is of approximately equal ability, the probability of winning the game may be more than .50 if the team is highly spirited and wishes to beat its rival and salvage an otherwise poor season. Of course, it could be less than .50 if the 10 losses have so demoralized the team that it can hardly face the humiliation of playing another game. Thus, although the independence of events is an important characteristic in assessing probabilities, in practice, it is sometimes difficult to determine if events are independent or not.

mutually exclusive events   Two events may also be mutually exclusive.

> Two events, A and B, of the same idealized experiment are considered to be **mutually exclusive** if they share no elementary events, that is, A and B are disjoint sets ($A \cap B = \emptyset$).

This implies that if one event has occurred, the other has not. Consider the event A of drawing a king on a single draw from that special deck composed only of the four jacks, queens, and kings. Abbreviate the cards by giving them two initials, the first for the denomination and the second for the suit (e.g., the King of Spades by KS, etc.). Since event A is drawing a king, set A contains four elements (all the kings):

$$A = \{KS, KC, KH, KD\}$$

Now let event B be drawing a queen in a single draw. Set B also contains four elements:

$$B = \{QS, QC, QH, QD\}$$

Note first that there is no element in A which is also in B. Therefore, A and B are disjoint sets and consequently $A \cap B = \emptyset$. Note also that if on a single draw A occurs, B has not occurred; if you draw a king you do not also draw a queen. In this case, drawing a king and drawing a queen are mutually exclusive events.

In contrast, consider now the events of drawing a king (event A) and drawing a red card (event B) from this special deck:

$$A = \{KH, KD, KS, KC\}$$
$$B = \{KH, KD, QH, QD, JH, JD\}$$

These events are not mutually exclusive because they have two common elements, $\{KH, KD\}$, therefore $\#(A \cap B) = 2$ not 0, and A and B are not disjoint. Further, it is not necessarily true that if A occurs B does not occur; because if the king of hearts or diamonds is drawn, then both event A and event B have simultaneously occurred.

Therefore, two events are mutually exclusive if their sets are disjoint and the occurrence of one event precludes the occurrence of the other.

independence and mutually exclusive events compared Although the ideas of independent and mutually exclusive events appear to be very similar, they should not be confused. The difference between them is that mutually exclusive refers to the sharing or not sharing of elements of sets whereas independence is defined in terms of the probabilities of two events. Therefore,

Mutually Exclusive Events: $A \cap B = \emptyset$
Independent Events: $\qquad P(B \mid A) = P(B)$

probability of complex events

PROBABILITY OF A ∩ B

What is the probability of $A \cap B$?

The probability that two events, A and B, both occur is

$$P(A \cap B) = P(A)P(B \mid A)$$

This means that the probability that both A and B occur is the probability of A times the probability of B given that A has occurred.

In the special case when A and B are independent events, $P(B \mid A) = P(B)$ (which is the definition of independent events). Therefore, substituting $P(B)$ for $P(B \mid A)$ in the above expression, we have the following:

The probability that two *independent* events A and B both occur is

$$P(A \cap B) = P(A)P(B)$$

For example, recall the deck of 12 face cards used in a previous sample, and consider determining the probability of drawing two kings in succession without replacement. Restated, this amounts to finding the probability of obtaining a king on the first draw (event A) *and* obtaining a king on the second draw (event B). Thus, the task is to compute the probability that both A and B occur, which can be symbolically stated in terms of their intersection

$$P(A \cap B)$$

The formula given above states that the required probability will be the product of the probability of A times the conditional probability of B given that A has occurred. The probability of drawing a king on the first trial is simply $\frac{4}{12}$ since there are four kings in the deck of 12 cards. The conditional probability of drawing a king on the second trial given that a king has already been drawn and not replaced is $\frac{3}{11}$ since three kings would remain in the deck which would now contain 11 cards. Thus, the required probability is

$$P(A \cap B) = P(A)P(B \mid A)$$

$$P(A \cap B) = \frac{4}{12} \cdot \frac{3}{11} = \frac{12}{132} = .09$$

Thus, on the average one could expect to draw two consecutive kings without replacement only 9 times in 100 such two-card draws.

Why are the probabilities multiplied? Consider the solution to the above problem in more detail. The task is to determine the probability of $A \cap B$, which by the laws of classical probability should be given by the number of ways $A \cap B$ can occur divided by the total number of two-card sequences in the sample space. Symbolically,

$$P(A \cap B) = \frac{\#(A \cap B)}{\#(S)}$$

First, how many ways can $A \cap B$ occur? Simply stated, there are four ways a king could be obtained on the first draw (one way for each king in the deck), and *for each one of those four ways* there exist three possible ways a king could be selected on the second trial given that one was picked on the first draw. Since there are three ways of getting a king on the second trial for *each* of the four ways of getting a king on the first, there are four threes or 4 × 3 ways of getting two consecutive kings without replacement. These 12 ways of obtaining two kings are enumerated in Table 7–2. In short, $\#(A \cap B)$ is simply $\#(A) \times \#(B \mid A)$, so

$$\#(A \cap B) = \#(A) \times \#(B \mid A) = 4 \times 3 = 12.$$

Now, how many total possible outcomes are there in this situation? The logic is the same: There are 12 possible outcomes on the first draw (one for each card in the deck), and for *each* of these 12 outcomes there are 11 possible results (one for each of the remaining 11 cards) on the second draw. Thus,

$$\#(S) = \#(S_A) \times \#(S_B) = 12 \times 11 = 132,$$

where S_A and S_B are the sample spaces for events A and B, respectively.

The desired probability is given by dividing the number of outcomes satisfying the complex event by the total number of possible outcomes in the idealized experiment. As determined above, this amounts to

$$P(A \cap B) = \frac{\#(A \cap B)}{\#(S)} = \frac{\#(A) \times \#(B \mid A)}{\#(S_A) \times \#(S_B)} = \frac{4 \times 3}{12 \times 11} = \frac{12}{132}$$

$$P(A \cap B) = P(A) \times P(B \mid A) = \frac{4}{12} \times \frac{3}{11} = \frac{12}{132}$$

7–2 The Number of Ways of Getting Two Consecutive Kings, $(A \cap B)$.		
First Draw	**Second Draw**	**Number of Ways**
King of Spades	$\left\{\begin{array}{l}\text{King of Clubs}\\\text{King of Hearts}\\\text{King of Diamonds}\end{array}\right.$	3
King of Clubs	$\left\{\begin{array}{l}\text{King of Spades}\\\text{King of Hearts}\\\text{King of Diamonds}\end{array}\right.$	3
King of Hearts	$\left\{\begin{array}{l}\text{King of Spades}\\\text{King of Clubs}\\\text{King of Diamonds}\end{array}\right.$	3
King of Diamonds	$\left\{\begin{array}{l}\text{King of Spades}\\\text{King of Clubs}\\\text{King of Hearts}\end{array}\right.$	3
[First Draw (A)] $\times$ [Second Draw $(B \mid A)$] = [Total $(A \cap B)$] 4 $\qquad \times \qquad$ 3 $\qquad = \qquad$ 12		

Observe that the first part of the above expression is $P(A)$ and the second part is the conditional probability of B given A, $P(B \mid A)$, and that the probability of the intersection of two events equals the probability of A times the conditional probability of B given A. In the case being illustrated, the probability of drawing two consecutive kings is $\frac{4}{12} \times \frac{3}{11} = \frac{12}{132} = .09$. This means that if you were to repeatedly draw two consecutive cards from the special deck, on the average you might expect that 9 of every 100 such pairs would be a pair of kings.

example Suppose you arrange to play a game of racket ball with a classmate. Your partner warns that a 5 P.M. game is chancey since afternoon laboratory classes run late about 50% of the time. Moreover, the probability is only .60 that a court will be available at 5 P.M. What is the probability that the two of you play your game at 5 P.M.?

Define event A to be "your partner is able to play at 5 P.M.," and event B to be "a court is available." Thus, the complex event of having a partner *and* a court free is

$$P(A \cap B) = P(A)P(B \mid A)$$

Since the probability of a free court is not altered by whether your partner can play, A and B are independent, and $P(B \mid A) = P(B)$. Therefore, the required probability is expressed

$$P(A \cap B) = P(A)P(B)$$

Since $P(A)$ is the probability that your partner can play, which is .50, and since $P(B)$ is the probability that a court is free, which is .60,

$$P(A \cap B) = P(A)P(B) = (.50)(.60) = .30$$

In words, the likelihood that you have a racket ball game at 5 P.M. is .30, or on 3 of every 10 such occasions.

discussion   Please note that one needs to remember only that

$$P(A \cap B) = P(A)P(B \mid A)$$

This formula includes the case in which A and B are independent when $P(B \mid A) = P(B)$. Second, the real problem in using this expression for the probability of the intersection of two events is translating the verbal statement of the problem into events A and B, and then determining if the intersection of A and B is required. Most often, the intersection of A and B is needed if the problem states (or could be restated to say) that both A *and* B must occur to satisfy the complex condition. The key word is "and":

(1) You must draw a king on the first try *and* on the second.
(2) Your partner must finish in time *and* the court must be free.

The word "and" signifies that the joint occurrence of A and B is required, and thus $A \cap B$ is an appropriate description of the problem.

expression for conditional probability   The previous discussion can provide an expression for the conditional probability of B given A. For example,

$$P(A \cap B) = P(A)P(B \mid A)$$

Dividing by $P(A)$ and transposing, we have

$$P(B \mid A) = \frac{P(A \cap B)}{P(A)}$$

Therefore, the conditional probability of B given A equals the probability that A and B both occur divided by the probability of A. In symbols:

$$P(B \mid A) = \frac{P(A \cap B)}{P(A)}$$

If the probability that your team wins a two-game basketball tournament is .15 $[P(A \cap B) = .15]$ and the probability of winning your first game is .50 $[P(A) = .50]$, then before the tournament begins you can speculate that the probability that you win the tournament given that you win the first game is

$$P(B \mid A) = \frac{P(A \cap B)}{P(A)} = \frac{.15}{.50} = .30$$

PROBABILITY OF A ∪ B

The probability of the occurrence of either one of two events, A or B, that is, $A \cup B$, is

$$P(A \cup B) = P(A) + P(B) - P(A \cap B)$$

This states that the probability that either A or B occurs equals the probability of A plus the probability of B minus the probability that both A and B occur [i.e., $P(A \cap B)$]. However, the probability of $A \cap B$ is zero if A and B are mutually exclusive. (This is because $A \cap B = \emptyset$ and $P(\emptyset) = .00$). Therefore, if A and B are mutually exclusive events, the preceding formula is simplified:

If A and B are *mutually exclusive*, the probability that either A or B occurs is

$$P(A \cup B) = P(A) + P(B)$$

This states that if A and B are mutually exclusive the probability that either A or B occurs is the sum of the probabilities of A and B. Let us examine the logic of this proposition with an example.

Return to the special deck of 12 face cards. What is the probability of selecting either a king or a red card in a single draw? If event A is drawing a king and event B is drawing a red card, then the question asks for the probability of A *or* B, which can be represented as the probability of the union of these events, $P(A \cup B)$.

The formula given above requires three probabilities. The probability of getting one of the four kings in a deck of 12 is $P(A) = \frac{4}{12}$. Since half the cards are red, $P(B) = \frac{1}{2}$. The probability of $A \cap B$ is simply the likelihood that both a king and a red card turn up, which could happen if either the king of hearts or king of diamonds is selected—2 of the 12 cards. Thus, $P(A \cap B) = \frac{2}{12}$. Therefore, the required probability is

$$P(A \cup B) = P(A) + P(B) - P(A \cap B)$$

$$= \frac{4}{12} + \frac{1}{2} - \frac{2}{12} = \frac{8}{12}$$

$$= .67$$

But what is the rationale of this formula? Why does one add the probabilities of A and B, and why must their intersection be subtracted? Consider the example in more detail. The problem is to determine the probability of the union of A with B, and according to the laws of classical probability this should equal the number of outcomes in $A \cup B$ divided by the total number of outcomes on a single draw:

$$P(A \cup B) = \frac{\#(A \cup B)}{\#(S)}$$

If the cards are abbreviated as before (e.g., Queen of Diamonds = QD), then the possible outcomes for events A(a king) and B(a red card) are

$$\#(A) = (KH, KD, KS, KC) = 4$$
$$\#(B) = (KH, KD, QH, QD, JH, JD) = 6$$

In order for an outcome to qualify for $A \cup B$ it must be in either A or in B. If one simply adds the outcomes in A to those in B, some outcomes will be counted twice—namely, those which are in both A and B, that is, in $A \cap B$. In this example, the outcomes in the intersection of A and B are KH and KD. If these shared outcomes are subtracted from the sum, the correct number of elements in $A \cup B$ is produced. Specifically,

$$\underbrace{\#(A)}_{} \qquad \underbrace{+\#(B)}_{} \qquad \underbrace{-\#(A \cap B)}_{}$$
$$(KH + KD + KS + KC) + (K\!\!\!/H + K\!\!\!/D + QH + QD + JH + JD) - (K\!\!\!/H + K\!\!\!/D)$$
$$KH + KD + KS + KC + QH + QD + JH + JD$$

are the eight outcomes which are either a king or a red card. Thus,

$$\#(A \cup B) = \#(A) + \#(B) - \#(A \cap B) = 4 + 6 - 2 = 8$$

The probability of $A \cup B$ is $\#(A \cup B)$ divided by $\#(S) = 12$ because there are 12 cards available for the single draw. Thus,

$$P(A \cup B) = \frac{\#(A) + \#(B) - \#(A \cap B)}{\#(S)}$$

$$= \frac{\#(A)}{\#(S)} + \frac{\#(B)}{\#(S)} - \frac{\#(A \cap B)}{\#(S)} = \frac{4}{12} + \frac{6}{12} - \frac{2}{12} = \frac{8}{12} = .67$$

$$P(A \cup B) = P(A) + P(B) - P(A \cap B)$$

example Suppose a student applied to two graduate schools, A and B, and assessed the chances of getting into each as $P(A) = .10$ and $P(B) = .25$. What is the probability of getting into either school A or school B? Since either A or B satisfies the required outcome, the probability is given by

$$P(A \cup B) = P(A) + P(B) - P(A \cap B) = .10 + .25 - (.10)(.25) = .325$$

example What is the probability of getting an odd number or a six in a single roll of a die? If A is the event of getting an odd number and B the event of getting a six, then the required probability is

$$P(A \cup B) = P(A) + P(B) - P(A \cap B) = \tfrac{3}{6} + \tfrac{1}{6} - 0 = \tfrac{4}{6}$$

Note that A and B are mutually exclusive and therefore the $P(A \cap B) = 0$.

discussion Once again, only the first formula needs to be remembered since for the case in which A and B are mutually exclusive one merely sets one of the terms equal to zero rather than changing the nature of the formula.

The word "or" in a verbal statement of a problem tends to imply that the union of two or more events is required, just as the presence of the word "and" signals the intersection of two or more events. Thus, the above discussion on the probability of the union of two events dealt with

(1) either a king *or* a red card,
(2) getting accepted at either school A *or* B, and
(3) rolling an odd number *or* a six.

Although the two probabilistic laws described above have been stated only in terms of two events, the formulas can be generalized to cases involving more than two events. For example, if A, B, and C are **independent**, then

$$P(A \cap B \cap C) = P(A)P(B)P(C)$$

If A, B, and C are all **mutually exclusive**, then

$$P(A \cup B \cup C) = P(A) + P(B) + P(C)$$

example Consider a last example which involves a combination of union and intersection. What is the probability of selecting either an ace or a king on the first draw and a red card or a face card (J, Q, K) on the second draw from an ordinary deck of 52 cards if selection is performed with replacement? Let

$$A = \text{an ace on the first draw}$$
$$B = \text{a king on the first draw}$$
$$C = \text{a red card on the second draw}$$
$$D = \text{a face card on the second draw}$$

Reducing the statement of the problem to symbols, the required complex event is (A *or* B) *and* (C *or* D), and thus the probability is

$$P[(A \cup B) \cap (C \cup D)]$$

First observe that the two events $(A \cup B)$ and $(C \cup D)$ are independent since the selection is performed with replacement. Further, A and B are mutually exclusive whereas C and D are not. Therefore, expanding the above expression,

$$P[(A \cup B) \cap (C \cup D)] = [P(A) + P(B)] \times [P(C) + P(D) - P(C \cap D)]$$

Now,

$$P(A) = \tfrac{4}{52} = \tfrac{1}{13}$$
$$P(B) = \tfrac{4}{52} = \tfrac{1}{13}$$
$$P(C) = \tfrac{26}{52} = \tfrac{1}{2}$$
$$P(D) = \tfrac{12}{52} = \tfrac{3}{13}, \text{ and}$$
$$P(C \cap D) = P(C)P(D) = (\tfrac{1}{2})(\tfrac{3}{13}) = \tfrac{3}{26}$$

Hence, the result is

$$[\tfrac{1}{13} + \tfrac{1}{13}][\tfrac{1}{2} + \tfrac{3}{13} - \tfrac{3}{26}] = (\tfrac{2}{13})(\tfrac{8}{13}) = \tfrac{16}{169} = .095$$

methods of counting

Since the classical definition of probability rests on the principle of taking the ratio of the number of elementary events in A divided by the number of elementary events in S, it is necessary to be able to assess the number of outcomes in a complex event in some manner other than enumerating each of them. Determining how many different basketball teams can be put on the court if you have ten players each of whom can play any position is very tedious if one has to write out all 252 five-player teams. Therefore, some counting methods are required to facilitate this task.

PERMUTATIONS

A **permutation** of a set of objects or events is an ordered sequence. The number of ordered sequences of r objects which can be selected from a total of n objects is symbolized by

$$_nP_r$$

which is read "the number of permutations of n things taken r at a time."

If one has four objects, A, B, C, and D, then $ABCD$, $ACBD$, $ADBC$, $ADCB$ are some of the 24 possible permutations of the four objects taken four at a time. If these four objects were taken two at a time, then AB, BA, AC, CA, AD, DA BC, CB, etc., are some of the 12 permutations of four objects taken two at a time. Note that the definition states "ordered sequences." That means that AB and BA are two different permutations, i.e., order makes a difference.

The number of permutations of n things taken r at a time, $_nP_r$, equals

$$_nP_r = \frac{n!}{(n-r)!}$$

This expression involves the symbol $n!$, read "n factorial," which is defined as

$$n! = n(n-1)(n-2)(n-3)\ldots(1)$$

Thus, $5! = (5)(4)(3)(2)(1) = 120$. Remember that $0! = 1$.

If $r = n$ in the expresssion for the number of permutations, the number of permutations of n things (taken n at a time) equals

$$_nP_n = \frac{n!}{(n-n)!} = \frac{n!}{0!} = n!$$

Let us examine the logic behind these expressions.

Suppose one has five objects, A, B, C, D, and E. Consider first the number of permutations of these five objects taken five at a time, i.e., $_nP_n = {_5P_5}$. Think of the task as having to fill five positions. There are five possible objects with which to fill the first position. For each one of those five selections, the second position may be filled with any one of the four remaining objects, since an ordered sequence does not permit selecting with replacement. This means that there are $(5)(4) = 20$ ways of filling the first two positions. Note that one multiplies because *for each one* of the first five possibilities, there exists four ways to fill the second. Thus, there will be five four's or $5 \times 4 = 20$ permutations of the first two positions. Continuing, the third position may be filled with any one of the three remaining objects, there are two ways to fill the fourth, and only one object (or way) remains for the last position. Therefore, the total number of ordered sequences or permutations of five things is

$$(5)(4)(3)(2)(1) = 5! = 120$$

More generally, there are $n!$ permutations of n things (taken n at a time),

$$_nP_n = n!$$

Now consider the number of permutations of five things taken only three at a time, i.e., $_nP_r = {_5P_3}$. There are five ways to fill the first position, four ways to fill the second position, and three ways to fill the third position and that is all. Thus one multiplies

$$_nP_r = n(n-1)(n-2)\ldots(n-r+1) = (5)(4)(3) = 60$$

The 60 permutations of 5 things taken 3 at a time are enumerated in Table 7–3.

7–3 The Sixty Permutations and Ten Combinations (Underlined) of Five Things Taken Three at a Time.

ABC	*ABD*	*ABE*	*ACD*	*ACE*
ACB	*ADB*	*AEB*	*ADC*	*AEC*
BCA	*BAD*	*BAE*	*CAD*	*CAE*
BAC	*BDA*	*BEA*	*CDA*	*CEA*
CAB	*DAB*	*EAB*	*DAC*	*EAC*
CBA	*DBA*	*EBA*	*DCA*	*ECA*
ADE	*BCD*	*BCE*	*BDE*	*CDE*
AED	*BDC*	*BEC*	*BED*	*CED*
DAE	*CBD*	*CBE*	*DBE*	*DCE*
DEA	*CDB*	*CEB*	*DEB*	*DEC*
EAD	*DBC*	*EBC*	*EBD*	*ECD*
EDA	*DCB*	*ECB*	*EDB*	*EDC*

However, mathematically the same result is arrived at by dividing $n!$ by $(n - r)!$:

$$_nP_r = \frac{n!}{(n - r)!} = \frac{(5)(4)(3)(\cancel{2})(\cancel{1})}{(\cancel{2})(\cancel{1})} = (5)(4)(3) = 60$$

Thus, the expression for the number of permutations of n things taken r at a time is

$$_nP_r = n(n - 1)(n - 2)\ldots(n - r + 1) = \frac{n!}{(n - r)!}$$

example What is the probability of picking first, second, and third in a race involving seven horses? There is only one way to pick the three horses and assign them to the proper places (event A) but there are $_7P_3$ ways of ordering three of seven horses. The required probability is

$$P(A) = \frac{\#(A)}{\#(S)} = \frac{1}{_7P_3} = \frac{1}{\dfrac{7!}{(7 - 3)!}} = \frac{1}{\dfrac{(7)(6)(5)(\cancel{4})(\cancel{3})(\cancel{2})(\cancel{1})}{(\cancel{4})(\cancel{3})(\cancel{2})(\cancel{1})}} = \frac{1}{(7)(6)(5)} = \frac{1}{210}$$

$$P(A) = .0048$$

Therefore, if there was a crowd of 10,000 people, none of whom had any information on the horses and all of whom guessed randomly, on the average 48 people would pick the first three horses to finish in order.

COMBINATIONS [2]

A **combination** is any set of objects or events regardless of their internal order. The number of groups of r objects that can be selected from n objects is symbolized by $_nC_r$ and given by

$$_nC_r = \frac{n!}{(n-r)!\,r!}$$

When the number of combinations of n things taken n at a time is desired, only one combination exists. Note also that while AB and BA are two different *permutations* of A and B, they are the *same combination;* permutations are ordered sequences while combinations are subsets and are not defined with respect to the order of their elements. Consider the logic of determining $_nC_r$.

Recall that the number of permutations of n objects taken r at a time is

$$_nP_r = \frac{n!}{(n-r)!}$$

Thus, if $n = 5$ and $r = 3$,

$$_5P_3 = \frac{5!}{2!} = 60$$

The number of combinations, however, is much less than 60, because many of the permutations are just reorderings of a single combination. Table 7–3 presents the 60 permutations of five things taken three at a time, but they are arranged into groups corresponding to the ten combinations. It can be seen that there are six permutations *for every one combination* (underlined in the table). In general, if objects are to be taken r at a time there will be $r!$ permutations for every combination. Thus, since there are three elements in each group, there are $3! = (3)(2)(1) = 6$ permutations for each combination as indicated by the groupings of six in Table 7–3. Just as one divides the number of inches by 12 in order to obtain length in feet, one divides the number of permutations by $r!$ in order to obtain the number of combinations since there are $r!$ permutations for every combination. Therefore, the expression for combinations is

$$_nC_r = \frac{_nP_r}{r!} = \frac{\dfrac{n!}{(n-r)!}}{r!} = \frac{n!}{(n-r)!\,r!}$$

example   A football coach has seven guards on the team. If it does not make any difference who plays the right or the left position, how

[2] This text uses the symbol $_nC_r$ for the number of combinations of n things taken r at a time, while some other books use $\binom{n}{r}$.

many different pairs of guards can be fielded? Since order is unimportant, this amounts to asking how many combinations of seven things taken two at a time are there?

$$_7C_2 = \frac{7!}{5!2!} = \frac{(7)(6)(5)(4)(3)(2)(1)}{(5)(4)(3)(2)(1)(2)(1)} = 21$$

example   What is the probability of being dealt a poker hand (five cards) containing all spades? If A is the event of being dealt all spades, one must get any of the many combinations of 13 cards in that suit taken five at a time. The sample space S includes the number of five-card hands in a deck of 52 cards. The required probability is

$$P(A) = \frac{_{13}C_5}{_{52}C_5} = \frac{\dfrac{13!}{8!5!}}{\dfrac{52!}{47!5!}} = \frac{(13)(12)(11)(10)(9)}{(52)(51)(50)(49)(48)}$$

$$P(A) = .0005$$

BINOMIAL PROBABILITY

A special application of determining the number of combinations occurs when one desires the probability of obtaining a certain percentage of a specified event in a set of independent trials. For example, in six tosses of a coin, what is the probability of obtaining exactly two heads? It is important to notice that the question does not specify the order in which the heads and tails must appear. It only requires that exactly two of the six tosses be heads. Therefore, the solution to this problem may be achieved by first ascertaining the probability of any single sequence of two heads and four tails and then determining how many such sequences are possible.

One potential sequence is (H, H, T, T, T, T). The probability of a head on any single flip is $\frac{1}{2}$ and the probability of a tail is also $\frac{1}{2}$. The probability of getting two heads in succession is $(\frac{1}{2})(\frac{1}{2})$, of two heads followed by a tail is $(\frac{1}{2})(\frac{1}{2})(\frac{1}{2})$, and of (H, H, T, T, T, T) is $(\frac{1}{2})(\frac{1}{2})(\frac{1}{2})(\frac{1}{2})(\frac{1}{2})(\frac{1}{2}) = \frac{1}{64}$.

Further, the probability of the sequence (T, T, T, H, H, T) is also

$$(\tfrac{1}{2})(\tfrac{1}{2})(\tfrac{1}{2})(\tfrac{1}{2})(\tfrac{1}{2})(\tfrac{1}{2}) = \tfrac{1}{64}$$

and the probability of *any* particular sequence of two heads and four tails is $\frac{1}{64}$.

How many such sequences of two heads and four tails are there? It happens that the number of sequences of two heads in six tosses is the same as the number of combinations of six things taken two at a time:

$$_6C_2 = \frac{6!}{2!(6-2)!} = 15$$

Therefore, since the event of two heads in six flips can occur in 15 different ways each with a probability of $\frac{1}{64}$, the required answer is given by the sum of these 15 probabilities (since they are mutually exclusive) or

$$\tfrac{1}{64} + \tfrac{1}{64} + \cdots + \tfrac{1}{64} = 15(\tfrac{1}{64}) = \tfrac{15}{64}$$

This problem is an example of **binomial probability**, and the process of finding its solution may be formalized into a general expression.

> In a sequence of n independent trials that have only two outcomes (arbitrarily call them "success" and "failure") with the probability p of a success and probability q of a failure (note that $q = 1 - p$) the probability of exactly r successes in n trials is
>
> $$_nC_r p^r q^{n-r}$$
>
> or
>
> $$\frac{n!}{r!(n-r)!} p^r q^{n-r}$$

To illustrate further, suppose an urn contained one red and three green balls. If the ball is returned to the urn after each drawing, what is the probability of selecting three reds in five tries? A "success" is defined as the selection of a red ball. Since on any one trial only one of the four balls in the urn is red, the probability of a success is one-fourth ($p = \frac{1}{4}$). Since $q = 1 - p$ and since three of the four balls available on any one trial are "failures," $q = \frac{3}{4}$. The required event is to obtain three red balls ($r = 3$) in five draws ($n = 5$). Therefore, the desired probability is

$$\frac{n!}{r!(n-r)!} p^r q^{n-r}$$

$$\frac{5!}{3!(5-3)!} \left(\frac{1}{4}\right)^3 \left(\frac{3}{4}\right)^{5-3} = \frac{90}{1024} = .088$$

FORMULAS

1. **Classical probability:**

   a. $P(A) = \dfrac{\#(A)}{\#(S)}$

   b. $P(\emptyset) = \dfrac{\#(\emptyset)}{\#(S)} = \dfrac{0}{\#(S)} = 0$

   c. $P(S) = \dfrac{\#(S)}{\#(S)} = 1.00$

2. Probability of an intersection:

 a. $P(A \cap B) = P(A)P(B \mid A)$

 b. If A and B are independent [i.e., $P(B \mid A) = P(B)$], then $P(A \cap B) = P(A)P(B)$.

3. Conditional probability:

$$P(B \mid A) = \frac{P(A \cap B)}{P(A)}$$

4. Probability of a union:

 a. $P(A \cup B) = P(A) + P(B) - P(A \cap B)$

 b. If A and B are mutually exclusive (i.e., $A \cap B = \emptyset$), then $P(A \cup B) = P(A) + P(B)$.

5. Permutations:

 a. $_nP_r = \dfrac{n!}{(n - r)!}$

 b. $_nP_n = n!$

6. Combinations:

$$_nC_r = \frac{n!}{(n - r)!r!}$$

7. Binomial probability, the probability of r successes in n independent trials:

$$P(r, n, p) = \frac{n!}{(n - r)!r!} p^r q^{n-r}$$

in which p = the probability of a success,
q = the probability of a failure, ($q = 1 - p$)

EXERCISES

 1. Determine which of the following events are mutually exclusive:
   (a) flipping a head, flipping a tail with one toss of a fair coin.
   (b) rolling a three or greater, rolling an even number with a die.
   (c) drawing a red card, drawing an ace.

2. Determine which of the following events are independent:
   (a) flipping a head on the first toss and a tail on the second toss of a coin.
   (b) selecting an ace and then selecting a king when drawing is done with replacement. When drawing is done without replacement.
   (c) having a boy as a first child and having a girl as a second.

3. What is the relationship between conditional probability and independence?

4. Determine the following probabilities:
   (a) In a deck of 12 cards (4 jacks, 4 queens, 4 kings), what is the probability of drawing a jack or a queen? A red card or a jack?
   (b) What is the probability of obtaining either (1) at least three, or, (2) less than two in a single roll of a die? At least three or an even number in a single roll of a die?
   (c) What is the probability of rolling two successive 6's with a die?
   (d) If an urn contains three red and four green balls, what is the probability of selecting a green ball given that a red ball has been drawn on the first selection and not replaced? And replaced? If drawing is without replacement, what is the probability of selecting two successive green balls? A red and then a green ball?

5. Determine the following permutations:
   (a) $_6P_6$ (b) $_5P_3$ (c) $_7P_4$

6. If a room has 6 chairs, how many different seating arrangements are there if 12 people come in?

7. Determine the following combinations:
   (a) $_6C_6$ (b) $_6C_3$ and $_6C_4$ (c) $_8C_4$

8. How many different relay teams of four swimmers could a coach put together with seven swimmers to choose from? If the order of swimming made a difference, then how many teams could be put together?

9. What is the probability of being dealt a five-card hand composed of all clubs? Of one suit?

10. What is the probability of naming the three top horses (regardless of specific position) in a field of 8? What is the probability of correctly designating first, second, and third positions from the field of 8? Given that you have picked the top three horses, what is the probability of correctly assigning them to the first three positions?

11. Suppose seven infants are familiarized with a given visual stimulus. Later they are permitted to look at that familiar pattern and two other stimuli that represent two degrees of similarity to the familiar one. The "discrepancy theory" predicts that looking time should be an inverted-U function of magnitude of discrepancy and the probability of this ordering of response is 1/12. What is the probability that exactly four of the seven infants should respond in this way? Four or more of the seven infants?[3]

---

[3] Inspired by R. B. McCall and J. Kagan, "Stimulus-Schema Discrepancy and Attention in the Infant." *Journal of Experimental Child Psychology*, 1967, V, 381–390.

INTRODUCTION TO HYPOTHESIS TESTING: SAMPLING DISTRIBUTIONS AND PROBABILITY

8

The previous chapter provided an introduction to probability. This chapter emphasizes the concept of probability and its application to the task of drawing statistical inferences. Since statistical inference consists of invoking probability statements to help make decisions about the population on the basis of a sample of observations, this discussion concerns the adequacy of the sample as a faithful representation of the population, the sampling distribution as an index of the amount of sampling error, and how the concept of probability as relative frequency can be used to make probability statements about the likelihood of certain events.

sampling and sampling distributions

The task of statistical inference is to make a decision about what exists in a large group of cases (i.e., the population) on the basis of observations made from a small subset of cases (i.e., the sample). Since estimates are to be made from information provided by the sample, the methods used to select this subset of cases are vital to the accuracy of inference.

METHODS OF SAMPLING

Recall that a **population** is an identifiable group of individuals or events. Characteristics of populations are known as **parameters**. A subset of a population is a **sample**, and quantities computed on a sample are called **statistics**. Often a statistic is used to estimate the value of a parameter. Although unbiasedness has been discussed as one attribute of a good estimator, a statistic used to estimate a parameter is no better than the sample upon which it is computed. There are many ways to select a sample and one type is called simple random sampling.

> A **simple random sample** is one in which all elements of the population have an equal probability of being selected.

Suppose you wanted a random sample of students at your university for an opinion poll on the quality and appropriateness of their educational experience. You might obtain a list of all students in the school, go to a **random number table**, and select a sample of 50. A random number table (Table J) is located in Appendix II of this book and consists of rows and columns of random numbers. The numbers are random in the sense that for any single digit position, each of the 10 numbers from 0 to 9 had an equal opportunity to occupy that position. This means that every digit was selected independently of every other digit. Further, not only are all the single digits "random," but all two-, three-, or N-digit numbers are also "random."

It should be observed that if you read down a one-digit column in the table you may feel that these numbers are not very random at all. This is because what most people regard as random is not what "random" in the statistical sense means. For example, if you were to write what you thought was a random sequence of 0's and 1's, you might write 01001001011101, etc. Most people are very hesitant to put more than three of a kind in succession (e.g., 000 or 111). Yet, in any random selection of four 0 and 1 digits, the probability of 0000 or 1111 is .125 or 125 in every 1000 such sets of four. Look at the first column of numbers in the random number table and observe such a statistically random sequence by letting even numbers be "0" and odd numbers be "1."

To use the table in getting a sample of 50 from a list of 3000 students, assign each student a number between 1 and 3000. Then go to the random number table and mentally block the table off into four-digit columns. Read down the columns until you obtain 50 four-digit numbers that fall between 0001 and 3000 inclusive. The students assigned numbers corresponding to these 50 numbers constitute a randomly selected sample.

In most cases described in this text, **independent random sampling** is required.

Independence in sampling implies that the selection of any element for inclusion in the sample does not alter the likelihood of drawing any other element of the population into the sample. In almost all cases in which random sampling is required in this text, the implication is that the elements have been independently selected.[1]

Since random sampling is the basis for most of the procedures of statistical inference discussed in this text, it would be wise to consider the characteristics of samples that actually are taken in research. For example, suppose one wanted to sample the population of a given town by selecting every two hundredth name in the telephone book. Would this be a random sample of townsfolk, i.e., does each person in the town have an equal opportunity to be selected? This would not be a random sample of townsfolk since people who do not own a phone are systematically excluded by this procedure. Now there are two things one can do to correct the situation. First, a list of all people could be obtained from the city government or census bureau, and the random number table employed. But, this might be a very time-consuming task, and it assumes the availability of the necessary list of all people in the town. The second possibility is to change the definition of the population in accordance with the nature of the sample. Since you cannot get a random sample of "all town people," change the population to "all telephone-owning town people" and discuss the results and conclusions in terms of this group rather than in terms of all residents. The important point is for the researcher to be aware of precisely what population the sample was selected from and to limit conclusions to that population.

The tediousness of obtaining a truly random sample is so inhibiting that researchers frequently do not select random samples, but nevertheless treat their samples statistically as if they were random. For example, a group of rats provided by an animal supplier is not a random selection of rats. Rats are raised in cages set on tiers, some of which are closer to the light than others, and the amount of illumination in the rat's rearing experience can influence some types of later behavior. Further, when the rats arrive at the laboratory and are assigned to experimental groups, it is sometimes tempting to place the first 10 in one group, the second 10 in the next, etc. But, it happens that the more curious and active rats frequently come over to the side of the shipping box when it is opened. These rats are more accessible and easier to pick up. They are thus selected first and go into the first group if the above procedure is carried out. It is a good idea to use

---

[1] Sometimes it is important for an investigator to insure that certain segments of the population are represented in the sample. The political pollsters, for example, attempt to sample the voting public in such a way that each area of the country, each ethnic group, each religious sect, etc. is appropriately represented. Thus, if 10% of the population is Catholic, 10% of the sample would be randomly selected from Catholic voters. Such a sample is called a **proportional stratified random sample**. Since all of the procedures outlined in this text are appropriate for simple random samples, stratified sampling and its associated statistical procedures will not be considered further.

a random number table to determine group assignments, or at least to alternate by assigning one rat to the first group, the next to the second, etc.

Another form of bias in sampling occurs when volunteers are used. College students who volunteer for experiments are probably somewhat different in terms of academic concern, motivation, etc., than those students who do not volunteer. Who volunteers can be an interesting issue in its own right, and it determines what kind of research can and cannot be done. For example, some developmental psychologists are dependent upon parents to volunteer their infants for observation. It is likely that highly educated parents are more receptive to "science's need for subjects" than are more minimally educated parents. Thus, the sample one obtains is not a random selection of parents because it may contain a preponderance of highly educated families.

How can one safeguard against such bias in one's sample? The best way is simply to be cautious, well read, and aware of what one is doing. In addition, it is advisable to measure the sample you have selected on several dimensions (e.g., age, education, "normality," etc.) appropriate to the research (as long as the measurement of these traits does not influence the subjects in any way) so that readers can judge whether this sample has characteristics similar to the population you want to discuss. The guiding principle is to insure that inferences and generalizations are made to the appropriate population.

SAMPLING DISTRIBUTIONS AND SAMPLING ERROR

Even when the sample is random and appropriate, it is likely to be different from the population just because it is a sample of considerably fewer cases than are contained in the population and because specific individuals differ from one another.

Suppose there are 20 students in your statistics class and the professor springs a surprise quiz consisting of 10 questions. The scores of the 20 students comprise the population of raw scores and are presented at the left in Table 8–1. Now suppose a random sample of $N = 4$ students is taken for the purpose of estimating the population mean (i.e., the mean of the 20 students which is actually 3.90). The first such sample of four students provides the scores (1, 5, 9, 0) which have a mean of 3.75, as indicated in Table 8–1. But suppose another random sample of $N = 4$ was selected and its mean is 2.25. Looking down the right-hand column of means in Table 8–1 for 10 randomly selected samples from the population, one can see that even randomly selected samples from the same population vary in the value of their mean one to another. Moreover, not one sample yields a mean that precisely equals the population mean. Why do samples differ from one another?

In selecting a random sample the implication is that each subject in the

8–1 A Population Distribution of Raw Scores, Ten Observed Sample Distributions, and an Empirical Sampling Distribution of the Mean

Population Distribution of Raw Scores		10 Observed Sample Distributions ($N = 4$)	Empirical Sampling Distribution of the $\overline{X}$'s
6	2	(1, 5, 9, 0)	3.75
9	5	(0, 3, 1, 5)	2.25
0	1	(5, 8, 3, 0)	4.00
3	2	(1, 5, 0, 7)	3.25
1	1	(7, 6, 1, 3)	4.25
5	2	(3, 2, 1, 7)	3.25
7	7	(2, 0, 3, 5)	2.50
7	8	(1, 2, 1, 1)	1.25
1	1	(2, 7, 1, 7)	4.25
3	7	(9, 7, 6, 2)	6.00
$\mu = 3.90, \sigma = 2.88$			Mean of $\overline{X}$'s = 3.48 Standard Deviation of $\overline{X}$'s = 1.31

population had an equal *opportunity* to be drawn into the sample, but this does not say that the sample itself will faithfully reflect the population characteristics. One could randomly select a sample that happened to contain many exceptionally bright students. Therefore, random samples will differ one from another just because they are samples composed of different individuals.

Returning to Table 8–1, we see that the means computed on the 10 samples could themselves be considered scores in a distribution of means. Notice that the 10 means have an average of 3.48 and a standard deviation of 1.31. Such a distribution has a special name and function in statistics.

The distribution of a statistic is called a **sampling distribution**.

Since a mean is a statistic, the distribution of the 10 sample means in Table 8–1 is an **empirical sampling distribution**. It is called "empirical" because these 10 means were actually observed by collecting 10 samples and computing $\overline{X}$ for each group. A **theoretical sampling distribution** is a theoretical distribution of a statistic. If samples of size 4 were continually drawn and the mean computed on each one, as the sampling continued the distribution of means would approach the theoretical sampling distribution of the mean for samples of size 4. Actually, sampling distributions are determined mathematically and not by repeated sampling as described above, but the results of the two approaches are very close.

The sampling distribution represents the third type of distribution to be considered in this discussion. There is a **population distribution** which is the distribution of scores in the population. Usually, this is a theoretical distribution because in actual practice the population is not available. Second, when a sample from the population is selected, this subgroup of scores forms the observed **sample distribution**. It is from this distribution that various statistics may be computed and used to estimate what exists in the population distribution. The **sampling distribution** is a theoretical distribution of a statistic for samples of size N drawn from the population distribution. Like the population distribution, it is theoretical, but in contrast to both the population and observed sample distributions, it is a distribution of a statistic based upon a sample of size N rather than simple raw observations. The empirical analogues of these three distributions are found in the three columns of Table 8–1. It will be important to maintain the distinction between these three distributions.

standard error of the mean   Just as a distribution of scores has certain characteristics (e.g., mean and variance), so, too, does a sampling distribution. For example, the empirical sampling distribution of the mean presented in the third column of Table 8–1 has a mean (3.48) and a standard deviation (1.31). However, researchers almost never actually collect an empirical sampling distribution; rather, the parameters of a theoretical sampling distribution are of interest. For example, the mean of the theoretical sampling distribution is symbolized by $\mu_{\bar{x}}$. The Greek μ is used to indicate that the mean of the theoretical sampling distribution is a parameter not a statistic, and the subscript $\bar{x}$ signifies that it is the population mean of means. The symbol $\mu_{\bar{x}}$ is to be distinguished from μ_x which represents the mean of the population distribution of raw scores. It happens that the mean of the theoretical sampling distribution of means equals the mean of the population distribution of raw scores:

$$\mu_{\bar{x}} = \mu_x = \mu$$

The symbol μ without a subscript is customarily used to indicate this value.

In addition to a mean, the theoretical sampling distribution of means has a standard deviation which is symbolized by $\sigma_{\bar{x}}$.

> The standard deviation of a sampling distribution of a statistic is called the **standard error** of that statistic.

Consequently, the standard deviation of the sampling distribution of the mean is known as the **standard error of the mean**.

It is exceptionally important for you to have a firm grasp of the meaning of a standard error. Consider the standard error of the mean, $\sigma_{\bar{x}}$. We have said that the mean of one sample of scores will not likely equal the mean of another sample of scores, even if those samples are both randomly selected from the same population. The fact that means differ in value from one sample to another simply testifies to the fact that there is variability in such a distribution of means. Since the standard deviation is a numerical index of variability, the standard deviation of the sampling distribution of means, $\sigma_{\bar{x}}$, is a numerical index of the extent to which means will vary from one sample to another. More generally, the standard error is an index of the amount of **sampling error** with respect to a given statistic. Thus, if $\sigma_{\bar{x}} = 5$ for samples of 20 males on a reading test but $\sigma_{\bar{x}} = 10$ for samples of 20 females on the same test, there is more sampling error for males than females. This implies that the more-or-less random variation between means due to differences in the nature of one sample versus another is greater for males than females.

It was stated above that the mean of the theoretical sampling distribution of the mean is identical to the mean of the population distribution of raw scores, $\mu_{\bar{x}} = \mu_x = \mu$. In contrast, the standard deviation of the sampling distribution of the mean (the standard error of the mean) is not identical (though it is related) to the standard deviation of the population distribution of raw scores.

> The standard error of the mean, $\sigma_{\bar{x}}$, equals the standard deviation of the population of raw scores divided by the square root of the size of the sample upon which the means are based:

$$\sigma_{\bar{x}} = \frac{\sigma_x}{\sqrt{N}}$$

If the standard deviation of the population of raw scores was $\sigma_x = 2.88$ and the sample size was $N = 4$, the theoretical standard error of the mean would be

$$\sigma_{\bar{x}} = \frac{\sigma_x}{\sqrt{N}} = \frac{2.88}{\sqrt{4}} = 1.44$$

estimating $\sigma_{\bar{x}}$ with $s_{\bar{x}}$ Thus far, the standard error of the mean has been expressed as a function of the standard deviation of the population of raw scores. The population standard deviation of raw scores may be estimated by the standard deviation of the observed sample of raw scores, and thus $\sigma_{\bar{x}}$ may be estimated by $s_{\bar{x}}$.

> Since s_x estimates σ_x, an estimate of the standard error of the mean is given by

$$s_{\bar{x}} = \frac{s_x}{\sqrt{N}}$$

which can also be expressed in terms of the raw scores of the sample as

$$s_{\bar{x}} = \sqrt{\frac{N \sum X_i^2 - (\sum X_i)^2}{N^2(N-1)}}$$

in which N is the size of the sample of X's.

Two things should be noticed about the standard error of the mean as expressed by $s_{\bar{x}} = s_x/\sqrt{N}$. First, all that is required to calculate $s_{\bar{x}}$ is the standard deviation and the N from a single sample of cases, yet $s_{\bar{x}}$ represents an estimate of the amount of random sampling variation in means from all possible samples of size N from the population of raw scores. Thus, it is not necessary to select several samples in order to estimate the sampling error of the mean; $s_{\bar{x}}$ estimates $\sigma_{\bar{x}}$ on the basis of just a single sample.

Second, observe that the formula for $s_{\bar{x}}$ states that the standard deviation of the sample must be divided by the square root of N: $s_{\bar{x}} = s_x/\sqrt{N}$. Therefore, the variability of means from sample to sample will always be smaller than the variability of raw scores. Also note that as N becomes larger, $s_{\bar{x}}$ becomes smaller. Thus, the variability of sample means decreases as the size of the sample increases. Consequently, for large samples one expects $\bar{X}$, the estimate of the population mean μ, to be less variable from sample to sample, and thus a more accurate estimate of μ than if the sample size were smaller. In short, when parameters must be estimated, it is a good idea to have as large a sample as is feasible.

other standard errors   The sampling distribution and standard error of the mean have been discussed in detail, but a sampling distribution and standard error exist for any statistic. In each case the logic is the same. Random samples differ in their characteristics, and any statistic will vary somewhat from sample to sample. The theoretical sampling distribution is the distribution of a particular statistic computed on all possible samples of size N, and the standard error of that statistic is the standard deviation of its sampling distribution.

sampling distributions and normality   Many of the procedures described in this and remaining chapters rest on the assumption that the sampling distribution of means is normal in form. This is the case if one of two conditions is met.

Given random sampling, the sampling distribution of the mean
   1. is a normal distribution if the population distribution of the raw scores is normal.
   2. approaches a normal distribution if the size of the sample is large.

If the population distribution is normal, the sampling distribution of the mean will also be normal. However, since one rarely has the population at one's disposal, how can one know if the population distribution is normal? One way to make an educated guess is to determine whether a random sample from the population is normally distributed. Some variables are usually not normally distributed because there are a few extreme scores. For example, IQ's of all 21-year olds are probably normally distributed but IQ's of all 21-year-old college students are not because low or extremely low scores are not represented as frequently in college groups as extremely high scores. Family income, the latency for a rat to move out of a startbox in a maze, and percent correct on a relatively easy exam are variables that are not usually normally distributed. Notice that the above variables are bounded on one end of their scales (e.g., $0 income, 0 sec., 100% correct). If the scores tend to fall near the bounded end of the scale, the distribution is likely to be skewed. Fortunately, many of the variables measured in social sciences can be assumed to be normally distributed. When variables are not normal, other statistical techniques may be used (see Chapter 13).

A second way to obtain a normal sampling distribution of the mean is to select a large enough sample. The sampling distribution of the mean will approach a normal distribution as the sample size increases, *even though the population distribution is not normal*. Just how many cases constitute a sufficiently large sample depends upon many factors, one of which is the extent of the departure from normality of the population distribution. If the population distribution does not deviate too much from normality, a sample of size $N = 2$ might produce a sampling distribution of the mean that is quite normal, whereas if the non-normality in the population is severe, N's of 20, 30, or several 100 might be necessary. In short, the sampling distribution of the mean will approach a normal form if the size of the sample is large.

One of the reasons why normality is necessary for the statistical procedures to be described is the following fact:

> If the population distribution is normal and the observations are independent and randomly selected, the sample mean and variance (and standard deviation) are independent across samples.

Two variables (e.g., $\overline{X}$ and s^2) are independent if they are unrelated to one another. In this case, if many samples were obtained from a normal population, the distribution of variances for samples having a mean of 10, for example, would be approximately the same as for samples having a mean of 12 or some other value. The independence of the mean and variance of a normal distribution will be important later.

Let's review. Most of the statistical procedures to be described subsequently are dependent upon several principles. Some of these include: (a) Samples are drawn at random with independent observations. (b) The sampling distribution represents a distribution of a statistic and its standard deviation (standard error) is an expression of the extent to which the statistic will vary from one sample to another (i.e., sampling error). (c) The sampling distribution of the mean is normal if the population is normal or the sample is large. (d) The mean and standard deviation of a random sample from a normal population are independent.

probability and its application to hypothesis testing

The purpose of inferential statistics is to assist in making inferences and judgments about what exists on the basis of only partial evidence. This is accomplished by using probability. In a way, most people use subjective probability every day. You want to go to the football game this afternoon, but someone has warned that it is going to rain. You look outside an hour before the game and while there are clouds, it is not threatening. You make a subjective judgment about the likelihood that it will rain based only upon your quick look out the window.

The weatherman reports there is a 70% chance of rain tomorrow, and the sports broadcaster announces that odds on Fleet Foot in the fourth race at Belmont are 3:2. In each of these examples a statement of probability is made on the basis of only partial evidence.

In scientific research, probability statements are also used to make inferences and judgments on the basis of only partial information. For example, a social psychologist was interested in the extent to which people could be made to inflict pain on a colleague by the application of social pressure to conform.[2] The social psychologist's experiment was structured so that a male "subject" would join three other men in what was described as an important learning experiment. In this experiment the subject and two other fellows were to teach the other person a simple laboratory task by administering electric shock to the "learner" for his incorrect responses. Actually, though unknown to the subject, the three other people were collaborators of the experimenter. In fact the entire situation, shock, learning, etc., was staged for the subject. Forty subjects were urged by their "colleagues" to turn up the purported shock level as high as possible because it "was essential to the experiment." The "learner" grimaced and squirmed in accordance with the level of shock the subject thought he was administering. Another 40 subjects were not pressured to elevate the presumed shock level. The results showed that those subjects who were not admonished by their colleagues to turn up the shock set their shock controls at an average intensity reading of approximately 3.5 arbitrary units while those subjects who were pressured averaged a shock level of approximately 14 arbitrary units,

[2] S. Milgram, "Group Pressure and Action against a Person," *Journal of Abnormal and Social Psychology*, 1964, LXIX, 137–143.

even though the "learner" screamed and gyrated in response to this much "shock." This experiment showed that for the subjects tested, social pressure seemed to result in the administration of almost three times as much "shock" as when no social pressure was applied.

But, how much confidence can we place in the results of this one study? Was this outcome simply a fluke, an unlikely chance result that would not happen again if the experiment were repeated? Would all groups of men in the population from which this sample was taken have responded essentially in the same way? Of course, there is no certain method of determining the answers to these questions short of testing every person in the population, an alternative that is almost always impossible. Therefore, we must quantify our uncertainty about what truly exists in the population and adopt some conventions for deciding what to conclude. The fundamental tool in this process is **probability**, the quantification of uncertainty.

More specifically, the task of statistical inference in the above experiment is to decide whether the mean of 14 is sufficiently greater than the mean of 3.5 to warrant the conclusion that the social pressure actually had an effect. Although 14 is substantially more than 3.5, it still could be a "chance" result. Not all members of the pressured group raised the purported shock level higher than each member of the non-pressured group, and some members of the non-pressured group presumably set the shock level higher than even the average of 14 observed for the other experimental condition. After all, suppose one just sampled two groups of 40 subjects and did not pressure either of the groups— that is, subjects from both groups were treated in precisely the same way. Even in this case we would not expect the average of these two groups to be exactly the same because of sampling error. The job of probability in statistical inference is to quantify the likelihood of just such a possibility. That is, how often in 100 such experiments in which two groups of 40 subjects were treated exactly alike would we expect a difference as large as 14 versus 3.5? If the answer is "not very often," then it is probably unreasonable to suppose this was simply a chance result, and one would conclude that the social pressuring probably caused the subjects to increase the amount of shock they were willing to administer. On the other hand, if the difference of 14 versus 3.5 is likely to happen, even if the social pressure had no effect whatsoever, then one would have to conclude that the experiment provides no evidence that social pressure is effective in altering the amount of shock men will give to their colleagues.

Scientists prefer to use probability as an index of the likelihood of events rather than their personal and subjective feelings of how probable something is. The numerical probability is public knowledge (all scientists can observe and understand it), the probability of one event can be easily compared with the probability of a different event, and certain conventions can be adopted about how high or low the probability must be in order to make one decision or another. Therefore, a knowledge of the concept of probability is essential to understanding the process of statistical inference and decision making in science.

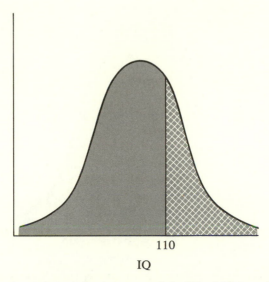

110

IQ

Fig. 8–1. The theoretical relative frequency of the IQ's of 10-year-old American children. The probability of a randomly selected child who has an IQ higher than 110 is indicated by the proportion of the total shaded area represented by the cross-hatched area.

PROBABILITY AND RELATIVE FREQUENCY

The determination of a simple probability really implies an **idealized sort of experiment**. In flipping a coin, one actually assumes an experiment in which the coin was tossed over and over again. There are two possible outcomes to a single flip of a coin: a head or a tail. It is assumed that both results are equally likely. On any single throw, either a head or a tail will occur, but over the long range of such flips of a coin, the ratio of heads to all possible outcomes will approach $\frac{1}{2} = .50$.

Thus, probability is **theoretical relative frequency**, the relative frequency of score values in a theoretical distribution based upon an unlimited number of cases. This implies that the probability of different events can be determined from theoretical distributions.

For example, suppose Figure 8–1 represents the theoretical relative frequency distribution of IQ of 10-year-old American children. Now consider the probability that a child selected at random from this population would have an IQ greater than 110. According to the conception of probability discussed above, this probability value should be given by the theoretical relative frequency of scores that exceed 110. The approach to determining the probability here rests on equating the **area** (shaded portion) existing between the curve and the abscissa with the concept of **theoretical relative frequency,** just as was done in Chapter 4. If the shaded portions under the curve in Figure 8–1 represent theoretical relative frequency, then that proportion of the total area which exists between 110 and

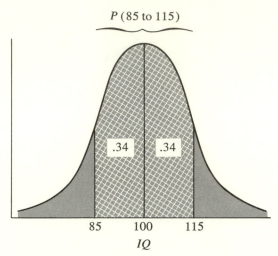

Fig. 8–2.   The proportion of the total shaded area that is cross-hatched represents the probability of randomly selecting a child with an IQ between 85 and 115.

$+\infty$ (indicated in the figure by cross-hatching) symbolizes the theoretical relative frequency of children having scores greater than 110. Therefore:

> The proportion of the total area under the curve of a theoretical relative frequency distribution that exists between any two points represents the probability of obtaining the events contained within the interval delimited by those two points.

For example, consider the probability that a child randomly selected from the population would have an IQ between 85 and 115. This probability is given by the proportion of the total area that exists between IQ's of 85 and 115 as illustrated in Figure 8–2.

The standard normal distribution (z) described in Chapter 4 and presented in Table A of Appendix II is a theoretical relative frequency distribution for the normal distribution having $\mu = 0$ and $\sigma = 1$, and based upon unlimited samplings. The percentiles listed in Table A correspond not only to the proportion of cases existing between two points but also to the probability of obtaining a score value located between these two points. There are many theoretical relative frequency distributions other than the standard normal whose percentiles are also tabled. These distributions will form the basis for making probabilistic statements as outlined in the remainder of this book.[3]

[3] The equation for a theoretical relative frequency distribution, such as the standard normal and several other distributions to be considered, is known as a **probability** or **density function**. To determine the probability of the occurrence of events located between any two points on the dimension, this function is integrated between these points by the methods of calculus. The values in Table A and other tables in this book represent the results of such a process.

hypothesis testing

The purpose of presenting discussions of sampling distributions and probability as theoretical relative frequency is because these two concepts are the basis of statistical inference. Although the specific techniques of statistical inference vary depending upon the research question being asked, the logic of the general approach is quite similar in these diverse cases. In order to illustrate this logic and the terminology that accompanies it, a relatively simple example will be used. In subsequent chapters, problems closer to those encountered in social science will be presented.

AN INFORMAL EXAMPLE

Suppose it is known that for the population of rats used for experimentation in a given laboratory the mean number of errorless trials in 200 attempts at a maze is 125, and the standard deviation is 10.5. In symbols, $\mu = 125$ and $\sigma_x = 10.5$. Now suppose that a psychologist has a hunch that injecting a certain drug before each daily testing session might alter performance, but doesn't know whether it will improve or retard it. The psychologist decides to make some relatively informal observations, first on just one rat and then on a small group of rats to which the drug was administered. If their performance is sufficiently different from what was expected of animals which are not drugged, then a formal experiment will be conducted comparing a large group of drugged with a large group of non-drugged animals.

First, the psychologist randomly selects one animal from the population of rats in the laboratory and then administers the drug to this experimental subject each day of the learning experiment. If this one drugged animal performs quite differently from the mean of the "normal" population, it is possible that the drug has some effect on learning performance in this situation. The psychologist will then give the drug to a group of rats to test this notion further. If the animal does not perform much differently than one would expect a non-drugged animal to do, this simple experiment provides no evidence that the drug has an effect.

Suppose the drugged animal scores 148 errorless trials. While this is clearly better than the population mean of 125, is it sufficiently different to warrant pursuing this line of research? How differently would this animal have to have performed to be "sufficiently different" from what would be expected of non-drugged subjects?

The strategy the scientist employs is quite simple. Suppose the drug actually has no effect. Then, the experimental animal should perform like a randomly selected member of the population of non-drugged animals which has a mean $\mu = 125$ and a standard deviation $\sigma = 10.5$. But if the experimental animal scores so well or so poorly that one would expect less than 5% of the non-drugged animals to behave so extremely, then the scientist will be encouraged in the belief that the drug might have an effect.

The psychologist has proposed a rather simple statistical problem of determining whether a score of 148 falls below the $P_{.025}$ or above the $P_{.975}$ percentile points of the distribution of non-drugged animals. Since 2.5% of the distribution falls below $P_{.025}$ and 2.5% falls above $P_{.975}$, if the experimental animal's score exceeds these percentile points it would have performed at a level that would have characterized less than 5% of the non-drugged animals. In this event, one might suspect the drug was effective.

Obviously, the scientist could go to the files of data on non-drugged animals, construct a frequency distribution, determine the percentile rank corresponding to a score value of 148, and then observe whether this percentile rank was more extreme than $P_{.025}$ or $P_{.975}$. However, assuming that the distribution of scores in this population is normal in form, the scientist could use the standard normal distribution to ascertain the percentile rank of a score of 148. Recall that

$$z_i = \frac{X_i - \mu}{\sigma}$$

translates any score in a normal distribution (e.g., $X_i =$ the experimental animal's score of 148, assuming the drug had no effect and it was thus a member of the normal population of non-drugged animals) into standard normal units. Since the parameters of that population are $\mu = 125$ and $\sigma = 10.5$, then

$$z = \frac{X_i - \mu}{\sigma} = \frac{148 - 125}{10.5} = \frac{23}{10.5} = 2.19$$

This implies that if the experimental subject were a member of the non-drugged population, it would have performed 2.19 standard deviation units above the mean. Looking at Table A of Appendix II, we see that a $z = 2.19$ falls at $P_{.9857}$ (i.e., 98.57% of the cases would fall below such a value) in a normal distribution with these parameters. Since this is more extreme than the scientist's arbitrary cutoff of $P_{.975}$, the decision is that the drug might have an effect.

However, recall that theoretical relative frequency may also be interpreted in terms of probability. Thus, the probability that the experimental animal should score 148 if the drug had no effect (i.e., it was actually like a member of the non-drugged population) was less than .05. In fact, the probability was $1 - .9857 = .0143$ that a non-drugged animal should score as high or higher than it did. Since it was so improbable that a non-drugged animal should score this differently, perhaps this subject was not behaving as a non-drugged animal would because the drug was having an effect upon its performance.

Buoyed by this result, the scientist decides to randomly select 20 rats from the laboratory population and determine their performance under the presumed influence of the drug. Essentially the same logic as before is used: If the mean of the group of drugged animals is sufficiently different from what would be expected of non-drugged animals, the notion that the drug affects this behavior is supported. Otherwise, there is no evidence favoring such a claim. The scientist tentatively assumes that the drug has no effect—that is, that the group of 20 subjects may be conceived to be comparable to a randomly selected group of 20 non-drugged subjects. If their performance exceeds $P_{.025}$ or $P_{.975}$, the conclusion is that it is not very likely that they were comparable to non-drugged animals since their performance would have been too atypical of this group. Thus, perhaps the drug had some effect on them. Otherwise, the experiment provides no support for such a notion.

The 20 animals score an average of 130. Statistically, this situation looks just like the previous case, except that now there is a group of subjects with a mean score rather than a single subject with one raw score. The problem demands that an observed mean (i.e., $\overline{X} = 130$) be transformed into standard normal units (i.e., z). The translation formula derives from the fact that the expression

$$z = \frac{X_i - \mu}{\sigma}$$

is perfectly general. It can be read: Any observation minus the population mean of those observations divided by the population standard deviation of those observations will equal z. In the first example, "observation" was a single score and the "population of observations" was the distribution of all non-drugged animals. Now, simply permit "a group mean" (i.e., $\overline{X}$) to be the observation and the theoretical distribution of means (i.e., the sampling distribution of the mean) be the "population of observations." Hence, the observation will be $\overline{X} = 130$, the mean of such observations will be $\mu_{\overline{x}} = 125$ (since $\mu_{\overline{x}} = \mu_x = \mu$), and the standard deviation of such observations will be the standard deviation of the sampling distribution of means (i.e., the standard error of the mean) which will equal $\sigma_x/\sqrt{N} = 10.5/\sqrt{20}$. Thus, the observed mean of 20 subjects may be translated into standard deviation units by

$$z = \frac{\overline{X} - \mu_{\overline{x}}}{\sigma_{\overline{x}}} = \frac{\overline{X} - \mu}{\sigma_{\overline{x}}/\sqrt{N}}$$

$$z = \frac{130 - 125}{10.5/\sqrt{20}} = 2.13$$

Looking again at Table A in Appendix II, we see that the percentile rank corresponding to a $z = 2.13$ is $P_{.9834}$ since 98.34% of the cases of a normal distribution would be expected to fall below such a value. Hence, the probability is indeed less than .05 that a group of 20 non-drugged rats would score so extremely. Since this is relatively improbable, perhaps these animals were made atypical by the drug.

Notice that although the formulas which were required to translate the observed value (X_i or $\overline{X}$) into standard normal units differed slightly in these two examples, the basic logic of the general procedure was the same. Randomly select a subject or a group of subjects and tentatively assume that, despite the fact that they receive the drug, they are no different than non-drugged animals. Arbitrarily select some percentiles (or probabilities) that define behavior that would provoke the interpretation that these experimental subjects might be different from non-drugged subjects. Translate a summary statistic of their performance (e.g., X_i, $\overline{X}$) into a form compatible with a theoretical relative frequency distribution and determine its percentile rank. If that rank exceeds the arbitrary limits set above, suspect that the tentative assumption that these subjects were just like non-drugged animals may have been wrong since their performance was very atypical or improbable. The next chapter examines the details of this logic.

FORMULAS

1. Standard Score Form:

$$z = \frac{X - \mu}{\sigma_x} \qquad z = \frac{\overline{X} - \mu}{\sigma_{\overline{x}}}$$

2. Standard Error of the Mean:

$$\sigma_{\overline{x}} = \frac{\sigma_x}{\sqrt{N}} \qquad \text{(population)}$$

$$s_{\overline{x}} = \frac{s_x}{\sqrt{N}} \qquad \text{(sample)}$$

EXERCISES

1. Discuss the appropriateness of the following samples for the stated populations.
   (a) Suppose a researcher in education wanted to test the effectiveness of two different teaching methods on college students in a university, using one method with an 8 A.M. class and the other with a 2 P.M. class.
   (b) A social psychologist is investigating patterns of group dynamics in the context of a jury simulation experiment to find the factors involved in the change of attitudes that transpires during jury debate in young adults. The psychology department requires that all students taking "Introduction to Psychology" serve in an experiment. Eighty students select the jury simulation experiment from the twenty possible research projects available to them.
   (c) An advertiser wants to know if people like the new style of package that Wonderease Soap Powder comes in. The package has just been displayed on color television, so the advertiser quickly sets up a telephone survey to inquire whether those people who saw the commercial liked the new packaging.

2. A population of 10 scores is listed in this exercise.

$$X_i = 2, 4, 4, 5, 5, 6, 7, 7, 8, 10$$

Write each score on a piece of paper and place it in a hat. Randomly select 10 samples of size 4 from this population and compute the mean (replace the selected numbers after each drawing of 4). Create an *empirical* sampling distribution of the mean from these data. Estimate the *theoretical* standard error of the mean first by using the standard deviation of the first sample you select in an appropriate formula and then by computing the standard deviation of the 10 samples you collected. How do you explain the differences in these values? Of what importance is the size of the sample in this process?

3. If the population standard deviation were as given below, what would be the standard error of the sampling distribution of the mean for samples of size N?

(a) If $\sigma_x = 12$, $N = 16$
(b) If $\sigma_x = 10$, $N = 25$
(c) If $\sigma_x = 8$, $N = 36$

4. The sampling distribution of the mean is normal in form if either one of two conditions is met. What are they?

5. Under what circumstances are the mean and variance independent?

6. What is the relationship between an "idealized experiment," probability, and theoretical relative frequency?

7. In a normal distribution with $\mu = 50$ and $\sigma_x = 10$, what is the probability of randomly sampling a subject who scores

(a) 60 or higher?
(b) 72 or higher?
(c) 41 or lower?
(d) between 47 and 58?

8. Assuming a normal population distribution with $\mu = 80$, $\sigma_x = 20$, what is the probability of randomly sampling the following groups of subjects

(a) $\bar{X} = 92$ or higher, $N = 4$?
(b) $\bar{X} = 88$ or higher, $N = 16$?
(c) $\bar{X} = 75$ or lower, $N = 25$?
(d) $\bar{X}$ between 73 and 84, $N = 9$?

INTRODUCTION TO HYPOTHESIS TESTING: TERMINOLOGY AND THEORY

9

In the previous chapter, sampling distributions and the concept of probability as relative frequency were introduced and illustrated with two simple examples in which the learning performance of a drugged rat or group of rats was compared with a non-drugged population. These illustrations were presented informally and phrased in common language. The purpose of this chapter is to recast one of these examples in more traditional statistical language, and to consider additional aspects of the statistical theory of hypothesis testing in preparation for applying these techniques to more conventional situations in social science.

statistical terminology

It will be helpful to summarize the last example presented in Chapter 8 before introducing formal statistical terms for the concepts and processes involved in it. Recall that the psychologist wished to compare the learning performance of a group of 20 drugged rats to a population of non-drugged rats which had a population mean of $\mu = 125$ correct responses with a population standard deviation of $\sigma_x = 10.5$. The experimental procedure permitted the making of two *assumptions*. First, the sample of 20 animals was randomly selected from the population of non-drugged animals, and second, the distribution of scores in this population was normal in form. Then, the psychologist *hypothesized* at least temporarily, that the drug actually had no effect on learning performance and that the group of 20 drugged rats would perform just like a group of 20 non-drugged animals (since they were random selections from that population). If this hypothesis were true, then the mean performance of this small sample should not be unusually deviant from the non-drugged population mean, $\mu = 125$. Before the experiment the scientist established some *decision rules* such that if the mean of the drugged animals was a value that fell between $P_{.025}$ and $P_{.975}$ for the sampling distribution of means based upon non-drugged animals, there would be no cause to dispute the hypothesis that the drug has no effect, since such a result would be a reasonable outcome for non-drugged animals. On the other hand, what would happen if the observed mean for the drugged group was so different from the population mean of non-drugged animals that such a value should be expected of non-drugged rats in only 5% *or less of such samples*? The scientist would question the hypothesis that the drug had no effect and then would conduct the experiment, observe the sample mean of drugged rats to be $\overline{X} = 130$, and *computationally translate* that value into standard normal deviates (since the population distribution was normal in form) by the formula

$$z = \frac{\overline{X} - \mu}{\sigma_x/\sqrt{N}} = \frac{130 - 125}{10.5/\sqrt{20}} = 2.13$$

The value, $z = 2.13$, corresponded to a percentile rank of $P_{.9834}$ in the standard normal distribution. This was judged to be quite different from what might have been expected of non-drugged rats, since the probability of observing a mean as extreme as $\overline{X} = 130$ is less than .05. Thus, the scientist *decides* that the drug might actually have an effect on learning performance. We will now apply more formal terminology to the concepts and processes described in this example.

FORMAL EXAMPLE

statistical assumptions and hypotheses Statistical inference as described above requires defining a statistical context by making some assumptions. In the example, the assumptions were that the rats were randomly and independently selected from a non-drugged population and that the sampling distribution of the mean is normal in form. The latter assumption is met if the population distribution of raw scores is normal or if N is large. Although the scientist attempted to actually sample rats randomly and did have some previously collected information about the normality of the population distribution, one can seldom be certain that these assumptions are, in fact, the case. Rather, certain characteristics of the situation must be assumed to be true.

Next, the psychologist "pretended" that the drug actually had no effect.

Of course, the drug could have some influence, but the scientist temporarily supposed that it did not. In this step of the process, the psychologist considers two hypotheses about what is true. Such hypotheses are mutually contradictory (e.g., either the drug has an effect or it does not), and most often they exhaust the possibilities. Finally, one of the hypotheses is tentatively held to be true.

> The hypothesis that is tentatively held to be true is called the **null hypothesis** and is customarily symbolized by H_0. The **alternative hypothesis** is represented by H_1.

In the present example the null and alternative hypotheses may be stated:

H_0: The observed mean is computed on a sample drawn from a population with $\mu = 125$ (i.e., the drug has no effect).

H_1: The observed mean is computed on a sample drawn from a population with $\mu \neq 125$ (i.e., the drug has some effect).

The assumptions and hypotheses are crucial to the statistical logic. If it is assumed that the sample of 20 rats is randomly selected from the population of non-drugged rats and if the null hypothesis that the drug has no effect is tentatively held to be true, then the sample of 20 drugged animals should behave like a typical sample of 20 non-drugged rats. By further assuming that the population distribution is normal in form, the sampling distribution of the mean will also be normal, and the percentiles of the standard normal distribution can be used to determine the probability that a random sample of 20 non-drugged rats should have a mean as deviant from $\mu = 125$ as the observed average of 130. If the probability is small that non-drugged animals would have a mean of 130, then perhaps the hypothesis of no drug effect which was tentatively held true at the beginning is actually false and should be rejected.

There are important differences between assumptions and hypotheses. While both assumptions and hypotheses are statements about what is true in nature and are often phrased in terms of population parameters, hypotheses represent a set of two or more contradictory and often exhaustive possibilities, only one of which can actually be the case. Thus, while all assumptions are presumed to be true, only one of the hypotheses can be true. Moreover, one of the hypotheses is temporarily held to be true (i.e., the null hypothesis), and it is the reasonableness of this hypothesis which is being tested by these statistical procedures. The logic is as follows: Tentatively hold the null hypothesis to be true (i.e., the drug has no effect). If the results of the analysis could have reasonably occurred given that assumption (i.e., the mean of the drugged group could probably have been scored by a non-drugged group), there is no reason to question the validity of that hypothesis of no drug effect. If the analysis indicates that the likelihood is very small that a non-drugged group could have produced this mean, the null hypothesis is rejected in favor of the alternative hypothesis. Notice that the assumptions of random sampling and normality remain constant and are assumed true regardless of the outcome of the experiment; only the null hypothesis is tentatively held and then either rejected or not rejected.

significance level   The assumptions and hypotheses determine the statistical context and logic for making a decision, but they do not answer the question of *how different* the sample mean must be from the population mean before one will reject the null hypothesis. This decision is cast in terms of probability: If the probability that the observed sample mean could be produced by a non-drugged group is very small, less than a certain value, then one will reject the null hypothesis. That "certain probability value" is the significance level of the test of the null hypothesis:

> The **significance level** (or **critical level**), symbolized by α (read "alpha"), is the probability value that forms the boundary between rejecting or not rejecting the null hypothesis.

In social science research the precise value of α is customarily taken to be .05. This implies that if the probability is less than .05 that the observed mean for drugged rats could have been obtained by non-drugged animals, the null hypothesis that the drug has no effect will be rejected, and this result is said to be "significant at the .05 level" or that "$p < .05$."

In the current example, the population mean is $\mu = 125$. Random samples of size 20 selected from the population of non-drugged animals will probably not have a mean which precisely equals this population value. That is, the sampling distribution of means describes the values of sample means likely to be obtained if the drug has no effect (i.e., H_0 is true). The researcher chooses a significance level of .05, which implies that unless the observed mean is so different from the population μ of 125 such that it would be expected of non-drugged animals less than 5% of the time, the researcher will not challenge the validity of H_0. However, if it was improbable (i.e., $p < .05$), the null hypothesis will be rejected and the conclusion will be that the drug probably did exert some influence. The significance level, in this case .05, represents the probability value that separates a decision to reject from a decision not to reject the null hypothesis.

decision rules   Once the significance level has been established, it is clear how improbable the observed result must be under the null hypothesis before that hypothesis is rejected. The significance level can then be used to formulate decision rules which are simply statements, phrased in terms of the statistics to be calculated, which dictate precisely when the null hypothesis will be rejected and when it will not.

> **Decision rules** are statements that designate the statistical conditions necessary for rejecting the null hypothesis.

Decision rules represent a formalization of the decision process based upon the significance level, but they are stated in terms of the statistics to be computed rather than in terms of probability. In the example above, the researcher selected the .05 level of significance. This implies that the null hypothesis will be rejected only if the observed sample mean deviates from the mean of the population of non-drugged animals to an extent likely to occur in non-drugged samples less than 5% of the time. The sampling distribution of the mean represents a theoretical relative frequency distribution of means based upon all possible samples of 20 non-drugged rats. Since the observed mean could be extremely high or low relative to the non-drugged population mean of 125, $P_{.025}$ and $P_{.975}$ of the sampling distribution of the mean define a range of values which in the long run would include 95% of the means of non-drugged samples and exclude 5%, $2\frac{1}{2}\%$ because they are extremely low and $2\frac{1}{2}\%$ because they are extremely high. Since the sampling distribution of the mean is normal in form, the standard normal distribution may be used to translate these percentile ranks into percentile points (i.e., z values). Looking at Table A in Appendix II and remembering that the standard normal is a symmetrical distribution about $z = 0$, one searches for the z value such that .025 of the distribution lies to its right (i.e., more extreme). Scanning the right-most column for .0250, one finds the corresponding z to be 1.96. Thus, $P_{.025}$ and $P_{.975}$ correspond to points $z = -1.96$ and $z = 1.96$.

This process is pictured in Figure 9–1. The normal distribution presented in this graph represents the theoretical sampling distribution of means for samples ($N = 20$) from the non-drugged population, but it is expressed in terms of standard normal deviates. Thus, the population mean ($\mu = 125$) is represented by $z = 0$. Since $P_{.025}$ and $P_{.975}$ correspond to $z = -1.96$ and $z = 1.96$, respectively, these points include 95% of the possible sample means, $47\frac{1}{2}\%$ on each side of $z = 0$. Thus, the shaded areas each contain $2\frac{1}{2}\%$ of the cases, and together constitute the 5% extreme sample means that would result in rejecting the null hypothesis. Since the observed sample mean ($\overline{X} = 130$) will be translated into a z value equivalent, it will be readily apparent whether the null hypothesis should be rejected. The formal statement of the decision rules is:

If z is between -1.96 and $+1.96$, do not reject H_0.
If z is less than or equal to -1.96 or greater than or equal to $+1.96$, reject H_0.

The same statements can be expressed symbolically by using the symbols $<$ ("less than"), $>$ ("greater than"), $\geq$ ("greater than or equal to"), etc.:

If $-1.96 < z < +1.96$, do not reject H_0.
If $z \leq -1.96$ or $z \geq +1.96$, reject H_0.

The z values of ± 1.96 in this example are called **critical values**, because they

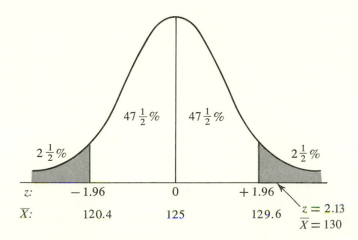

Fig. 9–1.   The sampling distribution of the mean expressed in standard normal
deviates (z) and sample means ($\overline{X}$).

separate z values that will result in a decision to reject or not to reject the null
hypothesis. Thus, the shaded areas in Figure 9–1 define the **critical region** or
region of rejection of the null hypothesis.

computation   The statistical procedures take advantage
of theoretical relative frequency distributions for which percentiles are already
available. In the example we have been considering, the standard normal was
used but there will be other theoretical distributions employed in different
contexts later in the text. The technique involves converting the observed statistic
(e.g., the mean) into a standard normal deviate so that this value can be compared with the critical values previously established. In this case, $\overline{X} = 130$ was
equivalent to $z = 2.13$.

In order to discriminate observed from critical values of the standardized
variable, subscripts are often used. In our example,

$$z_{\text{obs}} = 2.13$$

represents the value corresponding to the observed data while

$$z_{\text{crit}} = \pm 1.96$$

indicates the critical values of z.

decision   In the example, $z = 2.13$ falls within the
critical region (Fig. 9–1) which dictates that the null hypothesis is to be
rejected. This implies that the obtained mean of 130 ($z = 2.13$) would be
expected to occur in less than 5% of such samples of 20 non-drugged rats.

Consequently, since it is unlikely that a value should occur merely as a function of sampling error in picking some rats as opposed to others, the null hypothesis of no drug effect is rejected.

It is important that one understands the relationship between the logic of this statistical process and the concept of sampling error introduced in the previous chapter. Assuming the drug has no effect (i.e., H_0 is true), the statistical procedure compares the observed mean with the sampling distribution of means for the non-drugged population. This sampling distribution reflects the extent of sampling error for means derived on samples of size 20. The standard deviation of this sampling distribution of the mean is a numerical index of the amount of sampling error one would expect—the extent to which the mean of one sample will differ from the mean of another sample, even if these samples are treated exactly alike. If the observed mean is not a likely value in this sampling distribution, we reject the null hypothesis. In that case, one can say that the observed mean was so discrepant from what would have been expected on the basis of sampling error that it was unlikely that a mean of this magnitude could be obtained merely by chance variation from sample to sample. On the other hand, if the observed value is not sufficient to reject the null hypothesis, one can conclude that the mean of the drugged animals could have occurred even if the drug had no effect, since it could have been reasonably expected to deviate from the population average on the basis of sampling error alone (random variation between samples, "chance," etc.).

This interpretation can be understood from a different standpoint by examining the formula for translating the observed mean into a standard normal deviate of the theoretical sampling distribution of the mean:

$$z = \frac{\overline{X} - \mu}{\sigma_{\overline{x}}}$$

The formula simply states that z is the ratio of the difference between the sample mean and the mean of the non-drugged population ($\overline{X} - \mu$) relative to the amount of expected sampling error as expressed by its numerical index, the standard error of the mean ($\sigma_{\overline{x}}$). It is for this reason that this formula is sometimes called a **critical ratio**.

In a sense, the statistical test simply asks how different was the observed mean from the population mean relative to the sampling error one might expect. As this ratio increases in size, one begins to suspect that the difference between observed and population means is probably not simply a function of random variation between samples, chance, or more precisely, sampling error.

Note that the wording of the decision to reject the null hypothesis (when this is appropriate) is *not* stated as "accepting the alternative hypothesis." One "rejects H_0"; one does *not* "accept H_1." The reason for this is that only one hypothesis, the null hypothesis, was tested. It was tentatively held to be true and the statistical procedures carried out to determine if the data were reasonable under these conditions. Since they were not, H_0 is rejected as probably not being a valid characterization of what really exists. Since it was H_0 that was tested, the decision is made in reference to H_0, not H_1.

Similarly, if the results do not warrant rejecting the null hypothesis, one does not "accept the null hypothesis." In this case, the results simply do not demand that one reject H_0. It may seem like quibbling to insist on a distinction between "not rejecting" and "accepting" the null hypothesis, but the failure to understand the difference often reflects a failure to understand the logic of this statistical procedure. Suppose the observed value of z is not in the critical region and thus is not large enough to reject the null hypothesis. This does not necessarily say that the drug has no effect. It may influence learning performance, but not very much. Thus, the difference it produces is not large enough relative to the amount of sampling error to produce a z value sufficient to reject the null hypothesis in a sample of this size. The same difference might lead to rejecting H_0 in a larger sample. This is one reason why one does not "prove" or "accept" the null hypothesis—one simply has no cause to reject it.

additional considerations

decision errors Generally, the purpose of statistical inference is to make an educated guess about what exists in a population when only a small subset of cases from that population has been studied. Since the decision is a guess, it might be wrong.

As one comes to understand the logic of hypothesis testing one also begins to see that it is an approximate method and one can certainly make the wrong decision. In fact, if the significance level is .05, in 5% of the cases in which the drug actually has no effect, the researcher will make a decision (erroneously) to reject the null hypothesis. This is part of the logic of the procedure. You observe a sample mean and ask how likely is it to obtain such a mean if the drug has no effect. You arbitrarily decide that if such a mean should occur less than 5% of the time, assuming H_0, you will suspect the null hypothesis is incorrect. But suppose the null hypothesis was quite correct. Then, in 5% of the cases in which you observe a mean that deviates so much from the population value—purely because of sampling error and random variation—you would follow the decision rules and reject the null hypothesis. But, of course, you would have made an erroneous decision about what really exists: the drug *actually* has no effect, but you have made a *decision* that it does. This is called a Type I Error.

A **Type I Error** occurs when the null hypothesis is rejected when it is, in fact, true. Given the validity of the null hypothesis, the probability that it is erroneously rejected by these procedures equals α, the significance level.

There is another type of error that can be made. Suppose the null hypothesis is *actually* wrong, that is, the drug does indeed have an effect; however, the *decision* process may result in not rejecting the null hypothesis when it should be rejected.

> A **Type II Error** occurs when the null hypothesis is not rejected when, in fact, it is false. The probability of this type of error is symbolized by β.

The decision-making process is diagrammed in Figure 9–2. The distribution labeled H_0 represents the distribution of means (for samples with $N = 20$) of non-drugged rats. The shaded areas in the tails of this distribution constitute the region of rejection. If the null hypothesis is actually true, then this shaded area represents the probability of a Type I Error since means in this region would provoke a decision to reject the null hypothesis when it is actually true. Now shift your attention to the distribution labeled H_1, the distribution of means for drugged rats. Assume that H_1 is, in fact, true and the drug has an effect. Because of the overlap in the distributions, it is possible that some sample means would fall close enough to the mean of the non-drugged population so that the psychologist in his decision process would commit a Type II Error by failing to reject H_0 when it was false. A mean at point a would be such a case. The area labeled β in Figure 9–2 corresponds to means for drugged rats for which the statistical process would erroneously declare that the drug had no effect. It represents the probability of a Type II Error. However, the distribution under H_1 is rarely available, and hence it is usually impossible to estimate the size of β.

There are two other areas to notice in Figure 9–2. The portion of H_0 that is not in the region of rejection represents the probability of correctly refusing to reject $H_0(p = 1 - \alpha)$. The portion of H_1 that is not part of β represents the probability of correctly rejecting $H_0(p = 1 - \beta)$. This latter probability is called the **power** of a test. Table 9–1 summarizes these points.

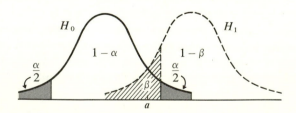

Fig. 9–2. Diagram of the relationship between Type I (α) and Type II (β) Errors and power ($1 - \beta$).

9–1   The Four Possible Outcomes of a Simple Decision Process and Their Associated Probabilities.

	Actual Situation	
	H_0 **is true**	H_0 **is false**
Reject H_0	*Type I Error* $p = \alpha$	*Correct Decision* $p = 1 - \beta$ (power)
Do Not Reject H_0	*Correct Decision* $p = 1 - \alpha$	*Type II Error* $p = \beta$

Decision

---

power of a statistical test   The power of a statistical test can be defined as follows:

The **power** of a statistical test is the probability that the test will correctly decide to reject H_0 when H_0 is indeed false.

In a sense this is a major requirement of a good statistical test. If H_0 is actually not true and should be rejected, we want to know that the statistical test we are using will come to that same conclusion. However, Type II Errors, in which the test concludes not to reject H_0 when H_0 is actually false, occur with a probability of β. Thus, the power of a test is $1 - \beta$. This means that the probability of correctly rejecting H_0 is $1 - \beta$. The actual value of this probability is difficult to obtain since it requires one to know the H_1 distribution. That is, one must already know what actually exists in nature. We rarely have this information — indeed, that is why we are performing the statistical test in the first place.

Obviously, researchers would like their statistical procedures to have as much power as possible. Despite the fact that we usually cannot precisely calculate the power of a statistical test, there are some ways of increasing this probability. First, **the power of a statistical test tends to increase as the significance level, α, increases**. Thus, a test performed at a significance level of .05 has more power than one at .01. Obviously, the less stringent the significance level, the more likely the null hypothesis will be rejected. But both correct and incorrect rejections will be more likely, so that simply having a larger value of α will increase the power but also increase the probability of a Type I Error.

Second, **the power of a test increases with sample size.** Thus, the likelihood of correctly rejecting H_0 is better for a sample of 30 than a sample of 20.

Third, **some statistical tests are more powerful than others.** For example, the techniques described in Chapters 10–12 are called parametric tests while those discussed in Chapter 13 are nonparametric tests. In general, given their assumptions, parametric tests are more powerful than nonparametric tests and are usually preferred. However, when the parametric assumptions cannot be made, nonparametric tests are sometimes used (see pages 298–328).

selecting the significance level It is now apparent that the significance level is the probability of erroneously rejecting the null hypothesis when it is, in fact, true (Type I Error). How does one go about setting this level? In a very real sense, the value of α reflects the investigator's feeling of how much error is tolerable in making a decision to reject H_0 on the one hand, balanced with how much power is wanted in the statistical test on the other. Ordinarily, social scientists accept the ".05 level of significance" as the value of α, but this is merely a convention that has grown up over the years and there is nothing fixed about it. When testing some hypotheses, other levels of significance might be adopted depending upon how critical it is to be wrong in rejecting the null hypothesis. For example, if you were a brain surgeon and were giving a test to determine whether a patient needed a very delicate type of surgery, it might be that you could not afford to risk an operation if the patient really didn't need one (i.e., if your diagnosis is wrong). Therefore, you might operate only if the probability is less than .01 or .001 that the test result is just a sampling error. However, the more unlikely you make the possibility of incorrectly rejecting the null hypothesis and performing the operation (Type I Error), the more likely a patient with a condition needing an operation will be diagnosed incorrectly as being able to do without it (incorrectly failing to reject H_0; a Type II Error). In any situation, it is important to remember that the level of significance is arbitrarily established on the basis of the researcher's tolerance for error in decision-making and the desire for statistical power. However, depending upon the circumstances, the reader may feel differently than the researcher about the relative sizes of error and power that the reader personally feels comfortable in accepting. Therefore, it might be a reasonable procedure to adopt a significance level but to report the actual probability found as a result of testing H_0, regardless of whether one rejects H_0 or not.

directional tests The test of the null hypothesis described in the drug example was a **non-directional test**. It was non-directional because the alternative hypothesis (H_1) did not specify the direction of the influence of the drug. Would it help or hinder learning? It only suggested the drug would influence performance, one way or the other. Consequently, the critical region was established so that extreme values in either direction would lead to a decision to reject H_0.

However, suppose this same drug had been found by other scientists to improve memory for simple visual stimuli in rats, and the psychologist wonders if its administration will also improve maze learning. Since it is very unlikely that the drug would actually hinder maze learning, the psychologist establishes the alternative hypothesis as

H_1: The observed mean is computed on a sample drawn from a population with $\mu > 125$, (i.e., the drug facilitates learning).

This is a **directional** hypothesis since it prescribes that the mean will be higher than 125.

In such an event, it would be unreasonable to divide the critical region into two parts so that extreme means in either direction would lead to rejecting the null hypothesis. Suppose the previous research information suggested that the probability is almost zero that drugged rats would exhibit an extremely low mean. Therefore, in order to maintain the significance level at .05, (i.e., the probability of erroneously rejecting the null hypothesis), the extreme 5% of the scores in the right-hand tail of the distribution constitutes the region of rejection. When looking in Table A of the standard normal, one searches for the z value such that .0500 of the area falls between it and the right-hand tail. This critical value is $z = 1.645$. A comparison of the regions of rejection for these non-directional and directional tests is presented in Figure 9–3.

Since a non-directional test locates the critical region in both tails of the theoretical distribution, it is frequently called a **two-tailed test**. Conversely, since a directional test locates the critical region in only one end of the distribution, it is called a **one-tailed test**.

In determining whether a test should be directional or non-directional, one considers whether there is other evidence or a theory which might predict the result. There needs to be some basis for presuming that a sample mean will deviate in only one direction from the population value. Then H_1 and the critical values are established in accordance with that prediction. However, this choice of a directional or non-directional test must be established before one knows the experimental result. Otherwise, if one waits to know the data and then decides to make a directional instead of a non-directional test, the theoretical probabilities involved in the significance level (e.g., $\alpha = .05$) are no longer appropriate. Therefore, the statistical hypotheses must be stated before the experimental observations are made.

Students frequently have difficulty understanding the rationale of making directional tests. One might look at Figure 9–3 and wonder, "If you have some reason for predicting that the sample mean will be greater than the mean of the

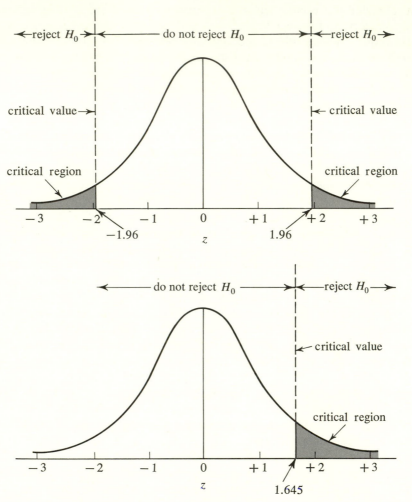

Fig. 9–3. Decision process for a non-directional (two-tailed) test (top) and a directional (one-tailed) test (bottom).

population of non-drugged rats, why does one select a lower critical value which seems to make it easier to reject the null hypothesis?" It seems like it should be the other way around: If you know that the difference between means will likely be positive (to the right of $z = 0$), then the critical value of z should be more stringent (i.e., further to the right) in order to balance out the advantage gained by being able to predict the direction of a difference. While it is easy to understand how Figure 9–3 gives this impression, the explanation for why there is an apparent "advantage" in rejecting the null hypothesis using one-tailed tests rests in the purpose of α, the significance level. Most of us, students and researchers, are interested in rejecting the null hypothesis. We want to have "significant" results. But, the significance level refers to the probability of rejecting the null hypothesis *by mistake*—that is, deciding there is a difference when no difference actually exists. The problem, then, is to conduct both a directional and a non-directional test at the .05 level of significance comparable to one another in terms of the probability of falsely rejecting H_0. If it is really the case that the difference between the drugged group mean and the non-drugged population mean could be positive or negative, then the region of rejection should include extreme scores on both sides of the population mean. Thus, a non-directional or two-tailed test can make an error in rejecting the null hypothesis by having extreme differences due to sampling error in either direction. However, if there is some reason to think that the sample mean will be larger than the population, either because there is empirical evidence or a theory that suggests this will be the case, there is very little chance that sampling error will produce extremely large negative differences. For example, experimental teaching methods are expected to improve test scores and almost never produce scores lower than the old teaching method. To use a two-tailed, non-directional alternative in this instance would really constitute a test at the .025 level of significance, because it is known that extreme negative differences will not occur. Therefore, in order to insure that the probability of a Type I Error is indeed the value of α, it is necessary to place all of the critical region in the right-hand tail. Then, there will still be a .05 probability of a mean being extreme for reasons of sampling error alone.

hypothesis testing when σ_x is estimated by s_x

STUDENT'S t DISTRIBUTION

The expression used above which translated a sample mean into a standard normal deviate is

$$z = \frac{\bar{X} - \mu}{\sigma_{\bar{x}}}$$

In this case z is a standard normal deviate (if the sampling distribution of the mean is normal), μ is the population mean of the sampling distribution of $\bar{X}$'s determined for all possible samples of size N from the population, and $\sigma_{\bar{x}}$ is the theoretical standard deviation of such $\bar{X}$'s. Up to this point, the formulas presented have always involved a parameter, for example $\sigma_{\bar{x}}$. Regrettably, the value of this parameter is usually not available, so it must be estimated.

The standard error of the sampling distribution of the mean, $s_{\bar{x}}$, which can be calculated on the basis of a single sample of scores ($s_{\bar{x}} = s_x/\sqrt{N}$), may be used for this estimation. However, when $s_{\bar{x}}$ is invoked to estimate $\sigma_{\bar{x}}$, the accuracy of $s_{\bar{x}}$ as an estimator and thus the accuracy of the probability value derived from the standard normal distribution depends upon the size of the sample, N. If the sample is quite large ($N > 50$ or 100), the probabilities derived from using the standard normal distribution as described above are fairly accurate. But, most samples in social science are not so large, and it happens that when $\sigma_{\bar{x}}$ is estimated by $s_{\bar{x}}$ calculated on a small sample, the standard normal does not provide sufficiently accurate probabilities. Fortunately, another theoretical sampling distribution exists, the Student's t distribution, which is appropriate for these situations.

The **Student's t distribution** is a theoretical sampling distribution developed by W. S. Gosset who wrote under the name of "Student." When scores are transformed in the following way, the Student's t distribution is appropriate rather than the standard normal:

$$t = \frac{\bar{X} - \mu}{s_{\bar{x}}} = \frac{\bar{X} - \mu}{s_x/\sqrt{N}}$$

Notice that except for substituting t for z and $s_{\bar{x}}$ for $\sigma_{\bar{x}}$, the formula is of the same form as that used in the examples above. The t distribution, however, differs from the normal. In addition to permitting the parameter $\sigma_{\bar{x}}$ to be estimated by the sample statistic $s_{\bar{x}}$, there is a different t distribution for each size of sample upon which $s_{\bar{x}}$ is computed. The appropriate t distribution is determined not by the sample size, N, but by its **degrees of freedom**, $N - 1$ in

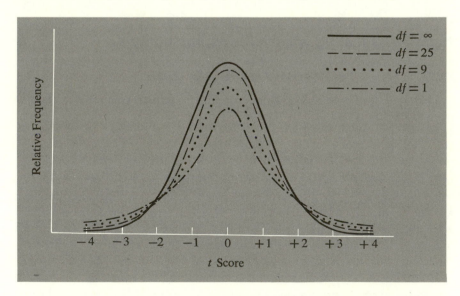

Fig. 9–4. The t distribution for various degrees of freedom. With an infinite number of degrees of freedom, the t and the standard normal (z) distributions are identical.

this case. Figure 9–4 shows the t distribution for several degrees of freedom. It also depicts the standard normal ($df = \infty$). Notice that the t and z distributions are quite different when the sample size (and thus degrees of freedom) is small, but as the number of degrees of freedom increases the t distribution becomes more and more like the normal. In fact, when the sample size is allowed to be theoretically infinite, the t and standard normal distributions are identical.[1]

degrees of freedom   Undoubtedly, one of the most difficult concepts for students to grasp, but also one of the most necessary, is that of degrees of freedom. Unfortunately, it is not easy to provide a clear, concise definition.

> The number of **degrees of freedom (df)** for any statistic is the number of components in its calculation that are free to vary.

The meaning of this definition is best explained by considering some examples. In a sense, every statistic in a specific context has a certain number of degrees of freedom associated with it. For example, the sample mean, $\bar{X}$, has N degrees of freedom. How does one know that? In words, the number of degrees of freedom equals the number of components in the calculation of $\bar{X}$ which are free to vary— which implies they can take on different values. Begin by examining the formula for the mean:

$$\bar{X} = \frac{\sum X_i}{N}$$

The first question to ask is which components of this formula can vary at all and which cannot. When calculating a mean from any specified sample of scores, the N does not vary. It is a constant, fixed in value for this sample. In contrast, the scores, X_i, which compose the $\sum X_i$ do take on different values—they are free to vary or assume any possible value given knowledge of N. Moreover, each of the scores could assume any possible value, and knowing the values of all but one score does not tell us the value of that last score. If there are five scores, and we know four of them, (3, 7, 5, 2, ?), there is no way for us to determine the value of "?." Thus, we must know all N scores to calculate the mean. It is in this sense that all N scores are free to vary (i.e., take on any values), and thus the degrees of freedom for the statistic, $\bar{X}$, is simply N.

---

[1] Some texts suggest that if the sample size is 30 or more, the normal and t distributions are similar enough so that the normal distribution (z) may be used even though $s_{\bar{x}}$ has been estimated. While an examination of the tables for z and t in the appendix certainly indicates a great degree of correspondence between the normal and t for samples of 30 or more, it will be the policy of this book to suggest that the t distribution always be used when a parameter is being estimated regardless of sample size. This policy results in greater accuracy in determining probabilities and somewhat less confusion.

The task becomes more complicated when we consider the number of degrees of freedom for the variance. Again, begin with the formula:

$$s_x^2 = \frac{\Sigma(X_i - \overline{X})^2}{N - 1}$$

Neither the sample size, N, nor the mean, $\overline{X}$ is free to vary. For any specified sample, they are constants. However, the deviations between each score and the mean $(X_i - \overline{X})$ take on different values depending upon the scores in the distribution. How many of these N deviations are free to vary? It happens that all but one of these deviations are free to vary, due to the fact that the sum of the deviations of scores about their own mean is always zero, $\Sigma(X_i - \overline{X}) = 0$. Knowing $N - 1$ of these deviations, you can always determine the last one because its value is such that the sum of all the deviations is zero. For example, consider the following distribution: 5, 7, 9. The mean is 7. Note what happens if any two of the deviations are computed:

X_i	$\overline{X}$	$(X_i - \overline{X})$
5	7	−2
7	7	0
9	7	?

The chart shows that two of the deviations are −2 and 0. Recall now, however, that the sum of the deviations from the mean is always zero [i.e., $\Sigma(X_i - \overline{X}) = 0$]. Since this is true, the third deviation must be such that when added to the others the sum is zero:

$$-2 + 0 + \text{(last deviation)} = \quad 0$$
$$\text{last deviation} = +2$$

It is in this sense that the last deviation to be computed, regardless of which particular score in the distribution is remaining, is not free to vary but is determined. Knowing $N - 1$ of the deviations, you can determine the precise value of the last deviation. Therefore, only $N - 1$ deviations are free to vary— free to take on any value. Thus, the number of degrees of freedom for the sample variance is $df = N - 1$.

The degrees of freedom for t are also $N - 1$. The formula for t is

$$t = \frac{\overline{X} - \mu}{s_x/\sqrt{N}}$$

The population mean, the mean for this sample, and N are all constants. Thus, the degrees of freedom for t are the degrees of freedom for s_x which we have seen is $N - 1$. When selecting the proper critical values for a statistical test involving the t distribution, one must know the degrees of freedom for t. The present application of the t distribution dictates that t have $N - 1$ degrees of freedom. Other applications of t discussed in the next chapter may have different numbers of df associated with them.

Notice also that whenever a statistic is used to estimate a population value, it is likely that the denominator for that statistic will contain the degrees of freedom. Since we frequently use s_x to estimate σ_x, we divide $\sum(X_i - \bar{X})^2$ by its degrees of freedom, $N - 1$, rather than simply by N. Similarly, for the standard error of estimate whose degrees of freedom equal $N - 2$:

$$s_{y.x} = \sqrt{\frac{\sum(Y_i - \tilde{Y})^2}{N - 2}}$$

The number of degrees of freedom for any statistic is also related to the number of parameters that must be estimated in order to calculate the statistic. For example, $\bar{X}$ is an estimate of the population mean and this estimate must be determined before the standard deviation can be calculated. The number of degrees of freedom for the standard deviation is the number of cases involved (i.e., N) minus the number of parameters being estimated (i.e., 1): $df = N - 1$. The standard error of estimate in the context of regression has $N - 2$ degrees of freedom because the $\tilde{Y}$ in the numerator $[\sum(Y_i - \tilde{Y})^2]$ can only be determined if the regression constants a and b are known. The estimation of these two values implies that the number of degrees of freedom for $s_{y.x}$ equals $N - 2$.

APPLICATION OF THE t DISTRIBUTION

Suppose the researcher decided to randomly select a sample of 20 rats and give each of them the drug prior to a daily testing session; but, suppose that the standard deviation of the population of non-drugged rats is not available. The population distribution is still regarded as being normal in form with $\mu = 125$. The researcher wishes to test the hypothesis that the observed mean is computed on a sample drawn from a population with $\mu = 125$.

The expression

$$t = \frac{\bar{X} - \mu}{s_x/\sqrt{N}}, \, df = N - 1$$

changes the unit and origin of the distribution of sample means into standardized t units when $s_x/\sqrt{N}$ is used to estimate $\sigma_{\bar{x}}$. With certain assumptions similar to those invoked to use the standard normal, the t distribution may be employed in the same manner as has been demonstrated with the standard normal distribution. The t distribution is found in Table B of Appendix II. Since it is somewhat different from the standard normal, it deserves a brief examination. In general, the table consists of the critical values of t for various significance levels at each of several degrees of freedom. The degrees of freedom are located in the left-most column. To their right one finds various values of t for different significance levels. Since the t distribution (like the z) is symmetrical, a two-tailed test at the .05 level at $N - 1 = 20 - 1 = 19$ degrees of freedom implies that $2\frac{1}{2}\%$ of such t's fall to the left of -2.093 and $2\frac{1}{2}\%$ fall to the right of $+2.093$. If a one-tailed test at 19 df at the .01 level of significance were appropriate, the entire 1% of the area under the curve would fall to the right of 2.539. Thus, the t table gives the critical values of t for various degrees of freedom and levels of significance for both directional and non-directional tests.

One should observe two additional things about t. First, for any given level of significance the value of t that is required to reject H_0 (critical value of t) becomes smaller as the number of degrees of freedom increases. Consider the third column for a two-tailed test at the .05 level of significance. With only one degree of freedom, $t = 12.706$ is required to reject H_0, whereas $t = 4.303$ is needed if the $df = 2$. If there are an infinite number of degrees of freedom, $t = 1.96$ is required which is precisely the value of the standard normal distribution for this situation. Thus, as the number of degrees of freedom increases the critical value of t decreases until it approaches the same value that the standard normal would dictate.

Second, the smaller the standard error the more likely the null hypothesis will be rejected. This cannot be seen from the t table but it can be appreciated by examining the expression for t:

$$t = \frac{\overline{X} - \mu}{s_{\overline{x}}}$$

Since the ratio of two quantities becomes larger as the denominator becomes smaller, it can be seen that the value of t grows larger as the standard error $(s_{\overline{x}})$ of the mean becomes smaller. Thus, the smaller the standard error the more likely the null hypothesis will be rejected when it is false.

A formal presentation of the solution to this hypothesis testing problem follows. Its format may be used as a model to follow when formal hypothesis testing solutions are required.

problem   If the mean number of correct trials of the population of non-drugged rats is 125, does the mean $\overline{X}$ of a random sample of 20 rats that are given a drug differ sufficiently from that population to warrant the conclusion that the drug has an effect on learning performance?

hypotheses

H_0: $\overline{X}$ is computed on a sample from a population with $\mu = 125$
H_1: $\overline{X}$ is computed on a sample from a population with $\mu \neq 125$

assumptions It is assumed (1) the rats are randomly and independently sampled, and (2) the population of non-drugged rats is normal with $\mu = 125$.

significance level Assume the .05 level.

critical values Since the alternative hypothesis H_1 was non-directional and $\alpha = .05$, t values must be selected so that $2\frac{1}{2}\%$ of the t distribution falls to the left of one and $2\frac{1}{2}\%$ falls to the right of the other critical value. Looking in Table B with $N - 1 = 20 - 1 = 19$ df, these critical values are -2.093 and $+2.093$.

decision rules

If t is between -2.093 and $+2.093$, do not reject H_0.

If t is less than or equal to -2.093 or greater than or equal to $+2.093$, reject H_0.

computation Suppose the experiment is conducted, the observed mean is 130, and the standard deviation is 9.5. Placing these values into the expression for t one obtains

$$t_{\text{obs}} = \frac{\bar{X} - \mu}{s_x/\sqrt{N}} = \frac{130 - 125}{9.5/\sqrt{20}} = 2.35$$

decision The observed t of 2.35 exceeds the critical values and falls within the province of the second decision rule to reject H_0. It is concluded that given the expected amount of variability in means of samples of size 20, the mean of 130 is too deviant from $\mu = 125$. Thus if the null hypothesis of no drug effect were true, this would be a very unlikely result. Since a mean as extreme as 130 would not likely occur by chance or sampling error alone, the hypothesis of no drug effect is rejected at the $p < .05$ level. The experimenter concludes that the drug may have an effect on learning performance.

summary of hypothesis testing The researcher is faced with the problem of deciding whether the results obtained in an experiment represent chance or sampling variability, or whether the factors isolated or manipulated actually produced differences. On the basis of sample data, the scientist must make a decision about what exists in a population not available for study. First, certain assumptions about the sampling procedures and the parameters of the populations are made. Second, usually two mutually exclusive hypotheses are offered about the population that reflect in statistical terms the researcher's scientific question. One of these hypotheses, the null hypothesis, is tentatively assumed to be true. Third, a significance level is selected; then, as a function of the nature of the alternative hypothesis, the significance level and the particular theoretical distribution to be used, critical values and decision rules are established. Fourth, the experiment is conducted and the salient aspects of the data converted into the chosen standardized theoretical distribution. Fifth, the observed transformed statistic is compared with the decision rules, and a decision to reject or not reject the null hypothesis is made. If the observed result deviated so much from what would be expected if the null hypothesis were true that it fell in the area of rejection, the tenability of the null hypothesis would be in doubt and it would be rejected. Conversely, if the observed value did not deviate markedly from what would be expected if the null hypothesis were true, the null hypothesis would not be rejected, and it would be concluded that the observed results apparently deviate from the hypothesized parametric values merely as a function of sampling error.

CONFIDENCE INTERVALS FOR THE MEAN

Suppose that a psychologist in a school system wanted to know what the average IQ of the students was in a given high school. It is rather expensive to give an IQ test to each student in the school so a random sample of 25 students is tested. Suppose the sample mean is 109 with a standard deviation of 15.

If the psychologist were required to estimate with one value the mean IQ in the population of all students in the high school, the estimate would be 109. After all, the sample mean is an unbiased estimator of the population mean, and if the sample were indeed random, one would feel somewhat confident that the sample mean of 109 was near the population mean. However, if you were to ask the psychologist whether the population mean was exactly 109, the answer would certainly be no. Well, how close is 109 to the population value?

An approach to answering this question is to give a range of values such that one feels reasonably confident that the interval limited by these values includes the population mean. For example, the psychologist might say that the population mean would likely be within 6 points of the sample mean, and thus the interval of 103–115 is likely to contain the population mean. It would be helpful to be more precise about this procedure such that one could make a probability statement concerning just how "confident" one was that the suggested interval actually contained the population mean. The procedure for determining such an interval is analogous to that discussed on pages 110–111 with respect to predicting from a regression line.

The interval to be constructed is called a **confidence interval** and the values describing the boundaries of such an interval are the **confidence limits**. The degree of "confidence" in the proposition that the stated interval actually contains the population mean is indicated by a probability value. Of course, one would expect that a very large interval would more likely contain the population value than a very small one (everything else being equal), and thus potentially there are any number of confidence intervals, each having a particular probability associated with it. The most commonly used confidence intervals are the "95% confidence interval" and the "99% confidence interval."

To understand how a 95% confidence interval is determined, consider the data from the above example. The sample mean was 109 and the standard deviation was 15 for a sample of $N = 25$. Now consider the distribution of such sample means—the sampling distribution of the mean. Given the data at hand, the sample mean of 109 is a good estimate of the mean of the sampling distribution of the mean (i.e., the population mean), and $s_x/\sqrt{N} = 15/\sqrt{25} = 3$ is an estimate of the standard deviation of this distribution of means (i.e., the standard error of the mean, $s_{\bar{x}}$). Now recall from the section on "Sampling Distributions and Normality" that under most circumstances the sampling distribution of the mean is normal in form. Lastly, remember from the section on the "Standard Normal Distribution" in Chapter 4 (see Table A) that in a normal distribution 95% of the cases fall between -1.96 and $+1.96$ standard deviation units of the mean. However, since we are *estimating* the standard error of the mean, the t distribution rather than the standard normal gives a better approximation to the correct number of standard deviation units for the required probability. When one refers to the t table (Table B) with $df = N - 1 = 25 - 1 = 24$, under two-tailed tests one finds that 95% of the cases should fall within ± 2.064 standard deviation units of the mean. Thus, since the sampling distribution of the mean is normal with estimated mean 109 and standard deviation (i.e., $s_{\bar{x}}$) of 3, then 95% of such sample means should fall within $\pm 2.064 s_{\bar{x}}$ or $2.064(3) = \pm 6.192$ points of the mean. Consequently, one might say that 95% of the means from samples of size 25 drawn from a population having $\mu = 109$ would fall between

$$\bar{X} - 2.064 s_{\bar{x}} = 109 - 2.064(3) = 102.808$$

and

$$\bar{X} + 2.064 s_{\bar{x}} = 109 + 2.064(3) = 115.192$$

This interval may also be interpreted to imply that the probability is .95 that the interval of 102.808 to 115.192 contains the population mean. Consider another way to view this interval. Suppose a 95% confidence interval is computed on each sample drawn from this population. If new samples were continually drawn and such intervals calculated, on the average 95% of such intervals would include the population mean value within their limits.

Suppose one wanted to be especially cautious and construct an interval such that 99 times out of 100 it would include the population mean. Following the same logic as above, one would go to the t table and find the t value for a two-tailed test at .01 with $df = 24$. The value listed is 2.797, and this indicates that

99% of the cases in a distribution of such sample means are likely to fall within $\pm 2.797 s_{\bar{x}}$ of the mean. Consequently, the 99% confidence limits would be

$$\bar{X} - 2.797 s_{\bar{x}} = 109 - 2.797(3) = 100.609$$

and

$$\bar{X} + 2.797 s_{\bar{x}} = 109 + 2.797(3) = 117.391$$

Note that the probability statement applies to the interval and not to the population mean. The population mean is a fixed value whereas the sample mean and the confidence interval are different from sample to sample. Therefore, the statement that "the probability is p that the population value falls within the interval" is technically bad form because it implies that the value of μ varies and might or might not happen to land in the stated interval. Actually, it is the interval which is variable, and thus a statement with a more correct connotation is that the "probability is p that the interval includes the population value."

FORMULAS

1. Standard Form for a Score

$$z = \frac{X - \mu}{\sigma}$$

2. Standard Form for a Mean

$$z = \frac{\bar{X} - \mu}{\sigma_{\bar{x}}}, \qquad \sigma_{\bar{x}} = \frac{\sigma}{\sqrt{N}}$$

N = Number of cases in the sample for $\bar{X}$

3. Standard Form for a Mean, Parameter Estimated

$$t = \frac{\bar{X} - \mu}{s_{\bar{x}}}, \qquad s_{\bar{x}} = \frac{s_x}{\sqrt{N}}$$

N = Number of cases in the sample for $\bar{X}$

$$df = N - 1$$

4. Confidence Limits for the Mean (*P* percent confidence)

$$\bar{X} - t_{P/2}(s_{\bar{x}})$$
$$\bar{X} + t_{P/2}(s_{\bar{x}})$$

EXERCISES

1. What is the basis of deciding between a directional and a non-directional alternative?

2. What considerations go into selecting the value of α?

3. What is the difference between statistical assumptions and hypotheses?

4. Some people say that a statistical test helps to decide whether an observed experimental outcome was just a "chance result." Explain what they mean.

5. Why is $(\bar{X} - \mu)/\sigma_{\bar{x}}$ called a "critical ratio"?

6. Why does a statistician never "accept H_1"? Accept H_0?

7. Distinguish between the two types of decision errors.

8. What is the relationship between α and β?

9. What is the power of a statistical test?

10. When do you use the standard normal (i.e., z) and when do you use the t distribution as the theoretical relative frequency distribution for making a statistical test?

11. List the assumptions, hypotheses, significance level (adopt the .05 level), critical values, decision rules, computation, and interpretation of the following tests of hypotheses.
    (a) Determine whether a mean of 84 based upon a sample of 25 is significantly different from a population mean of 81 with a standard deviation of 10.
    (b) What difference would it make if in Example *a* above you did not know the population standard deviation but you did know that the sample $s_x = 10$?
    (c) Suppose males in a given area of the world average 62 inches in height. One tribe in the same area and of comparable genetic stock pierces the lips and molds the heads of their young children while the other tribes do not. The natives believe this piercing and molding makes their males grow stronger. A psychological theory also suggests that a moderate amount of stress given in infancy produces skeletally larger adults. The average height of the 36 adult males in this special tribe is 64.5 inches and the standard deviation is 7. Is this information consistent with the theory and tribal beliefs? Why do these data not constitute proof that the piercing and molding causes this height advantage?[2]
    (d) The average IQ of male students at State University who have at least one older brother or sister is 113. A random sample of 121 first-born males was similarly tested and found to have a mean IQ of 117 with a standard deviation of 16. Is it reasonable to conclude that first-born male students have a different IQ than later borns?

12. Determine 95% and 99% confidence intervals for the following cases:

    (a) $\bar{X} = 28$, $s_{\bar{x}} = 4$, $N = 30$
    (b) $\bar{X} = 152$, $s_{\bar{x}} = 12$, $N = 16$
    (c) $\sum X = 2400$, $s_x = 20$, $N = 64$
    (d) $\bar{X} = 72$, $\sigma_{\bar{x}} = 5$

---

[2] Adapted from research reported by T. K. Landauer and J. W. M. Whiting, "Infantile Stimulation and Adult Stature of Human Males," *American Anthropologist*, 1964, LXVI, 1007–1028.

ELEMENTARY TECHNIQUES OF HYPOTHESIS TESTING

10

The general logic for hypothesis testing was discussed in Chapters 8 and 9. In short, a hypothesis is made about a characteristic of the population. This hypothesis is tentatively held to be true, and then data are collected to determine whether the results are likely to occur within the expected range of sampling error. If the results do not deviate markedly from what would be expected on the basis of sampling variations, there is no reason to doubt the validity of the hypothesis previously supposed to be true. If the results do deviate markedly from what would be expected on this basis, perhaps the hypothesis is not true.

The illustration of this procedure involved comparing the known mean number of correct trials of the population of normal rats in a simple learning task with a group of rats which were given a drug before their learning trials. The question was whether the mean of the drugged sample differed "significantly" from the mean of the non-drugged population. If the observed mean differed by an amount that could not be attributed to sampling error, then perhaps the drug had an effect.

inferences about the difference between means

This illustration required that the sample mean for the drugged group be transformed into a t value by

$$t = \frac{\overline{X} - \mu}{s_{\overline{x}}}$$

However, good scientific methodology seldom permits a researcher to simply compare the performance of a random sample of subjects with a presumed value from some nebulous population as was done in the illustration. How do we know the population mean of non-drugged rats is really $\mu = 125$? Moreover, even if a very large group of non-drugged rats was tested and their mean was 125, that group of rats might have been assessed at a different time and under different circumstances than the drugged group. For example, maybe the assistant who tested the animals was just learning to do the job when evaluating the non-drugged animals, but was very experienced by the time the drugged animals were tested. Thus, the assistant might be more relaxed, skilled in handling the animals, or patient when testing the drugged subjects, which factors alone, regardless of the possible influence of the drug, could improve the performance of the drugged relative to the non-drugged animals.

the two-sample experiment   A more common procedure would be to randomly select two samples of 20 rats each. Before each daily testing session, the rats in one group would receive the drug while the animals in the other group would also be given an injection but it would consist of "physiological saline solution," a neutral, harmless, and ineffectual mild salt solution. Thus, each group would receive whatever stress was associated with being given an injection. Further, two assistants would be used to test the animals. One would inject the animals while the other would test them without knowing which animals had received the drug and which the saline. The two assistants would change roles on alternate days. In this way, differences between the groups could not be produced by the experimenter. Notice that the goal of these procedures is to insure that the only difference between the groups is the presence of the drug versus saline. Then, if there is a difference in their performance that cannot obviously be attributable to sampling error, one can conclude more certainly that the drug *caused* the difference. Observe also that statistical evaluation of the data is only one part of the research enterprise—all the proper and sophisticated statistics cannot make up for a poorly designed, carelessly executed experiment or set of observations.

Given that the experiment has been well designed and rigorously executed, how does one determine the probability that H_0 is true when there are two samples to be compared and no population parameters available? Consider again the previous formula:

$$t = \frac{\overline{X} - \mu}{s_{\overline{x}}}$$

This expression is quite general, and it can be read, "A value minus the population mean of such values all divided by an estimate of the standard error of such values is distributed as t, a theoretical sampling distribution." In the above expression, a "value" was a single sample mean, $\overline{X}$.

The point of the two-sample experiment just described is to ask whether the difference between the mean of the drugged group (call it $\overline{X}_1$) and the mean of the saline group (label it $\overline{X}_2$) could occur through sampling error alone. If the two groups performed exactly the same, then the difference between their means would be zero: $\overline{X}_1 - \overline{X}_2 = 0$. However, this difference is not likely to be precisely 0, but it will vary with sampling error. Thus, one desires the probability that the difference between the two groups, $(\overline{X}_1 - \overline{X}_2)$, could be just sampling error.

To obtain a formula for this question, simply permit the "value" in the above expression to be the difference between the two means, substituting $(\overline{X}_1 - \overline{X}_2)$ for $\overline{X}$ in the above formula. In words, the difference between two sample means minus the difference between the means of those two populations all divided by an estimate of the standard error of such a difference between sample means will be distributed as t. In symbols,

$$t = \frac{(\overline{X}_1 - \overline{X}_2) - (\mu_1 - \mu_2)}{s_{\bar{x}_1 - \bar{x}_2}}$$

where μ_1 is the mean of the population from which the first sample was drawn, μ_2 is the mean of the population from which the second sample was drawn, and $s_{\bar{x}_1 - \bar{x}_2}$ is an estimate of the standard error of the difference between two sample means.

More concretely, suppose we carry out the two-sample drug-versus-saline experiment described above. We calculate the mean learning performance for each group, and then determine the difference between these sample means, $\overline{X}_1 - \overline{X}_2$. This is the first term in the numerator of the formula given above. The second term $(\mu_1 - \mu_2)$ implies that each of the two samples is drawn from a separate population. The drugged animals come from a population with a mean of μ_1 and the saline animals are representatives of another population having a mean of μ_2. Now, stop to think what the purpose of the experiment is and how this statistical analysis will serve that purpose. We want to know whether the observed difference between sample means is too large to be simply attributable to sampling error. If it were sampling error, then the drug and saline solution would have equal effects on rats in the long run, that is, *in their respective populations.* Indeed, this is the null hypothesis—the drug and the saline do not have different effects on the mean of the populations. If this were true, there would be no difference between the means of those populations, or symbolically, $\mu_1 - \mu_2 = 0$. Since the logic of these statistical procedures demands that we tentatively hold the null hypothesis to be true, the term $\mu_1 - \mu_2$ will be zero under H_0.

The denominator of the formula is an estimate of the standard error of the difference between the sample means drawn from the same population. Under the null hypothesis, the populations of drugged and saline-injected animals are tentatively presumed to be identical. But even so, the mean of one sample will not precisely equal the mean of the other sample. They will differ somewhat from each other because of sampling error. One can conceptually imagine selecting two samples from a common population, computing the difference between their means, collecting another two samples, etc. These differences would form a distribution of differences between pairs of means. Since this is a distribution of the statistic $(\overline{X}_1 - \overline{X}_2)$, this would constitute an empirical sampling distribution, and its standard deviation would be the standard error of the difference between pairs of means drawn from a common population. This population standard error may be estimated by $s_{\overline{x}_1 - \overline{x}_2}$, which is calculated on the basis of sample data. This value reflects the extent to which two sample means from identical populations will differ from one another on the basis of sampling error alone.

Now let's put the formula back together and view it from the standpoint of the rationale of this statistical and experimental procedure. What we would like to know is whether the drug produces a different effect than neutral saline solution on the learning performance of rats. This question can be posed in the form of two mutually exclusive and exhaustive hypotheses stated in terms of the means of the populations of drugged rats and saline-injected rats. The null hypothesis is that the drug and saline solution have equivalent effects on their respective population means. Thus, $H_0: \mu_1 = \mu_2$. Conversely, the drug might affect learning differently than saline, in which case these population means would not be identical. Thus, $H_1: \mu_1 \neq \mu_2$. But, the statistical logic demands that we tentatively presume the null hypothesis to be true. This implies that we will suppose that we simply have two samples drawn from identical populations and that whatever difference we observe in their mean values is simply sampling error. Given the null hypothesis, at least for the moment, the formula reduces to

$$t = \frac{(\overline{X}_1 - \overline{X}_2) - \overbrace{(\mu_1 - \mu_2)}^{\text{equals 0 by } H_0}}{s_{\overline{x}_1 - \overline{x}_2}} = \frac{\overline{X}_1 - \overline{X}_2}{s_{\overline{x}_1 - \overline{x}_2}}$$

and now expresses the ratio of the observed difference between sample means relative to a measure of the expected sampling variation in such a difference. This ratio represents a value in the t distribution. Using Table B of Appendix II which lists critical values for the t distribution, we can determine the probability that the observed difference between means is simply sampling error. If this probability is small, suggesting that it is not likely that such a difference could be reasonably expected by sampling error alone, the null hypothesis that these samples come from identical populations may be rejected and one would conclude that the drug has some differential effect over saline. The logic is the same as in the previous two chapters, only the formula is different.

The task remaining is to determine an expression for $s_{x_1 - x_2}$. It happens that the standard error of the difference between means is somewhat different depending upon whether the scores in the two groups are **independent** or **correlated**. If a different set of subjects composes the two groups, the scores in these groups will be independent. However, if the same subjects were measured twice—such as before a treatment is administered and then again afterward—the scores in the two groups of measurements will be correlated. This happens because factors which determine the individual subject's performance will likely influence its value on both assessments. If children are to be given a special mathematics training program, it is likely that individual pupils who score high relative to the group before the training are likely to score high after it. Thus, the before and after scores will be correlated. In this event, the estimate of $s_{\bar{x}_1 - \bar{x}_2}$ based upon independent groups is not appropriate and special techniques are required. We will consider both cases.

THE DIFFERENCE BETWEEN MEANS— INDEPENDENT GROUPS

research question A developmental psychologist wondered whether visual experience with angles as opposed to curves is more important to rats in learning to discriminate between a circle and a triangle.[1] To test this issue, two groups of rats are reared in special cages, one group in a "square" world that has as few curves as possible but has many angles painted on the sides of the cage. The other group is reared in a "round" world which has as few angles present as possible but which has curves painted on the sides of the cage. The animals are reared individually in these special cages from the time their eyes open. They are tested as adults on a circle versus triangle discrimination by a procedure in which water is consistently located behind either a circle or a triangle. The measure of learning is the number of trials on which the rat makes a correct choice (ten trials per day for ten days for a total of 100 trials). A formal summary of the statistical treatment of this experiment is given in Table 10–1 and the details are discussed below.

statistical hypotheses The hypotheses are as follows:

$$H_0: \mu_1 = \mu_2$$
$$H_1: \mu_1 \neq \mu_2$$

in which μ_1 is the population mean for the square world and μ_2 for the round world group.

---

[1] Based upon but not identical to S. J. Cool, "Some Effects of Early Visual Environments on Adult Discrimination Abilities in the Rat," (Doctoral dissertation, University of Illinois, 1966); R. B. McCall and M. L. Lester, "Differential Enrichment Potential of Visual Experience with Angles vs. Curves," *Journal of Comparative and Physiological Psychology*, 1969, LXIX, 644–648.

10–1 Summary of the test of the difference between means for independent groups (the square vs. round world example).

Hypotheses

$H_0: \mu_1 = \mu_2$
$H_1: \mu_1 \neq \mu_2$ (non-directional)

Assumptions

1. The subjects are **independently** and **randomly** sampled.
2. The groups are **independent**.
3. The population variances are **homogeneous**.
4. The population distribution of $(\bar{X}_1 - \bar{X}_2)$ is **normal** in form.

Decision Rules   (from Table B)

Given: .05 significance level, a non-directional test, and $N_1 + N_2 - 2 = 17 + 15 - 2 = 30 \; df$

If $-2.042 < t_{\text{obs}} < 2.042$, do not reject H_0
If $t_{\text{obs}} \leq -2.042$ or if $t_{\text{obs}} \geq 2.042$, reject H_0

Computation

Square World (Group 1)	Round World (Group 2)
$\bar{X}_1 = 80$	$\bar{X}_2 = 75$
$s_1{}^2 = 16$	$s_2{}^2 = 18$
$N_1 = 17$	$N_2 = 15$

$$t_{\text{obs}} = \frac{\bar{X}_1 - \bar{X}_2}{\sqrt{\left[\dfrac{(N_1 - 1)s_1{}^2 + (N_2 - 1)s_2{}^2}{N_1 + N_2 - 2}\right] \cdot \left[\dfrac{1}{N_1} + \dfrac{1}{N_2}\right]}}$$

$$= \frac{80 - 75}{\sqrt{\left[\dfrac{(17 - 1)16 + (15 - 1)18}{17 + 15 - 2}\right] \cdot \left[\dfrac{1}{17} + \dfrac{1}{15}\right]}}$$

$$t_{\text{obs}} = 3.42$$

Decision

Reject H_0

Notice two things. First, the statistical hypotheses are stated in terms of population parameters not statistics. This is because the decision to be made really involves what is true about the populations, rats reared in square or round environments, not just about the two specific samples observed in this experiment. Second, the alternative hypothesis, H_1, does not specify whether μ_1 is greater or less than μ_2. It just states that the population means are different. This implies that the statistical test should be sensitive to differences in either direction, $\mu_1 > \mu_2$ and $\mu_1 < \mu_2$. In short, a non-directional or two-tailed test is required.

assumptions The subjects must be **randomly** and **independently** sampled. This means that each subject in the population has an equal opportunity of being selected and that the inclusion of one subject in the sample does not influence the probability of selecting any other member of the population. Second, these procedures are for the case in which the two groups of measurements are **independent** of one another. The next section will describe procedures which will handle the case of correlated groups.

Third, the population variances of the two groups are presumed to be equal, a characteristic called **homogeneity of variance**. Unfortunately, it is often difficult to decide whether this condition is met by the data to be analyzed. Since the variance of a sample from a population is not likely to equal the variance computed on another sample from that population, the issue becomes a question of how different can the two sample variances be before one suspects that their population parameters are not equal? While statistical tests are available which could be used to make this decision quite precisely, many statisticians feel their application to this problem is not very worthwhile. In addition, moderate violations of this assumption are possible—especially if the number of subjects is approximately the same in each group—without seriously biasing the results. If the number of observations in one group is the same as in another and there are at least five subjects in each group, one sample variance may be as much as twice the size of the other without markedly altering the results of the statistical analysis.[2] Thus, it is best to have equal numbers of subjects in each group and to have adequate sized samples, then heterogeneity of variance will not be a problem.

Finally the population sampling distribution of $(\overline{X}_1 - \overline{X}_2)$ must be **normal** in form in order to use the percentiles of the t distribution. This requirement is satisfied either if the two population distributions of raw scores are both normal or if the sample sizes are reasonably large regardless of the form of the population distributions.

---

[2] G. E. P. Box, "Some Theorems on Quadratic Forms Applied in the Study of Analysis of Variance Problems: II. Effect of inequality of variance and of correlations of errors in the two-way classification," *The Annals of Mathematical Statistics*, 1954, XXV, 484–498.

formula   The formula relating the difference between sample means to its standard error is

$$t = \frac{\overline{X}_1 - \overline{X}_2}{s_{\overline{x}_1 - \overline{x}_2}}$$

in which

$$s_{\overline{x}_1 - \overline{x}_2} = \sqrt{\left[\frac{(N_1 - 1)s_1{}^2 + (N_2 - 1)s_2{}^2}{N_1 + N_2 - 2}\right] \cdot \left[\frac{1}{N_1} + \frac{1}{N_2}\right]}$$

The standard error of the difference between means is estimated on the basis of the variances of the two samples. The degrees of freedom for t is the sum of the *df* for each sample variance:

$$df = (N_1 - 1) + (N_2 - 1) = N_1 + N_2 - 2$$

significance level   Employ the .05 level of significance.

critical values   The critical values will depend upon the degrees of freedom, the nature of the alternative hypothesis, and the level of significance. A glance at Table 10–1 shows that there are 17 and 15 subjects in the groups and thus the degrees of freedom are $(N_1 + N_2 - 2) = (17 + 15 - 2) = 30$. The alternative hypothesis is non-directional and the .05 level has been assumed. From Table B in Appendix II, the critical values are found to be 2.042 and -2.042.

decision rules   If the observed (computed) value of t is between -2.042 and $+2.042$ the null hypothesis of no difference will not be rejected. One would conclude that such a difference between means is well within the range of sampling error. In this event the results would not provide evidence supporting the effectiveness of differential rearing with curves and angles. Conversely, if the observed value of t is larger than or equal to 2.042 or less than or equal to -2.042 the null hypothesis will be rejected. The reasoning would be that the probability is too remote that such an observed difference in means merely reflects sampling error and that it is likely that the rearing conditions did affect performance. Symbolically:

$$\text{If } -2.042 < t_{\text{obs}} < 2.042, \text{ do not reject } H_0$$
$$\text{If } t_{\text{obs}} \leq -2.042 \text{ or if } t_{\text{obs}} \geq 2.042, \text{ reject } H_0$$

computation   The computation of the observed t proceeds by listing the relevant known information, the formula for t, the calculation of the components of the formula, and the computation of the result. This work is presented in Table 10–1. The $t_{\text{obs}} = 3.42$.

decision   The observed value of t conforms to the second decision rule, namely to reject H_0. The probability that such a difference between means could occur merely as a function of sampling error is so small that it is likely that the two samples have been drawn from two different populations. If the experiment is well conceived, the implication is that the differential rearing conditions produced this difference in observed means.

the difference between means—correlated groups

Sometimes the two means to be compared are both measured on the same subjects or on matched pairs of subjects (e.g., siblings, pairs of individuals matched for IQ, etc.). In either case, some of the factors that influence scores in one group will also influence them in the other group (especially those factors associated with individual subjects), and thus the scores in the two groups will be correlated to some extent. In this event, the assumption of independent groups cannot be met, and alternative procedures must be used.

research question   Suppose it is important to ascertain if stimulation of one area of the brain is more reinforcing to a rat than stimulation of another part. An electrode is sunk into each of these areas in each of 10 rats. After an initial training session, the rats are allowed to press two bars, one of which results in stimulation to one area of the brain and the other of which stimulates the second area. The number of presses on each bar is recorded, and the mean number of presses for stimulation in Area 1 is to be compared with the mean for Area 2. In addition, suppose a set of experiments by other investigators and a current theory strongly suggest that Area 1 should be more effective in producing responses than Area 2. Therefore, the research question asks if Area 1 is a better site for the reinforcing effects of brain stimulation than Area 2. A summary of the procedure for statistically testing these questions is presented in Table 10–2.

statistical hypotheses   Because theory and empirical evidence suggest that stimulation of Area 1 may be more reinforcing than stimulation of Area 2, the alternative hypothesis is directional rather than non-directional. That is, based upon other information (theory and data), if there is a difference between the two means the prediction is that the mean for Area 1 will be greater than for Area 2 rather than the reverse. The null hypothesis states that μ_1 either equals or is less than μ_2. Symbolically:

$$H_0: \mu_1 \leq \mu_2$$
$$H_1: \mu_1 > \mu_2$$

10–2 Summary of the test of the difference between means for correlated groups (the brain stimulation example).

Hypotheses

$H_0: \mu_1 \leq \mu_2$

$H_1: \mu_1 > \mu_2$ (directional)

Assumptions

1. The data take the form of pairs of scores, and these pairs of observations are **randomly** and **independently sampled**. Often these two observations are made on the same or closely matched subjects.
2. The population distribution of the D_i is **normal**.

Decision Rules (from Table B)

Given: .01 significance level, a directional test, and

$N - 1 = 10 - 1 = 9 \; df$

If $t_{obs} < 2.821$, do not reject H_0

If $t_{obs} \geq 2.821$, reject H_0

Computation

Subject	Area 1	Area 2	D_i	D_i^2
1	58	42	16	256
2	45	50	−5	25
3	61	23	38	1444
4	55	50	5	25
5	58	45	13	169
6	90	85	5	25
7	26	30	−4	16
8	35	20	15	225
9	42	50	−8	64
10	48	60	−12	144

$$\sum D_i = 63 \qquad \sum D_i^2 = 2393$$

$$\bar{D} = 6.3$$

$$t_{obs} = \frac{\sum D_i}{\sqrt{\dfrac{N \sum D_i^2 - (\sum D_i)^2}{N - 1}}}$$

$$t_{obs} = \frac{63}{\sqrt{\dfrac{10(2393) - (63)^2}{10 - 1}}}$$

$$t_{obs} = 1.34$$

Decision

Do not reject H_0

formula   The computational routine for this case differs from the preceding example and rests upon the following fact:

> The difference between two means equals the mean difference between pairs of scores.

This states that if the difference between each subject's two scores is computed and the mean of such differences calculated, this mean will equal the mean of the first group of scores minus the mean of the second. Applied to the current situation, if D_i represents the difference between the pair of scores for the ith subject $(X_{1i} - X_{2i})$, then if there were absolutely no difference between the two sample means (i.e., $\bar{X}_1 - \bar{X}_2 = 0$), $\bar{D}$ would also equal zero. Because of sampling error, $\bar{D}$ rarely would be exactly zero even if the two populations were identical. Therefore, under the null hypothesis that the means of the two samples are both estimates of the same population mean value, the sampling distribution of $\bar{D}$ should also have a mean of zero. Consequently, the statistical question reduces to the probability that $\bar{D}$ should deviate from zero relative to the sampling error of $\bar{D}$:

$$t_{\text{obs}} = \frac{\bar{D} - 0}{s_{\bar{D}}} = \frac{\sum D_i / N}{\sqrt{\dfrac{N \sum D_i^2 - (\sum D_i)^2}{N^2(N-1)}}} = \frac{\sum D_i}{\sqrt{\dfrac{N \sum D_i^2 - (\sum D_i)^2}{N-1}}}$$

The N in the above formula refers to the number of subjects (i.e., the number of pairs of scores). In this example (see Table 10–2), $N = 10$.

assumptions   The data consist of pairs of scores and it is usually presumed that the two sets of scores are correlated. Often this results from having the same or closely matched subjects contribute both scores. It is assumed that the pairs are **randomly and independently sampled** and that in the population the D_i are **normally** distributed.

significance level   Suppose that the implications of this study are such that it would be exceptionally undesirable to incorrectly reject the null hypothesis. Therefore, the .01 level of significance will be selected.

critical values   The test to be performed will involve a directional alternative. This means that the test is one-tailed in that the critical region constitutes only one of the two tails of the t distribution. Since additional information dictates that Area 1 should be better than Area 2, the converse possibility that Area 1 might be poorer in reinforcing bar pressing is so unlikely that the probability that this should occur is nearly zero. Under these conditions it is no longer appropriate to expect that a negative value of t might occur, and so the left-hand tail of the theoretical distribution is not included in the critical region. As a result, the critical value appropriate for this test is such that 1% of the area under the curve falls to its right. Looking in the table of t values with $N - 1 = 10 - 1 = 9$ degrees of freedom, one finds the .01 level, one-tailed critical value is 2.821.

decision rules   The decision rules are as follows:

If $t_{obs} < 2.821$, do not reject H_0
If $t_{obs} \geq 2.821$, reject H_0

computation   The raw data and computation are illustrated in Table 10–2.

decision   The observed value of t ($t_{obs} = 1.34$) is less than the critical value of 2.821, and according to the decision rules one does not reject the null hypothesis. This implies that an observed $\bar{D}$ of 6.3 is within the realm of sampling error for correlated samples of size 10 drawn from populations having the same mean. That is, if the two areas of the brain were identical in their reinforcing potential, with the amount of variability involved it would be quite possible to obtain a sample having a $\bar{D} = 6.3$.

The researcher must conclude that his data provide no evidence that stimulation of Area 1 has more potential reinforcing value than Area 2. This is not to say that the evidence disproves the proposition that Area 1 is better than Area 2. There is a difference between failing to support a proposition and disproving it.

What if Area 1 actually produced substantially fewer responses than Area 2, despite the prediction to the contrary? If a directional test had been selected before the experiment was conducted (and this decision must be made beforehand), then a large negative t would conform to the first decision rule which dictates that one not reject the null hypothesis. This would be the decision even if t were very large, such as 4.00.

inferences about correlation coefficients

In the previous section inferences about differences between means were considered. Actually, tests of the values of other population parameters can also be made. For example, one might be interested in inferences about the degree of relationship between two variables. This section is concerned with whether a significant relationship exists (whether the observed r could come from a population in which the parameter ρ is actually zero) and whether two r's drawn from independent groups of subjects are significantly different from one another.

THE SIGNIFICANCE OF r

Suppose a correlation of .58 were found between two variables. One might want to know if an r of this magnitude is merely an imperfect reflection of a population in which that relationship is actually zero, or whether an $r = .58$ faithfully mirrors a non-zero relationship in the population. It could be the case that in the population a relationship does not exist between two specified variables. In the course of sampling from such a population in which $\rho = .00$ it might be possible to observe a correlation of .58 or even higher, purely on the basis of sampling error. What is the probability that this could be the case?

research question   Some tests of infant development contain items that are designed to assess the amount and nature of vocalizations made by the infant. For example, a bell is rung in front of the infant and the presence and extent of the youngster's vocalization in response to this stimulus is measured. Although many items on such infant scales tend to assess motor development and do not seem to relate to later tested IQ, it might be reasonable to inquire whether there is a relationship between vocalization in 12-month-old female infants and verbal intelligence at six years of age.[3] A formal summary of the following procedure appears in Table 10–3.

statistical hypotheses   The data reveal a correlation of .58 between infant vocalization and childhood verbal intelligence for a group of 27 females. However, it is possible that in the population from which these children were sampled, no relationship actually exists, that is $\rho = .00$. In such an event, the observed relationship of .58 is merely a function of sampling error. Theoretically, it would be possible to continue to select sample after sample of size 27 and compute a correlation on each. The distribution of such sample r's forms the sampling distribution of the correlation coefficient, and its standard deviation is the standard error of r. The null hypothesis states that the observed value of r is typical of such a distribution of sample r's drawn from a population in which this correlation is actually .00. The alternative hypothesis dictates that the observed r is too extreme to be considered a member of such a sampling distribution, and thus it probably reflects a relationship of some non-zero magnitude in the population. Since there is no theory or empirical basis for predicting that such a relationship, if it exists, would be positive or negative, the alternative hypothesis is non-directional. In symbols,

$$H_0: \rho = .00$$
$$H_1: \rho \neq .00$$

[3] Inspired by J. Cameron, N. Livson, and Nancy Bayley, "Infant Vocalizations and Their Relationship to Mature Intelligence," *Science*, 1967, CLVII, 331–333; R. B. McCall, P. S. Hogarty, and N. Hurlburt, "Transitions in Infant Sensorimotor Development and the Prediction of Childhood IQ," *American Psychologist*, 1972, XXVII, 729–748; T. Moore, "Language and Intelligence: A Longitudinal Study of the First Eight Years," *Human Development*, 1967, X, 88–106.

10–3 Summary of the test of the significance of a correlation coefficient (the infant vocalization and IQ example).

Hypotheses

$H_0: \rho = .00$

$H_1: \rho \neq .00$ (non-directional)

Assumptions

1. The subjects are **randomly** and **independently** sampled.
2. The population distributions of both X and Y are **normal** in form.

Decision Rules (from Table C)

Given: $\alpha = .05$, a non-directional test, and $N - 2 = 27 - 2 = 25$ df

If $-.3809 < r_{obs} < .3809$, do not reject H_0
If $r_{obs} \leq -.3809$ or $r_{obs} \geq .3809$, reject H_0

Computation

$r_{obs} = .58$
$df = N - 2 = 27 - 2 = 25$

Decision

Reject H_0

---

statistical formula The formula relating a sample correlation coefficient to a theoretical sampling distribution of r's follows the same general pattern as the previous formulas:

$$t = \frac{r_{obs} - \rho}{s_r}$$

This states that a sample correlation r minus the population correlation ρ divided by an estimate of the standard error of sample correlations s_r is distributed as t with $N - 2$ degrees of freedom. Since the null hypothesis dictates that $\rho = 0$, this formula reduces to r/s_r. Substituting the computational expression for s_r and then making a few algebraic simplifications, one has

$$t = \frac{r_{obs}}{s_r} = \frac{r_{obs}}{\sqrt{\dfrac{1 - r_{obs}^2}{N - 2}}} = \frac{r_{obs}}{\dfrac{\sqrt{1 - r_{obs}^2}}{\sqrt{N - 2}}}$$

$$t = r_{obs} \frac{\sqrt{N - 2}}{\sqrt{1 - r_{obs}^2}} \qquad \text{with } df = N - 2$$

It is possible to substitute the observed value of r (in this case $r_{obs} = .58$) into the above formula, compute t_{obs} (which equals 3.56), and determine its probability under H_0 by looking in the table of t values as before. However, since this process is done so often and the value of t depends only upon r_{obs} and its degrees of freedom, critical values of r_{obs} for various df have been computed and are presented in Table C in Appendix II. To use the table, decide whether the alternative hypothesis requires a directional or non-directional test, select the significance level, and then locate the appropriate column. Then, find the row corresponding to the degrees of freedom ($df = N - 2$), and the critical value r_{crit} is given at the intersection of this row and column. For the present data, a non-directional test at the .05 level with $df = 27 - 2 = 25$ has a critical value of $r_{crit} = .3809$. Actually, since the sampling distribution is symmetrical and this is a non-directional test, there are two critical values, $-.3809$ and $+.3809$.

assumptions It is assumed that the subjects are randomly and independently sampled and that the population distributions of both X and Y are normal in form.[4] Notice that one can *compute* a correlation on two variables regardless of the nature of their distributions, but normality is required to accurately perform this *statistical test* of the significance of r.

significance level Adopt the .05 level.

critical values In this case, the critical values can be expressed in terms of r rather than t by using Table C. For a non-directional test at .05 with $df = N - 2 = 27 - 2 = 25$, the critical values of r are $-.3809$ and $+.3809$. Therefore,

If $-.3809 < r_{obs} < +.3809$, do not reject H_0
If $r_{obs} \leq -.3809$ or $r_{obs} \geq +.3809$, reject H_0

computation Once r_{obs} is determined, no further computation is required.

decision Since the observed r ($r_{obs} = .58$) exceeds the critical value of .3809, the second decision rule is used and H_0 is rejected. Consequently, the probability that an observed correlation of .58 could be drawn from a population in which the correlation between these two variables is actually zero is too remote to warrant the conclusion that an $r = .58$ could come from a population in which $\rho = 0$. Therefore, such a hypothesis is rejected with the implication that there is a relationship in the population between vocalization in infant girls and their six-year-old verbal intelligence.

---

[4] Technically, the joint distribution of X and Y is bivariate normal.

THE DIFFERENCE BETWEEN TWO
CORRELATIONS (INDEPENDENT SAMPLES)

research question   The preceding results were obtained from girls. It might be the case that the relationship between infant vocalization and six-year-old verbal IQ is stronger or weaker for girls than for boys. To examine this possibility, a sample of 18 boys was measured at 12 months and at six years of age in precisely the same manner as described previously for girls. While the correlation for girls was .58, the correlation for boys was $-.09$. What is the probability that such a difference in observed correlations could occur merely as a function of sampling error when, in fact, in the population there is no difference in the degree of this relationship between boys and girls? Note that the two correlations being considered, .58 and $-.09$, are computed on independent (i.e., different) groups of subjects. The following procedures apply only to this case. Similar but different techniques are required in the event that two correlations computed on the same group of subjects are to be compared.[5] A summary of the procedures for independent groups is given in Table 10–4.

statistical hypotheses   If there is really no difference in the degree of correlation for the two groups (sexes), then the correlation in the population for the boys should equal that parameter for girls ($\rho_1 = \rho_2$). On the other hand, if there is a difference in the magnitude of the relationship for the two groups, their population values should not be equal. The alternative in this case is non-directional (two-tailed) and the hypotheses are as follows:

$$H_0: \rho_1 = \rho_2$$
$$H_1: \rho_1 \neq \rho_2$$

formula   The test of these hypotheses is accomplished by first transforming the obtained correlation coefficients according to the following expression:

$$z_r = \tfrac{1}{2} \log_e (1 + r) - \tfrac{1}{2} \log_e (1 - r)$$

Fortunately, this formula has been computed for many values of r and tabled. This r to z transformation is given in Table D in Appendix II in the back of this book. To use the table, simply locate the value of r in the left-hand column and immediately to its right read the corresponding transformed value, z_r. In the case of $r_1 = .58$, the transformed value $z_{r_1} = .662$, and for $r_2 = -.09$ the z_{r_2} is $-.090$.

Once the r to z transformations have been made on each of the two values

---

[5] See G. A. Ferguson, *Statistical Analysis in Psychology and Education* (New York: McGraw-Hill, 1966), 188–189.

10–4 Summary of the test of the difference between two independent correlation coefficients (the vocalization—IQ example).

Hypotheses

$H_0: \rho_1 = \rho_2$
$H_1: \rho_1 \neq \rho_2$ (non-directional)

Assumptions

1. The subjects in each group are **randomly** and **independently** selected.
2. The two groups are **independent**.
3. The distributions of X and Y for each population are **normal** in form.
4. N_1 and N_2 are **both greater than 20.**

Decision Rules (from Table A)

Given: $\alpha = .05$ and a non-directional test

If $-1.96 < z_{obs} < 1.96$, do not reject H_0
If $z_{obs} \leq -1.96$ or $z_{obs} \geq 1.96$, reject H_0

Computation

Group 1 (Girls): $N_1 = 27, r_1 = .58, z_{r_1} = .662$ (from Table D)
Group 2 (Boys): $N_2 = 18, r_2 = -.09, z_{r_2} = -.090$

$$z_{obs} = \frac{z_{r_1} - z_{r_2}}{\sqrt{\dfrac{1}{N_1 - 3} + \dfrac{1}{N_2 - 3}}}$$

$$z_{obs} = \frac{.662 - (-.090)}{\sqrt{\dfrac{1}{27 - 3} + \dfrac{1}{18 - 3}}}$$

$$z_{obs} = 2.28$$

Decision

Reject H_0

of r, the difference between the transformed correlation coefficients (z_r) relative to the standard error of such differences is given by

$$z_{obs} = \frac{z_{r_1} - z_{r_2}}{\sqrt{\dfrac{1}{N_1 - 3} + \dfrac{1}{N_2 - 3}}}$$

Note that the distribution employed as the theoretical distribution is the standard normal (observe that z refers to the standard normal deviate and z_{r_i} refers to the transformed correlations). Because the standard normal is being used and not the t, it is necessary to have an adequate number of cases in the two samples. It is probably best to have N_1 and N_2 each greater than 20.

assumptions There are several assumptions required for performing this test. As always, the sample r's are computed on **randomly** and **independently** selected subjects. Second, it is necessary that the two samples are **independent**, involving different or unmatched subjects. If this condition were not met, the formula for the sampling error of the difference between correlation coefficients would not be appropriate for reasons similar to those discussed under the testing of the difference in means for independent versus correlated groups. Third, the X and Y distributions for both correlation coefficients must be **normal** in form. Fourth, the two **sample sizes must be greater than 20** in order for the statistical test to be accurate.

significance level Assume the .05 level.

critical values A non-directional test at the .05 level using the standard normal distribution requires an observed z_{obs} in excess of ± 1.96 (see Table A).

decision rules

If $-1.96 < z_{obs} < +1.96$, do not reject H_0
If $z_{obs} \leq -1.96$ or $z_{obs} \geq +1.96$, reject H_0

computation The computation is summarized in Table 10–4. Note that the information given in the problem is stated first. Then the r's are transformed to their corresponding z_r values with the use of Table D. The values are substituted into the formula and a $z_{obs} = 2.28$ obtained.

decision The observed value of z ($z_{obs} = 2.28$) exceeds the critical values of ± 1.96 and thus conforms to the second decision rule to reject H_0. This implies that the probability is very remote that two such correlation coefficients could be drawn from a common population purely on the basis of sampling error. Therefore, it is likely that these r's represent two populations that have different magnitudes of relationship between infant vocalization and later verbal intelligence. Specifically, it would appear that such a relationship is higher for girls than for boys.

COMPARISON OF $H_0: \rho = .00$ AND
$H_0: \rho_1 = \rho_2$

It is important to distinguish between testing the null hypothesis that a given correlation is zero ($H_0: \rho = .00$) and the null hypothesis that two correlations are equal ($H_0: \rho_1 = \rho_2$). Suppose the correlation for girls was .58 but the correlation for boys was .35. As illustrated, the $r = .58$ for girls is significant; that is, it is unlikely that such a value was computed on a sample drawn from a population that possesses no correlation at all ($\rho = .00$). More informally, the significant correlation for girls implies that there is a relationship between infant vocalization and verbal IQ for girls. However, if the correlation of $r = .35$ calculated on a sample of 18 boys is tested for the null hypothesis of $\rho = .00$, H_0 is not rejected, implying that the relationship is not significant for boys and that there is no evidence of a relationship between vocalization and verbal IQ for boys. Now, when the two correlations (.58 and .35) are compared to determine if they are significantly different from each other ($H_0: \rho_1 = \rho_2$), the test fails to reject the null hypothesis suggesting that the relationship is not different for boys and girls. But this combination of results does not seem to make sense. How is it possible that there is a relationship for girls but not for boys while boys and girls do not differ in the amount of this relationship?

This anomaly stems from the fact that tests of hypotheses often are interpreted in terms of a dichotomous decision. Either there is or there is not a relationship. Although sometimes it is useful to think in this manner, attempting to make a dichotomous decision is a somewhat artificial procedure when the tool employed to make that decision is a probability value that may range from .00 to 1.00 and ordinarily does not fall neatly into one of two distinct classifications. To illustrate more clearly by citing an extreme example, suppose that with a sample of 32 girls and 32 boys, the correlations were .35 and .34 respectively. With a non-directional test at the .05 level, the relationship would be judged "significant" for girls but not for boys, yet the two correlations certainly are not significantly different from each other. The lesson to be learned from this example is that one should refrain from making simple dichotomous decisions, especially when not rejecting the null hypothesis. Remember, not being able to reject H_0 does not entitle you to say that "there is no relationship." Rather, the evidence at hand is not sufficient to conclude that there is a relationship. In this case, the subtle difference between "not rejecting" (which is the appropriate conclusion) and "accepting" or worse yet, "proving" H_0, becomes important.

Another point illustrated by this example is that just because there is a relationship for girls but no evidence supporting a relationship for boys, does not necessarily imply that boys and girls are different in this regard. Performing a test of H_0: $\rho = 0$ separately on both boys and girls does not address the same statistical question as making a test of H_0: $\rho_1 = \rho_2$.

How does one interpret such a situation as described? The combination of results is ambiguous. The correlation of .58 for girls is substantial enough to warrant the conclusion that there is probably a relationship between vocalization and IQ for girls. However, the data may be interpreted as being inconclusive for boys (assuming $r = .35$) in that while the correlation is not substantial enough to warrant a significant rejection of the null hypothesis, the observed correlation was not so different from the substantial correlation of .58 for girls. Other interpretations are also possible.

A COMPARISON OF THE DIFFERENCE
BETWEEN MEANS AND CORRELATION

It will be instructive to compare the implications of a test of the difference between means and a test of the significance of a correlation. Fortunately, a very interesting comparison between testing for mean differences versus correlational procedures exists.[6] The relative role of heredity and environment as factors in development has been a focus of interest for psychologists for some time. More specifically, people have been concerned with whether heredity or environment is responsible for intelligence. One way to approach this issue is to investigate the IQ's of adopted children and their biological and foster mothers. In general, the results have shown a correlation of approximately .38 between a measure of intellectual performance for the biological mothers and one for their children, but a correlation of almost zero between an estimate of the IQ of the foster mothers based upon their years of education and the IQ of the children they reared. By itself, this information would appear to suggest that heredity may be more important than environment in determining intelligence. However, the mean IQ of the children was approximately 21 IQ points higher than the mean IQ of their biological parents, and their average IQ was close to what might be estimated for their rearing parents. Thus the children had an average IQ that was much more like their foster mothers than their biological mothers, evidence that seems to implicate environment in the determination of intelligence. How is this pattern of results possible and what does it say about the procedures for testing a difference between means in contrast to a correlation?

Consider the hypothetical data presented in Figure 10–1. These data have been exaggerated somewhat to illustrate the statistical point more clearly. Notice first that the scores are plotted according to their value with higher IQ

[6] This example suggested by results reported in M. Skodak and H. M. Skeels, "A Final Follow-Up Study of One Hundred Adopted Children," *Journal of Genetic Psychology*, 1949, LXXV, 85–125; M. P. Honzik, "Developmental Studies of Parent-Child Resemblance in Intelligence," *Child Development*, 1957, XXVIII, 215–228.

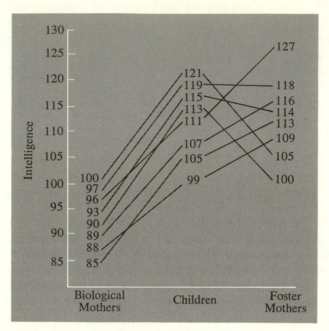

Fig. 10–1.   Diagram showing the different meaning of a correlation and the difference between means.

scores at the top, and that they are clustered into scores for biological mothers, children, and foster mothers. The lines connecting pairs of scores designate which biological mother goes with which child and which child goes with which foster mother. A correlation is high if the lines linking corresponding scores do not cross excessively. Notice that the children tend to line up within their group in much the same order that their biological mothers are assembled, and thus the correlation between biological mother and child in this hypothetical example is fairly high. However, the extensive crossing of lines relating child's IQ and foster mother's IQ suggests that the relative ordering of children and foster mothers is quite unpredictable and thus the correlation is low. In contrast, the general height (vertical distance from the X axis) of a group on this graph represents the relative score value (e.g., the mean) of the group. It is plain that the children are more like their foster mothers in this respect and less like their biological mothers. Therefore, in general it is quite possible that two groups of scores may have a correlation but no mean difference, a mean difference but no correlation, no correlation and no mean difference, or a correlation and a mean difference. Further, the correlations may be either positive or negative.

This example attempts to show that correlations and mean differences often present two distinct types of information, both of which are valuable to the interpretation of the general results. Very often, researchers only perform one of these two types of data analyses when, in fact, both could be performed and both could provide different types of information on the processes at work in the experiment or observation. For example, sometimes a test is given before a certain experimental treatment is introduced and then a posttest is given after the experimental treatment. Usually, the researcher looks for a difference in the means of the two groups of scores. Perhaps, an experimental teaching method has been used and the investigator wants to know if the group taught by this method has improved significantly over its performance prior to the experimental program. Suppose that some improvement was noted and the test of the difference between means is significant. If there is also a correlation between the pretest and posttest, then one can also presume that the program affected each student approximately to the same relative extent: The better students were still at the top of the group on the posttest, and so on. However, if there is no significant correlation, such a result would suggest that although the treatment did raise the mean of the group it seemed to influence some students relatively more than others so that their relative ranking within their group was disrupted. As a consequence, a researcher might wish to further investigate the characteristics of students who tended to show marked improvement versus those who did not.

Therefore, the difference between the means of two sets of scores and the correlation between those sets are two independent types of statistics, and they convey different messages about the events and processes being studied.

the interpretation of significance

It has become apparent that the appropriate interpretation of scientific results is a complex matter. Of paramount importance is the fact that statistical procedures provide the researcher with a set of tools that can help to interpret the results of experiments, but these procedures cannot replace the adequate collection of data under well-controlled conditions.

This proposition implies two important points. First, if the data are sloppily collected and inappropriate to the research question being posed, all the statistical significance in the world will not make the experiment worthwhile. Statistics do not improve the data or the experiment, they can only facilitate in revealing whatever conclusions lie hidden within that collection of measurements.

The second point is that "statistical significance" does not imply "scientific significance." That is, an experimenter may find emphatic differences between groups, but this information may be totally useless and uninformative. What is important or "scientifically significant" is difficult to define because scientists differ in their opinions on this subject. Further, a given item of data may be useless today but become very important in ten years or more. However, a result that has potential implications for a wide variety of issues (applied or theoretical) or relates to a broad spectrum of topics is an approximate definition of the second meaning of "significant research."

Thus, a great variety of factors are called upon to judge the significance of a scientific result, and such interpretations are made only after much experience with the methods of science and the facts of relevant phenomena.

PROBABILITY AND "SIGNIFICANCE"

There are several problems associated with declaring a difference simply as "significant" or "nonsignificant." First, the critical value used to make such a decision is based upon the significance level which the researcher arbitrarily selects. Thus, whether or not a statistical manipulation is "significant" depends upon the arbitrary selection of the probability of a Type I Error (see pages 191–94). Fortunately (or unfortunately) there is some communality among behavioral scientists as to what level that probability should be. Usually it is placed at .05, and sometimes (though rarely) at .01 or .001. The fact that many of the tables in the appendices of this book list only critical values corresponding to these significance levels attests to this practice.

However, as we have seen on page 226, the significant-nonsignificant dichotomy remains artificial. If a correlation of .43 is obtained with 22 subjects, it is deemed significant at the .05 level but a correlation of .42 would not be called significant. Certainly if one concludes that there is a relationship in the event of the correlation of .43 but that there is no relationship in the event of the correlation of .42 it is a gross oversimplification. This is particularly true in view of the potential influence of a single score on the magnitude of the correlation in a small sample as discussed in a previous chapter. Thus, a single subject could determine whether the relationship is significant or nonsignificant.

Despite the apparently artificial dichotomy between "significant" and "nonsignificant" results, techniques of statistical inference were developed largely for just this purpose—to decide whether or not an event had been observed that deviated from the limits of sampling error. To decide after a statistical evaluation that the observation "may be" or "may not be" a chance result is nearly to leave us where we started—with subjective decisions. Therefore, the custom of dichotomous decisions remains.

PROBABILITY AND N

The interpretation of statistical results also depends upon the number of subjects sampled because the critical value often varies with N. Suppose a correlation of .35 exists in the population and suppose that such a value was obtained in samples of various sizes. With a nondirectional test at .05, an r of .35 would be statistically significant only if 32 or more subjects were sampled. An examination of Table C shows that the value of r required for significance at .05 decreases as the number of subjects in the sample (i.e., degrees of freedom) increases. Notice that in a sample of 102 cases, a correlation of .195 is significant at the .05 level (two-tailed), but an $r = .75$ is not quite significant if only 7 subjects are involved. In general, the more subjects one samples the more likely it is that a significant result will be obtained if such a condition is actually present in the population, either in terms of correlations or mean differences.

On the one hand, this is as it should be. The probability value one obtains is intended to be a measure of the uncertainty in the situation. If a coin is tossed four times and it comes up heads on three of those tosses, one does not immediately conclude that the coin is biased. The coin might be biased, but how much money would you bet on such a proposition with only that much evidence? Not too much. On the other hand, if the coin is tossed 10,000 times, and 7,500 of those tosses result in a head, despite the fact that the same percentage of tosses were heads one would be far more confident in concluding that the coin is biased. Therefore, it is not unreasonable that the probability of a given event should be a function of the number of cases involved.

FORMULAS

1. Difference between means

a. Independent groups

$$t_{obs} = \frac{\overline{X}_1 - \overline{X}_2}{\sqrt{\left[\frac{(N_1 - 1)s_1^2 + (N_2 - 1)s_2^2}{N_1 + N_2 - 2}\right] \cdot \left[\frac{1}{N_1} + \frac{1}{N_2}\right]}}$$

$$df = N_1 + N_2 - 2$$

b. Correlated groups

$$t_{obs} = \frac{\sum D_i}{\sqrt{\frac{N \sum D_i^2 - (\sum D_i)^2}{N - 1}}}$$

$$df = N - 1$$

2. Correlations

a. Test that the correlation is zero

Look for the critical values of r in Table C.

b. Difference between two independent correlations

$$z_{obs} = \frac{z_{r_1} - z_{r_2}}{\sqrt{\dfrac{1}{N_1 - 3} + \dfrac{1}{N_2 - 3}}}$$

(Consult Table D for the r to z_r transformations)

EXERCISES

1. Why must it be assumed that the population distribution of the difference between means is normal and under what conditions can such an assumption be met?

2. Why is the test of the difference between means for independent groups not appropriate when the same subjects contribute to both groups of scores?

3. A theory suggests that when people experience cognitive dissonance, (e.g., conflicting motives or thoughts), they will attempt to reduce this dissonance by altering their perceptions of the circumstances. For example, college students were asked to perform a boring task for a long period of time. Then some were paid $20 and some were paid $1 to tell the next student that the task was really interesting and fun. Later, in private, they rated their own actual feelings about the task. The theory predicts that the group which was paid $20 will not experience as much dissonance when lying about the task because $20 is a fair wage for that kind of fib. They should rate the task as being quite boring. However, the group which was paid $1 should experience more dissonance about lying and as a consequence tend to view the task more favorably in order to justify the lie. The ratings (the higher the rating the more interesting the task) for the two groups are below.

   In view of the theory, evaluate these data[7] using the formal organization illustrated in this chapter.

$20	$1
3	4
1	8
2	6
4	9
0	3
5	6
4	7
5	10
1	4
3	8

[7] Inspired by L. C. Festinger and J. M. Carlsmith, "Cognitive Consequences of Forced Compliance," *Journal of Abnormal and Social Psychology*, 1959, LVIII, 203–210.

4. Mothers frequently claim that they can recognize the cries of their own babies, even in the first few days of their infant's life. Moreover, they apparently are able to distinguish between a pain and a hunger cry. A neonatologist set up the following experiment. Mothers listened to tape recorded sets of five cries from different babies, one of which was their own. They had to decide which of the five was their baby. Each mother heard 20 such comparisons, 10 in which the cries of the infants were associated with hunger and 10 in which the cries were produced by a slight pin prick to the foot. The researcher was confident on the basis of a theory and some other data that the mothers would be more successful in picking out their own infant when a hunger cry was involved, since they had more experience with that situation, than if the cries were expressions of pain. The data are below. Test the scientist's theory.

Number of Correct Identifications Out of 10		
Mother	Hunger Cry	Pain Cry
1	4	4
2	7	5
3	6	5
4	5	6
5	9	4
6	3	3
7	7	7
8	6	4

5. Suppose two types of psychotherapy were to be compared for their ability to alleviate anxiety. Two groups of 12 college students were selected from a large group of students in a freshman speech course. The 24 students were picked because through interviews, questionnaires, and physiological measurements they had the highest composite scores for anxiety about giving a speech. Each student then received ten sessions of therapy that followed one of two forms. One type, **behavior therapy**, attempted to teach the subject to relax and mentally associate this state of relaxation with the thought of giving a speech. The other group received **insight therapy** in which the therapist attempted to discern the causes for each person's anxiety and give the person insight into the problem. Later, each student had to give another speech and the same composite score of anxiety was measured. Below are the differences for each subject between the first and second score. High scores indicate a great deal of improvement. Evaluate these data in terms of the effectiveness of the two methods of therapy.[8]

[8] Inspired by G. L. Paul, *Insight vs. Desensitization in Psychotherapy: An Experiment in Anxiety Reduction* (Stanford: Stanford University Press, 1966).

Behavior Therapy	Insight Therapy
25	14
14	11
23	13
21	9
24	15
17	12
19	9
20	11
15	8
22	13
16	12
21	14

6. Construct a numerical example in which two groups of 8 scores are significantly different if the same 8 subjects each contributed a score to both groups (i.e., correlated groups) but they are obviously not significantly different if the same numbers were used but they were considered to be from independent groups of subjects.

7. Compute the correlation for the data in Exercise 4 and test to determine if the *r* is "significant."

8. Suppose that the correlation between the IQ's of 38 sets of identical twins is .87 and the correlation between 27 sets of fraternal twins is .53. Test the obvious theoretical prediction that the correlation is higher for identical than fraternal twins.[9]

9. Below are the data from a study comparing the improvement in reading performance in first grade as a function of two different teachers. Each child was given a pretest at the start of the reading program and a posttest after the training. The scores for these tests and the difference in the two scores for the students in each class follow:

	Teacher A		
Pupil	Pretest	Posttest	Difference
1	30	36	6
2	14	27	13
3	38	40	2
4	21	35	14
5	35	35	0
6	10	15	5
7	30	29	−1
8	32	41	9

[9] Inspired by L. Erlenmeyer-Kimling and Lissy F. Jarvik, "Genetics and Intelligence: A Review," *Science*, 1964, CXLII, 1477–1478.

Teacher B			
Pupil	Pretest	Posttest	Difference
1	34	49	15
2	21	30	9
3	16	20	4
4	38	63	25
5	27	44	17
6	25	30	5
7	31	50	19
8	15	12	-3
9	17	28	11
10	26	42	16

(a) Within each group, test to see if the pupils improved or declined between the pretest and posttest.

(b) Evaluate whether the teachers differed in their teaching effectiveness by testing the difference between the means of the two groups of difference scores.

(c) Correlate the pretest and posttest scores separately for each class. Test to determine if these correlations are significantly different from zero and whether they are different from one another.

(d) How do you interpret and explain the pattern of results obtained above, both in terms of their statistical reasonableness and in terms of what these data show about the two teachers?

SIMPLE ANALYSIS OF VARIANCE

Techniques that compare the difference between two means were examined in the previous chapter. The null hypothesis for those tests was that the two samples were drawn from populations having the same means ($H_0: \mu_1 = \mu_2$). However, very often a researcher wishes to compare means from more than just two samples and asks what the probability is that these several samples are drawn from populations having the same means ($H_0: \mu_1 = \mu_2 = \ldots = \mu_p$). A statistical procedure which addresses this broader question is called the analysis of variance.

Suppose a researcher was interested in the hypothesis that the pupil of the eye enlarges (dilates) when one looks at stimuli that are attractive to the viewer. To test this idea, suppose some male college students are either shown pictures of landscapes, sports action, or female pin-ups. A special camera photographs the eyes of the subjects every half second. Later, these pictures are projected on a large screen and the size of the pupil is measured. Each subject is given a score which corresponds to the amount of change in the size of his pupil while he watches the pictures. Those subjects viewing the pin-up pictures showed an average increase in pupil size of 17 units compared to increases of 9 and 4 units for those watching sports and landscape pictures, respectively.[1]

The statistical question is whether these observed differences between group means really reflect population differences provoked by the different pictures or whether these means could arise from three randomly sampled groups of

[1] Adapted from data presented by E. H. Hess, "Attitude and Pupil Size," *Scientific American*, 1965, CCXII, 46–54.

subjects from populations having the same mean and the observed differences between them are actually a function of sampling error. The null hypothesis is $H_0: \mu_1 = \mu_2 = \mu_3$.

In the previous chapter, techniques were presented for analyzing the difference between two means. It would be possible to perform such a test between each pair of means (AB, AC, BC) that can be formed from three samples (A, B, C). There are several reasons why this procedure is not only undesirable, but inappropriate. First, as the number of means to be compared increases, the number of pairs becomes quite large. For example, although there are only three pairs for three means, there are ten pairs for five means and 28 pairs for eight means. Therefore, the amount of computational labor increases rapidly as the number of means increases.

However, there are more serious reasons for not testing each pair of means. The second argument centers on the accuracy of the probabilistic statement that is to be made after testing a hypothesis. When two means are compared and the .05 level of significance is adopted, over many such comparisons one would expect only 5% of these differences between means to be as great or greater than the critical value under the null hypothesis. That is, if there were 100 pairs of means to be tested and each of the groups came from the same population, one would expect that on the average five of them would show a significant difference by chance or sampling error alone. Thus, as the number of t tests performed increases, so does the likelihood of obtaining at least one significant result purely by chance. Further, the significance level of a test of the null hypothesis, for example, .05, is meant to imply that an observed t that exceeds the critical value would occur in less than five of every 100 *independently* sampled pairs of means drawn from populations having the same mean. If several t tests are used to compare the differences between all possible pairs of a set of means, all the pairs are not mutually independent because each group in the set of k means is a member of $k - 1$ pairs. Therefore, the significance level appropriate for independent pairs of means is not appropriate when the pairs are not independent. You may appear to be using the .05 level, but the true significance level is some other value which cannot easily be determined.

A last criticism of using several t tests in this situation is that frequently the researcher wishes to ask a broader question than whether pairs of means are different. When the psychologist selected landscapes, sports scenes, and pin-ups to show the subjects, the purpose was to find out if pupil dilation was a function of the *collection* of these three types of stimuli, not merely whether it was different for members of the various pairs.[2] If sport scenes were significantly different from landscapes but no other pair-wise comparison was significant, what would

---

[2] When the researcher designates the specific stimuli in an example of this kind, the stimuli represent a **fixed factor**, whereas when the stimuli are random selections from a population it is called a **random factor**. Since the vast majority of experiments involve fixed factors, the analyses present in this text are appropriate for fixed rather than random factors.

one conclude about this *set* of three stimuli and pupil dilation? Thus, the question being asked is frequently broader than the information provided by separate tests between pairs of means.

For these reasons, the analysis of variance provides a more appropriate alternative to answering this type of question than a combination of several *t* tests between pairs of means.

the logic of the analysis of variance

GENERAL APPROACH

The purpose of the simple analysis of variance is to determine the probability that the means of several groups of scores deviate from one another merely by sampling error. The approach taken by the analysis of variance is to partition the variability in the total sample in much the same manner as was illustrated previously in the discussions of correlation and regression. In that context, the total variability of Y_i was divided into a portion attributable to X and a portion that was not associated with X. In the case of the analysis of variance the total variability in the scores is partitioned into a portion that reflects differences between the means of the groups and a portion that is not influenced by those differences in means.

The partitioning of variability is performed in such a way that two estimates of the variance of the scores in the population are computed. One of these estimates is based upon the deviation of the group means about the grand mean (mean over all scores in the total analysis). Its size will be influenced both by the variability of individual subjects (since their scores are involved in both the group and grand means) and, in addition, by any differences between group means. Because this variance estimate is based upon the deviation of group means about the grand mean, it is called a **between-groups estimate** of the population variance. In contrast, one could also base an estimate of the variance of the scores in the population on the deviation of scores about their respective group means. It can be shown that such an estimate is not influenced by differences in group means but only by the random variability of individual subjects. Since this estimate is determined by the deviation of scores within each group about their mean, it is known as the **within-groups estimate** of the population variance.

Conceptually, the two variance estimates differ only by virtue of the fact that the between-groups estimate is sensitive to differences between the group means while the within-groups estimate is not. As these group means become increasingly different from one another, the between-groups variance estimate grows large. However, the null hypothesis being tested is that in the population all the group means are equal (e.g., $H_0: \mu_1 = \mu_2 = \mu_3$). Since the null hypothesis is tentatively held to be true as part of the process of testing its validity, in theory, the between-groups estimate should have no contribution from population differences between means because the means are assumed to be equal to one another under H_0. Thus, given the null hypothesis, the between-groups estimate is influenced only by the same random variation in scores that determines the within-groups estimate.

Therefore, the analysis of variance provides two estimates of the population variance. Given the null hypothesis, both estimates should be identical to one another except for sampling error. The probability that two independent variance estimates differ from one another only by sampling error can be determined by taking the ratio of the two sample variances, in this case,

$$\frac{s^2_{between}}{s^2_{within}}$$

Under the null hypothesis that these variances estimate the same population value, their ratio has a known theoretical distribution called F, the percentiles of which are listed in Table E in the Appendix. If the ratio is so large that the probability is exceedingly small that $s^2_{between}$ and s^2_{within} estimate the same population variance, then one may assume that the additional influence of differences between group means has inflated the value of $s^2_{between}$, causing the F ratio to be unusually large. That is, the null hypothesis should be rejected.

Notice that although this technique is called the analysis of *variance*, its purpose is really to assess differences in group *means*. It accomplishes this goal by comparing pairs of variances, one of which can be influenced by differences in group means and one which cannot. The remainder of this section is devoted to expanding and clarifying this rationale.

NOTATION AND TERMINOLOGY

notation It will help to begin by specifying some notation that will serve as a convenient language with which to discuss these concepts. Table 11–1 presents this notation for the general case. Any score, X_{ij}, is written with two subscripts. The first or i subscript denotes the subject's number within its group and the second or j subscript indicates the group to which it belongs. Thus, X_{24} would be the second subject in the fourth group. Table 11–1 is arranged to show several subjects in each of the groups. Therefore, the i subscript runs up to n_1 for the first group, where n_1 indicates the total number of subjects in the first group. Similarly, n_2 indicates the number of subjects in the second group, and in general n_j denotes the number of subjects in the "jth group," a notation used to signify "some group" in the set. There are p groups so the number of subjects in the last group is n_p.

The total of all scores in group j is symbolized by T_j and the mean of the

11–1   General Notation for Simple Analysis of Variance.

	Group 1	Group 2	...	Group p	
	X_{11}	X_{12}	...	X_{1p}	
	X_{21}	X_{22}	...	X_{2p}	
	X_{31}	X_{32}	...	X_{3p}	
	X_{41}	X_{42}	...	X_{4p}	
	$\vdots$	$\vdots$	$\vdots$	$\vdots$	
	$X_{n_1 1}$	$X_{n_2 2}$	...	$X_{n_p p}$	
Group Totals	T_1	T_2 ...		T_p	Grand Total T
Group Means	$\overline{X}_1 = \dfrac{T_1}{n_1}$	$\overline{X}_2 = \dfrac{T_2}{n_2}$	... $\overline{X}_p = \dfrac{T_p}{n_p}$		Grand Mean $\overline{X}$

X_{ij} = score for the ith observation in the jth group
p = number of groups
n_j = number of subjects in the jth group
$N = n_1 + n_2 + \cdots + n_p = \sum\limits_{j=1}^{p} n_j$ = total number of subjects over all groups
T_j = total of all scores in group j
$\overline{X}_j$ = mean for group $j = T_j/n_j$
T = grand total over all subjects
$\overline{X}$ = grand mean = T/N

jth group is $\overline{X}_j = T_j/n_j$. Thus, $\overline{X}_1$ is the mean of the first group and $\overline{X}_p$ the mean of the last or pth group. In general, $\overline{X}_j$ is the mean of "some group" (the jth group). The grand mean, symbolized by $\overline{X}$ without any subscripts, is the mean of all the scores regardless of group. It can be expressed as

$$\overline{X} = \frac{T}{N}$$

in which T is the total of all scores and N is the total number of subjects in the design. One should note that the grand mean equals the average of the group means *only if all n_j are equal.*

classification terminology   The basis for classifying the different groups in the experiment is called a **factor**, and it is customary to assign a capital letter to such a factor. Therefore, in the present example, "type of picture" is a factor in this analysis and we shall label it "Factor A." The groups composing Factor A are known as **levels** and symbolized by corresponding lower case letters. In this case, the three levels of Factor A are landscapes, sport scenes, and pin-ups which we shall denote as a_1, a_2, and a_3, respectively.

variance terminology   The logic of the analysis of variance as briefly sketched above requires two estimates of the population variance, the within-groups and between-groups variance estimates. It will help to refine some terminology and notation about variances at this point. Previously, a sample variance (variance estimate) was defined to be

$$s^2 = \frac{\sum\limits_{i=1}^{n} (X_i - \bar{X})^2}{N - 1}$$

The numerator of this fraction is a sum of squared deviations about the mean, and thus it is known as a **sum of squares** symbolized by **SS**. The denominator is really the **degrees of freedom** associated with the sum of squares, and is therefore symbolized **df**. In these terms the variance estimate is really a type of average sum of squares and it is sometimes known as a **mean square** or **MS**. Consequently, a variance estimate can be symbolized by

$$MS = \frac{SS}{df} = \frac{\sum\limits_{i=1}^{n} (X_i - \bar{X})^2}{N - 1} = s^2$$

This merely constitutes a different vocabulary from what has been presented before. There is no important conceptual difference. The reason for this translation is that the new terms, sum of squares (SS) and mean square (MS), are customarily associated with the analysis of variance. Therefore, a variance estimate (e.g., s^2) in the context of the analysis of variance is called a mean square or MS.

hypotheses   The purpose of the analysis of variance is to estimate the probability that the means of the several groups differ from one another merely by sampling error. The null hypothesis is that in the population the group means are all equal and equal to the grand mean over all the groups. If μ_j represents the population mean for the jth group and μ is the population grand mean, then the null hypothesis is symbolized by

$$H_0: \mu_1 = \mu_2 = \cdots = \mu_p = \mu$$

The alternative hypothesis states that in the population the group means are not all equal which is best stated as follows:

$$H_1 : \text{Not } H_0$$

PARTITION OF VARIABILITY

derivation of MS   As indicated above in the general
discussion of rationale, the process underlying the mechanics of simple analysis
of variance is the partitioning of the total variability of scores into two components, one of which is sensitive to differences between group means while
the other is not. This partition is quite analogous to that discussed earlier in
the context of regression and correlation and illustrated again at the top of
Figure 11–1. Recall that the total variability in Y_i was divided into a portion

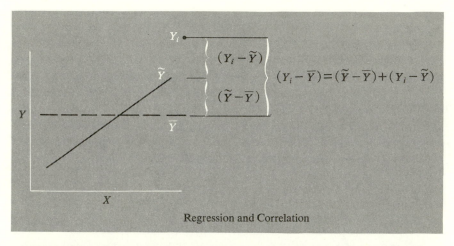

Regression and Correlation

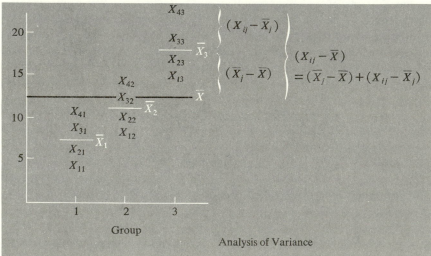

Analysis of Variance

Fig. 11–1.   Comparison of the partition of deviations in regression and correlation
with those in the analysis of variance.

that was associated with X and a portion that was not associated with X (i.e., "error"). For one particular score, the deviations are

$$(Y_i - \overline{Y}) \quad = \quad (\tilde{Y} - \overline{Y}) \quad + (Y_i - \tilde{Y})$$

$$\begin{pmatrix} \text{Total deviation} \\ \text{in } Y_i \end{pmatrix} = \begin{pmatrix} \text{Deviation} \\ \text{associated} \\ \text{with } X \end{pmatrix} + \quad (\text{Error})$$

This expression shows that the deviation in Y associated with X plus the deviation associated with error equals the total deviation of Y from the grand mean, $\overline{Y}$.

The bottom half of Figure 11–1 shows how similar the situation is within the context of the analysis of variance. The analysis of variance deals with the relation between groups of scores and some measure made on these subjects, call it X. If the groups represent different amounts of some thing (e.g., age, intelligence, food deprivation, light intensity, etc.), then the situations in regression and the analysis of variance are very similar. The bottom of Figure 11–1 shows the groups along the abscissa and the score values along the ordinate. The scores, X_{ij}, are placed in positions appropriate to their group and score value. The group means and grand mean are indicated in white. In a manner similar to the case of regression, the total deviations in the scores regardless of group affiliation, $(X_{ij} - \overline{X})$, is partitioned into components associated with the deviation of group means from the grand mean, $(\overline{X}_j - \overline{X})$, plus a portion due to random variability of the scores about their respective group means, $(X_{ij} - \overline{X}_j)$:

$$(X_{ij} - \overline{X}) \quad = \quad (\overline{X}_j - \overline{X}) \quad + \quad (X_{ij} - \overline{X}_j)$$

$$\begin{pmatrix} \text{Total deviation} \\ \text{in } X \end{pmatrix} = \begin{pmatrix} \text{Deviation between} \\ \text{group mean and} \\ \text{grand mean} \end{pmatrix} + \begin{pmatrix} \text{Deviation} \\ \text{within group} \end{pmatrix}$$

According to this expression, scores differ from one another for two reasons. First, scores are members of different groups, and if the group means differ from one another, the scores within the groups will, on the average, differ from scores in other groups by the same amount. Thus, the expression $(\overline{X}_j - \overline{X})$ simply reflects how much the mean of the jth group deviates from the grand mean. This is the **between-group** source of variability. Second, the scores within a group differ from one another—they do not all equal their group mean. This fact is expressed in the quantity, $(X_{ij} - \overline{X}_j)$, which is the difference between a score and its group mean. This is the **within-group** source of variability. Thus, scores differ from one another because they belong to different groups $(\overline{X}_j - \overline{X})$ and because of something unique to each subject which causes the score to differ from its own group mean $(X_{ij} - \overline{X}_j)$. Another way to express the same concept is to transform the above formula slightly by shifting the grand mean to the right side of the expression:

$$(X_{ij} - \overline{X}) = (\overline{X}_j - \overline{X}) + (X_{ij} - \overline{X}_j)$$
$$X_{ij} = \overline{X} + (\overline{X}_j - \overline{X}) + (X_{ij} - \overline{X}_j)$$

Now, any score X_{ij} may be "built up" by starting with the grand mean of all the scores $(\overline{X})$ and adding the amount of difference associated with being in the jth group $(\overline{X}_j - \overline{X})$ plus the amount of difference associated with that subject's unique deviation from the group mean $(X_{ij} - \overline{X}_j)$. If the grand mean is 10, the jth group mean is 14, and subject X_{ij} scores 2 units below the group mean, then $\overline{X}_j = 14$, $\overline{X} = 10$, $(\overline{X}_j - \overline{X}) = 4$, $(X_{ij} - \overline{X}_j) = -2$ and the score is given by

$$X_{ij} = \overline{X} + (\overline{X}_j - \overline{X}) + (X_{ij} - \overline{X}_j)$$
$$= 10 + 4 - 2$$
$$X_{ij} = 12$$

The above deviations represent contributions that a single score makes to the total variability in a sample of scores. To consider the variability over all samples, begin with

$$(X_{ij} - \overline{X}) = (\overline{X}_j - \overline{X}) + (X_{ij} - \overline{X}_j)$$

Then square each side and sum over the n_j scores within each group and over the p groups.

$$\sum_{j=1}^{p} \sum_{i=1}^{n_j} (X_{ij} - \overline{X})^2 = \sum_{j=1}^{p} \sum_{i=1}^{n_j} [(\overline{X}_j - \overline{X}) + (X_{ij} - \overline{X}_j)]^2$$

When these operations are carried out, the result is

$$\underbrace{\sum_{j=1}^{p} \sum_{i=1}^{n_j} (X_{ij} - \overline{X})^2}_{} = \underbrace{\sum_{j=1}^{p} n_j(\overline{X}_j - \overline{X})^2}_{} + \underbrace{\sum_{j=1}^{p} \sum_{i=1}^{n_j} (X_{ij} - \overline{X}_j)^2}_{}$$

$$\begin{pmatrix} \text{Total squared} \\ \text{deviations} \\ \text{in } X \end{pmatrix} = \begin{pmatrix} \text{Squared deviations} \\ \text{between group} \\ \text{means} \end{pmatrix} + \begin{pmatrix} \text{Squared deviations} \\ \text{within} \\ \text{groups} \end{pmatrix}$$

Notice that each component of the above expression is a sum of squared deviations (SS), and thus this expression can be written

$$SS_{\text{total}} = SS_{\text{between}} + SS_{\text{within}}$$

This statement indicates that the total sum of squares is composed of the sum of squared deviations of group means from their grand mean (SS_{between}) *plus* the sum of the squared deviations of scores from their respective group means (SS_{within}).

   Recall from the general rationale of the analysis of variance that rather than two **sums of squares**, one sensitive to group differences and the other not, two **mean squares** (*MS*) with these characteristics are required. A variance estimate is a sum of squares divided by its degrees of freedom. Therefore, the degrees of freedom for the sums of squares discussed above must be determined.

   For a sample variance, the degrees of freedom (*df*) equal one less than the number of cases considered for the sum of squares. In the notational scheme described at the beginning of this section, there are N total cases, n_j cases in the *j*th group, and a total of *p* groups. The total degrees of freedom in the sample is one less than the total number of cases in the sample or

$$df_{total} = N - 1$$

The degrees of freedom for $SS_{between}$ should be one less than the number of means in the total sample because $SS_{between}$ is the sum of the squared deviations of each mean about the grand mean. Since there are p means,

$$df_{between} = p - 1$$

Lastly, the SS_{within} is composed of the sum of the squared deviations of scores about their respective group means. Within any single group j the sum of squares has $n_j - 1$ degrees of freedom. When each of these within-group sum of squares is summed across all the groups to obtain SS_{within}, one also sums the degrees of freedom

$$\sum_{j=1}^{p} (n_j - 1)$$

Distributing the summation sign,

$$\sum_{j=1}^{p} n_j - \sum_{j=1}^{p} (1)$$

replacing the first term by its equivalent, N, and the second term by p (recall that the sum from 1 to p of a constant is p times the constant), one has that the degrees of freedom for SS_{within} are

$$df_{within} = N - p$$

It happens that the df_{total} equals the sum of the degrees of freedom for $SS_{between}$ plus SS_{within}:

$$df_{total} = df_{between} + df_{within}$$

Therefore, both the sum of squares and the degrees of freedom for the total sample are the sum of a between- and a within-group component.

To obtain a mean square, one simply divides a sum of squares by its degrees of freedom. Therefore, the mean square sensitive to between-group differences is

$$MS_{between} = \frac{SS_{between}}{df_{between}} = \frac{\sum_{j=1}^{p} n_j(\overline{X}_j - \overline{X})^2}{p-1}$$

and the mean square not sensitive to group differences (the MS_{within}) is

$$MS_{within} = \frac{SS_{within}}{df_{within}} = \frac{\sum_{j=1}^{p} \sum_{i=1}^{n_j} (X_{ij} - \overline{X}_j)^2}{N-p}$$

One must be careful *not* to suppose that, because

$$SS_{total} = SS_{between} + SS_{within}$$

and

$$df_{total} = df_{between} + df_{within}$$

that the total mean square equals the sum of the between and within mean squares. It does not.

comparison of $MS_{between}$ and MS_{within}   In the previous section, formulas for two variance estimates or mean squares were developed. The logic of the analysis of variance rests on the fact that one of these estimates ($MS_{between}$) can be influenced by population differences between the means of the several groups reflecting treatment effects while the other (MS_{within}) is not so influenced. This section attempts to make this vital discrimination more intuitive.

First, consider why two subjects from *different groups* do not score the same. Recall the example discussed at the beginning of the chapter. Suppose the amount of pupil dilation registered by the first subject in Group 1 (landscapes) was 10 and that of the first subject in Group 3 (pin-ups) was 16. Why are these two scores different? There are two major possibilities. First, one subject saw landscapes while the other viewed pin-up pictures, and maybe pin-up pictures affect pupil dilation more than landscapes. This contribution to differences between scores stems from possible **treatment effects.** A treatment effect occurs when the population mean corresponding to a given group in the analysis differs from the average of the population means for all groups. If the null hypothesis is true, there are no treatment effects because the population means of all groups are identical. But if H_1 is really the case, population group means will differ from one another and treatment effects are said to exist. Therefore, one reason two subjects do not score the same value is the possibility of treatment effects.

In addition to potential treatment effects, two people assessed under identical circumstances usually do not respond the same because of a variety of uncontrolled factors. For example, some subjects just respond more intensely than others, perhaps the test situation is just slightly different in temperature or apparatus position for one subject than another, or a multitude of other possibilities might exist. The entire collection of such potential causes, presumably unrelated to the differences in treatments, is denotatively called **error**. Therefore, differences or variability in scores between different groups may stem from treatment effects and/or error.

In contrast, consider why two scores from subjects in the *same* group are not identical. First, the two subjects each received the same treatment so that differences in treatment condition cannot be a determinant of variability within a group. However, all of those potential influences subsumed under the concept of error may still be operative. Therefore, in contrast to variability between groups, variability within groups is a function of error but not of treatment effects.

In brief,

$$MS_{between} \text{ reflects treatment effects + error}$$
$$MS_{within} \text{ reflects error}$$

It is important to remember that under the null hypothesis all treatment effects are presumed to be zero, so $MS_{between}$ and MS_{within} are both estimates of the common population variance. Since they are estimates, they will probably not precisely equal each other but will vary as a function of sampling error. But in the long run we would expect them to tend towards being equal.

The fact that $MS_{between}$ is sensitive to treatment effects whereas MS_{within} is not may be illustrated with a numerical example. Suppose one consulted a table of random numbers and selected three groups of five numbers each. Since these are random numbers, the three groups are analogous to three samples of size five drawn from a common population (sampling under the null hypothesis). These numbers are displayed in the top half of Table 11–2. The SS_{within} for each group is presented and the within-groups estimate is at the right: $MS_{within} = 7.33$. The group means are 4, 6, and 5 with a grand mean of 5. The between-groups variance estimate is computed below the listing of the groups and $MS_{between} = 5.0$.

Now suppose that there are group differences or treatment effects. To implement this condition, 3 units are added to each score in Group 2 and 12 units are added to each score in Group 3. This is equivalent to saying the sports photos are worth 3 extra units of pupillary change and the pin-ups are worth 12 extra units in comparison to landscapes.

Consider the two variance estimates presented in the lower half of Table 11–2. Notice that the MS_{within} is precisely the same as it was before the effects were introduced. This is a reflection of the fact that the variability of scores within a group is not influenced by adding a constant to each score in the group. How-

11–2 Numerical illustration of the fact that $MS_{between}$ is influenced by group differences while MS_{within} is not.

Group 1	Group 2	Group 3
$SS_1 = \sum(X_{i1} - \bar{X}_1)^2 \begin{cases} 7 \\ 5 \\ 3 \\ 4 \\ 1 \end{cases}$	$SS_2 = \sum(X_{i2} - \bar{X}_2)^2 \begin{cases} 2 \\ 6 \\ 9 \\ 9 \\ 4 \end{cases}$	$SS_3 = \sum(X_{i3} - \bar{X}_3)^2 \begin{cases} 9 \\ 3 \\ 5 \\ 6 \\ 2 \end{cases}$
$SS_1 = 20$	$SS_2 = 38$	$SS_3 = 30$
$df_1 = 4$	$df_2 = 4$	$df_3 = 4$

$$\underbrace{\bar{X}_1 = 4.0 \qquad\qquad \bar{X}_2 = 6.0 \qquad\qquad \bar{X}_3 = 5.0}$$

$$MS_{within} = \frac{SS_1 + SS_2 + SS_3}{df_1 + df_2 + df_3}$$

$$MS_{within} = \frac{20 + 38 + 30}{4 + 4 + 4} = 7.33$$

$$MS_{between} = \frac{\sum_{j=1}^{p} n_j(\bar{X}_j - \bar{X})^2}{p - 1}$$

$$MS_{between} = \frac{5(4 - 5)^2 + 5(6 - 5)^2 + 5(5 - 5)^2}{3 - 1} = 5.0$$

$$\bar{X} = 5.0$$

Treatment effect
(added to each score) 0   +3   +12

Group 1

$$
\left.\begin{array}{c} 7 \\ 5 \\ 3 \\ 4 \\ 1 \end{array}\right\}
$$

$SS_1 = 20$

$df_1 = 4$

$\bar{X}_1 = 4.0$

Group 2

$$
\left.\begin{array}{c} 5 \\ 9 \\ 12 \\ 12 \\ 7 \end{array}\right\}
$$

$SS_2 = 38$

$df_2 = 4$

$\bar{X}_2 = 9.0$

Group 3

$$
\left.\begin{array}{c} 21 \\ 15 \\ 17 \\ 18 \\ 14 \end{array}\right\}
$$

$SS_3 = 30$

$df_3 = 4$

$\bar{X}_3 = 17.0$

$$
MS_{\text{within}} = \frac{SS_1 + SS_2 + SS_3}{df_1 + df_2 + df_3}
$$

$$
MS_{\text{within}} = \frac{20 + 38 + 30}{4 + 4 + 4} = 7.33
$$

$$
\bar{X} = 10.0
$$

$$
MS_{\text{between}} = \frac{\sum_{j=1}^{p} n_j(\bar{X}_j - \bar{X})^2}{p - 1}
$$

$$
MS_{\text{between}} = \frac{5(4 - 10)^2 + 5(9 - 10)^2 + 5(17 - 10)^2}{3 - 1} = 215.0
$$

ever, the value of $MS_{between}$ was indeed changed as a function of the treatment effects. Now $MS_{between} = 215.0$. This is because a different constant was added to each of the three groups and thus to the three group means, and $MS_{between}$ is sensitive to these differences. It should be clear from this numerical example that the within-groups variance estimator is not influenced by differences in group means (i.e., treatment effects) whereas the between-groups estimate is influenced by treatment differences.

THE F TEST

The final step in the rationale of the analysis of variance is to compare the two variance estimates under the assumptions of the null hypothesis. Recall that the null hypothesis states that there are no treatment effects which implies that in the population the group means are all identical to one another and equal to the grand mean:

$$H_0: \mu_1 = \mu_2 = \cdots = \mu_p = \mu$$

The alternative hypothesis is that these conditions are not so; there are treatment effects and thus differences between group means:

$$H_1: \text{Not } H_0$$

If the null hypothesis is true, $MS_{between}$ and MS_{within} should both estimate the same parameter, just as they did in the numerical example above before treatment effects were added. Therefore, in the long run the ratio of these two variances or mean squares

$$F = \frac{MS_{between}}{MS_{within}}$$

should vary only with sampling error. The percentiles of the F distribution may be used in order to determine the probability of obtaining an F ratio of a specified size purely by sampling error. If the probability is very small that an observed F of this size is merely a function of sampling error, then perhaps the tentative assumption of the null hypothesis of no treatment effects is wrong. This is logical because $MS_{between}$ but not MS_{within} is influenced by treatment effects and a high F ratio means that $MS_{between}$ is large relative to MS_{within}.

The theoretical sampling distribution of the ratio of two independent variance estimates (e.g., $s^2_{between}$ and s^2_{within}) is called F, and the percentiles for this distribution are listed in Table E of Appendix II. However, just as there was a different t distribution for each number of degrees of freedom, there is a separate F distribution for each *combination* of degrees of freedom for the variance in the numerator and in the denominator of the F ratio.

independence The use of the F distribution in this fashion is based upon the assumption that the sample variances in the ratio are independent. When F was used previously, this requirement was assured because the variances were computed on different samples of subjects. In the case of the analysis of variance, the two mean squares are computed on the same subjects. The within-groups estimate is based upon all the scores in the total sample and the between-groups estimate is based upon the group and grand means to which each of these same scores contributes. Therefore, to use the F distribution in order to determine the probability of the null hypothesis, one must demonstrate that the two MS's are independent of one another.

As discussed previously, estimates of the population mean and variance based upon samples from populations that are normally distributed are independent. Thus, if the population of scores X_{ij} is normally distributed, $\overline{X}_j$ and s_j^2 are independent. Where several groups of scores are sampled from a normal population, the collection of all the group means ($\overline{X}_j$) is independent of the collection of all the group variances (s_j^2). $MS_{between}$ is based upon the $\overline{X}_j$ while MS_{within} involves the deviation of scores about their mean (e.g., s_j^2). Therefore, $MS_{between}$ and MS_{within} are two independent estimates of the population variance if the population is normally distributed.

Consequently, the ratio of two independent variances is distributed as F with $N_1 - 1$ and $N_2 - 1$ degrees of freedom, where $N_1 - 1$ is the degrees of freedom of the variance in the numerator and $N_2 - 1$ is the degrees of freedom of the variance in the denominator.

Table E in Appendix II in the back of this book lists the .05 (roman type) and .01 (boldface type) critical values for F's of various degrees of freedom. To locate a critical value, find the column of the table corresponding to the number of degrees of freedom for the variance in the numerator. Then locate the row corresponding to the degrees of freedom for the variance in the denominator of the ratio. Suppose there were 21 and 31 subjects in the groups for the variances in the numerator and denominator of the F ratio, respectively. There would be 20 and 30 degrees of freedom for the F ratio. Locate the intersection of the column labeled 20 and the row labeled 30 degrees of freedom. There are two values at that point. The first (roman type) is 1.93 and that is the critical value corresponding to a .05 level test. Below this figure you will find the value 2.55 (boldface type) which represents the .01 critical value.

the logic of the F test　　The logic of the F test can now be summarized:

(1) MS_{within} is an estimate of the population variance based upon the deviations of scores about their respective group means. It is not influenced by mean differences between groups (i.e., treatment effects).

(2) $MS_{between}$ is also an estimate of the population variance if the null hypothesis is true. It is based upon the deviations of group means about the grand mean.

Since it is influenced by any treatment effects that exist in the population, it is only an estimate of the same population variance if those treatment effects are zero, that is, if the null hypothesis is true.

(3) Since the two variance estimates are independent and since the logic of hypothesis testing demands that the null hypothesis be tentatively assumed true, the ratio of these two variance estimates is distributed as F:

$$F = \frac{MS_{\text{between}}}{MS_{\text{within}}}$$

(4) Since under conditions of the null hypothesis the two MS's are estimating the same population value, this ratio should approach a value of 1.0 in the long run.[3] The observed value of F is compared to the sampling distribution of such ratios to determine the probability that such an F value could be obtained merely by sampling error.

(5) If the observed F ratio is very large such that the probability is quite small that an F of this size should be obtained merely by chance, then perhaps the assumption of the null hypothesis (no treatment effects) was not appropriate. If there were treatment effects, MS_{between} would be sensitive to them but MS_{within} would not. Therefore, an improbably large F value might mean that treatment effects, in fact, do exist in the population and the null hypothesis should be rejected.

ASSUMPTIONS UNDERLYING THE ANALYSIS OF VARIANCE

Throughout the course of the previous discussion, several assumptions were made in order to perform the statistical manipulations necessary for the analysis. These assumptions are collected and outlined below.

1. random sampling and independence of groups

It is assumed that the groups involved in the analysis are composed of randomly and independently sampled subjects. Subjects must also be randomly assigned to treatment conditions. For example, as subjects arrive individually for an experiment, the researcher may randomly assign them to one of the treatment groups in the experiment (as opposed to considering the first 15 subjects as group 1). This random assignment guarantees the independence of the treatment groups. Sometimes this cannot be accomplished. For example, subjects cannot be randomly assigned to high, medium, and low levels of personal anxiety or to different income groups. The analysis of variance can still be used in these cases, but then the scientist cannot conclude that anxiety

---

[3] Actually, the ratio approaches 1.00 in the long run only as the number of subjects becomes very large.

(or income level) *caused* the observed results but rather it is only *associated* with such differences (see p. 135).

Occasionally it is desirable not to have independent groups but to measure the same subjects under each of several different conditions and to have the analysis determine if these correlated groups of scores have different means. There are procedures to perform this type of analysis which are called **repeated measures analyses of variance** because subjects are measured under more than one condition.[4] These analyses take into account the fact that if the same subjects contribute measures under more than one condition, the variability in those conditions may be correlated. Thus, an alternative method of estimating the error variance in the population must be used. The difference between independent groups and repeated measures analyses of variance is analogous to the difference between the *t* test for means from independent versus correlated groups. The analysis of variance procedures outlined in this text all require independent groups.

2. homogeneity of within-group variances

It is assumed that the populations from which the groups are drawn have equal variances. In symbols,

$$\sigma_1^2 = \sigma_2^2 = \cdots = \sigma_p^2$$

A similar assumption was made in Chapter 10 for the *t* test between the means of two groups. One reason for this assumption is that it enables MS_{within} to be an appropriate pooling of the variability about each group mean into a single estimate of the population variance. Without homogeneity of variance, one group with a very high variance might contribute disproportionately to this single estimate, and MS_{within} would not be representative of the variability within each group.

There are procedures for testing the homogeneity of variances. The *F* distribution can be employed to test the difference between two sample variances, and there are methods that extend such a test to include several variances rather than just two.[5] However, some statisticians have argued that these procedures may be influenced by extraneous factors and therefore do not provide an entirely appropriate test of the homogeneity of variance.[6] Further, if a sufficient number of cases are sampled and the number of subjects in each group is the same, moderate violations of this assumption do not alter the result of the analysis of variance very much.

---

[4] B. J. Winer, *Statistical Principles in Experimental Design*, second edition (New York: McGraw-Hill, 1972). For a simplified discussion of the problems and assumptions in performing these analyses, see R. B. McCall and M. I. Appelbaum, "Bias in the Analysis of Repeated-Measures Designs: Some Alternative Approaches," *Child Development*, 1973, XLIV, 401–415.

[5] B. J. Winer, *Statistical Principles in Experimental Design*, second edition (New York: McGraw-Hill, 1972).

[6] W. L. Hays, *Statistics for the Social Sciences*, second edition (New York: Holt, Rinehart & Winston, 1973).

3. normality It is assumed that the distribution of each population is normal in form. This condition should be reflected in each of the groups sampled. Each should have a relatively normal distribution.

The assumption of normality is made so that the two variance estimates are independent, permitting the F test to be used. As discussed above, the mean and variance of a normal distribution are independent. The $MS_{between}$ is based upon the means of the groups and the MS_{within} is derived from the variability of scores about their respective means. If the means are independent from the variability of scores about these group means (as they are in a normal distribution), then the between-groups and within-groups variance estimates will be independent. Moreover, the probability levels for the F statistic are accurate only if the two variance estimates are based on normal distributions.

Violations of the assumption of normality are not terribly damaging if a sufficient number of cases are sampled and the departure from normality is not severe. If the distributions are decidedly not normal, and there are not many cases in each group, a nonparametric analysis may be performed. Some nonparametric techniques are presented in Chapter 13.[7]

computational procedures

GENERAL FORMAT

As we discovered in previous chapters, the definitional formulas for statistical quantities are not often the most convenient for computational purposes. Table 11–3 gives a general computational scheme for the simple analysis of variance. Part **i** lists the scores in the p groups and several quantities needed for the computations. Under each group is the total of all the scores for that group (T_j), the n_j, the mean ($\overline{X}_j$), the sum of squared scores ($\sum_{i=1}^{n_j} X_{ij}^2$), and the squared sum of the scores divided by n_j (T_j^2/n_j). (Remember the sum of squared scores ($\sum X^2$) is arrived at by squaring each score and then summing. The squared sum of the scores ($\sum X$)^2 divided by n_j is arrived at by first summing the scores, then squaring the sum and dividing by n_j.) To the right of these group quantities are the totals for the entire sample: The total of all scores (T, sum the T_j), the total number of cases (N, sum the n_j), the total sum of the squared scores

$$\sum_{j=1}^{p} \left(\sum_{i=1}^{n_j} X_{ij}^2 \right), \text{ sum the } \sum_{i=1}^{n_j} X_{ij}^2$$

and the squared sum of all the scores divided by n_j ($\sum_{j=1}^{p} T_j^2/n_j$, sum all the

---

[7] See also S. Siegel, *Nonparametric Statistics* (New York: McGraw-Hill, 1956); J. V. Bradley, *Distribution-Free Statistical Tests* (Englewood Cliffs: Prentice-Hall, 1968).

$T_j{}^2/n_j$). These are the basic quantities needed to calculate the sums of squares for the analysis of variance.

Part **ii** lists three intermediate quantities that will facilitate the computation of the *SS*. Quantity (I) consists of the squared total sum of scores divided by N ($T_{total}{}^2/N$, square T_{total} and divide by N); quantity (II) is simply the total sum of the squared scores as found previously

$$\sum_{j=1}^{p} \left(\sum_{i=1}^{n_j} X_{ij}{}^2 \right)$$

and quantity (III) is the total of the squared sum of scores divided by n_j, also calculated previously

$$\sum_{j=1}^{p} \frac{T_j{}^2}{n_j}$$

Part **iii** of the table lists the formulas for the three sums of squares, the three degrees of freedom, and the two mean squares required for the analysis of variance. Notice that the formulas for the *SS* are expressed in terms of the three intermediate quantities [(I), (II), (III)] previously computed. The degrees of freedom are determined by using p (the number of different groups) and N (the total number of subjects in the sample.)

Part **iv** of Table 11–3 presents the traditional analysis of variance summary table, a customary display of the information in a simple analysis of variance. The first column is labeled "Source" and this denotes the source of the variance estimate. This is followed by the degrees of freedom, sums of squares, mean squares, and F ratio.

NUMERICAL EXAMPLE

research question Some years ago it was discovered that if a person were wired up so that "brain waves," EEG, heart rate, respiration rate, eye movements, etc. were recorded, it was possible to determine from the pattern of these measures when the person was dreaming.[8] With this method of detecting when a person was dreaming it was then possible to determine whether or not people who were accustomed to dreaming could suddenly do without dreaming. An interesting question about the opportunity to dream is whether deprivation of dreaming would have any effects on personality during the waking day. If normal adults seem to need to dream, perhaps they would become anxious and irritable if the opportunity to dream were curtailed. Consider the following hypothetical experiment.[9] Suppose one group of subjects

[8] For example, see N. Kleitman, "Patterns of Dreaming," *Scientific American*, 1960, CCIII, 82–88.
[9] Based upon, but not identical to W. Dement, "The Effect of Dream Deprivation," *Science*, 1960, CXXXI, 1705–1707.

11–3 General computational procedures.

i.	Group 1	Group 2	...	Group p	...	Total Sample
	X_{11}	X_{12}	...	X_{1p}		
	X_{21}	X_{22}	...	X_{2p}		
	X_{31}	X_{32}	...	X_{3p}		
	...	...		...		
	X_{n_11}	X_{n_22}	...	X_{n_pp}		
Sums	$T_1 = \sum_{i=1}^{n_1} X_{i1}$	$T_2 = \sum_{i=1}^{n_2} X_{i2}$	...	$T_p = \sum_{i=1}^{n_p} X_{ip}$	...	$T = \sum_{j=1}^{p} T_j$
n_j	n_1	n_2	...	n_p	...	$N = \sum_{j=1}^{p} n_j$
Means	$\bar{X}_1 = \dfrac{T_1}{n_1}$	$\bar{X}_2 = \dfrac{T_2}{n_2}$	...	$\bar{X}_p = \dfrac{T_p}{n_p}$	...	
Sum of squared scores	$\sum_{i=1}^{n_1} X_{i1}{}^2$	$\sum_{i=1}^{n_2} X_{i2}{}^2$	...	$\sum_{i=1}^{n_p} X_{ip}{}^2$	...	$\sum_{j=1}^{p}\left(\sum_{i=1}^{n_j} X_{ij}{}^2\right)$
Squared sum of scores divided by n_j	$\dfrac{T_1^2}{n_1}$	$\dfrac{T_2^2}{n_2}$	...	$\dfrac{T_p^2}{n_p}$	...	$\sum_{j=1}^{p}\left(\dfrac{T_j^2}{n_j}\right)$

ii.

$$(I) = \frac{T^2}{N} \qquad (II) = \sum_{j=1}^{p}\left(\sum_{i=1}^{n_j} X_{ij}^2\right) \qquad (III) = \sum_{j=1}^{p}\left(\frac{T_j^2}{n_j}\right)$$

iii.

$$SS_{\text{between}} = (III) - (I) \qquad df_{\text{between}} = p - 1 \qquad MS_{\text{between}} = \frac{SS_{\text{between}}}{df_{\text{between}}}$$

$$SS_{\text{within}} = (II) - (III) \qquad df_{\text{within}} = N - p \qquad MS_{\text{within}} = \frac{SS_{\text{within}}}{df_{\text{within}}}$$

$$SS_{\text{total}} = (II) - (I) \qquad df_{\text{total}} = N - 1$$

iv.

Summary Table

Source	df	SS	MS	F
Between groups	$p - 1$	SS_{between}	MS_{between}	$\dfrac{MS_{\text{between}}}{MS_{\text{within}}}$
Within groups	$N - p$	SS_{within}	MS_{within}	
Total	$N - 1$	SS_{total}		

had their sleep interrupted several times during the evening but never during or immediately before a dream. A second group was aroused an equal number of times, but on two occasions during each evening this wakening was at the onset of a dream. Lastly, a third group was awakened an equal number of times but these subjects were always aroused only when they started to dream. Therefore, three groups of subjects were characterized by either no, some, or much dream interruption. These procedures were followed for six consecutive nights. During each day the subjects were interviewed and given some personality tests that were designed to evaluate how anxious and irritable the subjects were. High scores indicated a very upset individual. The score for each subject was the total irritability over the six-day period. The hypothetical results are presented in Tables 11–4 and 11–5. The means for the three groups: no, some, and much interruption, were 4.00, 8.00, and 17.75, respectively. This seems to indicate that the prevention of dreaming produces increased irritability and anxiety in normal adults. But, the observed differences between means could

---

11–4   Summary of the numerical example of a simple analysis of variance (the dream example).

Hypotheses

$$H_0: \mu_1 = \mu_2 = \mu_3 = \mu$$
$$H_1: \text{Not } H_0$$

Assumptions

1. The subjects are **randomly** and **independently** sampled.
2. The groups are **independent** from one another.
3. The population variances for the groups are **homogeneous** (i.e., $\sigma_1{}^2 = \sigma_2{}^2 = \sigma_3{}^2$).
4. The population distributions are **normal** in form.

Decision Rules (from Table E)

Given: .05 significance level, $df = 2, 12$

If $F_{\text{obs}} < 3.88$, do not reject H_0
If $F_{\text{obs}} \geq 3.88$, reject H_0

Computation

See Table 11–5

$$F_{\text{obs}} = 24.50$$

Decision

Reject H_0

be a function of sampling error, there being no real difference among these three groups in the population. The analysis of variance addresses itself to this question: Given the null hypothesis of no differences in the population means, what is the probability that the observed difference between these three sample means is merely a function of sampling error? The details of this analysis are described below and summarized in Table 11–4.

statistical hypotheses   The question above boils down to determining the probability that the population means for the three groups are in fact equal and thus equal to the grand mean. Symbolically stated, the null hypothesis is

$$H_0: \mu_1 = \mu_2 = \mu_3 = \mu$$

The alternative is

$$H_1: \text{Not } H_0$$

assumptions   The assumptions underlying this test have been explained on pages 252–254.

significance level   Adopt $\alpha = .05$.

critical values   The computational work presented in Table 11–5 shows that in this case the numerator of the F ratio has 2 degrees of freedom and the denominator has 12. At $\alpha = .05$ with $df = 2/12$, the critical value for F is 3.88 according to Table E. Notice that no mention is made of whether the test is directional or non-directional. In the analysis of variance this issue is more complicated than for other tests of significance. Consequently, in this text all analysis of variance tests will be non-directional (procedures for directional tests are beyond the scope of this text[10]).

decision rules   The decision rules are:

If $F_{obs} < 3.88$, do not reject H_0
If $F_{obs} \geq 3.88$, reject H_0

computation   The calculations are presented in Table 11–5, following the general procedures set forth in Table 11–3.

interpretation   The observed $F = 24.50$. Clearly, this is greater than the required value of 3.88 at $\alpha = .05$. In fact, as presented at the

[10] B. J. Winer, op.cit.

11–5 Computational example.

	Group 1 (no interruption)	Group 2 (some interruption)	Group 3 (much interruption)	Total Sample
	7 5 3 4 1	5 9 12 12 7 3	21 15 17 18	
i. Totals	$T_1 = (7 + 5 + \cdots + 1)$ $= 20$	$T_2 = (5 + 9 + \cdots + 3)$ $= 48$	$T_3 = (21 + 15 + \cdots + 18)$ $= 71$	$T = \sum_{j=1}^{p} T_j = 139$
n_j	$n_1 = 5$	$n_2 = 6$	$n_3 = 4$	$N = \sum_{j=1}^{p} n_j = 15$
Means	$\bar{X}_1 = \dfrac{20}{5} = 4.00$	$\bar{X}_2 = \dfrac{48}{6} = 8.00$	$\bar{X}_3 = \dfrac{71}{4} = 17.75$	
Sum of squared scores	$\sum X_{i1}^{2} = 100$	$\sum X_{i2}^{2} = 452$	$\sum X_{i3}^{2} = 1279$	$\sum_{j=1}^{p} \left(\sum_{i=1}^{n_j} X_{ij}^{2} \right) = 1831$
Squared sum of scores divided by n_j	$\dfrac{T_1^{2}}{n_1} = \dfrac{(20)^2}{5} = 80$	$\dfrac{T_2^{2}}{n_2} = \dfrac{(48)^2}{6} = 384$	$\dfrac{T_3^{2}}{n_3} = \dfrac{(71)^2}{4} = 1260.25$	$\sum_{j=1}^{p} \left(\dfrac{T_j^{2}}{n_j} \right) = 1724.25$

ii. $(I) = \dfrac{T^2}{N} = \dfrac{(139)^2}{15} = 1288.07$ $(II) = \displaystyle\sum_{j=1}^{p}\left(\sum_{i=1}^{n_j} X_{ij}^{2}\right) = 1831$ $(III) = \displaystyle\sum_{j=1}^{p}\left(\dfrac{T_j^{2}}{n_j}\right) = 1724.25$

iii.
$SS_{\text{between}} = (III) - (I) = 1724.25 - 1288.07 = 436.18$ $df = p - 1 = 3 - 1 = 2$
$SS_{\text{within}} = (II) - (III) = 1831 - 1724.25\ = 106.75$ $df = N - p = 15 - 3 = 12$
$SS_{\text{total}} = (II) - (I) = 1831 - 1288.07\ = 542.93$ $df = N - 1 = 15 - 1 = 14$

$$MS_{\text{between}} = \dfrac{SS_{\text{between}}}{df_{\text{between}}} = \dfrac{436.18}{2} = 218.09$$

$$MS_{\text{within}} = \dfrac{SS_{\text{within}}}{df_{\text{within}}} = \dfrac{106.75}{12} = 8.90$$

iv.

Summary Table

Source	df	SS	MS	F
Between groups	2	436.18	218.09	$\dfrac{MS_{\text{between}}}{MS_{\text{within}}} = \dfrac{218.09}{8.90} = 24.50**$
Within groups	12	106.75	8.90	
Total	14	542.93		

Critical values $(df = 2, 12)$ $*F_{.05} = 3.88, p < .05$
$**F_{.01} = 6.93, p < .01$

bottom of Table 11–5, the observed value exceeds the critical value for these degrees of freedom when the significance level is .01. Customarily, the .05 level is used as the *minimum* significance level for stating that the data suggest the rejection of the null hypothesis. However, the researcher may indicate when the *F* exceeds the critical value at a higher level of significance. Frequently, the value of *F* is followed by * or ** or *** if it exceeds the critical value for $\alpha = .05$, .01, or .001, respectively. Thus, since 24.50 is larger than the critical value for $\alpha = .01$, this fact is indicated by writing the *F* value in the summary table as 24.50**. (Actually, $F_{obs} = 24.50$ exceeds the .001 level, but our table only gives the .01 critical values.)

The obtained *F* value results in rejection of the null hypothesis. This means the probability that the three means (4, 8, and 17.75) differ merely by sampling error is very small. Therefore, it is likely that the between-groups variance estimate was influenced by treatment effects and the population group means probably do differ from one another. The conclusion is that it is likely that the interruption and prevention of dreaming in adults leads to increased anxiety and irritability.

the relationship between the analysis of variance and other statistics

F AND t

If the analysis of variance is simply an extension of the *t* test to accommodate to more than just two groups, then there should be some relationship between *t* and *F*. More specifically, there should be some relationship between the results using the independent-groups *t* test and the analysis of variance when only two groups are to be compared.

The general nature of the relationship between *F* and *t* is

$$F_{1,v} = t_v^2$$

in which the subscripts indicate the degrees of freedom.

This relationship applies both to the observed values of *F* and *t* when comparing just two groups and also to the critical values.

Suppose one considers only the first two groups of scores in the experiment on the interruption of dreaming as presented in Table 11–5. One could perform a *t* test or an analysis of variance to test the difference between these two groups. It happens that because $F_{1,v} = t_v^2$, the two analyses would yield the same general result. For example, at $\alpha = .05$ (nondirectional) and with 17 *df*, the critical value of *t* is $t_{crit} = 2.11$. At the same significance level with degrees of freedom equal to 1 and 17, the required F is $F_{crit} = 4.45$. If $F_{1,v} = t_v^2$, then the following should hold:

$$4.45 \overset{?}{=} (2.11)^2$$

It does. In addition, the observed values of F and t hold the same relationship:

$$F_{obs} = (t_{obs})^2$$

Therefore, F and t are directly related and the analysis of variance is an extension of the t test between means to more than two groups.

EXERCISES

1. The following sets of numbers were obtained from a random number table.

Group 1	Group 2	Group 3
1	6	1
4	2	2
4	1	2
9	3	4
3	0	3
		7
		9

   (a) Compute the analysis of variance.
   (b) Add three to each score in Group 2 and six to each score in Group 3. This process is analogous to the existence of what in the population? Now, compute the analysis of variance again and explain any differences between this result and that found in Part (a).
   (c) Return to the original numbers as given above and add 20 to the last score in each group. Recompute the analysis of variance and explain any differences you observe.

2. Suppose the "error" component of your score is 4, the grand mean is 13, and the treatment effect associated with your group is -3. What is your score?

3. Explain how the partition of variability in the analysis of variance is analogous to the partition of variability in regression and correlation.

4. An experiment was designed to test the possibility that the expectancy teachers have about their children somehow becomes translated into actions that help to pro-

duce the expected characteristics (i.e., it is a self-fulfilling expectancy).[11] Children in the first grade of an elementary school were all given an intelligence test, but the teachers in the school thought it was a test for "late bloomers," children who would show sudden spurts of intellectual growth. The experimenters then selected three small groups of children *at random* and wrote to the teachers that the test showed the members in Group 1 probably would not demonstrate any particularly large growth spurts in the next year, the members of Group 2 would show a moderate amount, and those in the third group would show a great deal of advancement in the next year. Remember, the children were actually picked at random for these groups. A year later, the children were tested again. The difference in IQ is given below. Test the hypothesis that there were no differences among the groups in IQ change.

Group 1	Group 2	Group 3
3	10	14
2	4	25
6	1	10
0	14	19
1	5	15
5	3	9
	9	18

[11] Based upon but not identical to a study by R. Rosenthal and Lenore F. Jacobson, "Teacher Expectations for the Disadvantaged," *Scientific American*, 1968, CCXVIII, 19–23.

TWO-FACTOR ANALYSIS OF VARIANCE

12

The simple analysis of variance as described in Chapter 11 tests the likelihood that several sample means are actually diverse reflections of the same population mean and differ only because of sampling. It was assumed that these groups represented some type of one-dimensional classification: different amounts of food deprivation, different teaching programs, different makes of cars, etc. The point is that the several groups could be classified as being different levels or types of a *single* category of events, treatments, stimuli, etc.

purpose and rationale

TWO-FACTOR CLASSIFICATION

In actual practice, scientists more frequently view the groups involved in their experiments as belonging to more than one classification, and it is the purpose of this chapter to consider the extension of simple analysis of variance to the case in which the groups fall into a two-way classification scheme. For example, suppose one were interested in the question of whether vicarious reward or punishment would influence the extent to which children will imitate a model.

Consider the following experiment.[1] Forty boys and forty girls are randomly selected from a given school. Each child sees a movie in which an adult hits, pounds, pushes, and otherwise assaults a large plastic doll with a weighted base (called a Bobo doll). Half of the children of each sex see a film in which the adult aggressor is rewarded by another adult with praise and congratulations for the vicious attack while half of the children see the aggressor punished with verbal reprimands for violent behavior. After seeing the movie, all children are brought into a room with several age-appropriate toys including the Bobo doll. In a ten-minute play session, the number of imitated aggressive responses to the Bobo doll are counted. There are four groups in this experiment: (1) boys who see the aggressor rewarded, (2) boys who see the aggressor punished, (3) girls who see the aggressor rewarded, and (4) girls who see the aggressor punished. These four groups do not represent different levels of a single dimension, but rather each group belongs both to a classification based upon the sex of its subjects and to a classification based upon seeing the aggressor rewarded or punished.

If a single classification scheme is called a **factor** and each division within it a **level** (though these divisions need not necessarily represent different *amounts* of that factor—e.g., the sex factor with levels male and female), then the above example represents a **two-factor** experiment or **design** with two levels of each factor. Designating a factor by a capital letter and each level by a subscripted lower case letter of the same character, the example described above can be expressed in a tabular fashion as follows:

		Factor B **(Vicarious Reinforcement)**	
		b_1 **(reward)**	b_2 **(punishment)**
Factor A **(Sex)**	a_1 **(males)**	males who see aggressor rewarded	males who see aggressor punished
	a_2 **(females)**	females who see aggressor rewarded	females who see aggressor punished

Suppose the average number of imitative aggressive responses for each of the four groups was as follows:

[1] Similar to A. Bandura, D. Ross, and S. A. Ross, "Imitation of Film-Mediated Aggressive Models," *Journal of Abnormal and Social Psychology*, 1963, LXVI, 3–11.

		Factor *B* (Vicarious Reinforcement)		
		b_1 (reward)	b_2 (punishment)	
Factor *A* (Sex)	a_1 (males)	25	5	15
	a_2 (females)	19	3	11
		22	4	13

In addition to the group means, the "marginal" numbers represent the mean number of imitative responses for males (15) and females (11) "collapsed over" (i.e., disregarding the different) reinforcement conditions, and the mean number for subjects watching a rewarded aggressor (22) and a punished aggressor (4) "collapsed over" sex of subject. The grand mean number of responses over all subjects is 13.

Three types of questions could be asked about data collected in accordance with this classification scheme. First, is there a significant difference between the levels of **Factor *A***? In this case, on the average, do boys imitate aggressive behavior more than girls? Specifically, does the difference between the means of 15 and 11 represent a difference that exists in the population or is this observed result merely a function of sampling error? Second, is there a significant difference between the levels of **Factor *B***? In this case, does the vicarious experience of seeing the aggressor rewarded or punished influence the extent to which children will imitate? Is the difference between the means of 22 and 4 within the realm of sampling error? Third, is there an **interaction** between the sex of the child and the type of vicarious reinforcement such that the effect of rewarding or punishing the aggressor is different for boys than for girls? Alternatively, such a result may be interpreted to mean that the difference in the tendency to imitate aggressive behavior between boys and girls is different depending upon whether the aggressor is rewarded or punished.

The possible differences between levels of Factor *A* or levels of Factor *B* collapsed over the other factor are called **main effects,** while a potential joint result of both these factors is known as an **interaction.** The meaning of these terms can be appreciated best by examining graphs of possible results of the two-factor example just described. In Figure 12–1, Graph A depicts the case in

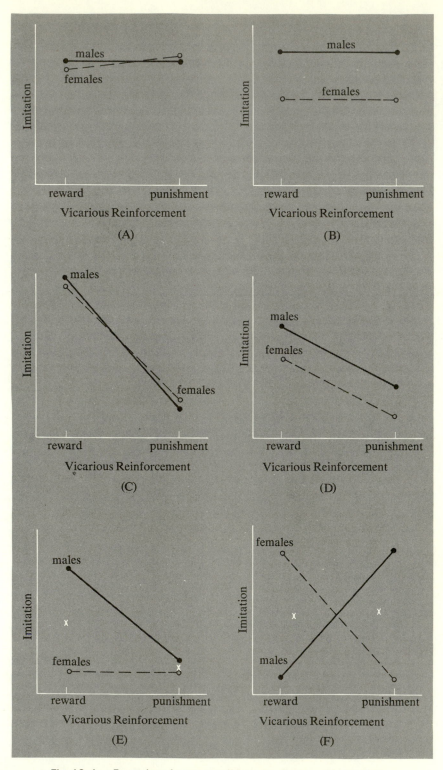

Fig. 12–1.   Examples of some possible main effects and interactions.

which all the means are approximately the same and there are no main effects and no interaction. Graph B describes one main effect: males imitate more than females. Notice that the reward and punishment conditions did not appear to influence the amount of imitation. Graph C illustrates a main effect for vicarious reinforcement with no effects for sex and no interaction. In short, children of both sexes imitated more if the aggressor was rewarded than if the aggressor was punished and the amount of imitation was the same for both sexes.

In Graph D, there appears to be an effect both for reinforcement and for sex of the child. In general, males imitated more than females and the reward condition generated more imitation than the punishment condition. There is no interaction in Graph D because the difference between males and females is about the same within each of the reinforcement conditions. Another way to say this is that the lines for each sex are approximately parallel indicating that the reinforcement conditions had a comparable effect on both sexes.

Graphs E and F depict interactions between sex and vicarious reinforcement.

The nature of an **interaction** is such that the effect for one factor is not the same under all conditions of the other factor.

In Graph E, whether the model was rewarded or punished made a difference for males but not for females. In Graph F, the influence for vicarious reinforcement had opposite effects for the two sexes. A rewarded aggressor produced more imitation in females than a punished aggressor, but the reverse was true for males. Notice that there is no main effect for vicarious reinforcement nor for sex. That is, if males and females are averaged separately within the reward and then within the punishment conditions, these means (indicated by white x's in Graph F, Figure 12–1) are not different from one another. Similarly, if the reward and punishment means are averaged separately within each sex, they are not different. Thus, Graph F depicts an interaction with no main effects.

In summary, a **main effect** is a difference in means for a given factor disregarding the other factor. For example, males may imitate more than females. An **interaction** occurs when the effect for a factor is different for different levels of the other factor. For example, the effect of vicarious reinforcement may depend on or **interact** with the sex of the child. Males may imitate a rewarded aggressor more than a punished one but females will not imitate either type of aggressor very much.

From another point of view, an interaction may be thought of as occurring when a specific combination of levels of factors generates a result that would not be predicted on the basis of knowledge of the effects of each factor separately. An analogy from chemistry provides a vivid illustration.[2] Suppose you

[2] The author is indebted to R. M. Liebert for calling this example to his attention. Of course, someone could predict the result of mixing HCl and NaOH on the basis of his familiarity with these chemicals. From a superficial standpoint, however, the example is analogous to statistical interaction.

had two beakers, each filled with a liquid. Specifically, one beaker contains hydrochloric acid (HCl); if a nickel were dropped into the acid it would likely dissolve leaving a copper coin. Suppose the other beaker contains sodium hydroxide (NaOH). If ground beef were placed into this solution it would disappear in a short while. Both beakers contain highly toxic substances that have severe effects on common substances. If the two solutions were mixed, one might suspect that the effects would be even more deleterious. Actually, however, the mixing of HCl and NaOH produces salty water (NaCl + H_2O or salt and water) after a time, and, except for the taste, may be drunk with relative safety. Here is an instance in which the combination of two factors each of which has a known deteriorating property is not a simple addition of effects which make the combination even more damaging. Rather, when the chemicals are mixed they **interact** in such a way that their effect is quite unlike what might have been predicted merely on the basis of knowing what each chemical does by itself. Thus, one way to conceive of a statistical interaction is that it occurs when the result of the joint influence of two factors is not what one would have predicted on the basis of knowing the separate effects of each factor.

In many analysis of variance designs, any possible combination of results can occur. There may be one or two significant main effects with or without an interaction or there may be an interaction and no main effects. However, when an interaction is found to be significant, generally one ignores the significance or insignificance of the main effects. That is, if there is an interaction, that fact means that the influence of one factor differed depending upon the level of the other factor. Since a main effect represents a difference in means for one factor collapsed over the levels of the other factor, the occurrence of an interaction indicates that collapsing over the other factor is not meaningful since the effects for Factor A are not the same within each level of Factor B. For example, consider Graph E in Figure 12–1. The small x's indicate the means for the reward and punishment conditions collapsed over the sex of the subject. It might be the case that the difference between these two means (the x's) is significant, and one would conclude that a rewarded aggressor produces more imitation than a punished aggressor. However, if the interaction depicted in that graph is also significant, it says that vicarious reinforcement makes a difference only for males and not for females, thus qualifying the general interpretation of the main effect for reinforcement. Consequently, if an interaction is significant, generally any main effects that are also significant are disregarded.[3] The reverse

---

[3] This general "rule" does have an exception in the event that an interaction exists but all levels of one group are significantly higher than the corresponding levels of the other group. The analysis would yield a main effect and an interaction. For example, suppose in Graph E of Figure 12–1 the line for males was substantially higher than for females under each of the reinforcement conditions. If the males evidenced more imitation than females under reward and under punishment conditions in addition to having the pattern difference displayed in Graph E, then the main effect for sex as well as the interaction would be meaningful. Determining if a main effect should be interpreted when an interaction is also present is a complex issue and beyond the scope of this text.

of this situation occurs in Graph F. Here the white x's are not different and it is likely there would not be a significant main effect for reinforcement. But, looking at the graph, it would be wrong to conclude that reinforcement had no influence on imitation—its influence depends on the sex of the subject and these differences are masked when the two sexes are averaged within reward and within punishment conditions. Therefore, if an interaction is significant, considerable care must be taken in interpreting the nature of main effects for factors involved in that interaction.

THE LOGIC OF TWO-FACTOR ANALYSIS OF VARIANCE [4]

The logic of two-factor analysis of variance is a direct extension of the rationale underlying simple analysis of variance. To review, in simple analysis of variance the total sum of squares was partitioned into two components, each of which provided an estimate of the variability in the population if the null hypothesis that the population mean of each group is the same value is true. However, one of these variance estimates was based upon the deviations of the group means about the grand mean (between-groups estimate) while the other was derived on the basis of the deviations of the scores about their respective group means (within-groups estimate). If the null hypothesis is true, these are both estimates of the same population value. However, since the between-groups estimate involves the group means, its size will depend upon the extent that the group means differ from one another. Consequently, if the between-groups estimate is very large relative to the within-groups estimate (which is not influenced by differences between group means), then one might conclude that the tentative presumption that these groups were all samples from the same population (i.e., the null hypothesis) may not be true. The ratio of the between- to within-groups estimate is distributed as F, and by determining the percentile of the observed ratio in this theoretical relative frequency distribution one can assign a probability to the possibility of obtaining such a ratio by sampling error alone. If the probability is sufficiently small, the null hypothesis of no difference between the population means is rejected.

In two-factor analysis of variance, the total sum of squares is usually partitioned into four components. Just as for simple analysis of variance, the variance estimates are called **mean squares** (MS). In the case of a double classification, the four mean squares all estimate the same population variance if the population means are all equal (i.e., the null hypothesis is true).[5] Consider these several sources of variability and their variance estimates.

One estimate of the variability in the population (symbolized by MS_A) is

---

[4] This discussion will be restricted to fixed factors, independent groups, and equal cell sizes as discussed later.

[5] Technically, there are several null hypotheses as discussed in the following material.

based upon the deviations of the means for the levels of Factor A (collapsed over Factor B) about the grand mean. This estimate is analogous to the between-groups estimate in a simple analysis of variance involving only the groups of Factor A. In the sex-reinforcement example presented above, this estimate would be based upon the deviations of the means for males (15) and females (11) about the grand mean (13). As such, its size is sensitive to differences between the means of the levels of Factor A. However, under the null hypothesis, differences between these means are merely a reflection of sampling error.

A second estimate of the variability in the population (symbolized by MS_B) is based upon the deviations of the means for the levels of Factor B (collapsed over Factor A) about the grand mean. As such, it is analogous to MS_A except that the means for the levels of Factor B are used. In the example, this estimate would be based upon the deviations of the reward (22) and punishment (4) means about the grand mean (11). This estimate is sensitive to differences between the means for Factor B.

A third estimate of the variability in the population (symbolized by MS_{AB}) is based upon the deviations of each group mean from what would be predicted on the basis of the knowledge of the two main effects. This mean square is sensitive to the possible interaction between Factors A and B.

Finally, the fourth estimate of the population variability is derived in the same manner as the within-groups estimate in simple analysis of variance (MS_{within}). It is based upon the deviations of each score from its respective group mean. As such, it is not sensitive to differences between groups or between levels of factors. Therefore, the within-groups estimate will be used as a standard against which the size of the other estimates may be evaluated.

The ratio of the mean square for Factor A divided by the mean square within-groups provides a test of the null hypothesis that the means of the levels of A differ from one another merely as a function of sampling error. Under the null hypothesis, the size of this ratio should not be very large since both variances presumably estimate the same value. However, since MS_A is sensitive to differences between the means for Factor A but MS_{within} is not, the ratio will be large to the extent that those means deviate from one another. If they are very different, the ratio will be so large that the probability that these deviations derive merely from sampling error is exceedingly remote, and the null hypothesis may be rejected. The conclusion would be that the means for the levels of Factor A are "significantly different" from one another.

Similarly, the ratio of the mean square for Factor B divided by MS_{within} reflects the extent to which the means for the levels of Factor B differ from one another. The general rationale for testing the null hypothesis that such differences are merely a function of sampling error is similar to that just described for Factor A.

Analogously, the ratio of MS_{AB} divided by MS_{within} tests the proposition that an interaction between Factors A and B exists in the population.

In short, the logic of double classification analysis of variance is a direct extension of that employed for simple analysis of variance. The total sum of squares is partitioned into components that are each sensitive to different aspects of the classification scheme. Under the null hypothesis, all the groups in the design are randomly selected and have the same population mean. If this is true, the sample means of the groups and the means for the levels of the two factors should deviate only by sampling error. Since MS_A, MS_B, and MS_{AB} are sensitive to different characteristics of the design while MS_{within} is not influenced by these characteristics, the ratio of each of the three mean squares to MS_{within} provides an F ratio that tests the null hypothesis that selected means differ only to an extent expected by sampling error.

derivation of formulas

NOTATION AND TERMINOLOGY

The raw score notation follows the general plan described for the simple one-factor analysis of variance except that an additional subscript is necessary. This notation is summarized in Table 12–1. A single score is indicated by X_{ijk} which represents the ith individual in the jth level of Factor A and the kth level of Factor B. There are a total of p levels of Factor A and q levels of Factor B. It will be assumed that there are an equal number of subjects in each of the jk groups and this number is n.[6]

Any group in the experiment is called a **cell** of the design, and the location of any cell is determined by the intersection of a specific row and column as indicated in Table 12–1. Thus, the intersection of the jth row and the kth column defines the jkth cell. The total of all the subjects in that cell is represented by T_{jk} and the mean of that group is written $\overline{X}_{jk}$. Therefore, the total of all the scores in cell 23 (read "cell two-three") is given by T_{23} and the mean of this cell is $\overline{X}_{23} = T_{23}/n$. The total of all the scores in a given row is $T_{j.}$ in which j indicates the row and the dot (located where the column designation should be) signifies that the scores have been summed over all columns. Thus, the mean of the third row is written as $\overline{X}_{3.} = T_{3.}/nq$ since there are q groups each containing n subjects in each row. Similarly, the mean of the second column is defined by $\overline{X}_{.2} = T_{.2}/np$ or in the kth column $X_{.k} = T_{.k}/np$. The dot now indicates scores have been summed over all rows. The grand total and mean (i.e., over all rows and columns) are written $T_{..}$ and $\overline{X}_{..}$.

---

[6] The two-factor techniques described in this text demand that there are an equal number of subjects per cell and that n is greater than 1. Special procedures do exist for the case in which the groups do not have equal numbers of subjects and/or $n = 1$. See, for example, B. J. Winer, *Statistical Principles in Experimental Design*, second edition (New York: McGraw-Hill, 1972).

12–1 Summary of Raw Score Notation for the Two-Factor Analysis of Variance.

		Factor B			Row Means
		b_1	b_2 $\quad \cdots$	b_q	
Factor A	a_1	X_{111} X_{211} X_{311} $\vdots$ X_{n11}	X_{112} $\quad\cdots$ X_{212} $\quad\cdots$ X_{312} $\quad\cdots$ $\vdots$ X_{n12} $\quad\cdots$	X_{11q} X_{21q} X_{31q} $\vdots$ X_{n1q}	
		$\bar{X}_{11} = \dfrac{T_{11}}{n}$	$\bar{X}_{12} = \dfrac{T_{12}}{n} \ \cdots$	$\bar{X}_{1q} = \dfrac{T_{1q}}{n}$	$\bar{X}_{1\cdot} = \dfrac{T_{1\cdot}}{nq}$
	a_2	X_{121} X_{221} X_{321} $\vdots$ X_{n21}	X_{122} $\quad\cdots$ X_{222} $\quad\cdots$ X_{322} $\quad\cdots$ $\vdots$ X_{n22} $\quad\cdots$	X_{12q} X_{22q} X_{32q} $\vdots$ X_{n2q}	
		$\bar{X}_{21} = \dfrac{T_{21}}{n}$	$\bar{X}_{22} = \dfrac{T_{22}}{n} \ \cdots$	$\bar{X}_{2q} = \dfrac{T_{2q}}{n}$	$\bar{X}_{2\cdot} = \dfrac{T_{2\cdot}}{nq}$
	$\vdots$	$\vdots$	$\vdots \qquad \cdots$	$\vdots$	$\vdots$
	a_p	X_{1p1} X_{2p1} X_{3p1} $\vdots$ X_{np1}	X_{1p2} $\quad\cdots$ X_{2p2} $\quad\cdots$ X_{3p2} $\quad\cdots$ $\vdots$ X_{np2} $\quad\cdots$	X_{1pq} X_{2pq} X_{3pq} $\vdots$ X_{npq}	
		$\bar{X}_{p1} = \dfrac{T_{p1}}{n}$	$\bar{X}_{p2} = \dfrac{T_{p2}}{n} \ \cdots$	$\bar{X}_{pq} = \dfrac{T_{pq}}{n}$	$\bar{X}_{p\cdot} = \dfrac{T_{p\cdot}}{nq}$
Column Means		$\bar{X}_{\cdot 1} = \dfrac{T_{\cdot 1}}{np}$	$\bar{X}_{\cdot 2} = \dfrac{T_{\cdot 2}}{np} \ \cdots$	$\bar{X}_{\cdot q} = \dfrac{T_{\cdot q}}{np}$	**Grand Mean** $\bar{X}_{\cdot\cdot} = \dfrac{T_{\cdot\cdot}}{npq}$

n = the number of subjects in each group

a_j = the jth level of Factor A

p = the number of levels of Factor A

b_k = the kth level of Factor B

q = the number of levels of Factor B

X_{ijk} = the ith score in the jkth group

T_{jk} = the total of all scores in the jkth group

$\bar{X}_{jk}$ = the mean of the jkth group

THE PARTITION OF VARIABILITY

In simple analysis of variance, the total variability of scores was partitioned into two parts, a between- and a within-groups component. This partitioning can be conceptualized in the following way. Why do scores differ from one another? One reason is that scores represent different groups or treatments which may be associated with different average response levels. Thus, there may be average between-group differences. A second reason is that even within a group, all subjects do not usually score the same value because of individual differences and measurement error. So there is variability within groups. Consequently, subjects differ in score value from one another (SS_{total}) because they belong to different groups in the design ($SS_{between}$) and because of individual differences and measurement error (SS_{within}). Symbolically,

$$SS_{total} = SS_{between} + SS_{within}$$

Turning to the case of a two-factor design, we can again ask why subjects differ in score value. Subjects may differ because of average group differences, but the group differences are now more complicated than before because there are two classification schemes. A subject belongs to a level in Factor A which may be associated with a higher or lower average score, and the subject belongs to a level of Factor B which may also be associated with a certain average score. In addition, there might be something special about being in the combination of a certain level of Factor A and Factor B which is associated with an average score that would not have been predicted solely on the basis of Factors A and B alone. Finally, subjects vary within groups as a function of individual differences and measurement error. Therefore, in two-factor analysis of variance, subjects differ in score value from one another because of group differences due to Factor A (SS_A), Factor B (SS_B), and the interaction of Factors A and B (SS_{AB}), in addition to individual differences and measurement error (SS_{within}). Symbolically,

$$SS_{total} = SS_A + SS_B + SS_{AB} + SS_{within}$$

Consider a numerical example as an illustration of these sources of variability in score value. Suppose Bill is a male in the experiment described above and was shown the movie in which the adult's aggressive behavior was rewarded. Look at Table 12–2 which presents this experimental design along with the means for the groups. Bill is a member of the male-reward group located in the top-left corner. Suppose Bill's score is 28. We can now ask, why do individual subjects in the experiment not all score the same value? If they did, everyone would have scored the grand mean which equalled 13. Why did Bill, for example, score 28 and not 13? To what shall we attribute the difference between any score X_{ijk} and the grand mean $\overline{X}_{..}$? In Bill's case,

$$\overline{X}_{ijk} - \overline{X}_{..} = 28 - 13 = 15$$

12–2   Means for the Example Described in the Text.

| | | Factor *B*
(Vicarious Reinforcement) | |
		b_1 (reward)	b_2 (punishment)	
Factor *A* (Sex)	a_1 (males)	25	5	15
	a_2 (females)	19	3	11
		22	4	13

First of all, Bill is a male and males tend to score a little higher than females. Specifically, according to Table 12–2, males averaged 15 whereas the grand mean over all subjects was 13. Therefore, one source of variability resides in the difference between the mean of the level of Factor *A* ($\overline{X}_{j.}$) and the grand mean ($\overline{X}_{..}$). In Bill's case,

$$(\overline{X}_{j.} - \overline{X}_{..}) = 15 - 13 = 2$$

which suggests that 2 points of the 15-point difference between Bill and the grand mean is because Bill is a male. Generally, one source of variability in score values is Factor *A*—whether the subject is a male or a female.

A second source is the fact that Bill saw the model rewarded whereas some other children saw the same behavior punished. Notice in Table 12–2 that the reward condition averaged 22 relative to the grand mean of 13. Therefore, another source of variability is the difference between the mean of the level of Factor *B* ($\overline{X}_{.k}$) and the grand mean ($\overline{X}_{..}$). For Bill,

$$(\overline{X}_{.k} - \overline{X}_{..}) = 22 - 13 = 9$$

which suggests that 9 points of the 15-point difference between Bill and the grand mean came from the fact that Bill was in the reward group. Being in one level or the other of Factor *B* is associated with some difference in score value.

Third, perhaps there is something special about the combination of being a male and seeing the model rewarded that is associated with a particular average score. For example, although males may display more aggressive behavior than females and seeing an adult rewarded for aggressiveness produces somewhat more imitated aggression than if the adult were punished, maybe in addition males are *especially* influenced by observing rewarded adult aggression—more than we might expect solely because they are males and because they saw rewarded versus punished aggressive behavior. For example, we have already seen that being a male was associated with an average score that was 2 points higher than the grand mean and that seeing the model rewarded was associated with an average that was 9 points higher than the grand mean. Based upon these values, the male-reward condition should have a mean that is $2 + 9 = 11$ points above the grand mean which would be an average of $13 + 11 = 24$. Actually, Table 12–2 indicates that the male-reward group had an average score of 25, 1 point higher than what one would have predicted on the basis of differences associated with Factor A and Factor B. This 1-point difference is variability associated with the AB interaction. Generally, the interaction variability derives from the difference between the particular group mean and the grand mean $(\overline{X}_{jk} - \overline{X}_{..})$ minus the effects for Factor A $(\overline{X}_{j.} - \overline{X}_{..})$ and Factor B $(\overline{X}_{.k} - \overline{X}_{..})$. Algebraically, this reduces to

$$(\overline{X}_{jk} - \overline{X}_{..}) - (\overline{X}_{j.} - \overline{X}_{..}) - (\overline{X}_{.k} - \overline{X}_{..})$$
$$\overline{X}_{jk} - \overline{X}_{..} - \overline{X}_{j.} + \overline{X}_{..} - \overline{X}_{.k} + \overline{X}_{..}$$
$$\overline{X}_{jk} - \overline{X}_{j.} - \overline{X}_{.k} + \overline{X}_{..}$$

Applied to Bill,

$$25 - 15 - 22 + 13 = 1$$

which implies that 1 point of the 15-point difference between Bill's score and the grand mean is associated with the specific combination of being a male who saw aggression rewarded—namely, the AB interaction.

The combination of the differences associated with Factor $A(+2)$, Factor $B(+9)$ and the AB interaction $(+1)$ in conjunction with the grand mean (13) accounts for how Bill's male-reward group had a mean of 25:

$$2 + 9 + 1 + 13 = 25$$

But, not everyone in that group had a score of 25. Bill scored 28. Therefore, the final reason why subjects score differently from one to another resides in the collection of individual differences and measurement error that is unique to each subject in the experiment. This source of variability is reflected in the difference between an individual subject's score and the group mean $(X_{ijk} - \overline{X}_{jk})$, which in Bill's case was $28 - 25 = 3$.

We can now conclude that individuals vary in score value $(X_{ijk} - \overline{X}_{..})$ as a function of which level of Factor A a subject is in $(\overline{X}_{j.} - \overline{X}_{..})$, which level of Factor B $(\overline{X}_{.k} - \overline{X}_{..})$, which combination of Factors A and B $(\overline{X}_{jk} - \overline{X}_{j.} - \overline{X}_{.k} + \overline{X}_{..})$, and individual differences and measurement error which produce differences between individual subjects and their respective group means $(X_{ijk} - \overline{X}_{jk})$. Algebraically, this statement can be expressed as

$$\underbrace{(X_{ijk} - \overline{X}_{..})}_{\text{total}} = \underbrace{(\overline{X}_{j.} - \overline{X}_{..})}_{A} + \underbrace{(\overline{X}_{.k} - \overline{X}_{..})}_{B}$$

$$+ \underbrace{(\overline{X}_{jk} - \overline{X}_{j.} - \overline{X}_{.k} + \overline{X}_{..})}_{AB} + \underbrace{(X_{ijk} - \overline{X}_{jk})}_{\text{within}}$$

In Bill's case,

$$28 - 13 = (15 - 13) + (22 - 13) + (25 - 15 - 22 + 13) + (28 - 25)$$
$$15 = \quad 2 \quad + \quad 9 \quad + \quad 1 \quad + \quad 3$$
$$15 = 15$$

sums of squares   Variability is expressed in terms of *squared* deviations summed over all subjects—that is, sums of squares. When the algebraic statement above is squared and summed over all subjects, the left side becomes $\sum\limits_{i=1}^{n} \sum\limits_{j=1}^{p} \sum\limits_{k=1}^{q} (X_{ijk} - \overline{X}_{..})^2$ which is the total sum of squares, SS_{total}. When the right side is squared and summed, all the cross product terms disappear and the total expression reduces to

$$SS_{\text{total}} = SS_A + SS_B + SS_{AB} + SS_{\text{within}}$$

This is what is meant by partitioning. The total sum of squares is divided into separate components which sum to SS_{total} and which represent different sources of variability (Factor A, Factor B, AB interaction, within groups).

degrees of freedom   As before, the variance estimates (mean squares, MS) are obtained by dividing each of these sums of squares by its appropriate degrees of freedom. The total sum of squares involves the squared deviation of each score from the grand mean. Thus, the number of degrees of freedom for SS_{total} will be one less than the total number of observations in the entire design. If there are n subjects per group and pq groups, the total number of subjects is npq, which may be abbreviated by N. Therefore,

$$df_{\text{total}} = npq - 1 = N - 1$$

The sum of squares for Factor A involves the squared deviation of each of the Factor A means from the grand mean. There are p such means, so the degrees of freedom for the Factor A variance estimate is

$$df_A = p - 1$$

Similarly, Factor B has q levels, so the degrees of freedom is

$$df_B = q - 1$$

Determining the degrees of freedom for interaction is slightly less intuitive. This sum of squares involves the cell means, but the grand mean and all marginal means (means for all levels of the main factors) are also involved. Therefore, the task is to determine how many cell means in the table are free to vary given the grand mean and all marginal means. Consider, for example, a 3 × 2 table:

?	?		10
			20
10	15	20	15

A little thought indicates that once the values for any two cells in a row are established—for example, the ones with question marks—then the means of the remaining cells can be determined. The open cells must have a value that would make the average within that row (or column) equal to the given marginal average. Therefore, in the above example, there are two degrees of freedom for interaction. It happens that the number of cells free to vary is always the product of (the number of rows minus one) times (the number of columns minus one) because one vacant cell in any row (or column) can be determined. Consequently, the degrees of freedom for interaction are

$$df_{AB} = (p - 1)(q - 1)$$

The sum of squares within groups is composed of the squared deviations of the scores about their own mean. Within any one group, $n - 1$ of those scores are free to vary. Since there are pq groups in the design, the degrees of freedom for SS_{within} are

$$df_{within} = pq(n - 1)$$
$$= pqn - pq$$
$$df_{within} = N - pq$$

Notice that just as was the case for the sums of squares, the degrees of freedom for the total equals the sum of the degrees of freedom for the component sources of variability:

$$df_{total} = df_A + df_B + df_{AB} + df_{within}$$

mean squares The mean squares for the several sources of variability are given by the sums of squares divided by their respective degrees of freedom:

$$MS_A = \frac{SS_A}{df_A}$$

$$MS_B = \frac{SS_B}{df_B}$$

$$MS_{AB} = \frac{SS_{AB}}{df_{AB}}$$

$$MS_{\text{within}} = \frac{SS_{\text{within}}}{df_{\text{within}}}$$

F ratios Once the mean squares have been determined, F ratios may be constructed to test the significance of the several possible treatment effects. The following F ratios may be formed:

$$F_A = \frac{MS_A}{MS_{\text{within}}}$$

$$F_B = \frac{MS_B}{MS_{\text{within}}}$$

$$F_{AB} = \frac{MS_{AB}}{MS_{\text{within}}}$$

In each case, under the null hypothesis the numerator and denominator are both estimates of the same population value. However, the numerators (in contrast to MS_{within}) are sensitive to differences between particular sets of group means. To the extent that these means differ from one another, the numerator of the F ratio will become large relative to its denominator. If the resulting ratio is so large that the probability is very small that an observed value of its size could be reasonably expected under the null hypothesis, then H_0 is rejected and one concludes that the differences between the means of the effect being considered are so great that they are not likely to be merely a result of sampling differences.[7]

NUMERICAL ILLUSTRATION OF TREATMENT EFFECTS

It will be helpful to observe in a numerical example how the presence of treatment effects, that is, large differences between group and grand means, is reflected in the results of an analysis of variance.

[7] A discussion of the assumptions required for this analysis appears in a later section.

Table 12–3 presents a 2×2 analysis of variance using randomly selected numbers between 0 and 10 as the scores. Since the numbers are random, it can be assumed that the null hypotheses are true and that in the population the group means are all equal. With certain additional assumptions, the population variance could be estimated by variances computed on these data in a variety of ways. It should not matter if variability is appropriately computed by taking scores about their cell means, means for the levels of one factor or another about the grand mean, etc. They should all estimate the same population variance. While these different estimates will probably not equal one another, if H_0 is true they should deviate from each other only by sampling error.

The sum of squares for Factor A reflects the extent to which the means for levels of A deviate from the grand mean. The $SS_A = 12.80$. Similarly, the sum of squares for Factor B reflects the deviations of the means for the levels of B about the grand mean. The $SS_B = 7.20$. The interaction sum of squares represents the degree to which the cell means deviate from the grand mean less the treatment effects for the respective levels of A and B. In this case, $SS_{AB} = 3.20$. Finally, the sum of squares within groups is computed by taking the squared deviation of each score about its own group mean. The $SS_{\text{within}} = 75.60$. The lower portion of Table 12–3 presents the traditional summary of the analysis of variance. The mean squares (MS) are calculated by dividing the SS by its degrees of freedom (df), and the F's are obtained by dividing the MS for A, B, or AB by the MS_{within}. Since according to the F table given in Table E of the Appendix the critical value for F with 1 and 16 degrees of freedom is 4.49 at $p < .05$, none of the effects in this example is significant.

Now consider the analysis presented in Table 12–4. The same numbers are used except that 10 has been added to each score in both the b_2 groups. This is analogous to introducing a treatment effect for Factor B. Observe how the several sums of squares respond to this specific manipulation. First, as one might expect, the sum of squares for Factor B increases considerably as a function of this change (and so does the total sum of squares). However, notice that the sums of squares for A, AB, and within groups do not change. This example illustrates how a selective introduction of a specific main effect is reflected only in the appropriate sum of squares.

Now turn to the analysis presented in Table 12–5. Here, the same random numbers (i.e., without treatment effects) used in Table 12–3 were modified by adding 10 only to the scores in the upper right-hand cell, ab_{12}. Since this difference is not added to the entire b_2 level (as was just done in Table 12–4) but only to b_2 within the a_1 level, the result should be an interaction between Factors A and B since the pattern of results for the levels of B depends upon or interacts with the level of A. As anticipated, the analysis shows an increase in the sum of squares for interaction, SS_{AB}, but observe that the sums of squares for A and B also increase. Only the SS_{within} remains uninfluenced by this change.

12–3 Two-Factor Analysis of Variance with No Effects.

Factor B

	b_1	b_2
a_1	5 4 3 4 2	8 9 4 2 5
	$\overline{X}_{11} = 3.6$	$\overline{X}_{12} = 5.6$

$\overline{X}_{1.} = 4.6$

Factor A

a_2	6 7 5 8 4	6 9 5 9 3
	$\overline{X}_{21} = 6.0$	$\overline{X}_{22} = 6.4$

$\overline{X}_{2.} = 6.2$

$\overline{X}_{.1} = 4.8$ $\overline{X}_{.2} = 6.0$ $\overline{X}_{..} = 5.4$

$$SS_A = nq \sum_{j=1}^{p} (\overline{X}_{j.} - \overline{X}_{..})^2$$
$$= (5)(2)[(4.6 - 5.4)^2 + (6.2 - 5.4)^2]$$
$$SS_A = 12.80$$

$$SS_B = np \sum_{k=1}^{q} (\overline{X}_{.k} - \overline{X}_{..})^2$$
$$= (5)(2)[(4.8 - 5.4)^2 + (6.0 - 5.4)^2]$$
$$SS_B = 7.20$$

Interaction

$$SS_{AB} = n \sum_{j=1}^{p} \sum_{k=1}^{q} (\overline{X}_{jk} - \overline{X}_{j.} - \overline{X}_{.k} + \overline{X}_{..})^2$$
$$= 5[(3.6 - 4.6 - 4.8 + 5.4)^2 + (5.6 - 4.6 - 6.0 + 5.4)^2$$
$$+ (6.0 - 6.2 - 4.8 + 5.4)^2 + (6.4 - 6.2 - 6.0 + 5.4)^2]$$
$$SS_{AB} = 3.20$$

Within Groups

$$SS_{\text{within}} = \sum_{i=1}^{n} \sum_{j=1}^{p} \sum_{k=1}^{q} (X_{ijk} - \overline{X}_{jk})^2$$
$$SS_{\text{within}} = 75.60$$

Source	df	SS	$MS = \dfrac{SS}{df}$	$F = \dfrac{MS}{MS_{\text{within}}}$
A	$p - 1 = 1$	12.80	12.80	2.71
B	$q - 1 = 1$	7.20	7.20	1.52
AB	$(p - 1)(q - 1) = 1$	3.20	3.20	.68
Within	$N - pq = 16$	75.60	4.72	
Total	$N - 1 = 19$	98.80		

12–4 Sample Two-Factor Diagram with a Treatment Effect Added to b_2

Factor B

	b_1	b_2 (+ 10)

Factor A

a_1

5	18
4	19
3	14
4	12
2	15
$\overline{X}_{11} = 3.6$	$\overline{X}_{12} = 15.6$

$\overline{X}_{1.} = 9.6$

a_2

6	16
7	19
5	15
8	19
4	13
$\overline{X}_{21} = 6.0$	$\overline{X}_{22} = 16.4$

$\overline{X}_{2.} = 11.2$

$\overline{X}_{.1} = 4.8$ $\overline{X}_{.2} = 16.0$ $\overline{X}_{..} = 10.4$

$$SS_A = nq \sum_{j=1}^{p} (\overline{X}_{j.} - \overline{X}_{..})^2$$
$$= (5)(2)[(9.6 - 10.4)^2 + (11.2 - 10.4)^2]$$
$$SS_A = 12.80$$

$$SS_B = np \sum_{k=1}^{q} (\overline{X}_{.k} - \overline{X}_{..})^2$$
$$= (5)(2)[(4.8 - 10.4)^2 + (16.0 - 10.4)^2]$$
$$SS_B = 627.20$$

Interaction

$$SS_{AB} = n \sum_{j=1}^{p} \sum_{k=1}^{q} (\overline{X}_{jk} - \overline{X}_{j.} - \overline{X}_{.k} + \overline{X}_{..})^2$$
$$= 5[(3.6 - 9.6 - 4.8 + 10.4)^2 + (15.6 - 9.6 - 16.0 + 10.4)^2$$
$$+ (6.0 - 11.2 - 4.8 + 10.4)^2 + (16.4 - 11.2 - 16.0 + 10.4)^2]$$
$$SS_{AB} = 3.20$$

Within Groups

$$SS_{\text{within}} = \sum_{i=1}^{n} \sum_{j=1}^{p} \sum_{k=1}^{q} (X_{ijk} - \overline{X}_{jk})^2$$
$$SS_{\text{within}} = 75.60$$

Source	df	SS	$MS = \dfrac{SS}{df}$	$F = \dfrac{MS}{MS_{\text{within}}}$
A	$p - 1 = 1$	12.80	12.80	2.71
B	$q - 1 = 1$	627.20	627.20	132.89
AB	$(p - 1)(q - 1) = 1$	3.20	3.20	.68
Within	$N - pq = 16$	75.60	4.72	
Total	$N - 1 = 19$	718.80		

12–5 Sample Two-Factor Design with a Treatment Effect Added to Cell ab_{12}

Factor B

	b_1	b_2	
a_1	5 4 3 4 2	(+10) 18 19 14 12 15	$\overline{X}_{1.} = 9.6$
	$\overline{X}_{11} = 3.6$	$\overline{X}_{12} = 15.6$	

Factor A

$$SS_A = nq \sum_{j=1}^{p} (\overline{X}_{j.} - \overline{X}_{..})^2$$
$$= (5)(2)[(9.6 - 7.9)^2 + (6.2 - 7.9)^2]$$
$$SS_A = 57.80$$

a_2	6 7 5 8 4	6 9 5 9 3	$\overline{X}_{2.} = 6.2$
	$\overline{X}_{21} = 6.0$	$\overline{X}_{22} = 6.4$	

| $\overline{X}_{.1} = 4.8$ | $\overline{X}_{.2} = 11.0$ | $\overline{X}_{..} = 7.9$ |

$$SS_B = np \sum_{k=1}^{q} (\overline{X}_{.k} - \overline{X}_{..})^2$$
$$= (5)(2)[(4.8 - 7.9)^2 + (11.0 - 7.9)^2]$$
$$SS_B = 192.20$$

Interaction

$$SS_{AB} = n \sum_{j=1}^{p} \sum_{k=1}^{q} (\overline{X}_{jk} - \overline{X}_{j.} - \overline{X}_{.k} + \overline{X}_{..})^2$$
$$= 5[(3.6 - 9.6 - 4.8 + 7.9)^2 + (15.6 - 9.6 - 11.0 + 7.9)^2$$
$$+ (6.0 - 6.2 - 4.8 + 7.9)^2 + (6.4 - 6.2 - 11.0 + 7.9)^2]$$
$$SS_{AB} = 168.20$$

Within Groups

$$SS_{\text{within}} = \sum_{i=1}^{n} \sum_{j=1}^{p} \sum_{k=1}^{q} (X_{ijk} - \overline{X}_{jk})^2$$
$$SS_{\text{within}} = 75.60$$

Source	df	SS	$MS = \dfrac{SS}{df}$	$F = \dfrac{MS}{MS_{\text{within}}}$
A	$p - 1 = 1$	57.80	57.80	12.24
B	$q - 1 = 1$	192.20	192.20	40.72
AB	$(p - 1)(q - 1) = 1$	168.20	168.20	35.63
Within	$N - pq = 16$	75.60	4.72	
Total	$N - 1 = 19$	493.80		

The inflation of SS_A and SS_B in response to the increment of a single cell results from the fact that such a manipulation does indeed change the means of the respective levels of A and B. The SS_{within} is not altered because adding a constant to any group of scores does not change the variability of those particular scores about their mean.

These comparisons illustrate how the analysis of variance is sensitive to different types of treatment effects. It shows how the SS_A and SS_B reflect differences in the marginal means, how SS_{AB} is changed when some but not all cells within a single level of one factor are altered, and how SS_{within} remains uninfluenced by changes in cell or level means. Consequently, if the null hypothesis is true and the groups are all random samples having the same population mean, these sums of squares all estimate the same value. However, to the extent that treatment effects exist for A, B, and/or AB, their respective mean squares will be inflated, but the mean square within groups will not be altered because it is not sensitive to differences between cell or level means. Consequently, the three F ratios, $\dfrac{MS_A}{MS_{within}}$, $\dfrac{MS_B}{MS_{within}}$, and $\dfrac{MS_{AB}}{MS_{within}}$, will test the existence of treatment effects in the population.

The above examples also demonstrate that when a significant interaction exists, significant effects for Factor A or Factor B may not be too meaningful. Recall that in Table 12–5 only cell ab_{12} was deliberately incremented, yet the sum of squares for Factors A and B as well as for the AB interaction were increased. Thus, the existence of interactions of some forms may also produce significant main effects even when only one cell is markedly different from the others. When a significant interaction is obtained, the data should be graphed in order to interpret the results.

ASSUMPTIONS UNDERLYING TWO-FACTOR ANALYSIS OF VARIANCE

Two-factor analysis of variance makes some of the same assumptions that are required in a single-factor analysis and for the same reasons.

First, the subjects must be **randomly and independently sampled**. Moreover, they should be randomly assigned to treatment conditions, though there are situations when this is not possible (e.g., when subject classification factors are used, such as sex, income level, blood type, etc.). Second, the groups in the design must be **independent** from one another. These assumptions are necessary so that the variability within each group is not correlated with the variability within another group. While all the analysis-of-variance procedures described in this text assume independent groups, techniques do exist for handling situations in which the groups are not independent, such as a before-after experiment in which the same subjects are measured before and then after a special treatment is administered.[8]

Additional assumptions are that the population distributions of each group in the design are **normal** in form and have equal variances (i.e., **homogeneity of variance**). The assumption of normality is made so that the variance estimates in the F ratio are independent, and so that the probabilities of the F distribution are appropriate. Homogeneity of variance is needed so that MS_{within} represents an appropriate pooling of the variability within each group of the design.

The procedures also assume that the factors involved in the design are **fixed**. There are two types of factors, **random** and **fixed**. A random factor is one for which the levels are randomly selected. For example, suppose a researcher were interested in the effects of a new teaching program versus an old teaching program at schools in a particular school system. If the school system is very large, perhaps not all the schools will be analyzed. Consequently, three of them are *randomly* selected and compose the three levels of the Factor A (schools) in the analysis. In this case, Factor A (schools) would be a random factor. However, if the researcher designated which particular schools were to be entered into the analysis, perhaps because of their size, socioeconomic makeup, geographical location, etc., then these schools would not be random selections from the population of schools but represent some "fixed" set of schools. Factor A (schools) would then be a fixed factor. It is possible to have a two-factor analysis of variance in which one factor is fixed and the other is random. This is called a **mixed model**. The procedures outlined in this text are only applicable to the **fixed model** (both factors are fixed), since this is the most common of the three designs. Techniques for analyzing the random and mixed models can be found elsewhere.[9]

Finally, the techniques outlined here have assumed that there are an **equal number of cases** in each group and that there is **more than one observation per cell**. Again, procedures do exist for the case in which the cells have unequal n.[10]

computation

COMPUTATIONAL FORMULAS

Just as with previous techniques, the definitional formulas are not the most convenient ones to use for computational purposes. A more satisfactory set of

---

[8] See "Repeated Measures Designs," B. J. Winer, *Statistical Principles in Experimental Design*, second edition (New York: McGraw-Hill, 1972). Also R. B. McCall and M. I. Appelbaum, "Bias in the Analysis of Repeated Measures Designs: Some Alternative Approaches," *Child Development*, 1973, XLIV, 401–415.

[9] Winer, op.cit.

[10] *Ibid.*

computational procedures is outlined in Table 12–6. Recall that $n =$ the number of subjects in each group, N is the total number of subjects in the design, $p =$ the number of levels of Factor A, $q =$ the number of levels of Factor B, and $X_{ijk} =$ the score for the ith subject in the jth level of A and kth level of B.

Part **i** of Table 12–6 displays the various cell, row, and column totals (sums). T_{jk} is the total for the jkth cell, $T_{j.}$ is the total for the jth level of A summed over all levels of B, $T_{.k}$ is the total for the kth level of B summed over all levels of A, and $T_{..}$ is the grand total accumulated over all observations in all conditions. If the data are laid out in rows and columns, all that has been done so far is to obtain the sum of scores within each group (T_{jk}) and for rows $(T_{j.})$ and columns $(T_{.k})$.

Part **ii** presents five quantities that facilitate the computation of the analysis of variance. Quantity (I) is the grand total squared, then divided by the total N in the design. Quantity (II) is simply the sum of all squared scores. Quantity (III) is the sum of the squared total for each level of Factor A divided by nq, and Quantity (IV) is the sum of the squared totals for each level of Factor B divided by np. Quantity (V) is the sum of the squares of all cell totals divided by n.

Part **iii** presents the formulas for obtaining all the necessary entries in the analysis of variance summary table. Notice that the sums of squares are computed quite easily by adding and subtracting the intermediate quantities displayed in Part **ii**. The sum of the degrees of freedom and the sum of the SS should equal df_{total} and SS_{total}, respectively.

FORMAL EXAMPLE

The issue of nature-nurture (the relative contributions of heredity and environment to the behavior of organisms) has been a popular topic for many years. Not too long ago, people believed that most development was predetermined by the genes and that growth was merely the unfolding of the plan of the genes. Now, the most common position is called interactionism. This theory states that the roles of heredity and environment are conceived to work in concert. One cannot talk about the role of heredity without specifying the environment and vice versa. In short, heredity and environment interact to produce the behavior we observe.

One illustration of the notion of interactionism is that the same environmental experience affects different species in dissimilar ways. For example, suppose twelve dogs from each of four different breeds (basenji, shetland sheepdog, wire-haired fox terrier, beagle) were either indulged or disciplined between the third and eighth week of their lives.[11] The indulged animals were encouraged in

---

[11] Inspired by but not identical to D. G. Freedman, "Constitutional and Environmental Interactions in Rearing of Four Breeds of Dogs," *Science*, 1958, CXXVII, 585–586.

12–6 Computational Formulas for Two-Factor Analysis of Variance

i. Table of Totals

		Factor B				Row Totals
		b_1	b_2	$\cdots$	b_q	
Factor A	a_1	T_{11}	T_{12}	$\cdots$	T_{1q}	$T_{1.}$
	a_2	T_{21}	T_{22}	$\cdots$	T_{2q}	$T_{2.}$
	$\cdots$	$\cdots$	$\cdots$	$\cdots$	$\cdots$	$\cdot$
	a_p	T_{p1}	T_{p2}	$\cdots$	T_{pq}	$T_{p.}$
Column Totals		$T_{.1}$	$T_{.2}$	$\cdots$	$T_{.q}$	$T_{..}$

ii. Intermediate Quantities

$$(\text{I}) = \frac{T_{..}^2}{N} \qquad (\text{II}) = \sum_{i=1}^{n}\sum_{j=1}^{p}\sum_{k=1}^{q} X_{ijk}^2 \qquad (\text{III}) = \frac{\sum_{j=1}^{p} T_{j.}^2}{nq}$$

$$(\text{IV}) = \frac{\sum_{k=1}^{q} T_{.k}^2}{np} \qquad (\text{V}) = \frac{\sum_{j=1}^{p}\sum_{k=1}^{q} T_{jk}^2}{n}$$

iii. Summary Table

Source	df	SS	MS	F
A	$p-1$	$(\text{III})-(\text{I})$	$\dfrac{SS_A}{df_A}$	$\dfrac{MS_A}{MS_{\text{within}}}$
B	$q-1$	$(\text{IV})-(\text{I})$	$\dfrac{SS_B}{df_B}$	$\dfrac{MS_B}{MS_{\text{within}}}$
AB	$(p-1)(q-1)$	$(\text{V})+(\text{I})-(\text{III})-(\text{IV})$	$\dfrac{SS_{AB}}{df_{AB}}$	$\dfrac{MS_{AB}}{MS_{\text{within}}}$
Within	$N-pq$	$(\text{II})-(\text{V})$	$\dfrac{SS_{\text{within}}}{df_{\text{within}}}$	
Total	$N-1$	$(\text{II})-(\text{I})$		

play, aggression, and climbing on their supine handler. In contrast, the disciplined dogs were restrained on their handler's lap, taught to sit, stay, come on command, etc. The indulged-disciplined treatment was inspired by reports that overindulged children often cannot inhibit their impulses in structured situations. Consequently, the test of the effects of these treatments was to take each animal into a room with the handler and a bowl of meat. The dog was hungry but the handler prevented it from eating for three minutes by hitting the animal on the rump with a rolled newspaper and shouting "no." After this period of restraint, the handler left the room and the length of time it took the dog to begin to eat the meat (latency) was recorded. Presumably, if the observations on children translate to dogs, the indulged animals should go to the food more quickly (record shorter latencies) than the disciplined dogs.

A simplified set of hypothetical data is presented in Part **i** of Table 12–7. Factor A (**rearing condition**) has two levels, indulged and disciplined. Factor B is **breed** and has four levels. Note that the "levels" of Factor B do not constitute a continuum but rather separate categories. Consider some possible results. It may be that the disciplined dogs will refrain from eating the food while the indulged will feast quickly. In this case, one would expect that the analysis of variance would yield a significant effect for Factor A. Another result might be that regardless of rearing condition, some breeds generally go to the food more rapidly than others, in which case there would be a significant effect for Factor B. Lastly, the effect of indulged or disciplined rearing may take different forms for the several breeds. For one breed the rearing treatment might make a difference, whereas for another it might not or it might even have an opposite effect. In this event, the analysis would yield a significant interaction between rearing and breed. If an interaction of this form were significant, then any main effects for rearing and breed would be re-evaluated and perhaps disregarded. Part **ii** of Table 12–7 gives the totals for each cell of the design and the marginal totals. Part **iii** presents the computation of the intermediate quantities, Part **iv** displays the calculation of the sums of squares and degrees of freedom, and the summary of the analysis is given in Part **v**.

In the present example, the critical values of F for 3 and 40 degrees of freedom are 2.84 and 4.31 for tests at the .05 and .01 levels, respectively. The observed F for interaction is 13.02, a value that exceeds the critical level at $p < .01$. The F's for the main effects are calculated for completeness of presentation. A formal summary of this analysis is presented in Table 12–8. Since there are three sources of variability to be tested, there are three sets of hypotheses, critical values, decision rules, etc. Moreover, notice that the hypotheses are now stated in terms of **treatment effects** as a notational convenience. Observe that the symbol α_1 represents the difference in the population between the mean for a_1 and the grand mean: $\alpha_1 = \mu_{a_1} - \mu$. Under the null hypothesis, the population means for a_1 and a_2 are presumed to be equal to each other and thus to the population grand mean. Therefore, since $\mu_{a_1} = \mu$ and $\mu_{a_2} = \mu$,

12–7 Computational Example of a Two-Factor Analysis of Variance.

i. Raw Data

	Factor B (breed)			
	b_1 (basenjis)	b_2 (shetland)	b_3 (terriers)	b_4 (beagles)
Factor A (rearing) a_1 (indulged)	1 4 3 1 2 2	7 10 10 9 6 8	6 9 7 8 5 10	9 7 10 10 8 9
a_2 (disciplined)	5 1 4 1 2 3	9 9 8 10 5 8	1 0 3 1 2 4	2 6 3 4 5 3

ii. Table of Totals

	b_1	b_2	b_3	b_4	
a_1	$T_{11} = (1 + \cdots + 2)$ $= 13$	$T_{12} = (7 + \cdots + 8)$ $= 50$	$T_{13} = (6 + \cdots + 10)$ $= 45$	$T_{14} = (9 + \cdots + 9)$ $= 53$	$T_{1.} = 161$
a_2	$T_{21} = (5 + \cdots + 3)$ $= 16$	$T_{22} = (9 + \cdots + 8)$ $= 49$	$T_{23} = (1 + \cdots + 4)$ $= 11$	$T_{24} = (2 + \cdots + 3)$ $= 23$	$T_{2.} = 99$
	$T_{.1} = 29$	$T_{.2} = 99$	$T_{.3} = 56$	$T_{.4} = 76$	$T_{..} = 260$

iii. Intermediate Quantities

$$(I) = \frac{T_{..}^2}{N} = \frac{(260)^2}{48} = 1408.3333$$

$$(II) = \sum_{i=1}^{n} \sum_{j=1}^{p} \sum_{k=1}^{q} X_{ijk}^2 = (1^2 + 4^2 + 3^2 + \cdots + 5^2 + 3^2) = 1896.0000$$

$$(III) = \frac{\sum_{j=1}^{p} T_{j.}^2}{nq} = \frac{(161^2 + 99^2)}{(6)(4)} = 1488.4167$$

$$(IV) = \frac{\sum_{k=1}^{q} T_{.k}^2}{np} = \frac{(29^2 + \cdots + 76^2)}{(6)(2)} = 1629.5000$$

$$(V) = \frac{\sum_{j=1}^{p} \sum_{k=1}^{q} T_{jk}^2}{n} = \frac{(13^2 + 16^2 + \cdots + 53^2 + 23^2)}{6} = 1801.6667$$

iv. Sums of Squares and Degrees of Freedom

$$SS_A = (III) - (I) = 1488.4167 - 1408.3333 = 80.0834$$
$$df_A = p - 1 = 2 - 1 = 1$$

$$SS_B = (IV) - (I) = 1629.5000 - 1408.3333 = 221.1667$$
$$df_B = q - 1 = 4 - 1 = 3$$

$$SS_{AB} = (V) + (I) - (III) - (IV) = 1801.6667 + 1408.3333$$
$$- 1488.4167 - 1629.5000 = 92.0833$$
$$df_{AB} = (p - 1)(q - 1) = (1)(3) = 3$$

$$SS_{within} = (II) - (V) = 1896.0000 - 1801.6667 = 94.3333$$
$$df_{within} = N - pq = 48 - (2)(4) = 40$$

$$SS_{total} = (II) - (I) = 1896.0000 - 1408.3333 = 487.6667$$
$$df_{total} = N - 1 = 48 - 1 = 47$$

v. Summary Table

Source	df	SS	MS	F
A (Rearing)	1	80.0834	80.0834	33.96**
B (Breed)	3	221.1667	73.7222	31.26**
AB (Rearing × Breed)	3	92.0833	30.6944	13.02**
Within	40	94.3333	2.3583	
Total	47	487.6667		

$**p < .01$

12–8   Summary of the Numerical Example of a Two-Factor Analysis of Variance (Rearing × Breed Example).

Hypotheses

Factor *A*	Factor *B*

$H_0: \alpha_1 = \alpha_2 = 0$ $H_0: \beta_1 = \beta_2 = \beta_3 = \beta_4 = 0$

$H_1:$ Not H_0 $H_1:$ Not H_0

AB Interaction

$H_0: \alpha\beta_{11} = \alpha\beta_{12} = \cdots = \alpha\beta_{24} = 0$

$H_1:$ Not H_0

Assumptions

1. The subjects are **randomly** and **independently sampled**.
2. The groups are **independent**.
3. The population distributions of each group are **normal** and have equal variances **(homogeneity of variance)**.
4. The factors are **fixed**, and there are *n* observations ($n > 1$) per group **(equal *n*'s)**.

Decision Rules (.05 level; from Table E)

		AB Interaction
Factor *A* ($df = 1/40$)	**Factor *B* ($df = 3/40$)**	**($df = 3/40$)**
Do not reject H_0 if: $F_{obs} < 4.08$	$F_{obs} < 2.84$	$F_{obs} < 2.84$
Reject H_0 if: $F_{obs} \geq 4.08$	$F_{obs} \geq 2.84$	$F_{obs} \geq 2.84$

Computation (See Table 12–7.)

$$F_{obs} = 33.96 \qquad F_{obs} = 31.26 \qquad F_{obs} = 13.02$$

Decision

Since the *F* for interaction exceeds the critical level the null hypothesis is rejected. It is concluded that the effects of indulgent and disciplined rearing are not the same for each breed of dog.

each treatment effect for Factor *A* will be zero, and consequently the null hypothesis can be written $H_0: \alpha_1 = \alpha_2 = 0$ with the alternative being $H_1:$ Not H_0. The same logic applies to the hypothesis for Factor *B* and the *AB* interaction.

A plot of the data, presented in Figure 12–2, will help to interpret the significant interaction. Note that the graph is not a polygon but a **bar graph** con-

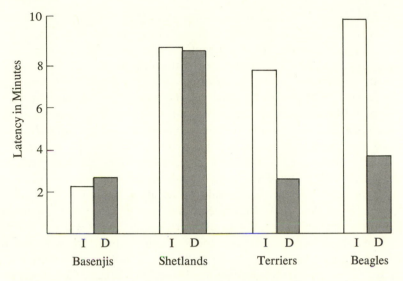

Fig. 12–2. Results for the Rearing (indulged, disciplined) × Breed experiment in which a significant interaction occurred.

sisting of bars for the indulged and disciplined groups within each breed. The vertical height of the bars represents the mean length of latency to eat the meat in the test situation. A tall bar indicates a long hesitation. The bar graph is used in this context rather than connected points because the abscissa (breed) represents discrete categories and not points along a continuum.

An interaction implies that differences between levels of one factor are not the same within each level of the other factor. In terms of the example, the difference between indulged and disciplined dogs is not the same within each breed of animal. Notice in the graph that the basenjis ate the food quickly, regardless of whether they were indulged or disciplined. The shetlands also showed little difference between rearing conditions but seemed to begin eating late in the period. In contrast, the rearing conditions did seem to affect the terriers and beagles since it appeared that the indulged dogs of these two breeds took longer to go to the food than their disciplined companions.

The significant interaction means that the indulged-disciplined manipulation affected some breeds differently from others. It is tempting to conclude more specifically that the rearing variable affected terriers and beagles but not basenjis or shetlands. Technically, the significant interaction does not apply to particular pairs of comparisons within the total design but rather indicates that the rearing treatment was different within the set of breeds observed, all four breeds considered at once. If the researcher had reason to be particularly concerned with some specific comparisons within a breed prior to the time of the experiment, the difference between means could be tested with a t test or other procedure for making **a priori comparisons** (i.e., before the fact) within the total design. However, most frequently a theory or other justification for examining specific pairs of means within a total design does not present itself prior to the experiment. Rather, it is often only after the results are available that the researcher decides to compare specific pairs. For example, suppose the scientist performing the above study did not have any specific reasons before the experiment for testing the difference between indulged and disciplined animals within any one particular breed. However, after the data were collected, it was noted that there was a significant interaction and the graph suggested that the rearing variable affected the terriers and beagles but not the others. The researcher might wonder if there would be significant differences between the two means for each of these two breeds. If now a simple t test is performed between these pairs of means, the resulting probability levels will not be appropriate. They are not correct because the researcher would probably not have tested them if the interaction was not significant or if in the graph there had not appeared to be a difference for some breeds and not others. Consequently, in the group of such **a posteriori comparisons** (i.e., after the fact) that this researcher makes, there would be a high number of significant differences even if the null hypotheses of no difference were actually true because this researcher only makes such tests when the data suggest that there will be a significant difference in a pair. It is in this sense that **a posteriori** tests "capitalize on chance" and some correction must be made in order to accommodate this. The theory behind choosing which correction to use in such after-the-fact comparisons is beyond the scope of this text, but the interested reader is referred to Winer's more advanced book on the analysis of variance.[12]

INTERPRETATION

The preceding example revealed a "significant" effect for the interaction between rearing treatment and breed of dog. Judging from the graph of this interaction, one might conclude that the difference in rearing treatment affects some breeds but not others. The fact that a "significant difference" was found indicates that the observed differences in group means are sufficiently large that it is likely that they did not occur simply because of sampling error. Nevertheless, these statistical procedures themselves do not guarantee that these factors *caused* the observed differences. The analysis only reports that the difference observed probably was not random. The design and execution of the experiment, not the statistics, comment upon the possible causal effects of the variables studied. Quite sizable and significant effects might have been produced not by

---

[12] Winer, *op. cit.*

breed or rearing, but by the behavior of the experimenter when preventing the dog from eating during the first three minutes of the test situation. Though it was not actually the case, suppose for the sake of the discussion that the experimenter tested all the shetlands first and really punished the dogs severely for going near the food. As a result, the dogs of both rearing groups tended to avoid the food, some for the entire ten-minute test situation. Feeling that the punishment was too severe, the experimenter could have tested the basenjis next and unconsciously reduced the level of punishment. However, since all the basenjis ate very quickly and since the experimenter sensed that none of the hypothesized rearing differences seemed to be appearing, it is possible that the experimenter might have subsequently punished the remaining disciplined dogs harder than the indulged animals and produced the rearing differences reported. Although this example is somewhat contrived to punctuate the point, experimenter bias has been found to influence the outcomes of experiments,[13] and it is entirely possible that the effects suggested by the example could be produced by this kind of "extraneous" variable if appropriate experimental procedures are not followed.

The point to remember is that the statistical procedures cannot discriminate between what effects are caused by the factors investigated or by other influences which have been allowed to operate. Causal inferences can be made only when the design of the experiment is such that if a difference is found there exists no possible cause for this difference other than the variables manipulated directly by the researcher. In short, statistics is a set of methods that serve to describe and quantify data in such a way that inferences may be made by an orderly process; the art of experimental design, not statistics, speaks to discerning the causes of the observed effects.

EXERCISES

1. Distinguish in your own words between a main effect and an interaction. Give three examples of an interaction in terms of common events.

2. If the different sums of squares add to SS_{total}, and the different degrees of freedom sum to df_{total}, do the different mean squares sum to a MS_{total}, and why?

3. The following is a rather random set of data:

---

[13] See, for example, R. Rosenthal, *Experimenter Effects in Behavioral Research* (New York: Appleton-Century-Crofts, 1966).

	Factor B	
	b_1	b_2
a_1	3 6 5 5	5 7 1 4
a_2	6 9 1 2	10 4 6 3

Factor A { (bracket spanning a_1 and a_2)

Compute the analysis of variance on these data. Now add 10 to each score in the a_2 level and recompute. Explain the differences and similarities in results between the first and second computation. Now take the original data and add 10 to each score in cell ab_{11} and recompute. Compare all three analyses and explain the similarities and differences.

4. An important social topic is the effects of marijuana. Twenty-four college men are selected, 12 of whom are regular users of marijuana, ordinary cigarettes, and alcohol and 12 who are regular users of cigarettes and alcohol but who have never tried marijuana before.[14] It is assumed that there are no other differences between these two groups of subjects (an assumption that may not be true). Within each group, user and non-user, six subjects smoked two marijuana cigarettes in the laboratory while six subjects smoked placebo cigarettes that taste and smell like marijuana but have no effect. A short time after smoking, all subjects took a set of perceptual-motor tests of skills required for driving. The researcher wanted to know if marijuana had more of an effect on driving skills than a placebo, if users responded differently from non-users, and if there was an interaction. The scores the subjects received are as follows:

Regular users receiving marijuana
42, 35, 48, 26, 55, 47

Regular users receiving placebo
35, 52, 43, 45, 49, 38

Naïve users receiving marijuana
60, 45, 55, 39, 47, 42

Naïve users receiving placebo
47, 42, 51, 37, 49, 48

[14] Data and results are hypothetical but represent an extrapolation of a study cautiously reported by A. T. Weil, N. E. Zinberg, and J. M. Nelson, "Clinical and Psychological Effects of Marihuana in Man," *Science*, 1968, CLXII, 1234–1242.

Evaluate these data with the analysis of variance. Draw up a formal summary of the analysis, display all computation, graph any results, and interpret the experiment.

5. Suppose the same researchers were interested in comparing the "high" achieved by subjects who are regular users versus those who are naïve to marijuana relative to subjects who are given placebos. Twenty-eight subjects participated, 14 who were regular users and 14 who were not (naïve). Half of each group smoked two marijuana cigarettes in the laboratory and half smoked two placebos. An elaborate system of questions and tasks was given a short time after the smoking took place, and the resultant score reflected the degree of "high" as reported by the subject and as evaluated by the clinical impressions of the attending physician. The greater the score, the greater the "high." Following the procedures of the previous question, evaluate and interpret the following data:

Regular user receiving marijuana

29, 33, 19, 23, 27, 21, 25

Regular user receiving placebo

17, 21, 19, 22, 18, 14, 23

Naïve user receiving marijuana

14, 10, 17, 9, 11, 13, 15

Naïve user receiving placebo

15, 12, 10, 16, 11, 12, 9

NONPARAMETRIC TECHNIQUES

13

parametric versus nonparametric tests

A variety of hypothesis testing techniques has been presented in the preceding chapters. In order to use these tests appropriately, several assumptions must hold about the population distributions. For example, the *t* test of the difference between two independent means requires that sampling is random and that the two population distributions are normal and have the same variance. Since one almost never has precise knowledge about the population, only guesses about the tenability of some of these assumptions can be made. Furthermore, there are times when certain of the assumptions simply cannot be met. For example, if a very easy examination is given to a class there may be many scores of 100% and only a few scores as low as 80%. This distribution would be markedly skewed to the left and decidedly not normal. Therefore, there is a need for statistical techniques that may be used when some of the assumptions required by the previously described procedures cannot be met.

The statistical techniques described in the previous chapters represent tests on the values of certain parameters (e.g., μ or ρ) and have made certain assumptions about other parameters (e.g., $\sigma_1^2 = \sigma_2^2 = \cdots = \sigma_p^2$), consequently they are collectively known as **parametric** statistical tests. Methods that do not test hypotheses about specific parameters and require different (and sometimes fewer) assumptions are known as **nonparametric** tests or **distribution-free** tests (because they do not require that scores are from a normal distribution, for example).

Although nonparametric tests are frequently used because certain assumptions cannot be made about the populations involved, a researcher may select a nonparametric technique to analyze data for other reasons as well. Sometimes the variables in question are measured with ordinal or even nominal scales (see Chapter 1). Parametric tests are not usually appropriate in such cases. For example, suppose an educator wants to correlate the scores from a new test of reading achievement with a teacher's rank ordering of pupils on reading proficiency. The teacher's rankings represent an ordinal scale, and a nonparametric index of the degree of relationship would be more appropriate than the Pearson r. Thus, when measurement is nominal or ordinal in character, a nonparametric test may be the only choice.

If nonparametric techniques do not require all the assumptions that parametric techniques do, then why are they not always used? Actually parametric rather than nonparametric procedures are more common and traditionally preferred when everything else is equal. One reason is that parametric tests are **robust** with respect to violations of some of their assumptions. That is, failure to have a perfectly normal distribution is really not very damaging to the accuracy of the probability values obtained with the t test or the analysis of variance. In fact, even rather substantial departures from normality have a relatively minor impact on the result of the test, especially if the sample size is large. Similar statements could be made about the robustness of these techniques when group variances are not equal. Consequently, moderate violations of the assumptions of normality and homogeneity of variance are often not strong reasons for choosing a nonparametric over a parametric test.

In addition, parametric methods usually have a greater **power-efficiency** than do nonparametric methods. Power-efficiency is a technical concept that refers to the probability that the test will reject the null hypothesis when that hypothesis is, in fact, false (correctly reject H_0).[1] If the difference between the central tendency of two groups is being considered, a t test is more likely to detect a population difference than is an appropriate nonparametric test for the given N's.

Another reason why parametric methods are often preferred is that they provide information that nonparametric methods do not. For example, in the two-factor analysis of variance, a test for an interaction may be made. It is more difficult to assess this type of effect with nonparametric methods.

A final consideration is more subtle. Frequently, parametric and nonparametric tests do not address themselves to precisely the same question and are sensitive to different aspects of the data. For example, if one wants to know whether the mean of one group differs from the mean of another in the population, a parametric test makes a rather direct assessment of this question, given the assumptions. A nonparametric test designed to make a similar evaluation may actually ask whether one distribution is different from another *in any*

---

[1] For a more detailed discussion of power-efficiency, see S. Siegel, *Nonparametric Statistics* (New York: McGraw-Hill, 1956), 20.

way, and distributions may differ not only in central tendency but also in variability, skewness, etc. Thus, although parametric and nonparametric tests are often intimately related, situations can occur in which a "significant" difference will be obtained with one technique and not with another because sometimes parametric and nonparametric tests evaluate slightly different aspects of the data.

In short, parametric tests possess the advantages of being somewhat robust with respect to violations of assumptions, having relatively more power-efficiency (everything else being equal), and sometimes providing relatively more information about a phenomenon (e.g., interactions in the analysis of variance). However, when departures from normality or homogeneity of variance are terribly severe, or when the data are nominal or ordinal, a nonparametric method may be more appropriate.

The techniques presented in this chapter are samples of some of the most common nonparametric methods. Many others exist and the interested reader is referred to books by Bradley and by Siegel[2] for more complete coverage of this area.

tests on independent samples

PEARSON CHI-SQUARE TESTS

purpose Occasionally, the social scientist collects independent and random samples of observations and wishes to compare them in terms of the similarity with which these observations are distributed among several discrete and mutually exclusive categories. Suppose that two or more groups of subjects are randomly selected. The two groups may be boys and girls, students and nonstudents, athletes and nonathletes, etc. Now, suppose the social scientist has a set of several discrete categories into which any particular subject may be classified. For example, subjects may be judged to have "warm," "neutral," or "cold" personalities or to have several levels of agreement or disagreement with a given statement or political figure. No matter what the classification system, the categories must be exhaustive and mutually exclusive so that each subject will belong to one and only one category.

To illustrate, suppose two samples were randomly selected, one composed of college males and the other of college females. All subjects were given a statement to read describing a "new morality" regarding heterosexual relationships. They

[2] J. V. Bradley, *Distribution-Free Statistical Tests* (Englewood Cliffs: Prentice-Hall, 1968). S. Siegel, *Nonparametric Statistics* (New York: McGraw-Hill, 1956).

were then asked if they approved, disapproved, or were neutral in their feeling about the statement. The data from such a set of observations might be displayed as follows.

	Men	Women	Total
Approve	58	35	93
Neutral	11	25	36
Disapprove	10	23	33
	79	83	162

Notice that the two samples, men and women, compose the columns, and the various categories of responses constitute the rows. The samples are independent and a person can only be tallied in one of the table's six cells. The illustrative data indicate, for example, that 79 men and 83 women were questioned, 93 people approved of the statement, and 25 women were neutral about it.

Sometimes this data format is called a **contingency table**. The research question is whether men and women differ in their relative distributions of responses to the statement. Another way to phrase this same question is to ask whether the distribution of responses is "contingent" or dependent upon the sex of the respondent.

In this and each of the following presentations of a statistical technique, a summary of the procedures is presented in tabular form (e.g., Table 13–1) and its details discussed in the text.

hypotheses   The statistical question that is to be asked is whether the groups differ in the relative distribution of observations among the different categories. The null hypothesis is that in the population the two groups do not differ in their relative frequency distributions of people among the categories. The alternative hypothesis is that the groups do differ. Notice that H_1 does not specify how they differ, but only that the two relative distributions are not the same in some way.

assumptions   First, it must be assumed that **the two samples are independent** from one another. This usually implies that different and unrelated sets of subjects are selected. Second, the subjects within each group must be **randomly** and **independently** sampled. Third, each observation must qualify for **one and only one category** in the classification scheme. Fourth, the **sample size must be relatively large.** The latter assumption will be discussed again below.

rationale and computation   The formula used to relate an appropriate statistic to a theoretical relative frequency distribution is based upon the difference between the frequencies which were actually observed for men and women relative to the frequencies that would be expected if men and women had the same population distributions of response to the morality statement. Once again, the null hypothesis is tentatively presumed to be true—men and women have the same population distribution. As usual, the observed data will not conform precisely with this hypothesized state of affairs. Is the difference between the observed and expected frequencies a reasonable outcome of sampling error? If not, reject the null hypothesis.

A major requirement of this technique is that one be able to determine what set of frequencies would exist in the samples of men and women if their population distributions were identical, that is, if the null hypothesis were true. Since one does not know what proportion of college students in the population, men and women combined, approve, disapprove, or are neutral relative to the statement, these proportions must be estimated from the observed data. For the data presented above, $\frac{93}{162} = 57.41\%$ of the college students approved of the statement. Since there were 79 men, 57.41% of 79 or 45.35 should have approved the statement if there were no differences in the distribution of response for the two sexes. The 45.35 men is an **expected frequency** for the cell "men-approve." The same process may be used to obtain the expected frequency of each cell in the table. The computation of expected frequencies is most often stated in the following terms:

> To compute the **expected frequency** for any cell, multiply the total for the row which contains the cell by the total for the column which contains the cell, and divide this product by the total number of cases in the table.

In terms of the "men-approve" cell, the expected frequency is given by

$$\frac{(93)(79)}{162} = 45.35$$

Since $\frac{93}{162}$ is the proportion of the total sample approving and 79 is the number of males in the sample, this method is identical to the logic described previously.

If the expected frequencies are computed in this manner for each cell, the observed frequencies (symbolized by O) and the expected frequencies (symbolized by E) for the sample data would be as follows:

	Men	Women
Approve	$O = 58$ $E = 45.35$	$O = 35$ $E = 47.65$
Neutral	$O = 11$ $E = 17.56$	$O = 25$ $E = 18.44$
Disapprove	$O = 10$ $E = 16.09$	$O = 23$ $E = 16.91$

If the calculation of the expected frequencies is correct, the row and column sums of the expected frequencies will equal the sums of the observed frequencies.

We now have a set of expected frequencies given that the null hypothesis of the equivalence of population distributions within the categories for the two groups is true and given the observed marginal values. Now the task is to determine some index of the extent to which the observed frequencies are consonant with the null hypothesis that the distributions for men and women are the same in the population. The following expression represents such an index and its sampling distribution approximates a theoretical distribution called **chi square** (χ^2):

$$\chi_{obs}^{2} = \sum_{j=1}^{r} \sum_{k=1}^{c} \frac{(O_{jk} - E_{jk})^2}{E_{jk}}$$

in which O_{jk} = the observed frequency in the cell corresponding to the intersection of the jth row and kth column,

E_{jk} = the expected frequency in the cell corresponding to the intersection of the jth row and kth column,

r = the number of rows, and

c = the number of columns

The formula simply directs one to take the difference between the observed and expected frequencies for each cell, square it, divide by the expected frequency, and sum these fractions over all cells. The resulting value is distributed as chi square with degrees of freedom

$$df = (r - 1)(c - 1)$$

where r is the number of rows and c the number of columns in the table of frequencies.

The percentiles of the chi square distribution for each number of degrees of freedom are known, and Table F in Appendix II lists values of chi square for selected percentiles (significance levels) at several df. In the present case, the

13–1 Formal Summary of $r \times c$ Chi Square Test
(Sex $\times$ Approval Example).

Hypotheses

H_0: Given the observed marginals, the distributions of frequencies in the population are not different for the groups.

H_1: Given the observed marginals, these distributions are different for the groups (nondirectional).

Assumptions

1. The subjects for each group are **randomly** and **independently** selected.
2. The **groups are independent.**
3. Each observation must qualify for **one and only one category.**
4. The sample size must be fairly large such that **no expected frequency is less than 5, for r or c greater than 2, or less than 10 if $r = c = 2$.**

Decision Rules (from Table F)

Given: .05, a nondirectional test with $df = (r - 1)(c - 1) = 2$

If $\chi_{obs}^2 < 5.99$, do not reject H_0

If $\chi_{obs}^2 \geq 5.99$, reject H_0

Computation (See text for data and details.)

$$\chi_{obs}^2 = \sum_{j=1}^{r} \sum_{k=1}^{c} \frac{(O_{jk} - E_{jk})^2}{E_{jk}}$$

in which O_{jk} = the observed frequency in the cell corresponding to the intersection of the jth row and kth column,

E_{jk} = the expected frequency in the cell corresponding to the jth row and kth column, determined by multiplying the total number of frequencies for the row and column which contain the cell and dividing by the number of frequencies in the table,

r = the number of rows, and

c = the number of columns

$\chi_{obs}^2 = 16.17$

Decision

Reject H_0

table of data has three rows and two columns, thus there are $(r - 1)(c - 1) = (3 - 1)(2 - 1) = 2$ degrees of freedom. The critical value for a nondirectional test at the .05 level of significance is 5.99. If the observed value of chi square, symbolized by χ_{obs}^2, exceeds the critical value, the null hypothesis, H_0, is rejected.

For the data presented, the calculation of χ^2 proceeds as follows:

$$\chi_{obs}^2 = \frac{(58 - 45.35)^2}{45.35} + \frac{(35 - 47.65)^2}{47.65} + \frac{(11 - 17.56)^2}{17.56}$$

$$+ \frac{(25 - 18.44)^2}{18.44} + \frac{(10 - 16.09)^2}{16.09} + \frac{(23 - 16.91)^2}{16.91}$$

$$\chi_{obs}^2 = 16.17$$

Since the observed value of 16.17 exceeds the critical value of 5.99 and, in fact, is beyond the critical value for a test at the .001 level, the null hypothesis is rejected. It can be concluded from the data that the distribution of approval-disapproval of the stated version of the new morality is different for the two sexes. Apparently, college men are more likely to endorse such a statement than are college women. (See Table 13–1 for a formal summary of this example.)

discussion When the assumptions were listed for performing such a test, it was noted that a large sample is required. The approximation to the theoretical chi square distribution is not very good for small samples and thus the probabilities are somewhat inaccurate. Obviously, the question becomes how large must the sample be for the approximation to be sufficiently close. Unfortunately, the closeness of the approximation is a function of many factors, and a single rule of thumb is not totally adequate. However, if a conservative guideline were needed, it would probably be best *not to have any expected frequency less than 5*. If the table is only 2 × 2 in size, then no expected frequency should be less than 10. Notice that the requirement is based upon the *expected* frequencies, not the observed frequencies.

MANN-WHITNEY *U* TEST FOR THE DIFFERENCE BETWEEN TWO POPULATIONS

purpose If two samples are randomly and independently selected, if there is an underlying continuous distribution, and if there is at least an ordinal scale of measurement, then the Mann-Whitney *U* test may be used to evaluate the difference between the two population distributions. The *U* test is one of the most popular alternatives to the parametric *t* test.

hypotheses The null hypothesis is that the populations from which the two samples are drawn are identical. The alternative hypothesis is that these two populations are not identical. Note that this is not equivalent to testing the difference between two population means because two distributions could be quite different in form but have identical means. Therefore, it is theoretically possible to obtain a statistically significant result with the U test when in fact the means are identical. From a practical standpoint, the general shapes of the distributions of two groups within a single experiment are not often markedly different. When the forms of the distributions are similar, the U test does compare the central tendencies of the groups. Thus, if the forms of the sample distributions are similar, the results of the U test are often interpreted in terms of differences in central tendency; if the forms of the distributions are not similar, the results must be viewed in terms of the difference between the distributions in general.

assumptions   The assumptions stated above are quite minimal. **Random** and **independent sampling** with **independent groups** is required. It is also assumed that there is an underlying **continuous scale of measurement**. This implies that the dependent variable is measured with a scale in which there are theoretically an infinite number of values between any two points (see page 10). Lastly, the **measurement scale must be at least ordinal** in character.

rationale and computation   The rationale for the test is based upon the premise that if two distributions of equal size are identical and if the observations from each group are lined up in rank order (i.e., smallest first), then the scores from the two groups should be well mixed in that ordered sequence. If they are well mixed, then the number of scores in Group A that precede each of the scores in Group B should equal within sampling error the number of scores in B that precede each of the scores in A. If the scores in Group A tend to be smaller in value than those in B, then more of the A scores will precede B scores when all the scores are rank ordered.

The statistic based upon an extension of this type of rationale is the Mann-Whitney U. Suppose that the sets of scores for Groups A and B are as follows:

$$A = \{5, 9, 17, 3\}$$
$$B = \{1, 8, 28, 20, 18\}$$

Now arrange the scores in order beginning with the smallest score but retain the group identity of each observation. Then assign each score a rank beginning with rank "1" for the smallest score:

Score	1	3	5	8	9	17	18	20	28
Group	B	A	A	B	A	A	B	B	B
Rank	1	2	3	4	5	6	7	8	9

Although the computation of U can be accomplished by using a summing technique alluded to above, a more convenient method requires that the total (T_j) of the ranks for one group be obtained. For the example just presented,

$$T_A = 2 + 3 + 5 + 6 = 16$$

The statistic U is then given by

$$U_{\text{obs}} = n_A n_B + \frac{n_A(n_A + 1)}{2} - T_A$$

in which n_A and n_B are the numbers of cases in Groups A and B, respectively. For the present example,

$$U_{\text{obs}} = 4(5) + \frac{4(4 + 1)}{2} - 16$$

$$U_{\text{obs}} = 14$$

n ≤ 20 If n for each group is 20 or less, Table G in Appendix II gives the critical values for U. A separate table is presented for different significance levels. In each case, the rows and columns represent different numbers of cases for the two groups (it makes no difference which group is used for the rows and which for the columns). At the intersection of the appropriate row and column, two values of U are given, one smaller than the other. These two values are a type of critical value such that if the observed U falls *between* these two values, H_0 is not rejected. If the observed value is less than or equal to the lower value in the table or greater than or equal to the larger value in the table, H_0 is rejected.

n > 20 If n for either group is greater than 20, then Table G cannot be used. It happens that with such a large sample, the observed value of U approaches a normal distribution with

$$\text{mean} = \frac{n_A n_B}{2}$$

and

$$\text{standard deviation} = \sqrt{\frac{(n_A)(n_B)(n_A + n_B + 1)}{12}}$$

Consequently, if the size of a group is greater than 20 and the difference in sample sizes of the two groups is not too great, the significance of U_{obs} may be determined by calculating

$$z = \frac{U_{\text{obs}} - (n_A n_B / 2)}{\sqrt{\dfrac{(n_A)(n_B)(n_A + n_B + 1)}{12}}}$$

which approaches the standard normal distribution. In this event, critical values may be obtained by consulting Table A.

ties Occasionally, the values of scores are tied.[3] For example, consider the set of scores {13, 15, 15, 18}. The score of 13 receives rank 1. The two scores of 15 are given the average of the next two ranks. These two ranks are ranks 2 and 3 and their average is 2.5. Consequently, the two scores of 15 each receive a rank of 2.5. Notice that the score of 18 is then assigned a rank of 4. It is not given a rank of 3 because this rank was used in the previous averaging. If three or more scores are tied, each score receives the average rank that these scores would have received if they were distinct. Similarly, the next score(s) begin with the next unused rank. An example of ranking with several ties follows:

Score	13	13	16	19	19	22	22	22	28	28	30
Rank	1.5	1.5	3	4.5	4.5	7	7	7	9.5	9.5	11

small sample illustration Freudian theory is based in part upon the premise that a person is born with certain innate drives and needs, one of which centers around the mouth, an oral need. Another important concept is that the energy system of an organism is closed, so that if a need is

---

[3] The method of handling tied observations suggested in this chapter is a common and convenient one, but it has certain technical liabilities. Most rank order statistics assume an underlying continuous distribution. If this is true, ties in scores result from imprecision of measurement. If more precise methods were available no ties would exist. Consequently, in this instance the occurrence of ties is not a true reflection of what really exists. The issue of just how to handle ties is not firmly resolved, and Bradley (*op. cit.*) presents a good though sophisticated discussion of the alternatives. One approach advocated by Siegel (*op. cit.*) is to use the average-rank technique presented in the text and correct for ties with special formulas. However, Siegel points out, the corrections do not change the result very much even when a large proportion of the scores are tied. Bradley notes that under some conditions the average-rank approach actually biases the outcome in one direction or another rather than yielding a result that is itself a type of average or medium approximation. One alternative to this problem is to treat the tie scores as if they were not tie scores, selecting the ranks in the manner *least* favorable to rejecting the null hypothesis. Then, rerank the observations, this time treating the ties in a manner *most* favorable to rejecting the null hypothesis. As a result, one obtains two test statistics, one most and one least favorable toward rejecting the null hypothesis. If both statistics fall into the region of rejection, the null hypothesis may be unambiguously rejected. If both fall outside the rejection region, the null hypothesis may not be rejected without ambiguity. However, if one value does and the other does not fall within the rejection region, no clear decision can be made. In short, most of the methods discussed in this chapter technically assume that no ties exist. Since ties are common in social science, some procedures must be followed to handle them, and the choice of which method to follow rests on technical considerations largely beyond the scope of this text. However, the careful student will note that the method of handling ties is an issue and will be sensitive to the possible qualifications their presence may make upon the accuracy of conclusions.

blocked from satisfaction the need does not dissipate but will express itself in other ways. For example, a person might be frustrated in oral needs as a young child and because of this dammed up need might perform a great deal of oral activity as an adult (e.g. by smoking). It would be reasonable under this theory to suppose that if during the early months of life oral needs (e.g., the need for sucking) were not exercised, and thus frustrated, there should be more oral activity later in order to make up for this frustration. Conversely, from a learning standpoint, if a person were not allowed to suck as an infant, one might not expect the person to learn to suck on other objects later in life.

For example, an experiment is run in which four infants are fed from special cups as soon as possible after birth.[4] Another six infants are fed on bottles throughout the course of infancy much as the average American child is. After eight months of these experiences, samples of the infants' behavior are made to determine how much of the time the infants suck their thumbs. These measures were expressed in terms of the proportion of time sucking during the observations.

The null hypothesis is that the population distribution for cup-fed babies is the same as for bottle-fed babies. The alternative hypothesis is that these distributions are different in some way.

The assumptions are that the **subjects are randomly and independently sampled** and that **the scale of measurement** (percent thumb sucking) **is continuous and of an ordinal nature.** The .05 level will be adopted.

The data are presented in the following table in which A indicates cup feeding and B bottle feeding. The scores are percentages.

Group	A	A	A	B	B	A	B	B	B	B
Score	3	5	6	9	10	12	13	13	16	24
Rank	1	2	3	4	5	6	7.5	7.5	9	10

U_{obs} is computed as follows:

$$U_{obs} = n_A n_B + \frac{n_A(n_A + 1)}{2} - T_A$$

$$= 4(6) + \frac{4(5)}{2} - 12$$

$$U_{obs} = 22$$

---

[4] Inspired by, but not identical to R. R. Sears and G. W. Wise, "Relation of Cup Feeding in Infancy to Thumbsucking and the Oral Drive," *American Journal of Orthopsychiatry*, 1950, XX, 123–138.

Looking at Table G for a two-tailed test at the .05 level, one finds the critical values of U for $n = 4,6$ are 2 and 22. The observed value of U is 22 and since this equals the critical value for U, H_0 is rejected. The distributions are probably different, and it would appear that cup-fed infants suck their thumbs less, though they presumably experience more frustration of their oral needs because of the reduced opportunity to suck.

large sample illustration   The same issue that motivated the above experiment inspired a similar experiment with dogs.[5] Dogs were randomly and independently sampled and arbitrarily assigned to one of two rearing conditions. As pups, the dogs were bottle-fed with nipples having either very large holes allowing the milk to flow freely or small holes which demanded more sucking in order for a dog to obtain a sufficient meal. After being weaned the dogs were tested for the amount of non-nutritive sucking they did in a structured situation. The logic of the experiment suggests that if there is an innate drive to suck, not having an opportunity to suck during rearing should frustrate this drive and lead to more oral behavior later. Thus, the dogs being fed through big holes should have a more frustrated need to suck because they did not suck as much during infancy. In contrast, the small-holes group had to suck a great deal, and all this oral activity presumably reduced the need for sucking behavior later. If a learning orientation is assumed, just the opposite predictions might be made. A great deal of sucking should produce a strong habit of sucking.

Twenty-five dogs were assigned to the little-hole group and 24 to the big-hole group. The subjects were randomly and independently selected and the amount of time spent in oral activity is on a continuous scale having ordinal properties. The null hypothesis is that the populations from which these two samples are drawn are identical. The alternative is that the population distributions are not identical in every respect.

Since the sample sizes are large (greater than 20), the standard normal approximation will be used. For a nondirectional alternative at the .05 level, the observed z must be less than or equal to -1.96 or greater than or equal to 1.96 in order to reject H_0.

The data and computation are presented in Table 13–2 and a formal summary of the procedure is presented in Table 13–3. The data are arranged in increasing order of score value within each group. Then, disregarding group affiliation, the scores are rank ordered, and the total of the ranks for the two groups is determined. The value of U_{obs} is computed in Table 13–2.

The formula approximating the standard normal is given in Table 13–3 and the corresponding values entered. The resulting observed z is 2.07 which complies with the second decision rule and the null hypothesis is rejected. The interpretation is that the groups probably do differ in the population and an examination of the data indicate that according to the Freudian orientation,

[5] Inspired by, but not identical to D. M. Levy, "Experiments on the Sucking Reflex and Social Behavior in Dogs," *American Journal of Orthopsychiatry*, 1934, IV, 203–224.

13–2 Data and Computation for Large-Sample Mann-Whitney U Test (Size of Nipple Hole Example).			
Little Holes		**Big Holes**	
Score	Rank	Score	Rank
8	2	3	1
10	3	22	9
11	4.5	27	10
11	4.5	29	11.5
12	6	30	13
18	7	36	14
21	8	51	23
29	11.5	51	23
45	15	51	23
46	16	59	26
49	18	65	27
49	18	74	30
49	18	76	31.5
50	20.5	76	31.5
50	20.5	81	33.5
57	25	83	35
71	28	96	40.5
73	29	98	42
81	33.5	122	44
89	36	135	45
90	37	142	46
93	38	159	47
94	39	183	48
96	40.5	190	49
109	43	$n_B = 24$	$T_B = 703.5$
$n_A = 25$	$T_A = 521.5$		

$$U_{obs} = n_A n_B + \frac{n_A(n_A + 1)}{2} - T_A$$

$$= 25(24) + \frac{25(25 + 1)}{2} - 521.5$$

$$U_{obs} = 403.5$$

13–3   Formal Summary of
Large-Sample Illustration of Mann-Whitney U Test
(Size of Nipple Hole Example).

Hypotheses

H_0: The population distributions from which the samples are drawn
are identical.

H_1: These populations are different in some way (nondirectional).

Assumptions

1. The observations are **randomly** and **independently** sampled, and the
two groups are **independent** from one another.
2. The underlying dimension of the scale of measurement is
continuous.

Decision Rules (from Table A)

Since the sample is large ($n > 20$), the standard normal approximation will be used. For a nondirectional test at .05, the decision
rules are

$$\text{If } -1.96 < z_{obs} < 1.96, \text{ do not reject } H_0$$
$$\text{If } z_{obs} \leq -1.96 \text{ or } z_{obs} \geq 1.96, \text{ reject } H_0$$

Computation

$$U_{obs} = n_A n_B + \frac{n_A(n_A + 1)}{2} - T_A$$

in which n_A and n_B = the number of subjects in samples A and B,
respectively, and T_A = the sum of the ranks for sample A. U_{obs} is calculated to be 403.5 in Table 13–2 for the illustrative data. The approximation to the standard normal distribution is given by

$$z_{obs} = \frac{U_{obs} - n_A n_B / 2}{\sqrt{\dfrac{(n_A)(n_B)(n_A + n_B + 1)}{12}}}$$

$$= \frac{403.5 - 24(25)/2}{\sqrt{\dfrac{(24)(25)(24 + 25 + 1)}{12}}}$$

$$z_{obs} = 2.07$$

Decision

H_0 is rejected.

dogs reared without much sucking opportunity (big-hole group) showed more oral behavior than the animals given much sucking opportunity (small-hole group) early in life.

KRUSKAL-WALLIS TEST FOR
k INDEPENDENT SAMPLES

purpose   The Mann-Whitney U test for two samples may be generalized to several independent samples. As such, the test for several groups would be analogous to the simple parametric analysis of variance but without making several of its assumptions. The most common approach to this kind of analysis is known as the Kruskal-Wallis test. To illustrate this procedure, suppose we have three groups of subjects which are each subjected to a different experimental treatment of some kind.

hypotheses   The null hypothesis is that the three samples have identical population distributions, while the alternative hypothesis is that their population distributions are different. If the distributions have the same form, then H_1 implies that the scores are higher or lower in some of the groups than in others.

assumptions   The three **independent groups** of subjects are **randomly selected**. Assume also that the dependent variable has a **continuous distribution**, and that it is measured with at least an **ordinal scale**. Finally, there should be **at least five observations per group** for an accurate estimation of the probability.[6]

rationale and computation   The method of handling data is similar to the Mann-Whitney test. Consider the following sample data.

Groups					
1		**2**		**3**	
Score	**Rank**	**Score**	**Rank**	**Score**	**Rank**
21	1	35	5	28	2
29	3	39	7	31	4
38	6	45	8	52	9
54	10	58	11	79	16
60	12.5	60	12.5	80	17
71	15	63	14	83	18
		89	19		
$n_1 = 6$	$T_1 = 47.5$	$n_2 = 7$	$T_2 = 76.5$	$n_3 = 6$	$T_3 = 66$

[6] For procedures to handle the case in which there are less than five observations in a group, see Siegel, *op. cit.*, 185–188.

The scores are arranged into groups in ascending order of score value. Then, without regard to group affiliation, all the observations are ranked, the smallest score value being assigned a rank of 1. If any scores are ties, each tie score receives the average of the ranks available for those scores. The ranks are totaled within each group, and this total is signified by T_j for the jth group.

The general rationale is that if the groups are distributed in the same way and with the same central tendency in the population, then the total of the ranks for the several samples should be approximately equal. To the extent that the scores in one group are higher than those in the others, the several totals will be unequal. Obviously, the totals are not likely to be precisely equal, but under the null hypothesis will differ only because of sampling error. When the differences in average ranks become so great that it is implausible to attribute them to error, the tentative assumption of the null hypothesis is rejected and the existence of treatment effects in the population is suspected.

This logic is translated into a formula for the statistic H which reflects the extent to which the sum of the ranks for the several groups differ from one another. The formula for H is

$$H_{\text{obs}} = \left[\frac{12}{N(N+1)}\right]\left[\sum_{j=1}^{k}\frac{T_j^2}{n_j}\right] - 3(N+1)$$

in which

k = the number of groups in the analysis
n_j = the number of observations in the jth group
$N = \sum n_j$, the total number of observations in the analysis
T_j = the total of the ranks in the jth group.

The formula directs one to sum the ranks and square this total separately for each group. Divide each squared total by the number of observations in that particular group, and sum across all groups to obtain

$$\sum_{j=1}^{k}\frac{T_j^2}{n_j}$$

Enter this and N into the above expression for H.

The sampling distribution of the statistic H has approximately the same form as chi square with $k - 1$ degrees of freedom (k = the number of groups). This approximation is close only when there are at least five observations per group and the accuracy of the approximation improves as N increases.

In the present case, there are three groups so the degrees of freedom for H is $k - 1 = 3 - 1 = 2$. The critical value of chi square for a nondirectional test with $df = 2$ is 5.99 as obtained from Table F. Thus, if H_{obs} is greater than or equal to 5.99, the null hypothesis of equivalence of population distributions will be rejected.

The computation for the data provided is straightforward.

$$H_{obs} = \left[\frac{12}{N(N+1)}\right]\left[\sum_{j=1}^{k}\frac{T_j^2}{n_j}\right] - 3(N+1)$$

$$= \left[\frac{12}{19(19+1)}\right]\left[\frac{(47.5)^2 \cdot}{6} + \frac{(76.5)^2}{7} + \frac{(66)^2}{6}\right] - 3(19+1)$$

$$H_{obs} = 1.20$$

Since the value of H_{obs} does not exceed the critical level, the observed differences between the samples are within the realm of sampling error and the null hypothesis of no population differences is not rejected.

example   In Chapter 12, a study was mentioned that involved showing a movie to young children and noting whether or not they would imitate the aggressive actions of an adult more if the adult was seen to be rewarded for such behavior.[7] The parallels to violence and aggression on television are obvious. Suppose there were three different groups of children in the experiment. All children saw a movie of an adult striking and otherwise assaulting a large doll, Bobo. After this behavior, the film depicted one of three consequences to the aggressor. Either the aggressor was rewarded with praise, punished with reprimands, or nothing at all happened. Each of the three groups of children saw a different ending to the movie. The question was whether this vicarious experience with reinforcement would determine the percentage of imitative aggressive behaviors in a ten-minute test situation in which each child was placed in a room with Bobo and other toys.

The hypothesis to be tested is that the population distributions for the three conditions in the experiment are identical. The alternative hypothesis is that these distributions are not the same in some way.

The assumptions for a Kruskal-Wallis test can be met. The subjects were randomly selected and assigned to independent groups. The dependent variable is the percent of responses the child makes which are imitations of the aggressor, and this variable is theoretically continuous and ordinal in nature.

Since there are three groups, the degrees of freedom for this test are $k - 1 = 3 - 1 = 2$. The test statistic H is distributed as chi square, and Table F shows the critical value for such a test to be 5.99. Thus, if the value of H_{obs} is greater than or equal to 5.99 the null hypothesis will be rejected.

The data and the computation of H_{obs} are presented in Table 13–4. H_{obs} is found to be 13.91 which exceeds the critical value at .05 (and at .01 as well), and H_0 is rejected. The analysis suggests that the populations from which these three groups are drawn do differ in some way, and an examination of the data

[7] Similar to A. Bandura, D. Ross, and S. A. Ross, "Imitation of Film-Mediated Aggressive Models," *Journal of Abnormal and Social Psychology*, 1963, LXVI, 3–11.

13–4   Data and Computation for the Kruskal-Wallis Test Example (Imitation Example).

Punished		Nothing		Rewarded	
Score (%)	Rank	Score (%)	Rank	Score (%)	Rank
0	1	2	3	8	13.5
1	2	3	5	12	16.5
3	5	4	7.5	13	18
3	5	6	10.5	16	20.5
4	7.5	7	12	19	22
5	9	10	15	21	23
6	10.5	12	16.5	22	24
8	13.5	14	19	23	25
		16	20.5		
$n_1 = 8$	$T_1 = 53.5$	$n_2 = 9$	$T_2 = 109$	$n_3 = 8$	$T_3 = 162.5$

$$H = \left[\frac{12}{N(N+1)}\right]\left[\sum_{j=1}^{k}\frac{T_j^2}{n_j}\right] - 3(N+1)$$

$$= \left[\frac{12}{25(25+1)}\right]\left[\frac{(53.5)^2}{8} + \frac{(109)^2}{9} + \frac{(162.5)^2}{8}\right] - 3(25+1)$$

$$H = 13.91$$

$$df = k - 1 = 3 - 1 = 2$$

implies that a child is more likely to imitate if positive consequences are perceived to derive from the aggressor's behavior. A formal summary of this analysis is presented in Table 13–5.

correlated samples

WILCOXON TEST FOR TWO CORRELATED SAMPLES

All of the tests described thus far in this chapter have been for independent samples, groups of observations on separate or unmatched subjects. Just as special procedures were required for the t test when the sets of observations were made on the same or matched subjects, so too a different nonparametric

---

13–5   Formal Summary of Kruskal-Wallis Test
(Imitation Example).

Hypotheses

H_0: The population distributions from which the groups are sampled
are identical.

H_1: These distributions are different in some way.

Assumptions

1. Subjects are **randomly and independently sampled** and divided into
k independent groups with all $n_j \geq 5$.
2. The underlying scale of measurement is **continuous** and it has at
least **ordinal** properties.

Decision Rules (from Table F)

Given: the .05 level of significance, a nondirectional test and that H is
distributed as chi square with $k - 1 = 3 - 1 = 2$ *df*

If $H_{obs} < 5.99$, do not reject H_0
If $H_{obs} \geq 5.99$, reject H_0

Computation (See Table 13–4.)

$$H_{obs} = \left[\frac{12}{N(N + 1)} \right] \left[\sum_{j=1}^{k} \frac{T_j^2}{n_j} \right] - 3(N + 1)$$

in which N = the total number of subjects in the experiment

n_j = the number of subjects in group j, and

T_j^2 = the square of the total of the ranks for scores in group j.

$H_{obs} = 13.91$

Decision

H_0 is rejected.

---

analysis must be made when the samples are not independent. One of the most
common nonparametric tests for this situation is the Wilcoxon test for correlated or matched samples.

purpose   If the same subjects are measured under two
conditions or if matched pairs of subjects each provide a score and if the
measurement is ordinal for both within-pair and between-pair differences, then
the Wilcoxon test may be used to test the null hypothesis that the population
distributions corresponding to the two types of observations are identical.

Suppose that a special program is designed to provide children with broadening sociocultural experiences. It is also of interest to observe whether this program improves children's language skills. Seven children are enrolled in the program and each is administered a test of linguistic development at the beginning and at the end of the program. The researcher wishes to know if there was any change in linguistic behavior even though no direct attempt was made to teach language.

hypotheses   The null hypothesis is that the population distributions under the two conditions are identical. The alternative hypothesis is that they are not identical. Usually, if the distributions are symmetrical, this is taken to mean that the central tendency of one distribution is higher than that of the other.

assumptions   There are a few assumptions which the Wilcoxon test makes but they are less restrictive than those required for the appropriate t test. First, the subjects must be **randomly and independently** selected. Second, the scale of measurement must at least be **ordinal** in nature. Also, if each subject is measured twice there will be two scores per subject, and these two values will probably differ. One could obtain a distribution of these differences, and the test assumes that these **differences also fall on an ordinal scale** (i.e., the differences may be ordered in magnitude).

rationale and computation   The procedure requires that the pairs of scores be subtracted in order to obtain their difference and that the algebraic sign of the difference be retained. Following this, the *absolute* values of the differences are assigned ranks starting with a rank of 1 for the smallest difference. Recall that the signs of the differences were retained but that the rankings were made without regard to sign. The ranks may now be attributed to positive and negative differences between the two groups. If there is no difference between the groups, then one would expect that the sum of the ranks associated with positive differences between the groups would be about equal to the sum of the ranks associated with negative differences between the groups. Since under this circumstance, the total of all ranks would be divided relatively evenly between positive and negative differences, the smaller of these two sums would take on its largest value under the null hypothesis of no difference. If there is a difference between groups, then either the positive or negative sum of ranks will be quite a bit smaller than the other. As the difference between groups increases, the smaller of the two sums gets smaller and smaller. The sampling distribution of this smaller sum is known, and when the observed total becomes sufficiently small as to be unlikely to have arisen solely because of sampling error, the null hypothesis of no difference is rejected.

Suppose the data presented in Table 13–6 are for the seven children in the hypothetical example of a sociocultural enrichment program:

			Differ-ence d_i	Absolute Differ-ence $|d_i|$	Rank Differ-ence	Signed Rank Dif-ference
				13–6 Hypothetical Data for Wilcoxon Test Example.		
Subject	Pretest	Posttest	Differ-ence d_i	Absolute Differ-ence $|d_i|$	Rank Differ-ence	Signed Rank Dif-ference
A	74	76	-2	2	3	-3
B	81	80	1	1	1.5	1.5
C	85	89	-4	4	6	-6
D	79	88	-9	9	7	-7
E	92	95	-3	3	4.5	-4.5
F	83	80	3	3	4.5	4.5
G	87	86	1	1	1.5	1.5
						$T_+ = 7.5$ $T_- = 20.5$ $W_{obs} = 7.5$

The seven subjects and their scores on the pretest and posttest are listed, and the difference between these scores, d_i, is computed. Then the absolute values of these differences are taken and ranked, assigning the rank of 1 to the lowest absolute difference. If a difference is zero, then it is dropped from the analysis and the total N (the number of *paired* observations) is reduced by the number of such zero differences. If some of the absolute differences are of equal value, these ties are assigned the average of the ranks that they would have received if they had been distinct.

After the absolute differences have been ranked, the last column of the above table merely repeats the rank that each matched pair received but the algebraic sign of the difference in score values is attached to the rank. Now, two quantities are computed, T_+ which is the total of the ranks having positive signs associated with them in the last column of the table and T_- which is the sum of those ranks having negative signs. The statistic of interest is W_{obs} which is simply the smaller of T_+ and T_-. If the two groups are similar to one another, these two totals will be about equal. As the difference between groups increases so does the difference between T_+ and T_-, and W_{obs} (the smaller of the two) takes on a smaller and smaller value. When W_{obs} becomes sufficiently small relative to its sampling distribution, H_0 is rejected.

For N (the number of *paired* observations sampled less the number of pairs having zero differences in scores) between 5 and 50, the critical values for the sampling distribution of W as a function of N for several levels of significance and for directional and nondirectional tests are presented in Table H. If W_{obs} *is less than or equal to* the tabled critical value, H_0 is rejected and a difference in the population is presumed. In the present illustration, $N = 7$, and if the test is taken to be nondirectional at the .05 level, the critical value is 2. Since W_{obs} is greater than this critical value, H_0 is not rejected and the observed differences between the pretest and posttest are attributed to sampling error.

For N greater than 50, an approximation to the standard normal may be used (actually the approximation is sufficiently good so that it can be employed with $N \geq 10$). The conversion to a standard normal deviate is given by the following:

$$z_{obs} = \frac{W_{obs} - N(N + 1)/4}{\sqrt{\dfrac{N(N + 1)(2N + 1)}{24}}}$$

For the sake of illustration, when the values obtained in the illustration are substituted into this expression one has

$$z_{obs} = \frac{7.5 - 7(7 + 1)/4}{\sqrt{\dfrac{7(7 + 1)[2(7) + 1]}{24}}}$$

$$z_{obs} = -1.10$$

For a nondirectional test, the critical values at the .05 level would be -1.96 and 1.96. If the observed value of z falls between -1.96 and 1.96, H_0 is not rejected. Since -1.10 does occur in this interval, these data do not provide evidence of a difference in the population. If the test were directional, the critical region would be entirely in the left-hand tail of the standard normal, with $z = -1.64$ as the critical value.

example   One fundamental principle in the sensorimotor development of organisms is the apparent close relationship between visual and auditory perceptual processes on the one hand and the opportunity for the organism to physically interact with its environment on the other. Some theorists have suggested that in order for visual and auditory stimuli to really have an effect on the organism, they must be associated with the feedback of physical interaction with the stimulus environment. One application of this theory was made in the following experiment.[8] Eight pairs of kittens, the members of any pair coming from the same litter, were reared in darkness until they were 10 weeks of age. They then received visual stimulation for only a short period each day under very special conditions. The two kittens of each pair were placed into a vertically oriented cylindrical apparatus with stripes painted on the side. One member of each pair was allowed to move about the apparatus at will. However, it wore a harness which was attached by means of a system of pulleys

[8] Inspired by, but not identical to R. Held and A. Hein, "Movement-Produced Stimulation in the Development of Visually-Guided Behaviors," *Journal of Comparative and Physiological Psychology*, 1963, LVI, 872–876.

and gears to a "gondola-like" carriage that held the other kitten. A post in the center of the apparatus prevented one member of the pair from seeing the other, and the circumstances were arranged so that the visual experience of the two kittens was quite similar. If the theory is correct, the freely active kitten should show faster development on visual-motor tasks than the kitten carried passively through the environment in the gondola. A series of tasks that measure visual-motor development was used and each subject received a score indicating proficiency on such a test battery.

The null hypothesis is that the population distributions for active and passive kittens are identical. The alternative hypothesis is that these distributions are not the same in some way.

It is assumed that the pairs of kittens are randomly and independently selected. The test battery yields a score such that the measurement within pairs and between differences in pairs is at least ordinal in character. While correlated data sets are most often produced by measuring each subject twice, in this experiment pairs of kittens from the same litter were used and each kitten contributed one score. Since we may presume that the scores of littermates are similar because of their similar genetic and early environmental circumstances, a pair of kittens is the observational unit and each pair produces two scores which contribute to two sets of correlated observations.

The data, computation, and formal summary for this example appear in Table 13–7. Notice that for pair D, the difference between the two kittens is zero and this fact eliminates the pair from the analysis. Consequently, the N is reduced from 8 to 7. The negative ranks have the smaller total ($T_- = 2$), and Table H reveals that the critical value for W is 2 for a nondirectional test at $\alpha = .05$. Since the observed and critical values are equal, the null hypothesis is rejected. This study supports the theory that feedback from physical interaction with the stimulus environment is a catalytic element in the enrichment potential of the sensory environment.

rank-order correlation

SPEARMAN RANK-ORDER CORRELATION COEFFICIENT

The Pearson product moment correlation coefficient introduced in Chapter 6 may be applied to ordinal as well as interval or ratio data. Often, if the data are markedly skewed, measurements made with an interval or ratio scale are transformed to ranks before the correlation is computed. When the Pearson product moment correlation is applied to rank orderings, it is called Spearman's rank-order correlation, and it is symbolized by r_s.

Suppose that a group of 15 nursery children were being observed by two

13–7   Summary for the Wilcoxon Test
(Sensorimotor Example).

Hypotheses

H_0: The population distributions for the two correlated groups of
observations are identical.

H_1: These two distributions are different in some way (nondirectional).

Assumptions

1. The pairs of observations are **randomly** and **independently selected,**
   but the two observations of a pair are made on the **same or matched
   subjects**.
2. **Ordinal measurement** is available both within pairs and between
   the N differences between members' scores (i.e., d_i).

Decision Rules (from Table H)

Given: the .05 level, $N = 7$ (see below), and a nondirectional
alternative

$\quad\quad$ If $W_{obs} > 2$, do not reject H_0
$\quad\quad$ If $W_{obs} \leq 2$, reject H_0

Computation

Pair	Active Kitten	Passive Kitten	d_i	$|d_i|$	Rank of $|d_i|$	Signed Rank of $|d_i|$
A	4	2	2	2	5	5
B	3	0	3	3	7	7
C	1	0	1	1	2	2
D	2	2	0	0	eliminated	
E	5	3	2	2	5	5
F	1	2	−1	1	2	−2
G	3	1	2	2	5	5
H	5	4	1	1	2	2

$N =$ number of pairs minus the number of zero differences $\quad$ $T_+ = 26$

$\quad\quad\quad\quad\quad\quad\quad\quad\quad\quad\quad\quad\quad\quad\quad\quad\quad\quad\quad\quad\quad T_- = 2$

$N = 8 - 1 = 7$ $\quad\quad\quad\quad\quad\quad\quad\quad\quad\quad\quad\quad\quad W_{obs} = 2$

Decision

$\quad$ H_0 is rejected.

judges who were asked to rank the children on their social aggressiveness. Thus, each judge would rank order the 15 children, assigning a rank of 1 to the child presumed to have the least aggressive behavior and a rank of 15 to the child presumed to have the most aggressive tendencies. The question is to what extent do the two judges agree in their ranking. The requirements for computing such an index are that the subjects are **randomly** sampled and the measurement is at least **ordinal**.

Suppose the data are:

Pupil	Judge I	Judge II	d_i	d_i^2
A	1	3	-2	4
B	4	4	0	0
C	5	8	-3	9
D	10	5	5	25
E	8	2	6	36
F	14	15	-1	1
G	7	9	-2	4
H	2	6	-4	16
I	12	14	-2	4
J	9	7	2	4
K	15	13	2	4
L	3	1	2	4
M	13	12	1	1
N	11	10	1	1
O	6	11	-5	25
$N = 15$			$\sum d_i = 0$	$\sum d_i^2 = 138$

In the present case, the raw data were themselves rank orderings of the subjects by two different judges. If the data were numbers of aggressive acts, for example, these measurements would have to be rank ordered before proceeding. Notice, however, that in contrast to some of the previous rank-order statistical tests, observations are *ranked only within, not across, a condition.* That is, for an index of relationship, each subject has two scores, one measuring one attribute (or made under one condition) and the other measuring another attribute. The observations are ranked for each attribute separately. Ties may be handled as before by assigning the average of the ranks that the tied observations would otherwise have received.

The method proceeds by computing the difference (d_i) between the ranks for each subject and then squaring each of these differences. The sum of the squared differences in ranks $\left(\sum\limits_{i=1}^{N} d_i^2\right)$ and the number of **pairs of observations (N)**, including those with zero differences, are entered into the following formula for r_S:

$$r_S = 1 - \left[\frac{6\left(\sum\limits_{i=1}^{N} d_i^2\right)}{N^3 - N}\right]$$

For the data presented above:

$$r_S = 1 - \left[\frac{6(138)}{15^3 - 15}\right]$$

$$r_S = .75$$

The formula given above for the Spearman rank-order correlation is a simplification of the formula for the Pearson product-moment correlation as applied to ranked data. It can be shown that when the Pearson formula is applied to data that have been ranked, the expression can be reduced to the formula given above for r_S. This means that if the Pearson formula were applied to the data above, a correlation of .75 would result. However, suppose a set of data measured on an interval or ratio scale were available and a Pearson correlation computed. Now, if these same data were subsequently transformed to ranks and the Spearman formula used, the Pearson and Spearman correlations would not be identical. In short, when applied to the same ranked data r and r_S will yield identical coefficients; but an r computed on interval or ratio data and an r_S computed on the rankings for that same data will not be identical (but probably will be quite close).

TESTING THE SIGNIFICANCE OF r_S

As with the Pearson r, it is desirable to be able to test the hypothesis that the observed value of r_S is really computed on a sample drawn from a population in which the correlation is actually zero and that the observed value is merely a function of sampling error.

Using the data presented in the previous section, the null hypothesis would be that the observed Spearman correlation of .75 is based upon a sample from a population in which the correlation is actually zero (that is, $H_0: \rho_S = 0$). The alternative hypothesis is that a nonzero correlation actually does exist in the population ($H_1: \rho_S \neq 0$). The assumptions are that the subjects were **randomly and independently** selected and that the measurement was at least **ordinal**.

Table I[9] lists critical values for the Spearman correlation for samples of

[9] The values in this table are exact for $N \leq 10$, but approximate for other values of N. Note also that the entries in the table may be regarded as + (positive) or − (negative).

size $N = 5$ to $N = 30$ for several levels of significance and for directional and nondirectional tests. If the observed correlation equals or exceeds the value in the table for specified N, α, and type of test (directional or nondirectional), the null hypothesis is rejected. For the present case, $N = 15$, $\alpha = .05$, and the alternative is directional since one would predict that the judges would tend to agree. Thus, the critical value of r_S is .447. Since the observed correlation of .75 is greater than the critical value, H_0 is rejected and it is concluded that the two judges do evidence some degree of concordance in their evaluations of the children.

For $N > 30$, the following expression translates r_S into an approximation to Student's t distribution with $N - 2$ degrees of freedom:

$$ t = \frac{r_S \sqrt{N - 2}}{\sqrt{1 - r_S^2}} $$

example   The following example illustrates the computation of r_S and a test to determine if the population correlation is zero.

Suppose a new test designed to diagnose reading skill has become available. Mrs. Smith, a reading consultant for a public school system, would like to use the test to screen children in the schools in order to select those that need remedial work. Since there are several hundred pupils, a single test must be used for this purpose. However, in order to evaluate whether the new test will serve this function, Mrs. Smith randomly selects 20 pupils and performs a comprehensive workup on each child based upon scores on several specialized tests, reading samples, and clinical techniques. As a result of this extensive evaluation, she ranks each of the 20 children in terms of general reading skills, a rank of 1 going to the least capable student. After this workup, she administers the new diagnostic test. She wants to know the degree of relationship between the test and her thorough evaluation and to test whether this correlation is significantly different from zero.

The assumptions are that the subjects were randomly and independently sampled and that the rankings and test scores both constitute ordinal scales. The null hypothesis for testing r_S is that the observed value deviates from a population correlation of zero only because of sampling error (H_0: $\rho_S = 0$). The directional alternative is that a positive relationship exists between the two forms of evaluation (H_1: $\rho_S > 0$).

The decision rules are based upon the critical values which are obtained from Table I. From the table with $N = 20$ and a directional test at the .05 level, the required value of r_S is .381. Thus, the decision rules are that if the observed value of r_S is greater than .381, reject H_0.

The data are presented in Table 13–8. Notice that the scores on the reading test must first be converted to ranks, while the teacher's evaluations are already

13–8 Data for the Spearman Rank-Order Correlation (Reading Example).

Pupil	Reading Test Score	Rank of Test Score	Teacher Ranking	d_i	d_i^2
A	38	1	11	−10	100
B	67	7	13	−6	36
C	72	10	5	5	25
D	43	2	10	−8	64
E	91	18	15	3	9
F	54	5	12	−7	49
G	63	6	9	−3	9
H	78	12	6	6	36
I	69	9	4	5	25
J	74	11	8	3	9
K	85	14	14	0	0
L	98	20	19	1	1
M	46	3	7	−4	16
N	52	4	3	1	1
O	68	8	1	7	49
P	80	13	16	−3	9
Q	93	19	17	2	4
R	87	16	20	−4	16
S	86	15	2	13	169
T	89	17	18	−1	1

$$N = 20, \quad \sum_{i=1}^{N} d_i^2 = 628$$

in this form. The value of d_i represents the difference *in ranks* for the two measures. The $N = 20$ and the $\sum_{i=1}^{N} d_i^2 = 628$.

Table 13-9 presents a formal summary of the procedure for testing the significance of r_S. The value of the correlation is found to be .528 with a critical value of .381. Since the observed value exceeds the critical value in the predicted direction, H_0 is rejected. It is concluded that the observed correlation probably does reflect a nonzero relationship in the population.

13-9 Summary of a Test of the Significance of the Spearman Rank-Order Correlation Coefficient (Reading Example).

Hypotheses

$$H_0 : \rho_S \leq 0$$
$$H_1 : \rho_S > 0 \text{ (directional)}$$

Assumptions

1. The sample is **randomly** and **independently** selected.
2. The measurement is at least **ordinal** in character.

Decision Rules (from Table I)

Given: a directional alternative, the .05 level, and $N = 20$

If $r_S < .381$, do not reject H_0.
If $r_S \geq .381$, reject H_0.

Computation

Given: $N = 20$ and $\sum_{i=1}^{N} d_i^2 = 628$ (from Table 13-8)

$$r_S = 1 - \left[\frac{6 \sum_{i=1}^{N} d_i^2}{N^3 - N} \right]$$

in which N = the number of pairs of scores including zero differences, and

d_i^2 = the squared difference in ranks for the ith pair of scores.

$$= 1 - \left[\frac{6(628)}{20^3 - 20} \right]$$

$$r_S = .528$$

Decision

Reject H_0.

discussion Because the approximations to theoretical sampling distributions for samples of intermediate size are somewhat less accurate than might be desired, some statisticians and researchers prefer another method of assessing rank correlation. This statistic is called Kendall's *tau*, and the procedures for testing its significance are more precise than for the Spearman coefficient. The Kendall procedure reflects a slightly different rationale, and thus the two coefficients are not precisely equivalent. Procedures for the use of "tau" are outlined in Siegel (*op. cit.*) and Bradley (*op. cit.*).

FORMULAS

1. Chi Square for r × c tables

$$\chi_{obs}^2 = \sum_{j=1}^{r} \sum_{k=1}^{c} \frac{(O_{jk} - E_{jk})^2}{E_{jk}}$$

in which

O_{jk} = the observed frequency of the jkth cell
E_{jk} = the expected frequency of the jkth cell
r = the number of rows
c = the number of columns

Refer to the Chi Square Distribution (Table F) with

$$df = (r - 1)(c - 1)$$

2. Mann-Whitney U Test for Two Independent Samples

a. For $n \leq 20$:

$$U_{obs} = n_A n_B + \frac{n_A(n_A + 1)}{2} - T_A$$

in which

n_A = the number of observations in Group A
n_B = the number of observations in Group B
T_A = the total of the ranks for Group A

Refer to the U Distribution (Table G) with n_A and n_B.

b. For $n > 20$:

$$z = \frac{U_{obs} - n_A n_B/2}{\sqrt{\dfrac{(n_A)(n_B)(n_A + n_B + 1)}{12}}}$$

in which U_{obs}, n_A, and n_B are defined above.
Refer to the Standard Normal Distribution (Table A).

3. Kruskal-Wallis Test for *k* Independent Samples

$$H_{obs} = \left[\frac{12}{N(N+1)} \right] \left[\sum_{j=1}^{k} \frac{T_j^2}{n_j} \right] - 3(N+1)$$

in which

k = the number of groups in the analysis
n_j = the number of observations in the *j*th group
$N = \sum n_j$, the total number of observations in the analysis
T_j = the total of the ranks in the *j*th group

Refer H_{obs} to the Chi Square Distribution (Table F) with

$$df = k - 1$$

4. Wilcoxon Test for Two Correlated Samples

a. For $N \leq 50$:

W_{obs} = the smaller of the sum of the ranks associated with positive differences in pairs of scores (T_+) and the sum of the ranks associated with negative differences (T_-).

Refer to the W Distribution (Table A).

b. For $N > 50$:

$$z_{obs} = \frac{W_{obs} - N(N+1)/4}{\sqrt{\dfrac{N(N+1)(2N+1)}{24}}}$$

in which W_{obs} is defined as above and

N = the number of pairs of observations having nonzero differences

Refer to Standard Normal Distribution (z).

5. Spearman Rank-Order Correlation Coefficient

$$r_S = 1 - \left[\frac{6 \left(\sum_{i=1}^{N} d_i^2 \right)}{N^3 - N} \right]$$

in which

N = the number of pairs of observations including zero differences
d_i = the difference in ranks for the *i*th pair of scores

a. For $N \leq 30$:

Refer to table of critical values for r_S (Table I).

b. For $N > 30$:

$$t = \frac{r_S \sqrt{N - 2}}{\sqrt{1 - r_S^2}}$$

Refer to Student's t Distribution (Table B) with

$$df = N - 2$$

EXERCISES

1. Under what conditions might a researcher prefer to use a nonparametric rather than a parametric statistical technique?

2. To what does power-efficiency refer? For a given N, are parametric tests or comparable nonparametric tests more powerful?

3. A sample of children was observed from 3 to 12 years of age and their IQ was tested periodically. It was found that 53 children showed increases in the general trend of their IQ's over this age period while 54 displayed essentially declining trends. The mothers of these children were seen in their homes during this period and the home visitor rated each mother on the extent to which she expected intellectual success and encouraged her child in its pursuit. The data follow:

		Amount of Maternal Aspiration		
		Low	Medium	High
IQ Trend over Age	Increased	9	16	28
	Decreased	32	10	12

Test the hypothesis that there is no difference in the distribution of maternal aspiration for intellectual success for the children that evidenced IQ increases from those showing declines.[10]

[10] Inspired by, but not identical to, R. B. McCall, M. I. Appelbaum, and P. S. Hogarty, "Developmental Changes in Mental Performance," *Monographs of the Society for Research in Child Development*, 1973, Serial No. 150.

4.

A	B	C
28	34	51
33	31	72
14	20	21
6	18	13
9	15	53
14	22	44
21	30	48
24	54	61

Above is a set of data. Perform the following nonparametric statistical tests on these data:

(a) Assume that Groups A, B, and C are independent random samples. Test the hypothesis that there is no difference between the population distributions for Groups A and B. For Groups A and C. For Groups B and C.

(b) Assuming that the three groups are independent, test the hypothesis that in the population these three groups do not differ.

(c) Conceptually, what is the difference between the questions in parts (a) and (b)? Is there an advantage to one over the other, and if so, what?

(d) Suppose that the first score in each group is a measure on a single subject before, during, and after a certain treatment. Test the hypothesis that the measurements in A are from a population distribution comparable to that from which the scores in B were drawn. Compare A and C for the same question. B and C.

(e) Compare the result you obtained for Group A vs. Group B when you tested it in Part (a) with the result when you tested it in Part (d). How do you explain any differences in the results of these two tests?

(f) Making the same assumptions as in Part (d), perform a Pearson product-moment correlation on Groups A and C, and then rank the data separately within each group. Perform both a Pearson and a Spearman correlation procedure on these rankings. Compare the results you obtained in these three cases and state the general conclusion that you have illustrated.

(g) Test the Spearman correlation computed in Part (f) above for the hypothesis that the correlation in the population is zero. Compute the Spearman correlation for the data in A and B and test this correlation in the same manner. Do the same for the data in B and C.

5. Consider the following practical situation. Suppose that a father comes home from work after a hard day and sits down with his wife and five-year-old child for dinner. The wife asks the husband, "How was your day, dear?" The retort is

"It was . . . ," in which ". . ." is a set of expletives not in the best social and child-rearing traditions. The mother may censor her husband in front of the child by saying, "Jim, you really shouldn't swear like that in front of Junior," or she could continue the conversation without commenting on the profanity. The question is, under which of these maternal response conditions is the child more likely to remember the profanity? Suppose it were possible to perform such a study in which some fathers were verbally censored while others were not.[11] Later, the child was asked what his father had said in response to the question of, "How

| | | Child's Memory of Profanity | | |
		None	Some	All
Mother's Response to Profanity	Censors Father	2	23	25
	No Response	13	22	14

was your day?" The responses are scored as either not remembering anything, remembering a portion of the father's response, or remembering all of it. The numbers of children responding at each level are presented in the table above. Test the hypothesis that the mother's response to the father's profanity does not influence the ability of the child to remember the event.

6. One hypothesis about thumbsucking in infants and children is that the behavior is a learned habit. An interesting question is how children come to learn it. It happens that all normal infants have a "rooting reflex" in which stroking the side of the mouth with a finger (for example) elicits a widening of the mouth, a turning of the head to the side of the tactile stimulus, and a propensity to suck the finger. This reflex is useful in helping the infant find the mother's breast. However, when an infant sleeps, it is customary to place the child on its stomach and its arms lie on each side of its head. The thumb may easily contact the side of the mouth, and the infant "roots" and sucks its thumb. Perhaps the infant learns the habit in this context. If infants could be prevented from rooting and sucking their thumbs when they go to sleep and wake up, presumably they would not develop as strong a habit for this behavior.[12] Suppose nylon mittens were put on the hands of nine infants just before they went to sleep and removed when they got up, thus preventing thumbsucking. Eleven other infants were reared without the gloves. In an observation period of several hours when the infants were nine months of age, the amount of time the infant spent thumbsucking was noted. The data follow. With the appropriate nonparametric technique, test the hypothesis that the wearing of mittens does not alter the amount of thumbsucking in the observation.

[11] Inspired by but not identical to R. M. Liebert and L. E. Fernandez, "Effects of Vicarious Consequences on Imitative Performance," *Child Development*, 170, XLI, 847–852.
[12] Inspired by but not identical to Lorna S. Benjamin, "The Beginning of Thumbsucking," *Child Development*, 1967, XXXVIII, 1079–1088.

Mittens	Control
4	7
10	15
6	7
14	8
1	8
0	16
5	11
13	11
9	35
	19
	21

7. Given the following data, calculate the means and medians for the two groups and use the parametric *t* test to compare the two groups. Then compute a Mann-Whitney *U* test on the same data. Compare the results of the two tests. Explain any differences and attempt to draw some conclusions about when nonparametric tests might be more appropriate than parametric tests. In what way is the difference between the mean and the median similar to the difference between a parametric and a nonparametric test in this example?

A	*B*
10	16
11	17
12	18
13	19
14	20
15	21
62	24

8. The concept of reminiscence in learning refers to the improvement in performance of a learned task after a period of "rest" following an initial practice period. The effect often appears in tasks requiring motor learning. For example, a pursuit rotor is a machine on which a spot of light moves in a circular pattern and the subject attempts to keep the point of a pencil-like stylus on the moving dot. The apparatus is such that it can monitor the length of time the point of the stylus is actually on the spot of light. Each of several randomly selected subjects is allowed 25 seconds of practice on the pursuit rotor and then given a rest of either .5, 1, or 3 minutes. This is followed by a test period on the rotor. The number of seconds in contact with the spot during the test is given for the three groups.[13]

[13] Inspired by but not identical to A. L. Irion, "Reminiscence in Pursuit-Rotor Learning as a Function of Length of Rest and Amount of Pre-Test Practice," *Journal of Experimental Psychology*, 1949, XXXIX, 492–499.

Using the appropriate nonparametric technique, test the hypothesis that the amount of rest does not alter postrest performance.

Rest in Minutes		
.5	1.0	3.0
21	32	42
32	55	58
26	62	63
49	24	71
51	53	56
41	35	13
19	59	65
27		54
		68

9. Twelve culturally deprived children are given an intensive preschool enrichment program in an attempt to raise their IQ's. They are tested first after one month of training and then at the end of the first year. The IQ's of the children for these two testings follow. By using the appropriate nonparametric technique, test the hypothesis that the program had no effect on the IQ's of the youngsters. (Would such a program likely retard IQ?).

Child	One Month	One Year
A	89	103
B	95	97
C	82	100
D	101	98
E	91	96
F	85	88
G	96	97
H	93	105
I	86	99
J	99	110
K	90	107
L	84	86

10. For the data in Exercise 9, using r_s, determine the degree of relationship between the first testing and the second for the 12 children. Test the hypothesis that in the population the relationship is zero. On psychological and educational grounds, how do you interpret the result observed in Exercise 9 in view of this additional information? (Would such correlations likely be negative?)

APPENDIX 1

APPENDIX 1

review of basic mathematics

Almost invariably a class in elementary statistics contains students whose mathematical backgrounds vary from a knowledge of high school algebra to facility with differential equations. This broad range of ability makes it difficult to begin a course in statistics unless some common level of mathematical experience can be assumed. This appendix contains a review of several basic mathematical concepts and operations including symbols, fractions, factorials, exponents, factoring, and square roots. Since this is meant to be a review, some students will not need to spend much time on this section while others would profit from a fairly serious study of this material.[1] It would be best for most students to check themselves by working the exercises at the end of the section.

SYMBOLS

The study of mathematics is greatly facilitated by the use of symbols. However, some students feel that their basic problem with mathematical material is precisely the symbolism. Actually, this problem occurs in part because the students do not take time to learn what the symbols mean. It will be helpful if readers do not proceed until they can readily interpret all the symbols presented to that point.

Most symbols will be introduced as they arise in the text. However, in addition to the signs of equality ($=$) and inequality ($\neq$) and those signs for the four basic mathematical operations ($+$, $-$, $\times$ and $\div$), the student should be intimately familiar with signs denoting inequalities. The symbol

$$>$$

means "is greater than." The expression

$$5 > 3$$

[1] Those students needing a more thorough review of the concepts presented in this section and additional material relevant to this text are referred to Helen Walker, *Mathematics Essential for Statistics* (New York: Holt, Rinehart and Winston, 1951); F. Ayers, Jr., *Schaum's Outline of Theory and Problems of First Year College Mathematics* (New York: Schaum, 1958).

is read "5 is greater than 3" and

$$a > b$$

is read "a is greater than b." Conversely, the symbol

$$<$$

means "is less than." The expression

$$3 < 5$$

is read "3 is less than 5" and

$$b < a$$

is read "b is less than a." Some students remember the difference between these two symbols by recalling that the open end of the symbol (as opposed to the vertex) is always next to the larger quantity.

Sometimes an expression of the following type will be encountered:

$$-1.96 < t < 1.96$$

This statement means that the value of t is greater than -1.96 but less than 1.96. More simply, t lies between -1.96 and 1.96. If one wants to state the opposite fact, namely that t falls outside this interval of -1.96 to 1.96, one customarily writes

$$t < -1.96 \text{ or } t > 1.96$$

Occasionally, it is desirable to write that some quantity is "greater than or equal to" some other quantity. This fact can be written with the symbol

$$\geq$$

To show that z assumes values of 2.56 or greater, write

$$z \geq 2.56$$

Similarly, the symbol

$$\leq$$

means "less than or equal to," and if z were less than or equal to zero one could write

$$z \leq 0$$

In a few places, we will use the symbolic expression

$$|X|$$

which is read the "absolute value of X." This simply means that regardless of whether X is a positive or negative number, $|X|$ equals its positive, or absolute value. Thus,

$$|-5| = 5 \quad \text{and} \quad |5| = 5$$

and if $W = 4$ and $Y = 7$,

$$|W - Y| = |4 - 7| = |-3| = 3$$

SIGNED NUMBERS

addition and subtraction   Almost any algebraic manipulation requires a knowledge of how to perform mathematical operations on negative numbers. Adding and subtracting with negative quantities is straightforward, especially if you remember that subtracting a negative number is equivalent to changing the sign of the number and adding.

$$4 - 3 = 1 \quad \text{or} \quad -3 + 4 = 1$$
$$7 - (-4) = 7 + 4 = 11$$
$$-a - (-b) = -a + b = b - a$$

multiplication   When multiplying a string of numbers the product is positive if there is an even number of negative values in the set of terms to be multiplied (0 is considered even):

$$(-4)(1)(2)(-3) = 24$$
$$(-a)(-b)(-c)(-d) = abcd$$

The product is negative if there is an odd number of negative values:

$$(-3)(2)(5) = -30$$
$$(-a)(b)(-c)(-d) = -abcd$$

division   The same rule applies to division. If there is an even number of negative values in the division, the result is positive:

$$\frac{-4}{-3} = 1.33$$

$$\frac{(-a)(b)}{-b} = a$$

If there is an odd number of negative values in the division, the result is negative:

$$\frac{6}{-3} = -2$$

$$\frac{c}{(-c)(d)} = -\frac{1}{d}$$

FRACTIONS

multiplication   The product of two or more fractions equals the product of the numerators divided by the product of the denominators:

$$\frac{1}{2} \cdot \frac{3}{5} = \frac{(1)(3)}{(2)(5)} = \frac{3}{10}$$

In general, multiply $\frac{a}{b}$ times $\frac{c}{d}$ as follows:

$$\frac{a}{b} \cdot \frac{c}{d} = \frac{ac}{bd}$$

division To divide one fraction by another, invert the divisor (the fraction you want to divide by) and multiply:

$$\tfrac{1}{2} \div \tfrac{1}{3} = \tfrac{1}{2} \cdot \tfrac{3}{1} = \tfrac{3}{2} = 1.5$$

In general,

$$\frac{a}{b} \div \frac{c}{d} = \frac{a}{b} \cdot \frac{d}{c} = \frac{ad}{bc}$$

cancellation If large numbers are involved in fractions or if one must multiply several fractions together, one can frequently simplify the computational labor by the process of cancellation in which terms in the numerator are "cancelled" with terms in the denominator. One form of cancellation is implicit in the "reduction" of fractions in which the numerator and denominator are first factored to their simplest form and then identical terms in the numerator and denominator are cancelled:

$$\frac{2}{4} = \frac{\not{2}}{(\not{2})(2)} = \frac{1}{2}$$

$$\frac{21}{147} = \frac{(3)(7)}{(49)(3)} = \frac{(\not{3})(\not{7})}{(\not{7})(7)(\not{3})} = \frac{1}{7}$$

Essentially the same process is involved when one has a string of fractions to be multiplied:

$$\left(\frac{\not{2}}{\not{3}}\right)\left(\frac{\not{3}}{\not{4}}\right) = \frac{1}{2}$$

$$\left(\frac{\not{3}}{\not{5}}\right)\left(\frac{\not{2}}{\not{3}}\right)\left(\frac{\not{5}}{\not{6}}\right) = \frac{1}{3}$$

Occasionally, the cancellation can become rather complicated:

$$\left(\frac{1}{\not{3}}\right)\left(\frac{\not{3}}{\not{8}}\right)\left(\frac{72}{35}\right)\left(\frac{\not{7}}{\not{3}}\right)\left(\frac{\not{5}}{\not{8}}\right)\left(\frac{\not{2}}{\not{3}}\right) = \frac{1}{4}$$

It is customary that

$$\frac{0}{n} = 0$$

and that

$$\frac{n}{0} = \text{undefined}$$

addition and subtraction   In order for one to add fractional quantities, the denominators of the two fractions must be equal. Thus, to add $\frac{1}{2}$ and $\frac{1}{3}$ it is necessary to change both fractions to sixths by multiplying the first by $\frac{3}{3}$ and the second by $\frac{2}{2}$:

$$\frac{1}{2} + \frac{1}{3} = ?$$

$$\frac{1}{2}(\frac{3}{3}) + \frac{1}{3}(\frac{2}{2}) = \frac{3}{6} + \frac{2}{6} = \frac{5}{6}$$

More generally, to add $\dfrac{a}{b} + \dfrac{c}{d}$,

$$\frac{a}{b} + \frac{c}{d} = \frac{a}{b}\left(\frac{d}{d}\right) + \frac{c}{d}\left(\frac{b}{b}\right) = \frac{ad}{bd} + \frac{cb}{bd} = \frac{ad + cb}{bd}$$

FACTORIALS

In some probability problems it is necessary to multiply a positive integer by each of the integers having a value less than that integer ending with 1. This string of multiplications of integers is called a *factorial* and the sign "!" following the largest integer in the string is used to indicate this operation. For example, 3!, read "three factorial," would equal

$$3! = 3 \cdot 2 \cdot 1 = 6$$

In general, $n!$ means

$$n! = n(n - 1)(n - 2)(n - 3) \cdots (1)$$

Note also by convention that

$$0! = 1$$

EXPONENTS

An exponent is a number written as a superscript to a base number which signifies that the base number should be multiplied together as many times as the exponent states. Therefore,

$$2^3 = 2 \cdot 2 \cdot 2 = 8$$

and more generally

$$n^r = \underbrace{n \cdot n \cdot n \cdots n}_{r \text{ times}}$$

Note also that

$$n^1 = n$$

and

$$n^0 = 1$$

addition and subtraction   Generally, numbers with exponents cannot be added or subtracted without first carrying out the exponentiation of each quantity. This is true even if the numbers have the same base. For example, $2^2 + 2^3$ is handled by performing the indicated exponentiation and then adding:

$$2^2 + 2^3 = 2 \cdot 2 + 2 \cdot 2 \cdot 2 = 4 + 8 = 12$$

multiplication   The product of two exponential quantities with the *same base number* equals that base number raised to the sum of the two exponents. For example,

$$(2^2)(2^3) = 2^{2+3} = 2^5$$

because

$$(2^2)(2^3) = (2 \cdot 2)(2 \cdot 2 \cdot 2) = 2^5$$

More generally,

$$(n^r)(n^s) = n^{r+s}$$

If the exponents *do not have the same base number* (e.g., $2^4 \times 3^4$), this procedure does not apply and the exponentiation should be carried out first.

division   The quotient of two exponential quantities with the same base number is that base raised to the difference between the exponent of the numerator and that of the denominator. For example,

$$\frac{2^3}{2^2} = 2^{3-2} = 2^1 = 2$$

More generally,

$$\frac{n^r}{n^s} = n^{r-s}$$

It is helpful to remember in this context that if s is larger than r in the expression n^r/n^s, then the result has a negative exponent. Negative exponents mean that a reciprocal $\left(\dfrac{1}{\text{number}}\right)$ is taken before the exponentiation is carried out. For example,

$$\frac{2^4}{2^7} = 2^{4-7} = 2^{-3} = \frac{1}{2^3} = \frac{1}{2 \cdot 2 \cdot 2} = \frac{1}{8}$$

fractions   A fraction raised to a power equals the ratio of the numerator raised to that power divided by the denominator raised to that power. For example,

$$\left(\frac{3}{5}\right)^2 = \frac{3^2}{5^2} = \frac{9}{25}$$

More generally,

$$\left(\frac{r}{s}\right)^n = \frac{r^n}{s^n}$$

binomial exponentiation   Many of the algebraic manipulations presented in this text require the student to understand the squaring of a binomial, such as, $(a + b)^2$:

$$(a + b)^2 = a^2 + 2ab + b^2$$

This result is obtained by taking the square of the first term in the binomial (e.g., a^2), plus 2 times the product of the two terms in the binomial ($2ab$), plus the square of the second term (b^2). A more common problem is to expand $(a - b)^2$. This is accomplished in the same way but with attention to the algebraic signs:

$$(a - b)^2 = a^2 + 2a(-b) + (-b)^2 = a^2 - 2ab + b^2$$

Again, the result equals the square of the first term (a^2), plus 2 times the product of the two terms [e.g., $2(a)(-b) = -2ab$], plus the square of the last term [$(-b)^2 = b^2$]. The student must remember that these procedures apply to any binomial regardless of the specific terms.

For example, quite frequently it will be necessary to expand $(X - \bar{X})^2$. The result is generated just as in the examples above:

$$(X - \bar{X})^2 = X^2 - 2X\bar{X} + \bar{X}^2$$

FACTORING AND SIMPLIFICATION

removing parentheses   Occasionally, algebraic expressions may be simplified by removing parentheses. When no multiplications or divisions are involved, one simply removes the parentheses and performs any required addition or subtraction:

$$a + (-b) = a - b$$

If a multiplication or division is involved, then one carries out this operation first. Note that $-(a + b)$ should be considered to be $(-1)(a + b)$. For example,

$$(a) - (-b) - (c + d) = a + b - c - d$$
$$a(b + c) = ab + ac$$
$$-a(b - c) = -ab + ac$$
$$\frac{1}{a}(ab - c) = b - \frac{c}{a}$$

transposing   Sometimes it is convenient to transpose a term from one side of an equation to the other. When the term to be transposed is added (or subtracted) to the expression on one side of the equation, it is transposed by subtracting (or adding) that term on both sides of the equation:

$$a - b = c$$
$$-a = -a$$
$$\overline{a - b - a = c - a}$$
$$-b = c - a$$

This amounts to placing the term (e.g., a) on the other side of the equation with a change of sign.

If the term to be transposed is involved in multiplication or division, the opposite operation (i.e., division or multiplication) must be used on both sides of the equation:

$$\frac{a}{b} = c$$
$$\left(\frac{a}{b}\right)\left(\frac{b}{1}\right) = c\left(\frac{b}{1}\right)$$
$$a = cb$$

complex factoring   Factoring an algebraic expression involves determining the simplest set of numbers which, when multiplied together, will yield the original number:

$$ab + ac = a(b + c)$$
$$-ab - ac = -a(b + c)$$

Factoring is often used to simplify algebraic expressions. Consider the following example:

$$\frac{-a(b - c) - (c - ab)}{a - 1}$$

Carrying out the appropriate multiplications in the numerator, one obtains

$$\frac{-ab - a(-c) - (c - ab)}{a - 1}$$

and simplifying the signs of certain expressions, one obtains

$$\frac{-ab + ac - c + ab}{a - 1}$$

By subtracting,

$$\frac{ac - c}{a - 1}$$

factoring,

$$\frac{c(a - 1)}{a - 1}$$

and dividing, one finds the expression reduces to

$$c$$

Sometimes in the course of simplifying an expression it helps to divide each term in the numerator by the denominator:

$$\frac{a - b}{c} = \frac{a}{c} - \frac{b}{c}$$

However, the student must discriminate. The above manipulation is correct but the following manipulations are *incorrect*.

$$\frac{c}{a - b} \neq \frac{c}{a} - \frac{c}{b}$$

$$\frac{a - b}{c - d} \neq \frac{a}{c} - \frac{b}{d}$$

ROOTS

double roots   It must be remembered that technically the square root of a^2 is $\pm a$ since both $(+a)^2$ and $(-a)^2$ equal a^2. Ordinarily, just the positive root is accepted as the answer, but there will be occasions in which it is necessary to remember that two roots do exist.

extracting the square root The square root of a number is frequently desired in statistical manipulations and it is quite helpful if the student can perform this operation without tables. The following is a description of how to proceed. Suppose the square root of 184.3 is desired. First, using the decimal point as a starting place, separate the digits into pairs working away from the decimal point in both directions:

$$1 \qquad 84.30 \qquad 00$$

Next, consider only the first group of digits, the "1" in this case. Pose the question, "What number when multiplied by itself will be less than or equal to 1?" The answer is "1." Write this as follows:

```
              1
      ┌──────────────────
   1  │   1    84.30    00
```

Continue the square-root operation as follows:

```
              1
      ┌──────────────────
   1  │   1    84.30    00
      │   1
      └──────────────
          0    84
```

Notice that the next *pair* of digits (8 and 4), not just the next single digit, was brought down. Now, double whatever number is currently in the answer (i.e., above the horizontal line) and place it to the left of the "84" (the preceding zero has been dropped):

```
              1      ?
      ┌──────────────────
   1  │   1    84.30    00
      │   1
      └──────────────
   2?     │    84
```

Notice that the 1 was doubled to 2 but another digit is required and that place is reserved with a question mark in two places, one in the answer and one in the current divisor. The question mark represents some digit such that the digit times the current divisor (2?) is as close as possible to, but less than or equal to 84. The "?" equals 3 because $3 \times 23 = 69$ which is less than 84. Just as in long division, the required number must be the largest such integer. In this case 4 is too large because $4 \times 24 = 96$ which is greater than 84, so 3 is the largest appropriate integer. After the familiar multiplication and subtraction, this procedure is repeated:

```
              1      3.?
      ┌──────────────────
   1  │   1    84.30    00
      │   1
      └──────────────
   23     │    84
          │    69
          └──────────────
   26?    │   1530
```

The current divisor of 26? has been obtained by doubling the current answer (13) and affixing an unknown digit (?). Again the question is what does "?" equal to make ? × 26? ≤ 1530? The answer is 5 because 5 × 265 = 1325 which is less than but close to 1530. The number 6 would be too large because 6 × 266 = 1596 > 1530.

```
              1        3.5       ?
    1  |  1       84.30      00
       |  1
       |————
          23 |  84
             |  69
             |————
         265 |  1530
             |  1325
             |————
        270? |  205       00
```

Notice that in order to obtain the next divisor the current answer is doubled but the decimal point is ignored. Thus, the current divisor is 270? not 27.0?. Again, note that a *pair* of zeros, not just one, was brought down into the remainder. The appropriate value for "?" is now 7:

```
              1        3.5       7
    1  |  1       84.30      00
       |  1
       |————
          23 |  84
             |  69
             |————
         265 |  1530
             |  1325
             |————
        2707 |  205       00
             |  189       49
             |————
                 15       51
```

In long division, to round the answer appropriately one frequently asks if two times the remainder is more than the divisor. If it is, one rounds the answer up, otherwise the answer remains as it is. Thus, one might be tempted to say, "Since twice the current remainder of 1551 is 3102 which is greater than 2707, round the answer to 13.58." This procedure does not always work in extracting square roots because the current divisor will not be the divisor in the next step. The best policy is to carry the extraction one step beyond the desired accuracy. If the answer is required only to tenths, 13.6 is the result.

table of squares and square roots   Appendix II, Table K in the back of this book lists the squares and square roots of each integer from 1 to 1000. The square of 28 is obtained simply by finding 28 in the first column headed N and looking to the next column labeled N^2 in that row to find the answer of 784. The square root of 28 is found in the third column which lists 5.2915 as the $\sqrt{N}$.

The precise number of interest may not be listed in Table K. For example, suppose one wanted to know the square root of 6.25. The table will actually provide the precise answer if one conceives of 6.25 as $\frac{625}{100}$. Since

$$\sqrt{\frac{625}{100}} = \frac{\sqrt{625}}{\sqrt{100}} = \frac{\sqrt{625}}{10}$$

one needs only to find the square root of 625 and divide it by 10. The table lists the square root of 625 to be 25, and dividing that by 10 yields the square root of 6.25 as 2.5.

To obtain the square root of 75300, think of 75300 as 100×753 and thus its square root as

$$\sqrt{(100)(753)} = \sqrt{100}\sqrt{753} = 10\sqrt{753}$$

The root listed for 753 is 27.4408 and 10 times this gives the desired answer of 274.408.

These illustrations show that if a number can be factored into two or more values which are available in the table, the square or square root of that number can be determined with a minimum of computation.

INTERPOLATION

Interpolation is a procedure with which one can obtain an approximate value corresponding to a value not listed in the table. For example, consider the square root of 13.67. Such a number is not listed in Table K of Appendix II. If the root is computed by the long method described previously, the answer is 3.6973. An approximation to this value can be obtained by interpolating within the square root table as illustrated in the following manner:

Number	Square Root	Difference		Partition of Difference	
13	3.6056				3.6056
		.1361	$\frac{2}{3}$	.0907	+ .0907
13.67					3.6963
14	3.7417		$\frac{1}{3}$	.0454	
				.1361	

The square root of 13 is 3.6056 and the square root of 14 is 3.7417 (as shown in Table K in Appendix II). Since the square root of 13.67 is desired, the result should fall somewhere between the root for 13 and the root for 14. In fact, the basic logic of interpolation is that the answer should fall between these two roots in the same ratio that 13.67 falls between 13 and 14. The table shows 13 and 14 and their corresponding square roots of 3.6056 and 3.7417. The number in question, 13.67, falls two-thirds of the way between 13 and 14. Thus, the difference in the roots for 13 and 14, namely .1361, is partitioned into two parts, two-thirds (.0907) and one-third (.0454). Since 13.67 falls two-thirds of the way between 13 and 14, two-thirds of the difference between the roots of 13 and 14 should be added to the root of 13 in order to approximate the square root of 13.67. This result is 3.6963. Notice that it is not identical to the correct answer of 3.6973, but for some purposes this approximation will be sufficiently accurate.

The application of the general procedure of interpolation is not limited to finding square roots. As the reader will note, there are many tables in the back of this book and interpolation may be used to obtain a value which is not listed in these other tables as well.

EXERCISES

1. Perform the indicated operations.

   a. $\frac{2}{7} + \frac{3}{7}$ e. $\frac{1}{2} - \frac{1}{3}$

   b. $\frac{3}{5} + \frac{3}{10}$ f. $\frac{5}{6} - \frac{1}{18}$

   c. $\frac{4}{9} + \frac{6}{11}$ g. $\frac{7}{9} - \frac{9}{20}$

   d. $\frac{7}{2} + \frac{3}{7}$

2. Perform the indicated operations.

   a. $\frac{2}{3} \cdot \frac{1}{3}$ d. $\frac{2}{3} \div \frac{3}{4}$

   b. $\frac{3}{7} \cdot \frac{2}{3}$ e. $\frac{4}{5} \div \frac{2}{3}$

   c. $\frac{27}{54} \cdot \frac{2}{3} \cdot \frac{15}{18} \cdot \frac{3}{5} \cdot 6$ f. $\frac{8}{11} \div \frac{5}{22}$

3. Simplify the following.

   a. $4!$ b. $\dfrac{5!}{3!}$ c. $\dfrac{3!\,6!}{9}$

4. Simplify the following.

   a. 3^3 g. $3^3 \div 3^3$

   b. $3^2 + 3^2$ h. $4^3 \div 4^2$

   c. $4^2 + 2^3$ i. $5^2 \div 3^2$

   d. $2^4 - 3^2$ j. $\left(\frac{3}{5}\right)^3$

   e. $2^3 \cdot 2^4$ k. $\left(\frac{2}{3}\right)^3 \div \left(\frac{4}{5}\right)^2$

   f. $3^2 \cdot 4^2$

5. Expand and simplify the following expressions.

   a. $(a + b)^2$ e. $\dfrac{(b - c)(-a) + (ab - c)}{a - 1}$

   b. $(a - b)^2$ f. $\dfrac{ca - b}{c}$

   c. $(X - \bar{X})^2$ g. $\dfrac{dab + cba}{ab(d - c)}$

   d. $(cd - ab)^2$

6. First, determine the square root without using tables and then use the tables to determine the square root of each of the following.

   a. 1444   e. 992.5

   b. 128,881   f. 118.2

   c. 4800   g. 11695

   d. .57

APPENDIX II
TABLES

Table A. Proportions of Area under the Standard Normal Curve

z			z			z		
0.00	.0000	.5000	0.55	.2088	.2912	1.10	.3643	.1357
0.01	.0040	.4960	0.56	.2123	.2877	1.11	.3665	.1335
0.02	.0080	.4920	0.57	.2157	.2843	1.12	.3686	.1314
0.03	.0120	.4880	0.58	.2190	.2810	1.13	.3708	.1292
0.04	.0160	.4840	0.59	.2224	.2776	1.14	.3729	.1271
0.05	.0199	.4801	0.60	.2257	.2743	1.15	.3749	.1251
0.06	.0239	.4761	0.61	.2291	.2709	1.16	.3770	.1230
0.07	.0279	.4721	0.62	.2324	.2676	1.17	.3790	.1210
0.08	.0319	.4681	0.63	.2357	.2643	1.18	.3810	.1190
0.09	.0359	.4641	0.64	.2389	.2611	1.19	.3830	.1170
0.10	.0398	.4602	0.65	.2422	.2578	1.20	.3849	.1151
0.11	.0438	.4562	0.66	.2454	.2546	1.21	.3869	.1131
0.12	.0478	.4522	0.67	.2486	.2514	1.22	.3888	.1112
0.13	.0517	.4483	0.68	.2517	.2483	1.23	.3907	.1093
0.14	.0557	.4443	0.69	.2549	.2451	1.24	.3925	.1075
0.15	.0596	.4404	0.70	.2580	.2420	1.25	.3944	.1056
0.16	.0636	.4364	0.71	.2611	.2389	1.26	.3962	.1038
0.17	.0675	.4325	0.72	.2642	.2358	1.27	.3980	.1020
0.18	.0714	.4286	0.73	.2673	.2327	1.28	.3997	.1003
0.19	.0753	.4247	0.74	.2704	.2296	1.29	.4015	.0985
0.20	.0793	.4207	0.75	.2734	.2266	1.30	.4032	.0968
0.21	.0832	.4168	0.76	.2764	.2236	1.31	.4049	.0951
0.22	.0871	.4129	0.77	.2794	.2206	1.32	.4066	.0934
0.23	.0910	.4090	0.78	.2823	.2177	1.33	.4082	.0918
0.24	.0948	.4052	0.79	.2852	.2148	1.34	.4099	.0901
0.25	.0987	.4013	0.80	.2881	.2119	1.35	.4115	.0885
0.26	.1026	.3974	0.81	.2910	.2090	1.36	.4131	.0869
0.27	.1064	.3936	0.82	.2939	.2061	1.37	.4147	.0853
0.28	.1103	.3897	0.83	.2967	.2033	1.38	.4162	.0838
0.29	.1141	.3859	0.84	.2995	.2005	1.39	.4177	.0823
0.30	.1179	.3821	0.85	.3023	.1977	1.40	.4192	.0808
0.31	.1217	.3783	0.86	.3051	.1949	1.41	.4207	.0793
0.32	.1255	.3745	0.87	.3078	.1922	1.42	.4222	.0778
0.33	.1293	.3707	0.88	.3106	.1894	1.43	.4236	.0764
0.34	.1331	.3669	0.89	.3133	.1867	1.44	.4251	.0749
0.35	.1368	.3632	0.90	.3159	.1841	1.45	.4265	.0735
0.36	.1406	.3594	0.91	.3186	.1814	1.46	.4279	.0721
0.37	.1443	.3557	0.92	.3212	.1788	1.47	.4292	.0708
0.38	.1480	.3520	0.93	.3238	.1762	1.48	.4306	.0694
0.39	.1517	.3483	0.94	.3264	.1736	1.49	.4319	.0681
0.40	.1554	.3446	0.95	.3289	.1711	1.50	.4332	.0668
0.41	.1591	.3409	0.96	.3315	.1685	1.51	.4345	.0655
0.42	.1628	.3372	0.97	.3340	.1660	1.52	.4357	.0643
0.43	.1664	.3336	0.98	.3365	.1635	1.53	.4370	.0630
0.44	.1700	.3300	0.99	.3389	.1611	1.54	.4382	.0618
0.45	.1736	.3264	1.00	.3413	.1587	1.55	.4394	.0606
0.46	.1772	.3228	1.01	.3438	.1562	1.56	.4406	.0594
0.47	.1808	.3192	1.02	.3461	.1539	1.57	.4418	.0582
0.48	.1844	.3156	1.03	.3485	.1515	1.58	.4429	.0571
0.49	.1879	.3121	1.04	.3508	.1492	1.59	.4441	.0559
0.50	.1915	.3085	1.05	.3531	.1469	1.60	.4452	.0548
0.51	.1950	.3050	1.06	.3554	.1446	1.61	.4463	.0537
0.52	.1985	.3015	1.07	.3577	.1423	1.62	.4474	.0526
0.53	.2019	.2981	1.08	.3599	.1401	1.63	.4484	.0516
0.54	.2054	.2946	1.09	.3621	.1379	1.64	.4495	.0505

Source: Runyon and Haber, *Fundamentals of Behavioral Statistics*, 2 ed., 1971, Addison-Wesley, Reading, Mass.

Table A (continued)

z			z			z		
1.65	.4505	.0495	2.22	.4868	.0132	2.79	.4974	.0026
1.66	.4515	.0485	2.23	.4871	.0129	2.80	.4974	.0026
1.67	.4525	.0475	2.24	.4875	.0125	2.81	.4975	.0025
1.68	.4535	.0465	2.25	.4878	.0122	2.82	.4976	.0024
1.69	.4545	.0455	2.26	.4881	.0119	2.83	.4977	.0023
1.70	.4554	.0446	2.27	.4884	.0116	2.84	.4977	.0023
1.71	.4564	.0436	2.28	.4887	.0113	2.85	.4978	.0022
1.72	.4573	.0427	2.29	.4890	.0110	2.86	.4979	.0021
1.73	.4582	.0418	2.30	.4893	.0107	2.87	.4979	.0021
1.74	.4591	.0409	2.31	.4896	.0104	2.88	.4980	.0020
1.75	.4599	.0401	2.32	.4898	.0102	2.89	.4981	.0019
1.76	.4608	.0392	2.33	.4901	.0099	2.90	.4981	.0019
1.77	.4616	.0384	2.34	.4904	.0096	2.91	.4982	.0018
1.78	.4625	.0375	2.35	.4906	.0094	2.92	.4982	.0018
1.79	.4633	.0367	2.36	.4909	.0091	2.93	.4983	.0017
1.80	.4641	.0359	2.37	.4911	.0089	2.94	.4984	.0016
1.81	.4649	.0351	2.38	.4913	.0087	2.95	.4984	.0016
1.82	.4656	.0344	2.39	.4916	.0084	2.96	.4985	.0015
1.83	.4664	.0336	2.40	.4918	.0082	2.97	.4985	.0015
1.84	.4671	.0329	2.41	.4920	.0080	2.98	.4986	.0014
1.85	.4678	.0322	2.42	.4922	.0078	2.99	.4986	.0014
1.86	.4686	.0314	2.43	.4925	.0075	3.00	.4987	.0013
1.87	.4693	.0307	2.44	.4927	.0073	3.01	.4987	.0013
1.88	.4699	.0301	2.45	.4929	.0071	3.02	.4987	.0013
1.89	.4706	.0294	2.46	.4931	.0069	3.03	.4988	.0012
1.90	.4713	.0287	2.47	.4932	.0068	3.04	.4988	.0012
1.91	.4719	.0281	2.48	.4934	.0066	3.05	.4989	.0011
1.92	.4726	.0274	2.49	.4936	.0064	3.06	.4989	.0011
1.93	.4732	.0268	2.50	.4938	.0062	3.07	.4989	.0011
1.94	.4738	.0262	2.51	.4940	.0060	3.08	.4990	.0010
1.95	.4744	.0256	2.52	.4941	.0059	3.09	.4990	.0010
1.96	.4750	.0250	2.53	.4943	.0057	3.10	.4990	.0010
1.97	.4756	.0244	2.54	.4945	.0055	3.11	.4991	.0009
1.98	.4761	.0239	2.55	.4946	.0054	3.12	.4991	.0009
1.99	.4767	.0233	2.56	.4948	.0052	3.13	.4991	.0009
2.00	.4772	.0228	2.57	.4949	.0051	3.14	.4992	.0008
2.01	.4778	.0222	2.58	.4951	.0049	3.15	.4992	.0008
2.02	.4783	.0217	2.59	.4952	.0048	3.16	.4992	.0008
2.03	.4788	.0212	2.60	.4953	.0047	3.17	.4992	.0008
2.04	.4793	.0207	2.61	.4955	.0045	3.18	.4993	.0007
2.05	.4798	.0202	2.62	.4956	.0044	3.19	.4993	.0007
2.06	.4803	.0197	2.63	.4957	.0043	3.20	.4993	.0007
2.07	.4808	.0192	2.64	.4959	.0041	3.21	.4993	.0007
2.08	.4812	.0188	2.65	.4960	.0040	3.22	.4994	.0006
2.09	.4817	.0183	2.66	.4961	.0039	3.23	.4994	.0006
2.10	.4821	.0179	2.67	.4962	.0038	3.24	.4994	.0006
2.11	.4826	.0174	2.68	.4963	.0037	3.25	.4994	.0006
2.12	.4830	.0170	2.69	.4964	.0036	3.30	.4995	.0005
2.13	.4834	.0166	2.70	.4965	.0035	3.35	.4996	.0004
2.14	.4838	.0162	2.71	.4966	.0034	3.40	.4997	.0003
2.15	.4842	.0158	2.72	.4967	.0033	3.45	.4997	.0003
2.16	.4846	.0154	2.73	.4968	.0032	3.50	.4998	.0002
2.17	.4850	.0150	2.74	.4969	.0031	3.60	.4998	.0002
2.18	.4854	.0146	2.75	.4970	.0030	3.70	.4999	.0001
2.19	.4857	.0143	2.76	.4971	.0029	3.80	.4999	.0001
2.20	.4861	.0139	2.77	.4972	.0028	3.90	.49995	.00005
2.21	.4864	.0136	2.78	.4973	.0027	4.00	.49997	.00003

Table B. Critical Values of *t*

df	Level of significance for a directional (one-tailed) test					
	.10	.05	.025	.01	.005	.0005
	Level of significance for a non-directional (two-tailed) test					
	.20	.10	.05	.02	.01	.001
1	3.078	6.314	12.706	31.821	63.657	636.619
2	1.886	2.920	4.303	6.965	9.925	31.598
3	1.638	2.353	3.182	4.541	5.841	12.941
4	1.533	2.132	2.776	3.747	4.604	8.610
5	1.476	2.015	2.571	3.365	4.032	6.859
6	1.440	1.943	2.447	3.143	3.707	5.959
7	1.415	1.895	2.365	2.998	3.499	5.405
8	1.397	1.860	2.306	2.896	3.355	5.041
9	1.383	1.833	2.262	2.821	3.250	4.781
10	1.372	1.812	2.228	2.764	3.169	4.587
11	1.363	1.796	2.201	2.718	3.106	4.437
12	1.356	1.782	2.179	2.681	3.055	4.318
13	1.350	1.771	2.160	2.650	3.012	4.221
14	1.345	1.761	2.145	2.624	2.977	4.140
15	1.341	1.753	2.131	2.602	2.947	4.073
16	1.337	1.746	2.120	2.583	2.921	4.015
17	1.333	1.740	2.110	2.567	2.898	3.965
18	1.330	1.734	2.101	2.552	2.878	3.922
19	1.328	1.729	2.093	2.539	2.861	3.883
20	1.325	1.725	2.086	2.528	2.845	3.850
21	1.323	1.721	2.080	2.518	2.831	3.819
22	1.321	1.717	2.074	2.508	2.819	3.792
23	1.319	1.714	2.069	2.500	2.807	3.767
24	1.318	1.711	2.064	2.492	2.797	3.745
25	1.316	1.708	2.060	2.485	2.787	3.725
26	1.315	1.706	2.056	2.479	2.779	3.707
27	1.314	1.703	2.052	2.473	2.771	3.690
28	1.313	1.701	2.048	2.467	2.763	3.674
29	1.311	1.699	2.045	2.462	2.756	3.659
30	1.310	1.697	2.042	2.457	2.750	3.646
40	1.303	1.684	2.021	2.423	2.704	3.551
60	1.296	1.671	2.000	2.390	2.660	3.460
120	1.289	1.658	1.980	2.358	2.617	3.373
∞	1.282	1.645	1.960	2.326	2.576	3.291

Source: Table B is taken from Table III of Fisher and Yates, *Statistical Tables for Biological, Agricultural and Medical Research*, published by Longman Group Ltd., London (previously published by Oliver and Boyd, Ltd., Edinburgh), and by permission of the authors and publishers.

The value listed in the table is the critical value of *t* for the number of degrees of freedom listed in the left column for a directional (one-tailed) or non-directional (two-tailed) test at the significance level indicated at the top of each column. If the observed *t* is *greater than or equal to* the tabled value, reject H_0. Since the *t* distribution is symmetrical about *t* = 0, these critical values represent both + and − values for non-directional tests.

Table **C**.   Critical Values of the Pearson Product Moment Correlation Coefficient

	Level of significance for a directional (one-tailed) test				
	.05	.025	.01	.005	.0005
	Level of significance for a non-directional (two-tailed) test				
$df = N-2$	.10	.05	.02	.01	.001
1	.9877	.9969	.9995	.9999	1.0000
2	.9000	.9500	.9800	.9900	.9990
3	.8054	.8783	.9343	.9587	.9912
4	.7293	.8114	.8822	.9172	.9741
5	.6694	.7545	.8329	.8745	.9507
6	.6215	.7067	.7887	.8343	.9249
7	.5822	.6664	.7498	.7977	.8982
8	.5494	.6319	.7155	.7646	.8721
9	.5214	.6021	.6851	.7348	.8471
10	.4973	.5760	.6581	.7079	.8233
11	.4762	.5529	.6339	.6835	.8010
12	.4575	.5324	.6120	.6614	.7800
13	.4409	.5139	.5923	.6411	.7603
14	.4259	.4973	.5742	.6226	.7420
15	.4124	.4821	.5577	.6055	.7246
16	.4000	.4683	.5425	.5897	.7084
17	.3887	.4555	.5285	.5751	.6932
18	.3783	.4438	.5155	.5614	.6787
19	.3687	.4329	.5034	.5487	.6652
20	.3598	.4227	.4921	.5368	.6524
25	.3233	.3809	.4451	.4869	.5974
30	.2960	.3494	.4093	.4487	.5541
35	.2746	.3246	.3810	.4182	.5189
40	.2573	.3044	.3578	.3932	.4896
45	.2428	.2875	.3384	.3721	.4648
50	.2306	.2732	.3218	.3541	.4433
60	.2108	.2500	.2948	.3248	.4078
70	.1954	.2319	.2737	.3017	.3799
80	.1829	.2172	.2565	.2830	.3568
90	.1726	.2050	.2422	.2673	.3375
100	.1638	.1946	.2301	.2540	.3211

Source: Table C is taken from Table VII of Fisher and Yates, *Statistical Tables for Biological, Agricultural, and Medical Research*, published by Longman Group Ltd., London (previously published by Oliver and Boyd, Ltd., Edinburgh), and by permission of the authors and publishers.

If the observed value of *r* is *greater than or equal to* the tabled value for the appropriate level of significance (columns) and degrees of freedom (rows), then reject H_0. The degrees of freedom are the number of pairs of scores minus two, or $N - 2$. The critical values in the table are both $+$ and $-$ for non-directional (two-tailed) tests.

Table **D**. Transformation of r to z_r

r	z_r	r	z_r	r	z_r	r	z_r	r	z_r
.000	.000	.200	.203	.400	.424	.600	.693	.800	1.099
.005	.005	.205	.208	.405	.430	.605	.701	.805	1.113
.010	.010	.210	.213	.410	.436	.610	.709	.810	1.127
.015	.015	.215	.218	.415	.442	.615	.717	.815	1.142
.020	.020	.220	.224	.420	.448	.620	.725	.820	1.157
.025	.025	.225	.229	.425	.454	.625	.733	.825	1.172
.030	.030	.230	.234	.430	.460	.630	.741	.830	1.188
.035	.035	.235	.239	.435	.466	.635	.750	.835	1.204
.040	.040	.240	.245	.440	.472	.640	.758	.840	1.221
.045	.045	.245	.250	.445	.478	.645	.767	.845	1.238
.050	.050	.250	.255	.450	.485	.650	.775	.850	1.256
.055	.055	.255	.261	.455	.491	.655	.784	.855	1.274
.060	.060	.260	.266	.460	.497	.660	.793	.860	1.293
.065	.065	.265	.271	.465	.504	.665	.802	.865	1.313
.070	.070	.270	.277	.470	.510	.670	.811	.870	1.333
.075	.075	.275	.282	.475	.517	.675	.820	.875	1.354
.080	.080	.280	.288	.480	.523	.680	.829	.880	1.376
.085	.085	.285	.293	.485	.530	.685	.838	.885	1.398
.090	.090	.290	.299	.490	.536	.690	.848	.890	1.422
.095	.095	.295	.304	.495	.543	.695	.858	.895	1.447
.100	.100	.300	.310	.500	.549	.700	.867	.900	1.472
.105	.105	.305	.315	.505	.556	.705	.877	.905	1.499
.110	.110	.310	.321	.510	.563	.710	.887	.910	1.528
.115	.116	.315	.326	.515	.570	.715	.897	.915	1.557
.120	.121	.320	.332	.520	.576	.720	.908	.920	1.589
.125	.126	.325	.337	.525	.583	.725	.918	.925	1.623
.130	.131	.330	.343	.530	.590	.730	.929	.930	1.658
.135	.136	.335	.348	.535	.597	.735	.940	.935	1.697
.140	.141	.340	.354	.540	.604	.740	.950	.940	1.738
.145	.146	.345	.360	.545	.611	.745	.962	.945	1.783
.150	.151	.350	.365	.550	.618	.750	.973	.950	1.832
.155	.156	.355	.371	.555	.626	.755	.984	.955	1.886
.160	.161	.360	.377	.560	.633	.760	.996	.960	1.946
.165	.167	.365	.383	.565	.640	.765	1.008	.965	2.014
.170	.172	.370	.388	.570	.648	.770	1.020	.970	2.092
.175	.177	.375	.394	.575	.655	.775	1.033	.975	2.185
.180	.182	.380	.400	.580	.662	.780	1.045	.980	2.298
.185	.187	.385	.406	.585	.670	.785	1.058	.985	2.443
.190	.192	.390	.412	.590	.678	.790	1.071	.990	2.647
.195	.198	.395	.418	.595	.685	.795	1.085	.995	2.994

Source: From Edwards, A. L., *Statistical Methods for the Behavioral Sciences*, 1965, Holt, Rinehart and Winston, New York.

Table E. Critical Values of F (.05 level in roman type, .01 level in bold face)

Each cell shows the .05 level value (roman type) over the .01 level value (bold face).

Degrees of freedom for the numerator

Denom. df	1	2	3	4	5	6	7	8	9	10	11	12	14	16	20	24	30	40	50	75	100	200	500	∞
1	161 / **4,052**	200 / **4,999**	216 / **5,403**	225 / **5,625**	230 / **5,764**	234 / **5,859**	237 / **5,928**	239 / **5,981**	241 / **6,022**	242 / **6,056**	243 / **6,082**	244 / **6,106**	245 / **6,142**	246 / **6,169**	248 / **6,208**	249 / **6,234**	250 / **6,261**	251 / **6,286**	252 / **6,302**	253 / **6,323**	253 / **6,334**	254 / **6,352**	254 / **6,361**	254 / **6,366**
2	18.51 / **98.49**	19.00 / **99.00**	19.16 / **99.17**	19.25 / **99.25**	19.30 / **99.30**	19.33 / **99.33**	19.36 / **99.36**	19.37 / **99.37**	19.38 / **99.39**	19.39 / **99.40**	19.40 / **99.41**	19.41 / **99.42**	19.42 / **99.43**	19.43 / **99.44**	19.44 / **99.45**	19.45 / **99.46**	19.46 / **99.47**	19.47 / **99.48**	19.47 / **99.48**	19.48 / **99.49**	19.49 / **99.49**	19.49 / **99.49**	19.50 / **99.50**	19.50 / **99.50**
3	10.13 / **34.12**	9.55 / **30.82**	9.28 / **29.46**	9.12 / **28.71**	9.01 / **28.24**	8.94 / **27.91**	8.88 / **27.67**	8.84 / **27.49**	8.81 / **27.34**	8.78 / **27.23**	8.76 / **27.13**	8.74 / **27.05**	8.71 / **26.92**	8.69 / **26.83**	8.66 / **26.69**	8.64 / **26.60**	8.62 / **26.50**	8.60 / **26.41**	8.58 / **26.35**	8.57 / **26.27**	8.56 / **26.23**	8.54 / **26.18**	8.54 / **26.14**	8.53 / **26.12**
4	7.71 / **21.20**	6.94 / **18.00**	6.59 / **16.69**	6.39 / **15.98**	6.26 / **15.52**	6.16 / **15.21**	6.09 / **14.98**	6.04 / **14.80**	6.00 / **14.66**	5.96 / **14.54**	5.93 / **14.45**	5.91 / **14.37**	5.87 / **14.24**	5.84 / **14.15**	5.80 / **14.02**	5.77 / **13.93**	5.74 / **13.83**	5.71 / **13.74**	5.70 / **13.69**	5.68 / **13.61**	5.66 / **13.57**	5.65 / **13.52**	5.64 / **13.48**	5.63 / **13.46**
5	6.61 / **16.26**	5.79 / **13.27**	5.41 / **12.06**	5.19 / **11.39**	5.05 / **10.97**	4.95 / **10.67**	4.88 / **10.45**	4.82 / **10.29**	4.78 / **10.15**	4.74 / **10.05**	4.70 / **9.96**	4.68 / **9.89**	4.64 / **9.77**	4.60 / **9.68**	4.56 / **9.55**	4.53 / **9.47**	4.50 / **9.38**	4.46 / **9.29**	4.44 / **9.24**	4.42 / **9.17**	4.40 / **9.13**	4.38 / **9.07**	4.37 / **9.04**	4.36 / **9.02**
6	5.99 / **13.74**	5.14 / **10.92**	4.76 / **9.78**	4.53 / **9.15**	4.39 / **8.75**	4.28 / **8.47**	4.21 / **8.26**	4.15 / **8.10**	4.10 / **7.98**	4.06 / **7.87**	4.03 / **7.79**	4.00 / **7.72**	3.96 / **7.60**	3.92 / **7.52**	3.87 / **7.39**	3.84 / **7.31**	3.81 / **7.23**	3.77 / **7.14**	3.75 / **7.09**	3.72 / **7.02**	3.71 / **6.99**	3.69 / **6.94**	3.68 / **6.90**	3.67 / **6.88**
7	5.59 / **12.25**	4.74 / **9.55**	4.35 / **8.45**	4.12 / **7.85**	3.97 / **7.46**	3.87 / **7.19**	3.79 / **7.00**	3.73 / **6.84**	3.68 / **6.71**	3.63 / **6.62**	3.60 / **6.54**	3.57 / **6.47**	3.52 / **6.35**	3.49 / **6.27**	3.44 / **6.15**	3.41 / **6.07**	3.38 / **5.98**	3.34 / **5.90**	3.32 / **5.85**	3.29 / **5.78**	3.28 / **5.75**	3.25 / **5.70**	3.24 / **5.67**	3.23 / **5.65**
8	5.32 / **11.26**	4.46 / **8.65**	4.07 / **7.59**	3.84 / **7.01**	3.69 / **6.63**	3.58 / **6.37**	3.50 / **6.19**	3.44 / **6.03**	3.39 / **5.91**	3.34 / **5.82**	3.31 / **5.74**	3.28 / **5.67**	3.23 / **5.56**	3.20 / **5.48**	3.15 / **5.36**	3.12 / **5.28**	3.08 / **5.20**	3.05 / **5.11**	3.03 / **5.06**	3.00 / **5.00**	2.98 / **4.96**	2.96 / **4.91**	2.94 / **4.88**	2.93 / **4.86**
9	5.12 / **10.56**	4.26 / **8.02**	3.86 / **6.99**	3.63 / **6.42**	3.48 / **6.06**	3.37 / **5.80**	3.29 / **5.62**	3.23 / **5.47**	3.18 / **5.35**	3.13 / **5.26**	3.10 / **5.18**	3.07 / **5.11**	3.02 / **5.00**	2.98 / **4.92**	2.93 / **4.80**	2.90 / **4.73**	2.86 / **4.64**	2.82 / **4.56**	2.80 / **4.51**	2.77 / **4.45**	2.76 / **4.41**	2.73 / **4.36**	2.72 / **4.33**	2.71 / **4.31**
10	4.96 / **10.04**	4.10 / **7.56**	3.71 / **6.55**	3.48 / **5.99**	3.33 / **5.64**	3.22 / **5.39**	3.14 / **5.21**	3.07 / **5.06**	3.02 / **4.95**	2.97 / **4.85**	2.94 / **4.78**	2.91 / **4.71**	2.86 / **4.60**	2.82 / **4.52**	2.77 / **4.41**	2.74 / **4.33**	2.70 / **4.25**	2.67 / **4.17**	2.64 / **4.12**	2.61 / **4.05**	2.59 / **4.01**	2.56 / **3.96**	2.55 / **3.93**	2.54 / **3.91**
11	4.84 / **9.65**	3.98 / **7.20**	3.59 / **6.22**	3.36 / **5.67**	3.20 / **5.32**	3.09 / **5.07**	3.01 / **4.88**	2.95 / **4.74**	2.90 / **4.63**	2.86 / **4.54**	2.82 / **4.46**	2.79 / **4.40**	2.74 / **4.29**	2.70 / **4.21**	2.65 / **4.10**	2.61 / **4.02**	2.57 / **3.94**	2.53 / **3.86**	2.50 / **3.80**	2.47 / **3.74**	2.45 / **3.70**	2.42 / **3.66**	2.41 / **3.62**	2.40 / **3.60**
12	4.75 / **9.33**	3.88 / **6.93**	3.49 / **5.95**	3.26 / **5.41**	3.11 / **5.06**	3.00 / **4.82**	2.92 / **4.65**	2.85 / **4.50**	2.80 / **4.39**	2.76 / **4.30**	2.72 / **4.22**	2.69 / **4.16**	2.64 / **4.05**	2.60 / **3.98**	2.54 / **3.86**	2.50 / **3.78**	2.46 / **3.70**	2.42 / **3.61**	2.40 / **3.56**	2.36 / **3.49**	2.35 / **3.46**	2.32 / **3.41**	2.31 / **3.38**	2.30 / **3.36**
13	4.67 / **9.07**	3.80 / **6.70**	3.41 / **5.74**	3.18 / **5.20**	3.02 / **4.86**	2.92 / **4.62**	2.84 / **4.44**	2.77 / **4.30**	2.72 / **4.19**	2.67 / **4.10**	2.63 / **4.02**	2.60 / **3.96**	2.55 / **3.85**	2.51 / **3.78**	2.46 / **3.67**	2.42 / **3.59**	2.38 / **3.51**	2.34 / **3.42**	2.32 / **3.37**	2.28 / **3.30**	2.26 / **3.27**	2.24 / **3.21**	2.22 / **3.18**	2.21 / **3.16**

Degrees of freedom for the denominator

Source: Reproduced by permission from *Statistical Methods*, 5th edition by George B. Snedecor, copyright 1956 by the Iowa State University Press.

The values in the table are the critical values of F for the degrees of freedom listed over the columns (the degrees of freedom for the numerator of the F ratio) and the degrees of freedom listed for the rows (the degrees of freedom for the denominator of the F ratio). The critical value for the .05 level of significance is presented first (roman type) followed by the critical value at the .01 level (bold face). If the observed value is *greater than or equal to* the tabled value, reject H_0. F values are always positive.

Table E (continued)

Degrees of freedom for the numerator

Degrees of freedom for the denominator	1	2	3	4	5	6	7	8	9	10	11	12	14	16	20	24	30	40	50	75	100	200	500	∞
14	4.60 / 8.86	3.74 / 6.51	3.34 / 5.56	3.11 / 5.03	2.96 / 4.69	2.85 / 4.46	2.77 / 4.28	2.70 / 4.14	2.65 / 4.03	2.60 / 3.94	2.56 / 3.86	2.53 / 3.80	2.48 / 3.70	2.44 / 3.62	2.39 / 3.51	2.35 / 3.43	2.31 / 3.34	2.27 / 3.26	2.24 / 3.21	2.21 / 3.14	2.19 / 3.11	2.16 / 3.06	2.14 / 3.02	2.13 / 3.00
15	4.54 / 8.68	3.68 / 6.36	3.29 / 5.42	3.06 / 4.89	2.90 / 4.56	2.79 / 4.32	2.70 / 4.14	2.64 / 4.00	2.59 / 3.89	2.55 / 3.80	2.51 / 3.73	2.48 / 3.67	2.43 / 3.56	2.39 / 3.48	2.33 / 3.36	2.29 / 3.29	2.25 / 3.20	2.21 / 3.12	2.18 / 3.07	2.15 / 3.00	2.12 / 2.97	2.10 / 2.92	2.08 / 2.89	2.07 / 2.87
16	4.49 / 8.53	3.63 / 6.23	3.24 / 5.29	3.01 / 4.77	2.85 / 4.44	2.74 / 4.20	2.66 / 4.03	2.59 / 3.89	2.54 / 3.78	2.49 / 3.69	2.45 / 3.61	2.42 / 3.55	2.37 / 3.45	2.33 / 3.37	2.28 / 3.25	2.24 / 3.18	2.20 / 3.10	2.16 / 3.01	2.13 / 2.96	2.09 / 2.98	2.07 / 2.86	2.04 / 2.80	2.02 / 2.77	2.01 / 2.75
17	4.45 / 8.40	3.59 / 6.11	3.20 / 5.18	2.96 / 4.67	2.81 / 4.34	2.70 / 4.10	2.62 / 3.93	2.55 / 3.79	2.50 / 3.68	2.45 / 3.59	2.41 / 3.52	2.38 / 3.45	2.33 / 3.35	2.29 / 3.27	2.23 / 3.16	2.19 / 3.08	2.15 / 3.00	2.11 / 2.92	2.08 / 2.86	2.04 / 2.79	2.02 / 2.76	1.99 / 2.70	1.97 / 2.67	1.96 / 2.65
18	4.41 / 8.28	3.55 / 6.01	3.16 / 5.09	2.93 / 4.58	2.77 / 4.25	2.66 / 4.01	2.58 / 3.85	2.51 / 3.71	2.46 / 3.60	2.41 / 3.51	2.37 / 3.44	2.34 / 3.37	2.29 / 3.27	2.25 / 3.19	2.19 / 3.07	2.15 / 3.00	2.11 / 2.91	2.07 / 2.83	2.04 / 2.78	2.00 / 2.71	1.98 / 2.68	1.95 / 2.62	1.93 / 2.59	1.92 / 2.57
19	4.38 / 8.18	3.52 / 5.93	3.13 / 5.01	2.90 / 4.50	2.74 / 4.17	2.63 / 3.94	2.55 / 3.77	2.48 / 3.63	2.43 / 3.52	2.38 / 3.43	2.34 / 3.36	2.31 / 3.30	2.26 / 3.19	2.21 / 3.12	2.15 / 3.00	2.11 / 2.92	2.07 / 2.84	2.02 / 2.76	2.00 / 2.70	1.96 / 2.63	1.94 / 2.60	1.91 / 2.54	1.90 / 2.51	1.88 / 2.49
20	4.35 / 8.10	3.49 / 5.85	3.10 / 4.94	2.87 / 4.43	2.71 / 4.10	2.60 / 3.87	2.52 / 3.71	2.45 / 3.56	2.40 / 3.45	2.35 / 3.37	2.31 / 3.30	2.28 / 3.23	2.23 / 3.13	2.18 / 3.05	2.12 / 2.94	2.08 / 2.86	2.04 / 2.77	1.99 / 2.69	1.96 / 2.63	1.92 / 2.56	1.90 / 2.53	1.87 / 2.47	1.85 / 2.44	1.84 / 2.42
21	4.32 / 8.02	3.47 / 5.78	3.07 / 4.87	2.84 / 4.37	2.68 / 4.04	2.57 / 3.81	2.49 / 3.65	2.42 / 3.51	2.37 / 3.40	2.32 / 3.31	2.28 / 3.24	2.25 / 3.17	2.20 / 3.07	2.15 / 2.99	2.09 / 2.88	2.05 / 2.80	2.00 / 2.72	1.96 / 2.63	1.93 / 2.58	1.89 / 2.51	1.87 / 2.47	1.84 / 2.42	1.82 / 2.38	1.81 / 2.36
22	4.30 / 7.94	3.44 / 5.72	3.05 / 4.82	2.82 / 4.31	2.66 / 3.99	2.55 / 3.76	2.47 / 3.59	2.40 / 3.45	2.35 / 3.35	2.30 / 3.26	2.26 / 3.18	2.23 / 3.12	2.18 / 3.02	2.13 / 2.94	2.07 / 2.83	2.03 / 2.75	1.98 / 2.67	1.93 / 2.58	1.91 / 2.53	1.87 / 2.46	1.84 / 2.42	1.81 / 2.37	1.80 / 2.33	1.78 / 2.31
23	4.28 / 7.88	3.42 / 5.66	3.03 / 4.76	2.80 / 4.26	2.64 / 3.94	2.53 / 3.71	2.45 / 3.54	2.38 / 3.41	2.32 / 3.30	2.28 / 3.21	2.24 / 3.14	2.20 / 3.07	2.14 / 2.97	2.10 / 2.89	2.04 / 2.78	2.00 / 2.70	1.96 / 2.62	1.91 / 2.53	1.88 / 2.48	1.84 / 2.41	1.82 / 2.37	1.79 / 2.32	1.77 / 2.28	1.76 / 2.26
24	4.26 / 7.82	3.40 / 5.61	3.01 / 4.72	2.78 / 4.22	2.62 / 3.90	2.51 / 3.67	2.43 / 3.50	2.36 / 3.36	2.30 / 3.25	2.26 / 3.17	2.22 / 3.09	2.18 / 3.03	2.13 / 2.93	2.09 / 2.85	2.02 / 2.74	1.98 / 2.66	1.94 / 2.58	1.89 / 2.49	1.86 / 2.44	1.82 / 2.36	1.80 / 2.33	1.76 / 2.27	1.74 / 2.23	1.73 / 2.21
25	4.24 / 7.77	3.38 / 5.57	2.99 / 4.68	2.76 / 4.18	2.60 / 3.86	2.49 / 3.63	2.41 / 3.46	2.34 / 3.32	2.28 / 3.21	2.24 / 3.13	2.20 / 3.05	2.16 / 2.99	2.11 / 2.89	2.06 / 2.81	2.00 / 2.70	1.96 / 2.62	1.92 / 2.54	1.87 / 2.45	1.84 / 2.40	1.80 / 2.32	1.77 / 2.29	1.74 / 2.23	1.72 / 2.19	1.71 / 2.17
26	4.22 / 7.72	3.37 / 5.53	2.98 / 4.64	2.74 / 4.14	2.59 / 3.82	2.47 / 3.59	2.39 / 3.42	2.32 / 3.29	2.27 / 3.17	2.22 / 3.09	2.18 / 3.02	2.15 / 2.96	2.10 / 2.86	2.05 / 2.77	1.99 / 2.66	1.95 / 2.58	1.90 / 2.50	1.85 / 2.41	1.82 / 2.36	1.78 / 2.28	1.76 / 2.25	1.72 / 2.19	1.70 / 2.15	1.69 / 2.13

The function, $F = e$ with exponent $2z$, is computed in part from Fisher's table VI (7). Additional entries are by interpolation, mostly graphical.

Table E (continued)

Degrees of freedom for the numerator

Denom.	1	2	3	4	5	6	7	8	9	10	11	12	14	16	20	24	30	40	50	75	100	200	500	∞
27	4.21 / 7.68	3.35 / 5.49	2.96 / 4.60	2.73 / 4.11	2.57 / 3.79	2.46 / 3.56	2.37 / 3.39	2.30 / 3.26	2.25 / 3.14	2.20 / 3.06	2.16 / 2.98	2.13 / 2.93	2.08 / 2.83	2.03 / 2.74	1.97 / 2.63	1.93 / 2.55	1.88 / 2.47	1.84 / 2.38	1.80 / 2.33	1.76 / 2.25	1.74 / 2.21	1.71 / 2.16	1.68 / 2.12	1.67 / 2.10
28	4.20 / 7.64	3.34 / 5.45	2.95 / 4.57	2.71 / 4.07	2.56 / 3.76	2.44 / 3.53	2.36 / 3.36	2.29 / 3.23	2.24 / 3.11	2.19 / 3.03	2.15 / 2.95	2.12 / 2.90	2.06 / 2.80	2.02 / 2.71	1.96 / 2.60	1.91 / 2.52	1.87 / 2.44	1.81 / 2.35	1.78 / 2.30	1.75 / 2.22	1.72 / 2.18	1.69 / 2.13	1.67 / 2.09	1.65 / 2.06
29	4.18 / 7.60	3.33 / 5.42	2.93 / 4.54	2.70 / 4.04	2.54 / 3.73	2.43 / 3.50	2.35 / 3.33	2.28 / 3.20	2.22 / 3.08	2.18 / 3.00	2.14 / 2.92	2.10 / 2.87	2.05 / 2.77	2.00 / 2.68	1.94 / 2.57	1.90 / 2.49	1.85 / 2.41	1.80 / 2.32	1.77 / 2.27	1.73 / 2.19	1.71 / 2.15	1.68 / 2.10	1.65 / 2.06	1.64 / 2.03
30	4.17 / 7.56	3.32 / 5.39	2.92 / 4.51	2.69 / 4.02	2.53 / 3.70	2.42 / 3.47	2.34 / 3.30	2.27 / 3.17	2.21 / 3.06	2.16 / 2.98	2.12 / 2.90	2.09 / 2.84	2.04 / 2.74	1.99 / 2.66	1.93 / 2.55	1.89 / 2.47	1.84 / 2.38	1.79 / 2.29	1.76 / 2.24	1.72 / 2.16	1.69 / 2.13	1.66 / 2.07	1.64 / 2.03	1.62 / 2.01
32	4.15 / 7.50	3.30 / 5.34	2.90 / 4.46	2.67 / 3.97	2.51 / 3.66	2.40 / 3.42	2.32 / 3.25	2.25 / 3.12	2.19 / 3.01	2.14 / 2.94	2.10 / 2.86	2.07 / 2.80	2.02 / 2.70	1.97 / 2.62	1.91 / 2.51	1.86 / 2.42	1.82 / 2.34	1.76 / 2.25	1.74 / 2.20	1.69 / 2.12	1.67 / 2.08	1.64 / 2.02	1.61 / 1.98	1.59 / 1.96
34	4.13 / 7.44	3.28 / 5.29	2.88 / 4.42	2.65 / 3.93	2.49 / 3.61	2.38 / 3.38	2.30 / 3.21	2.23 / 3.08	2.17 / 2.97	2.12 / 2.89	2.08 / 2.82	2.05 / 2.76	2.00 / 2.66	1.95 / 2.58	1.89 / 2.47	1.84 / 2.38	1.80 / 2.30	1.74 / 2.21	1.71 / 2.15	1.67 / 2.08	1.64 / 2.04	1.61 / 1.98	1.59 / 1.94	1.57 / 1.91
36	4.11 / 7.39	3.26 / 5.25	2.86 / 4.38	2.63 / 3.89	2.48 / 3.58	2.36 / 3.35	2.28 / 3.18	2.21 / 3.04	2.15 / 2.94	2.10 / 2.86	2.06 / 2.78	2.03 / 2.72	1.98 / 2.62	1.93 / 2.54	1.87 / 2.43	1.82 / 2.35	1.78 / 2.26	1.72 / 2.17	1.69 / 2.12	1.65 / 2.04	1.62 / 2.00	1.59 / 1.94	1.56 / 1.90	1.55 / 1.87
38	4.10 / 7.35	3.25 / 5.21	2.85 / 4.34	2.62 / 3.86	2.46 / 3.54	2.35 / 3.32	2.26 / 3.15	2.19 / 3.02	2.14 / 2.91	2.09 / 2.82	2.05 / 2.75	2.02 / 2.69	1.96 / 2.59	1.92 / 2.51	1.85 / 2.40	1.80 / 2.32	1.76 / 2.22	1.71 / 2.14	1.67 / 2.08	1.63 / 2.00	1.60 / 1.97	1.57 / 1.90	1.54 / 1.86	1.53 / 1.84
40	4.08 / 7.31	3.23 / 5.18	2.84 / 4.31	2.61 / 3.83	2.45 / 3.51	2.34 / 3.29	2.25 / 3.12	2.18 / 2.99	2.12 / 2.88	2.07 / 2.80	2.04 / 2.73	2.00 / 2.66	1.95 / 2.56	1.90 / 2.49	1.84 / 2.37	1.79 / 2.29	1.74 / 2.20	1.69 / 2.11	1.66 / 2.05	1.61 / 1.97	1.59 / 1.94	1.55 / 1.88	1.53 / 1.84	1.51 / 1.81
42	4.07 / 7.27	3.22 / 5.15	2.83 / 4.29	2.59 / 3.80	2.44 / 3.49	2.32 / 3.26	2.24 / 3.10	2.17 / 2.96	2.11 / 2.86	2.06 / 2.77	2.02 / 2.70	1.99 / 2.64	1.94 / 2.54	1.89 / 2.46	1.82 / 2.35	1.78 / 2.26	1.73 / 2.17	1.68 / 2.08	1.64 / 2.02	1.60 / 1.94	1.57 / 1.91	1.54 / 1.85	1.51 / 1.80	1.49 / 1.78
44	4.06 / 7.24	3.21 / 5.12	2.82 / 4.26	2.58 / 3.78	2.43 / 3.46	2.31 / 3.24	2.23 / 3.07	2.16 / 2.94	2.10 / 2.84	2.05 / 2.75	2.01 / 2.68	1.98 / 2.62	1.92 / 2.52	1.88 / 2.44	1.81 / 2.32	1.76 / 2.24	1.72 / 2.15	1.66 / 2.06	1.63 / 2.00	1.58 / 1.92	1.56 / 1.88	1.52 / 1.82	1.50 / 1.78	1.48 / 1.75
46	4.05 / 7.21	3.20 / 5.10	2.81 / 4.24	2.57 / 3.76	2.42 / 3.44	2.30 / 3.22	2.22 / 3.05	2.14 / 2.92	2.09 / 2.82	2.04 / 2.73	2.00 / 2.66	1.97 / 2.60	1.91 / 2.50	1.87 / 2.42	1.80 / 2.30	1.75 / 2.22	1.71 / 2.13	1.65 / 2.04	1.62 / 1.98	1.57 / 1.90	1.54 / 1.86	1.51 / 1.80	1.48 / 1.76	1.46 / 1.72
48	4.04 / 7.19	3.19 / 5.08	2.80 / 4.22	2.56 / 3.74	2.41 / 3.42	2.30 / 3.20	2.21 / 3.04	2.14 / 2.90	2.08 / 2.80	2.03 / 2.71	1.99 / 2.64	1.96 / 2.58	1.90 / 2.48	1.86 / 2.40	1.79 / 2.28	1.74 / 2.20	1.70 / 2.11	1.64 / 2.02	1.61 / 1.96	1.56 / 1.88	1.53 / 1.84	1.50 / 1.78	1.47 / 1.73	1.45 / 1.70

Degrees of freedom for the denominator

Table E (continued)

Denominator df \\ Numerator df	1	2	3	4	5	6	7	8	9	10	11	12	14	16	20	24	30	40	50	75	100	200	500	∞
50	4.03 / 7.17	3.18 / 5.06	2.79 / 4.20	2.56 / 3.72	2.40 / 3.41	2.29 / 3.18	2.20 / 3.02	2.13 / 2.88	2.07 / 2.78	2.02 / 2.70	1.98 / 2.62	1.95 / 2.56	1.90 / 2.46	1.85 / 2.39	1.78 / 2.26	1.74 / 2.18	1.69 / 2.10	1.63 / 2.00	1.60 / 1.94	1.55 / 1.86	1.52 / 1.82	1.48 / 1.76	1.46 / 1.71	1.44 / 1.68
55	4.02 / 7.12	3.17 / 5.01	2.78 / 4.16	2.54 / 3.68	2.38 / 3.37	2.27 / 3.15	2.18 / 2.98	2.11 / 2.85	2.05 / 2.75	2.00 / 2.66	1.97 / 2.59	1.93 / 2.53	1.88 / 2.43	1.83 / 2.35	1.76 / 2.23	1.72 / 2.15	1.67 / 2.06	1.61 / 1.96	1.58 / 1.90	1.52 / 1.82	1.50 / 1.78	1.46 / 1.71	1.43 / 1.66	1.41 / 1.64
60	4.00 / 7.08	3.15 / 4.98	2.76 / 4.13	2.52 / 3.65	2.37 / 3.34	2.25 / 3.12	2.17 / 2.95	2.10 / 2.82	2.04 / 2.72	1.99 / 2.63	1.95 / 2.56	1.92 / 2.50	1.86 / 2.40	1.81 / 2.32	1.75 / 2.20	1.70 / 2.12	1.65 / 2.03	1.59 / 1.93	1.56 / 1.87	1.50 / 1.79	1.48 / 1.74	1.44 / 1.68	1.41 / 1.63	1.39 / 1.60
65	3.99 / 7.04	3.14 / 4.95	2.75 / 4.10	2.51 / 3.62	2.36 / 3.31	2.24 / 3.09	2.15 / 2.93	2.08 / 2.79	2.02 / 2.70	1.98 / 2.61	1.94 / 2.54	1.90 / 2.47	1.85 / 2.37	1.80 / 2.30	1.73 / 2.18	1.68 / 2.09	1.63 / 2.00	1.57 / 1.90	1.54 / 1.84	1.49 / 1.76	1.46 / 1.71	1.42 / 1.64	1.39 / 1.60	1.37 / 1.56
70	3.98 / 7.01	3.13 / 4.92	2.74 / 4.08	2.50 / 3.60	2.35 / 3.29	2.23 / 3.07	2.14 / 2.91	2.07 / 2.77	2.01 / 2.67	1.97 / 2.59	1.93 / 2.51	1.89 / 2.45	1.84 / 2.35	1.79 / 2.28	1.72 / 2.15	1.67 / 2.07	1.62 / 1.98	1.56 / 1.88	1.53 / 1.82	1.47 / 1.74	1.45 / 1.69	1.40 / 1.62	1.37 / 1.56	1.35 / 1.53
80	3.96 / 6.96	3.11 / 4.88	2.72 / 4.04	2.48 / 3.56	2.33 / 3.25	2.21 / 3.04	2.12 / 2.87	2.05 / 2.74	1.99 / 2.64	1.95 / 2.55	1.91 / 2.48	1.88 / 2.41	1.82 / 2.32	1.77 / 2.24	1.70 / 2.11	1.65 / 2.03	1.60 / 1.94	1.54 / 1.84	1.51 / 1.78	1.45 / 1.70	1.42 / 1.65	1.38 / 1.57	1.35 / 1.52	1.32 / 1.49
100	3.94 / 6.90	3.09 / 4.82	2.70 / 3.98	2.46 / 3.51	2.30 / 3.20	2.19 / 2.99	2.10 / 2.82	2.03 / 2.69	1.97 / 2.59	1.92 / 2.51	1.88 / 2.43	1.85 / 2.36	1.79 / 2.26	1.75 / 2.19	1.68 / 2.06	1.63 / 1.98	1.57 / 1.89	1.51 / 1.79	1.48 / 1.73	1.42 / 1.64	1.39 / 1.59	1.34 / 1.51	1.30 / 1.46	1.28 / 1.43
125	3.92 / 6.84	3.07 / 4.78	2.68 / 3.94	2.44 / 3.47	2.29 / 3.17	2.17 / 2.95	2.08 / 2.79	2.01 / 2.65	1.95 / 2.56	1.90 / 2.47	1.86 / 2.40	1.83 / 2.33	1.77 / 2.23	1.72 / 2.15	1.65 / 2.03	1.60 / 1.94	1.55 / 1.85	1.49 / 1.75	1.45 / 1.68	1.39 / 1.59	1.36 / 1.54	1.31 / 1.46	1.27 / 1.40	1.25 / 1.37
150	3.91 / 6.81	3.06 / 4.75	2.67 / 3.91	2.43 / 3.44	2.27 / 3.14	2.16 / 2.92	2.07 / 2.76	2.00 / 2.62	1.94 / 2.53	1.89 / 2.44	1.85 / 2.37	1.82 / 2.30	1.76 / 2.20	1.71 / 2.12	1.64 / 2.00	1.59 / 1.91	1.54 / 1.83	1.47 / 1.72	1.44 / 1.66	1.37 / 1.56	1.34 / 1.51	1.29 / 1.43	1.25 / 1.37	1.22 / 1.33
200	3.89 / 6.76	3.04 / 4.71	2.65 / 3.88	2.41 / 3.41	2.26 / 3.11	2.14 / 2.90	2.05 / 2.73	1.98 / 2.60	1.92 / 2.50	1.87 / 2.41	1.83 / 2.34	1.80 / 2.28	1.74 / 2.17	1.69 / 2.09	1.62 / 1.97	1.57 / 1.88	1.52 / 1.79	1.45 / 1.69	1.42 / 1.62	1.35 / 1.53	1.32 / 1.48	1.26 / 1.39	1.22 / 1.33	1.19 / 1.28
400	3.86 / 6.70	3.02 / 4.66	2.62 / 3.83	2.39 / 3.36	2.23 / 3.06	2.12 / 2.85	2.03 / 2.69	1.96 / 2.55	1.90 / 2.46	1.85 / 2.37	1.81 / 2.29	1.78 / 2.23	1.72 / 2.12	1.67 / 2.04	1.60 / 1.92	1.54 / 1.84	1.49 / 1.74	1.42 / 1.64	1.38 / 1.57	1.32 / 1.47	1.28 / 1.42	1.22 / 1.32	1.16 / 1.24	1.13 / 1.19
1000	3.85 / 6.66	3.00 / 4.62	2.61 / 3.80	2.38 / 3.34	2.22 / 3.04	2.10 / 2.82	2.02 / 2.66	1.95 / 2.53	1.89 / 2.43	1.84 / 2.34	1.80 / 2.26	1.76 / 2.20	1.70 / 2.09	1.65 / 2.01	1.58 / 1.89	1.53 / 1.81	1.47 / 1.71	1.41 / 1.51	1.36 / 1.54	1.30 / 1.44	1.26 / 1.38	1.19 / 1.28	1.13 / 1.19	1.08 / 1.11
∞	3.84 / 6.64	2.99 / 4.60	2.60 / 3.78	2.37 / 3.32	2.21 / 3.02	2.09 / 2.80	2.01 / 2.64	1.94 / 2.51	1.88 / 2.41	1.83 / 2.32	1.79 / 2.24	1.75 / 2.18	1.69 / 2.07	1.64 / 1.99	1.57 / 1.87	1.52 / 1.79	1.46 / 1.69	1.40 / 1.59	1.35 / 1.52	1.28 / 1.41	1.24 / 1.36	1.17 / 1.25	1.11 / 1.15	1.00 / 1.00

Degrees of freedom for the numerator

Degrees of freedom for the denominator

Table **F.** Critical Values of Chi Square

	Level of significance for a directional test					
	.10	.05	.025	.01	.005	.0005
	Level of significance for a non-directional test					
df	.20	.10	.05	.02	.01	.001
1	1.64	2.71	3.84	5.41	6.64	10.83
2	3.22	4.60	5.99	7.82	9.21	13.82
3	4.64	6.25	7.82	9.84	11.34	16.27
4	5.99	7.78	9.49	11.67	13.28	18.46
5	7.29	9.24	11.07	13.39	15.09	20.52
6	8.56	10.64	12.59	15.03	16.81	22.46
7	9.80	12.02	14.07	16.62	18.48	24.32
8	11.03	13.36	15.51	18.17	20.09	26.12
9	12.24	14.68	16.92	19.68	21.67	27.88
10	13.44	15.99	18.31	21.16	23.21	29.59
11	14.63	17.28	19.68	22.62	24.72	31.26
12	15.81	18.55	21.03	24.05	26.22	32.91
13	16.98	19.81	22.36	25.47	27.69	34.53
14	18.15	21.06	23.68	26.87	29.14	36.12
15	19.31	22.31	25.00	28.26	30.58	37.70
16	20.46	23.54	26.30	29.63	32.00	39.29
17	21.62	24.77	27.59	31.00	33.41	40.75
18	22.76	25.99	28.87	32.35	34.80	42.31
19	23.90	27.20	30.14	33.69	36.19	43.82
20	25.04	28.41	31.41	35.02	37.57	45.32
21	26.17	29.62	32.67	36.34	38.93	46.80
22	27.30	30.81	33.92	37.66	40.29	48.27
23	28.43	32.01	35.17	38.97	41.64	49.73
24	29.55	33.20	36.42	40.27	42.98	51.18
25	30.68	34.38	37.65	41.57	44.31	52.62
26	31.80	35.56	38.88	42.86	45.64	54.05
27	32.91	36.74	40.11	44.14	46.96	55.48
28	34.03	37.92	41.34	45.42	48.28	56.89
29	35.14	39.09	42.69	46.69	49.59	58.30
30	36.25	40.26	43.77	47.96	50.89	59.70
32	38.47	42.59	46.19	50.49	53.49	62.49
34	40.68	44.90	48.60	53.00	56.06	65.25
36	42.88	47.21	51.00	55.49	58.62	67.99
38	45.08	49.51	53.38	57.97	61.16	70.70
40	47.27	51.81	55.76	60.44	63.69	73.40
44	51.64	56.37	60.48	65.34	68.71	78.75
48	55.99	60.91	65.17	70.20	73.68	84.04
52	60.33	65.42	69.83	75.02	78.62	89.27
56	64.66	69.92	74.47	79.82	83.51	94.46
60	68.97	74.40	79.08	84.58	88.38	99.61

Source: Table F is taken from Table IV of Fisher and Yates, *Statistical Tables for Biological, Agricultural and Medical Research*, published by Longman Group Ltd., London (previously published by Oliver and Boyd, Ltd., Edinburgh), and by permission of the authors and publishers.

The table lists the critical values of chi square for the degrees of freedom shown at the left for tests corresponding to those significance levels which head each column. If the observed value of χ_{obs}^2 is *greater than or equal to* the tabled value, reject H_0. All chi squares are positive.

Table G. Critical Values of the Mann-Whitney U for a Directional Test at .005 or a Non-directional Test at .01

n_B \ n_A	1	2	3	4	5	6	7	8	9	10	11	12	13	14	15	16	17	18	19	20
1	--	--	--	--	--	--	--	--	--	--	--	--	--	--	--	--	--	--	--	--
2	--	--	--	--	--	--	--	--	--	--	--	--	--	--	--	--	--	--	0/38	0/40
3	--	--	--	--	--	--	--	--	0/27	0/30	0/33	1/35	1/38	1/41	2/43	2/46	2/49	2/52	3/54	3/57
4	--	--	--	--	--	0/24	0/28	1/31	1/35	2/38	2/42	3/45	3/49	4/52	5/55	5/59	6/62	6/66	7/69	8/72
5	--	--	--	--	0/25	1/29	1/34	2/38	3/42	4/46	5/50	6/54	7/58	7/63	8/67	9/71	10/75	11/79	12/83	13/87
6	--	--	--	0/24	1/29	2/34	3/39	4/44	5/49	6/54	7/59	9/63	10/68	11/73	12/78	13/83	15/87	16/92	17/97	18/102
7	--	--	--	0/28	1/34	3/39	4/45	6/50	7/56	9/61	10/67	12/72	13/78	15/83	16/89	18/94	19/100	21/105	22/111	24/116
8	--	--	--	1/31	2/38	4/44	6/50	7/57	9/63	11/69	13/75	15/81	17/87	18/94	20/100	22/106	24/112	26/118	28/124	30/130
9	--	--	0/27	1/35	3/42	5/49	7/56	9/63	11/70	13/77	16/83	18/90	20/97	22/104	24/111	27/117	29/124	31/131	33/138	36/144
10	--	--	0/30	2/38	4/46	6/54	9/61	11/69	13/77	16/84	18/92	21/99	24/106	26/114	29/121	31/129	34/136	37/143	39/151	42/158
11	--	--	0/33	2/42	5/50	7/59	10/67	13/75	16/83	18/92	21/100	24/108	27/116	30/124	33/132	36/140	39/148	42/156	45/164	48/172
12	--	--	1/35	3/45	6/54	9/63	12/72	15/81	18/90	21/99	24/108	27/117	31/125	34/134	37/143	41/151	44/160	47/169	51/177	54/186
13	--	--	1/38	3/49	7/58	10/68	13/78	17/87	20/97	24/106	27/116	31/125	34/125	38/144	42/153	45/163	49/172	53/181	56/191	60/200
14	--	--	1/41	4/52	7/63	11/73	15/83	18/94	22/104	26/114	30/124	34/134	38/144	42/154	46/164	50/174	54/184	58/194	63/203	67/213
15	--	--	2/43	5/55	8/67	12/78	16/89	20/100	24/111	29/121	33/132	37/143	42/153	46/164	51/174	55/185	60/195	64/206	69/216	73/227
16	--	--	2/46	5/59	9/71	13/83	18/94	22/106	27/117	31/129	36/140	41/151	45/163	50/174	55/185	60/196	65/207	70/218	74/230	79/241
17	--	--	2/49	6/62	10/75	15/87	19/100	24/112	29/124	34/148	39/148	44/160	49/172	54/184	60/195	65/207	70/219	75/231	81/242	86/254
18	--	--	2/52	6/66	11/79	16/92	21/105	26/118	31/131	37/143	42/156	47/169	53/181	58/194	64/206	70/218	75/231	81/243	87/255	92/268
19	--	0/38	3/54	7/69	12/83	17/97	22/111	28/124	33/138	39/151	45/164	51/177	56/191	63/203	69/216	74/230	81/242	87/255	93/268	99/281
20	--	0/40	3/57	8/72	13/87	18/102	24/116	30/130	36/144	42/158	48/172	54/186	60/200	67/213	73/227	79/241	86/254	92/268	99/281	105/295

(Dashes in the body of the table indicate that no decision is possible at the stated level of significance.)

Source: From Mann, H. B., and Whitney, D. R., "On a test of whether one of two random variables is a stochastically larger than the other," *Annals of Mathematical Statistics,* 1947, **18,** 50-60, and Auble, D., "Extended tables for the Mann-Whitney statistic," *Bulletin of the*

Table **G.** Critical Values of the Mann-Whitney U for a Directional Test at .01 or a Non-directional Test at .02

n_B \ n_A	1	2	3	4	5	6	7	8	9	10	11	12	13	14	15	16	17	18	19	20
1	--	--	--	--	--	--	--	--	--	--	--	--	--	--	--	--	--	--	--	--
2	--	--	--	--	--	--	--	--	--	--	--	--	0 / 26	0 / 28	0 / 30	0 / 32	0 / 34	0 / 36	1 / 37	1 / 39
3	--	--	--	--	--	--	0 / 21	0 / 24	1 / 26	1 / 29	1 / 32	2 / 34	2 / 37	2 / 40	3 / 42	3 / 45	4 / 47	4 / 50	4 / 52	5 / 55
4	--	--	--	--	0 / 20	1 / 23	1 / 27	2 / 30	3 / 33	3 / 37	4 / 40	5 / 43	5 / 47	6 / 50	7 / 53	7 / 57	8 / 60	9 / 63	9 / 67	10 / 70
5	--	--	--	0 / 20	1 / 24	2 / 28	3 / 32	4 / 36	5 / 40	6 / 44	7 / 48	8 / 52	9 / 56	10 / 60	11 / 64	12 / 68	13 / 72	14 / 76	15 / 80	16 / 84
6	--	--	--	1 / 23	2 / 28	3 / 33	4 / 38	6 / 42	7 / 47	8 / 52	9 / 57	11 / 61	12 / 66	13 / 71	15 / 75	16 / 80	18 / 84	19 / 89	20 / 94	22 / 99
7	--	--	0 / 21	1 / 27	3 / 32	4 / 38	6 / 43	7 / 49	9 / 54	11 / 59	12 / 65	14 / 70	16 / 75	17 / 81	19 / 86	21 / 91	23 / 96	24 / 102	26 / 107	28 / 112
8	--	--	0 / 24	2 / 30	4 / 36	6 / 42	7 / 49	9 / 55	11 / 61	13 / 67	15 / 73	17 / 79	20 / 84	22 / 90	24 / 96	26 / 102	28 / 108	30 / 114	32 / 120	34 / 126
9	--	--	1 / 26	3 / 33	5 / 40	7 / 47	9 / 54	11 / 61	14 / 67	16 / 74	18 / 81	21 / 87	23 / 94	26 / 100	28 / 107	31 / 113	33 / 120	36 / 126	38 / 133	40 / 140
10	--	--	1 / 29	3 / 37	6 / 44	8 / 52	11 / 59	13 / 67	16 / 74	19 / 81	22 / 88	24 / 96	27 / 103	30 / 110	33 / 117	36 / 124	38 / 132	41 / 139	44 / 146	47 / 153
11	--	--	1 / 32	4 / 40	7 / 48	9 / 57	12 / 65	15 / 73	18 / 81	22 / 88	25 / 96	28 / 104	31 / 112	34 / 120	37 / 128	41 / 135	44 / 143	47 / 151	50 / 159	53 / 167
12	--	--	2 / 34	5 / 43	8 / 52	11 / 61	14 / 70	17 / 79	21 / 87	24 / 96	28 / 104	31 / 113	35 / 121	38 / 130	42 / 138	46 / 146	49 / 155	53 / 163	56 / 172	60 / 180
13	--	0 / 26	2 / 37	5 / 47	9 / 56	12 / 66	16 / 75	20 / 84	23 / 94	27 / 103	31 / 112	35 / 121	39 / 130	43 / 139	47 / 148	51 / 157	55 / 166	59 / 175	63 / 184	67 / 193
14	--	0 / 28	2 / 40	6 / 50	10 / 60	13 / 71	17 / 81	22 / 90	26 / 100	30 / 110	34 / 120	38 / 130	43 / 139	47 / 149	51 / 159	56 / 168	60 / 178	65 / 187	69 / 197	73 / 207
15	--	0 / 30	3 / 42	7 / 53	11 / 64	15 / 75	19 / 86	24 / 96	28 / 107	33 / 117	37 / 128	42 / 138	47 / 148	51 / 159	56 / 169	61 / 179	66 / 189	70 / 200	75 / 210	80 / 220
16	--	0 / 32	3 / 45	7 / 57	12 / 68	16 / 80	21 / 91	26 / 102	31 / 113	36 / 124	41 / 135	46 / 146	51 / 157	56 / 168	61 / 179	66 / 190	71 / 201	76 / 212	82 / 222	87 / 233
17	--	0 / 34	4 / 47	8 / 60	13 / 72	18 / 84	23 / 96	28 / 108	33 / 120	38 / 132	44 / 143	49 / 155	55 / 166	60 / 178	66 / 189	71 / 201	77 / 212	82 / 224	88 / 234	93 / 247
18	--	0 / 36	4 / 50	9 / 63	14 / 76	19 / 89	24 / 102	30 / 114	36 / 126	41 / 139	47 / 151	53 / 163	59 / 175	65 / 187	70 / 200	76 / 212	82 / 224	88 / 236	94 / 248	100 / 260
19	--	1 / 37	4 / 53	9 / 67	15 / 80	20 / 94	26 / 107	32 / 120	38 / 133	44 / 146	50 / 159	56 / 172	63 / 184	69 / 197	75 / 210	82 / 222	88 / 235	94 / 248	101 / 260	107 / 273
20	--	1 / 39	5 / 55	10 / 70	16 / 84	22 / 98	28 / 112	34 / 126	40 / 140	47 / 153	53 / 167	60 / 180	67 / 193	73 / 207	80 / 220	87 / 233	93 / 247	100 / 260	107 / 273	114 / 286

(Dashes in the body of the table indicate that no decision is possible at the stated level of significance.)

Institute of Educational Research at Indiana University, 1953, **1**, No. 2, as used in Runyon and Haber, *Fundamentals of Behavorial Statistics,* 1967, Addison-Wesley, Reading, Mass.

If the observed value of U falls between the two values presented in the table for n_A and n_B, do not reject H_0. Otherwise, reject H_0.

Table G. Critical Values of the Mann-Whitney U for a Directional Test at .025 or a Non-directional Test at .05

Each cell shows the upper value over the underlined lower value, written here as upper/lower.

$n_B \backslash n_A$	1	2	3	4	5	6	7	8	9	10	11	12	13	14	15	16	17	18	19	20
1	--	--	--	--	--	--	--	--	--	--	--	--	--	--	--	--	--	--	--	
2	--	--	--	--	--	--	--	0/16	0/18	0/20	0/22	1/23	1/25	1/27	1/29	1/31	2/32	2/34	2/36	
3	--	--	--	--	0/15	1/17	1/20	2/22	2/25	3/27	3/30	4/32	4/35	5/37	5/40	6/42	6/45	7/47	7/50	
4	--	--	--	0/16	1/19	2/22	3/25	4/28	4/32	5/35	6/38	7/41	8/44	9/47	10/50	11/53	11/57	12/60	13/63	
5	--	--	0/15	1/19	2/23	3/27	5/30	6/34	7/38	8/42	9/46	11/49	12/53	13/57	14/61	15/65	17/68	18/72	19/76	
6	--	--	1/17	2/22	3/27	5/31	6/36	8/40	10/44	11/49	13/53	14/58	16/62	17/67	19/71	21/75	22/80	24/84	25/89	
7	--	--	1/20	3/25	5/30	6/36	8/41	10/46	12/51	14/56	16/61	18/66	20/71	22/76	24/81	26/86	28/91	30/96	32/101	
8	--	0/16	2/22	4/28	6/34	8/40	10/46	13/51	15/57	17/63	19/69	22/74	24/80	26/86	29/91	31/97	34/102	36/108	38/114	
9	--	0/18	2/25	4/32	7/38	10/44	12/51	15/57	17/64	20/70	23/76	26/82	28/89	31/95	34/101	37/107	39/114	42/120	45/126	
10	--	0/20	3/27	5/35	8/42	11/49	14/56	17/63	20/70	23/77	26/84	29/91	33/97	36/104	39/111	42/118	45/125	48/132	52/138	55/145
11	--	0/22	3/30	6/38	9/46	13/53	16/61	19/69	23/76	26/84	30/91	33/99	37/106	40/114	44/121	47/129	51/136	55/143	58/151	62/158
12	--	1/23	4/32	7/41	11/49	14/58	18/66	22/74	26/82	29/91	33/99	37/107	41/115	45/123	49/131	53/139	57/147	61/155	65/163	69/171
13	--	1/25	4/35	8/44	12/53	16/62	20/71	24/80	28/89	33/97	37/106	41/115	45/124	50/132	54/141	59/149	63/158	67/167	72/175	76/184
14	--	1/27	5/37	9/47	13/57	17/67	22/76	26/86	31/95	36/104	40/114	45/123	50/132	55/141	59/151	64/160	67/171	74/178	78/188	83/197
15	--	1/29	5/40	10/50	14/61	19/71	24/81	29/91	34/101	39/111	44/121	49/131	54/141	59/151	64/161	70/170	75/180	80/190	85/200	90/210
16	--	1/31	6/42	11/53	15/65	21/75	26/86	31/97	37/107	42/118	47/129	53/139	59/149	64/160	70/170	75/181	81/191	86/202	92/212	98/222
17	--	2/32	6/45	11/57	17/68	22/80	28/91	34/102	39/114	45/125	51/136	57/147	63/158	67/171	75/180	81/191	87/202	93/213	99/224	105/235
18	--	2/34	7/47	12/60	18/72	24/84	30/96	36/108	42/120	48/132	55/143	61/155	67/167	74/178	80/190	86/202	93/213	99/225	106/236	112/248
19	--	2/36	7/50	13/63	19/76	25/89	32/101	38/114	45/126	52/138	58/151	65/163	72/175	78/188	85/200	92/212	99/224	106/236	113/248	119/261
20	--	2/38	8/52	13/67	20/80	27/93	34/106	41/119	48/132	55/145	62/158	69/171	76/184	83/197	90/210	98/222	105/235	112/248	119/261	127/273

(Dashes in the body of the table indicate that no decision is possible at the stated level of significance.)

Table G. Critical Values of the Mann-Whitney U for a Directional Test at .05 or a Non-directional Test at .10

n_B \ n_A	1	2	3	4	5	6	7	8	9	10	11	12	13	14	15	16	17	18	19	20
1	--	--	--	--	--	--	--	--	--	--	--	--	--	--	--	--	--	--	0/19	0/20
2	--	--	--	--	0/10	0/12	0/14	1/15	1/17	1/19	1/21	2/22	2/24	2/26	3/27	3/29	3/31	4/32	4/34	4/36
3	--	--	0/9	0/12	1/14	2/16	2/19	3/21	3/24	4/26	5/28	5/31	6/33	7/35	7/38	8/40	9/42	9/45	10/47	11/49
4	--	--	0/12	1/15	2/18	3/21	4/24	5/27	6/30	7/33	8/36	9/39	10/42	11/45	12/48	14/50	15/53	16/56	17/59	18/62
5	--	0/10	1/14	2/18	4/21	5/25	6/29	8/32	9/36	11/39	12/43	13/47	15/50	16/54	18/57	19/61	20/65	22/68	23/72	25/75
6	--	0/12	2/16	3/21	5/25	7/29	8/34	10/38	12/42	14/46	16/50	17/55	19/59	21/63	23/67	25/71	26/76	28/80	30/84	32/88
7	--	0/14	2/19	4/24	6/29	8/34	11/38	13/43	15/48	17/53	19/58	21/63	24/67	26/72	28/77	30/82	33/86	35/91	37/96	39/101
8	--	1/15	3/21	5/27	8/32	10/38	13/43	15/49	18/54	20/60	23/65	26/70	28/76	31/81	33/87	36/92	39/97	41/103	44/108	47/113
9	--	1/17	3/24	6/30	9/36	12/42	15/48	18/54	21/60	24/66	27/72	30/78	33/84	36/90	39/96	42/102	45/108	48/114	51/120	54/126
10	--	1/19	4/26	7/33	11/39	14/46	17/53	20/60	24/66	27/73	31/79	34/86	37/93	41/99	44/106	48/112	51/119	55/125	58/132	62/138
11	--	1/21	5/28	8/36	12/43	16/50	19/58	23/65	27/72	31/79	34/87	38/94	42/101	46/108	50/115	54/122	57/130	61/137	65/144	69/151
12	--	2/22	5/31	9/39	13/47	17/55	21/63	26/70	30/78	34/86	38/94	42/102	47/109	51/117	55/125	60/132	64/140	68/148	72/156	77/163
13	--	2/24	6/33	10/42	15/50	19/59	24/67	28/76	33/84	37/93	42/101	47/109	51/118	56/126	61/134	65/143	70/151	75/159	80/167	84/176
14	--	2/26	7/35	11/45	16/54	21/63	26/72	31/81	36/90	41/99	46/108	51/117	56/126	61/135	66/144	71/153	77/161	82/170	87/179	92/188
15	--	3/27	7/38	12/48	18/57	23/67	28/77	33/87	39/96	44/106	50/115	55/125	61/134	66/144	72/153	77/163	83/172	88/182	94/191	100/200
16	--	3/29	8/40	14/50	19/61	25/71	30/82	36/92	42/102	48/112	54/122	60/132	65/143	71/153	77/163	83/173	89/183	95/193	101/203	107/213
17	--	3/31	9/42	15/53	20/65	26/76	33/86	39/97	45/108	51/119	57/130	64/140	70/151	77/161	83/172	89/183	96/193	102/204	109/214	115/225
18	--	4/32	9/45	16/56	22/68	28/80	35/91	41/103	48/114	55/123	61/137	68/148	75/159	82/170	88/182	95/193	102/204	109/215	116/226	123/237
19	0/19	4/34	10/47	17/59	23/72	30/84	37/96	44/108	51/120	58/132	65/144	72/156	80/167	87/179	94/191	101/203	109/214	116/226	123/238	130/250
20	0/20	4/36	11/49	18/62	25/75	32/88	39/101	47/113	54/126	62/138	69/151	77/163	84/176	92/188	100/200	107/213	115/225	123/237	130/250	138/262

(Dashes in the body of the table indicate that no decision is possible at the stated level of significance.)

Table H.   Critical Values of *W* for the Wilcoxon Test

	Level of significance for a directional test					Level of significance for a directional test			
	.05	.025	.01	.005		.05	.025	.01	.005
	Level of significance for a non-directional test					Level of significance for a non-directional test			
N	.10	.05	.02	.01	*N*	.10	.05	.02	.01
5	0	--	--	--	28	130	116	101	91
6	2	0	--	--	29	140	126	110	100
7	3	2	0	--	30	151	137	120	109
8	5	3	1	0	31	163	147	130	118
9	8	5	3	1	32	175	159	140	128
10	10	8	5	3	33	187	170	151	138
11	13	10	7	5	34	200	182	162	148
12	17	13	9	7	35	213	195	173	159
13	21	17	12	9	36	227	208	185	171
14	25	21	15	12	37	241	221	198	182
15	30	25	19	15	38	256	235	211	194
16	35	29	23	19	39	271	249	224	207
17	41	34	27	23	40	286	264	238	220
18	47	40	32	27	41	302	279	252	233
19	53	46	37	32	42	319	294	266	247
20	60	52	43	37	43	336	310	281	261
21	67	58	49	42	44	353	327	296	276
22	75	65	55	48	45	371	343	312	291
23	83	73	62	54	46	389	361	328	307
24	91	81	69	61	47	407	378	345	322
25	100	89	76	68	48	426	396	362	339
26	110	98	84	75	49	446	415	379	355
27	119	107	92	83	50	466	434	397	373

Source: From F. Wilcoxon, S. Katte, and R. A. Wilcox, *Critical Values and Probability Levels for the Wilcoxon Rank Sum Test and the Wilcoxon Signed Rank Test,* New York, American Cyanamid Co., 1963, and F. Wilcoxon and R. A. Wilcox, *Some Rapid Approximate Statistical Procedures,* New York, Lederle Laboratories, 1964 as used in Runyon and Haber, *Fundamentals of Behavioral Statistics,* 1967, Addison-Wesley, Reading, Mass.

For a given *N* (the number of pairs of scores), if the observed value is *less than or equal to* the value in the table for the appropriate level of significance, then reject *H₀*.

Table I. Critical Values for the Spearman Rank-Order Correlation Coefficient

N	Significance level for a directional test at			
	.05	.025	.005	.001
	Significance level for a non-directional test at			
	.10	.05	.01	.002
5	.900	1.000		
6	.829	.886	1.000	
7	.715	.786	.929	1.000
8	.620	.715	.881	.953
9	.600	.700	.834	.917
10	.564	.649	.794	.879
11	.537	.619	.764	.855
12	.504	.588	.735	.826
13	.484	.561	.704	.797
14	.464	.539	.680	.772
15	.447	.522	.658	.750
16	.430	.503	.636	.730
17	.415	.488	.618	.711
18	.402	.474	.600	.693
19	.392	.460	.585	.676
20	.381	.447	.570	.661
21	.371	.437	.556	.647
22	.361	.426	.544	.633
23	.353	.417	.532	.620
24	.345	.407	.521	.608
25	.337	.399	.511	.597
26	.331	.391	.501	.587
27	.325	.383	.493	.577
28	.319	.376	.484	.567
29	.312	.369	.475	.558
30	.307	.363	.467	.549

Source: Glasser, G. J., and R. F. Winter, "Critical Values of the Coefficient of Rank Correlation for Testing the Hypothesis of Independence," *Biometrika,* **48,** 444 (1961).

If the observed value of r_s is *greater than or equal to* the tabled value for the appropriate level of significance, reject H_0. Note that the left-hand column is the number of pairs of scores, not the number of degrees of freedom. The critical values listed are both + and − for non-directional tests.

Table J. Random Numbers

22 17 68 65 84	68 95 23 92 35	87 02 22 57 51	61 09 43 95 06	58 24 82 03 47
19 36 27 59 46	13 79 93 37 55	39 77 32 77 09	85 52 05 30 62	47 83 51 62 74
16 77 23 02 77	09 61 87 25 21	28 06 24 25 93	16 71 13 59 78	23 05 47 47 25
78 43 76 71 61	20 44 90 32 64	97 67 63 99 61	46 38 03 93 22	69 81 21 99 21
03 28 28 26 08	73 37 32 04 05	69 30 16 09 05	88 69 58 28 99	35 07 44 75 47
93 22 53 64 39	07 10 63 76 35	87 03 04 79 88	08 13 13 85 51	55 34 57 72 69
78 76 58 54 74	92 38 70 96 92	52 06 79 79 45	82 63 18 27 44	69 66 92 19 09
23 68 35 26 00	99 53 93 61 28	52 70 05 48 34	56 65 05 61 86	90 92 10 70 80
15 39 25 70 99	93 86 52 77 65	15 33 59 05 28	22 87 26 07 47	86 96 98 29 06
58 71 96 30 24	18 46 23 34 27	85 13 99 24 44	49 18 09 79 49	74 16 32 23 02
57 35 27 33 72	24 53 63 94 09	41 10 76 47 91	44 04 95 49 66	39 60 04 59 81
48 50 86 54 48	22 06 34 72 52	82 21 15 65 20	33 29 94 71 11	15 91 29 12 03
61 96 48 95 03	07 16 39 33 66	98 56 10 56 79	77 21 30 27 12	90 49 22 23 62
36 93 89 41 26	29 70 83 63 51	99 74 20 52 36	87 09 41 15 09	98 60 16 03 03
18 87 00 42 31	57 90 12 02 07	23 47 37 17 31	54 08 01 88 63	39 41 88 92 10
88 56 53 27 59	33 35 72 67 47	77 34 55 45 70	08 18 27 38 90	16 95 86 70 75
09 72 95 84 29	49 41 31 06 70	42 38 06 45 18	64 84 73 31 65	52 53 37 97 15
12 96 88 17 31	65 19 69 02 83	60 75 86 90 68	24 64 19 35 51	56 61 87 39 12
85 94 57 24 16	92 09 84 38 76	22 00 27 69 85	29 81 94 78 70	21 94 47 90 12
38 64 43 59 98	98 77 87 68 07	91 51 67 62 44	40 98 05 93 78	23 32 65 41 18
53 44 09 42 72	00 41 86 79 79	68 47 22 00 20	35 55 31 51 51	00 83 63 22 55
40 76 66 26 84	57 99 99 90 37	36 63 32 08 58	37 40 13 68 97	87 64 81 07 83
02 17 79 18 05	12 59 52 57 02	22 07 90 47 03	28 14 11 30 79	20 69 22 40 98
95 17 82 06 53	31 51 10 96 46	92 06 88 07 77	56 11 50 81 69	40 23 72 51 39
35 76 22 42 92	96 11 83 44 80	34 68 35 48 77	33 42 40 90 60	73 96 53 97 86
26 29 13 56 41	85 47 04 66 08	34 72 57 59 13	82 43 80 46 15	38 26 61 70 04
77 80 20 75 82	72 82 32 99 90	63 95 73 76 63	89 73 44 99 05	48 67 26 43 18
46 40 66 44 52	91 36 74 43 53	30 82 13 54 00	78 45 63 98 35	55 03 36 67 68
37 56 08 18 09	77 53 84 46 47	31 91 18 95 58	24 16 74 11 53	44 10 13 85 57
61 65 61 68 66	37 27 47 39 19	84 83 70 07 48	53 21 40 06 71	95 06 79 88 54
93 43 69 64 07	34 18 04 52 35	56 27 09 24 86	61 85 53 83 45	19 90 70 99 00
21 96 60 12 99	11 20 99 45 18	48 13 93 55 34	18 37 79 49 90	65 97 38 20 46
95 20 47 97 97	27 37 83 28 71	00 06 41 41 74	45 89 09 39 84	51 67 11 52 49
97 86 21 78 73	10 65 81 92 59	58 76 17 14 97	04 76 62 16 17	17 95 70 45 80
69 92 06 34 13	59 71 74 17 32	27 55 10 24 19	23 71 82 13 74	63 52 52 01 41
04 31 17 21 56	33 73 99 19 87	26 72 39 27 67	53 77 57 68 93	60 61 97 22 61
61 06 98 03 91	87 14 77 43 96	43 00 65 98 50	45 60 33 01 07	98 99 46 50 47
85 93 85 86 88	72 87 08 62 40	16 06 10 89 20	23 21 34 74 97	76 38 03 29 63
21 74 32 47 45	73 96 07 94 52	09 65 90 77 47	25 76 16 19 33	53 05 70 53 30
15 69 53 82 80	79 96 23 53 10	65 39 07 16 29	45 33 02 43 70	02 87 40 41 45
02 89 08 04 49	20 21 14 68 86	87 63 93 95 17	11 29 01 95 80	35 14 97 35 33
87 18 15 89 79	85 43 01 72 73	08 61 74 51 69	89 74 39 82 15	94 51 33 41 67
98 83 71 94 22	59 97 50 99 52	08 52 85 08 40	87 80 61 65 31	91 51 80 32 44
10 08 58 21 66	72 68 49 29 31	89 85 84 46 06	59 73 19 85 23	65 09 29 75 63
47 90 56 10 08	88 02 84 27 83	42 29 72 23 19	66 56 45 65 79	20 71 53 20 25
22 85 61 68 90	49 64 92 85 44	16 40 12 89 88	50 14 49 81 06	01 82 77 45 12
67 80 43 79 33	12 83 11 41 16	25 58 19 68 70	77 02 54 00 52	53 43 37 15 26
27 62 50 96 72	79 44 61 40 15	14 53 40 65 39	27 31 58 50 28	11 39 03 34 25
33 78 80 87 15	38 30 06 38 21	14 47 47 07 26	54 96 87 53 32	40 36 40 96 76
13 13 92 66 99	47 24 49 57 74	32 25 43 62 17	10 97 11 69 84	99 63 22 32 98

Source: Table J is taken from Table XXXIII of Fisher and Yates, *Statistical Tables for Biological, Agricultural and Medical Research*, published by Longman Group Ltd., London (previously published by Oliver and Boyd, Ltd., Edinburgh), and by permission of the authors and publishers.

Table J (continued)

```
10 27 53 96 23   71 50 54 36 23   54 31 04 82 98   04 14 12 15 09   26 78 25 47 47
28 41 50 61 88   64 85 27 20 18   83 36 36 05 56   39 71 65 09 62   94 76 62 11 89
34 21 42 57 02   59 19 18 97 48   88 30 03 30 98   05 24 67 70 07   84 97 50 87 46
61 81 77 23 23   82 82 11 54 08   53 28 70 58 96   44 07 39 55 43   42 34 43 39 28
61 15 18 13 54   16 86 20 26 88   90 74 80 55 09   14 53 90 51 17   52 01 63 01 59

91 76 21 64 64   44 91 13 32 97   75 31 62 66 54   84 80 32 75 77   56 08 25 70 29
00 97 79 08 06   37 30 28 59 85   53 56 68 53 40   01 74 39 59 73   30 19 99 85 48
36 46 18 34 94   75 20 80 27 77   78 91 69 16 00   08 43 18 73 68   67 69 61 34 25
88 98 99 60 50   65 95 79 42 94   93 62 40 89 96   43 56 47 71 66   46 76 29 67 02
04 37 59 87 21   05 02 03 24 17   47 97 81 56 51   92 34 86 01 82   55 51 33 12 91

63 62 06 34 41   94 21 78 55 09   72 76 45 16 94   29 95 81 83 83   79 88 01 97 30
78 47 23 53 90   34 41 92 45 71   09 23 70 70 07   12 38 92 79 43   14 85 11 47 23
87 68 62 15 43   53 14 36 59 25   54 47 33 70 15   59 24 48 40 35   50 03 42 99 36
47 60 92 10 77   88 59 53 11 52   66 25 69 07 04   48 68 64 71 06   61 65 70 22 12
56 88 87 59 41   65 28 04 67 53   95 79 88 37 31   50 41 06 94 76   81 83 17 16 33

02 57 45 86 67   73 43 07 34 48   44 26 87 93 29   77 09 61 67 84   06 69 44 77 75
31 54 14 13 17   48 62 11 90 60   68 12 93 64 28   46 24 79 16 76   14 60 25 51 01
28 50 16 43 36   28 97 85 58 99   67 22 52 76 23   24 70 36 54 54   59 28 61 71 96
63 29 62 66 50   02 63 45 52 38   67 63 47 54 75   83 24 78 43 20   92 63 13 47 48
45 65 58 26 51   76 96 59 38 72   86 57 45 71 46   44 67 76 14 55   44 88 01 62 12

39 65 36 63 70   77 45 85 50 51   74 13 39 35 22   30 53 36 02 95   49 34 88 73 61
73 71 98 16 04   29 18 94 51 23   76 51 94 84 86   79 93 96 38 63   08 58 25 58 94
72 20 56 20 11   72 65 71 08 86   79 57 95 13 91   97 48 72 66 48   09 71 17 24 89
75 17 26 99 76   89 37 20 70 01   77 31 61 95 46   26 97 05 73 51   53 33 18 72 87
37 48 60 82 29   81 30 15 39 14   48 38 75 93 29   06 87 37 78 48   45 56 00 84 47

68 08 02 80 72   83 71 46 30 49   89 17 95 88 29   02 39 56 03 46   97 74 06 56 17
14 23 98 61 67   70 52 85 01 50   01 84 02 78 43   10 62 98 19 41   18 83 99 47 99
49 08 96 21 44   25 27 99 41 28   07 41 08 34 66   19 42 74 39 91   41 96 53 78 72
78 37 06 08 43   63 61 62 42 29   39 68 95 10 96   09 24 23 00 62   56 12 80 73 16
37 21 34 17 68   68 96 83 23 56   32 84 60 15 31   44 73 67 34 77   91 15 79 74 58

14 29 09 34 04   87 83 07 55 07   76 58 30 83 64   87 29 25 58 84   86 50 60 00 25
58 43 28 06 36   49 52 83 51 14   47 56 91 29 34   05 87 31 06 95   12 45 57 09 09
10 43 67 29 70   80 62 80 03 42   10 80 21 38 84   90 56 35 03 09   43 12 74 49 14
44 38 88 39 54   86 97 37 44 22   00 95 01 31 76   17 16 29 56 63   38 78 94 49 81
90 69 59 19 51   85 39 52 85 13   07 28 37 07 61   11 16 36 27 03   78 86 72 04 95

41 47 10 25 62   97 05 31 03 61   20 26 36 31 62   68 69 86 95 44   84 95 48 46 45
91 94 14 63 19   75 89 11 47 11   31 56 34 19 09   79 57 92 36 59   14 93 87 81 40
80 06 54 18 66   09 18 94 06 19   98 40 07 17 81   22 45 44 84 11   24 62 20 42 31
67 72 77 63 48   84 08 31 55 58   24 33 45 77 58   80 45 67 93 82   75 70 16 08 24
59 40 24 13 27   79 26 88 86 30   01 31 60 10 39   53 58 47 70 93   85 81 56 39 38

05 90 35 89 95   01 61 16 96 94   50 78 13 69 36   37 68 53 37 31   71 26 35 03 71
44 43 80 69 98   46 68 05 14 82   90 78 50 05 62   77 79 13 57 44   59 60 10 39 66
61 81 31 96 82   00 57 25 60 59   46 72 60 18 77   55 66 12 62 11   08 99 55 64 57
42 88 07 10 05   24 98 65 63 21   47 21 61 88 32   27 80 30 21 60   10 92 35 36 12
77 94 30 05 39   28 10 99 00 27   12 73 73 99 12   49 99 57 94 82   96 88 57 17 91

78 83 19 76 16   94 11 68 84 26   23 54 20 86 85   23 86 66 99 07   36 37 34 92 09
87 76 59 61 81   43 63 64 61 61   65 76 36 95 90   18 48 27 45 68   27 23 65 30 72
91 43 05 96 47   55 78 99 95 24   37 55 85 78 78   01 48 41 19 10   35 19 54 07 73
84 97 77 72 73   09 62 06 65 72   87 12 49 03 60   41 15 20 76 27   50 47 02 29 16
87 41 60 76 83   44 88 96 07 80   83 05 83 38 96   73 70 66 81 90   30 56 10 48 59
```

Table **K**.   Table of Squares and Square Roots

N	N^2	$\sqrt{N}$	N	N^2	$\sqrt{N}$
1	1	1.0000	41	1681	6.4031
2	4	1.4142	42	1764	6.4807
3	9	1.7321	43	1849	6.5574
4	16	2.0000	44	1936	6.6332
5	25	2.2361	45	2025	6.7082
6	36	2.4495	46	2116	6.7823
7	49	2.6458	47	2209	6.8557
8	64	2.8284	48	2304	6.9282
9	81	3.0000	49	2401	7.0000
10	100	3.1623	50	2500	7.0711
11	121	3.3166	51	2601	7.1414
12	144	3.4641	52	2704	7.2111
13	169	3.6056	53	2809	7.2801
14	196	3.7417	54	2916	7.3485
15	225	3.8730	55	3025	7.4162
16	256	4.0000	56	3136	7.4833
17	289	4.1231	57	3249	7.5498
18	324	4.2426	58	3364	7.6158
19	361	4.3589	59	3481	7.6811
20	400	4.4721	60	3600	7.7460
21	441	4.5826	61	3721	7.8102
22	484	4.6904	62	3844	7.8740
23	529	4.7958	63	3969	7.9373
24	576	4.8990	64	4096	8.0000
25	625	5.0000	65	4225	8.0623
26	676	5.0990	66	4356	8.1240
27	729	5.1962	67	4489	8.1854
28	784	5.2915	68	4624	8.2462
29	841	5.3852	69	4761	8.3066
30	900	5.4772	70	4900	8.3666
31	961	5.5678	71	5041	8.4261
32	1024	5.6569	72	5184	8.4853
33	1089	5.7446	73	5329	8.5440
34	1156	5.8310	74	5476	8.6023
35	1225	5.9161	75	5625	8.6603
36	1296	6.0000	76	5776	8.7178
37	1369	6.0828	77	5929	8.7750
38	1444	6.1644	78	6084	8.8318
39	1521	6.2450	79	6241	8.8882
40	1600	6.3246	80	6400	8.9443

Source: J. W. Dunlap and A. K. Kurtz, *Handbook of Statistical Monographs, Tables and Formulas.* New York: World Book Company, 1932, as used in A. L. Edwards, *Statistical Methods for the Behavioral Sciences*, 1954, Holt, Rinehart and Winston, New York.

Table **K** (continued)

N	N^2	$\sqrt{N}$	N	N^2	$\sqrt{N}$
81	6561	9.0000	121	14641	11.0000
82	6724	9.0554	122	14884	11.0454
83	6889	9.1104	123	15129	11.0905
84	7056	9.1652	124	15376	11.1355
85	7225	9.2195	125	15625	11.1803
86	7396	9.2736	126	15876	11.2250
87	7569	9.3274	127	16129	11.2694
88	7744	9.3808	128	16384	11.3137
89	7921	9.4340	129	16641	11.3578
90	8100	9.4868	130	16900	11.4018
91	8281	9.5394	131	17161	11.4455
92	8464	9.5917	132	17424	11.4891
93	8649	9.6437	133	17689	11.5326
94	8836	9.6954	134	17956	11.5758
95	9025	9.7468	135	18225	11.6190
96	9216	9.7980	136	18496	11.6619
97	9409	9.8489	137	18769	11.7047
98	9604	9.8995	138	19044	11.7473
99	9801	9.9499	139	19321	11.7898
100	10000	10.0000	140	19600	11.8322
101	10201	10.0499	141	19881	11.8743
102	10404	10.0995	142	20164	11.9164
103	10609	10.1489	143	20449	11.9583
104	10816	10.1980	144	20736	12.0000
105	11025	10.2470	145	21025	12.0416
106	11236	10.2956	146	21316	12.0830
107	11449	10.3441	147	21609	12.1244
108	11664	10.3923	148	21904	12.1655
109	11881	10.4403	149	22201	12.2066
110	12100	10.4881	150	22500	12.2474
111	12321	10.5357	151	22801	12.2882
112	12544	10.5830	152	23104	12.3288
113	12769	10.6301	153	23409	12.3693
114	12996	10.6771	154	23716	12.4097
115	13225	10.7238	155	24025	12.4499
116	13456	10.7703	156	24336	12.4900
117	13689	10.8167	157	24649	12.5300
118	13924	10.8628	158	24964	12.5698
119	14161	10.9087	159	25281	12.6095
120	14400	10.9545	160	25600	12.6491

Table **K** (continued)

N	N^2	$\sqrt{N}$	N	N^2	$\sqrt{N}$
161	25921	12.6886	201	40401	14.1774
162	26244	12.7279	202	40804	14.2127
163	26569	12.7671	203	41209	14.2478
164	26896	12.8062	204	41616	14.2829
165	27225	12.8452	205	42025	14.3178
166	27556	12.8841	206	42436	14.3527
167	27889	12.9228	207	42849	14.3875
168	28224	12.9615	208	43264	14.4222
169	28561	13.0000	209	43681	14.4568
170	28900	13.0384	210	44100	14.4914
171	29241	13.0767	211	44521	14.5258
172	29584	13.1149	212	44944	14.5602
173	29929	13.1529	213	45369	14.5945
174	30276	13.1909	214	45796	14.6287
175	30625	13.2288	215	46225	14.6629
176	30976	13.2665	216	46656	14.6969
177	31329	13.3041	217	47089	14.7309
178	31684	13.3417	218	47524	14.7648
179	32041	13.3791	219	47961	14.7986
180	32400	13.4164	220	48400	14.8324
181	32761	13.4536	221	48841	14.8661
182	33124	13.4907	222	49284	14.8997
183	33489	13.5277	223	49729	14.9332
184	33856	13.5647	224	50176	14.9666
185	34225	13.6015	225	50625	15.0000
186	34596	13.6382	226	51076	15.0333
187	34969	13.6748	227	51529	15.0665
188	35344	13.7113	228	51984	15.0997
189	35721	13.7477	229	52441	15.1327
190	36100	13.7840	230	52900	15.1658
191	36481	13.8203	231	53361	15.1987
192	36864	13.8564	232	53824	15.2315
193	37249	13.8924	233	54289	15.2643
194	37636	13.9284	234	54756	15.2971
195	38025	13.9642	235	55225	15.3297
196	38416	14.0000	236	55696	15.3623
197	38809	14.0357	237	56169	15.3948
198	39204	14.0712	238	56644	15.4272
199	39601	14.1067	239	57121	15.4596
200	40000	14.1421	240	57600	15.4919

Table **K** (continued)

N	N²	√N		N	N²	√N
241	58081	15.5242		281	78961	16.7631
242	58564	15.5563		282	79524	16.7929
243	59049	15.5885		283	80089	16.8226
244	59536	15.6205		284	80656	16.8523
245	60025	15.6525		285	81225	16.8819
246	60516	15.6844		286	81796	16.9115
247	61009	15.7162		287	82369	16.9411
248	61504	15.7480		288	82944	16.9706
249	62001	15.7797		289	83521	17.0000
250	62500	15.8114		290	84100	17 0294
251	63001	15.8430		291	84681	17.0587
252	63504	15.8745		292	85264	17.0880
253	64009	15.9060		293	85849	17.1172
254	64516	15.9374		294	86436	17.1464
255	65025	15.9687		295	87025	17.1756
256	65536	16.0000		296	87616	17.2047
257	66049	16.0312		297	88209	17.2337
258	66564	16.0624		298	88804	17.2627
259	67081	16.0935		299	89401	17.2916
260	67600	16.1245		300	90000	17.3205
261	68121	16.1555		301	90601	17.3494
262	68644	16.1864		302	91204	17.3781
263	69169	16.2173		303	91809	17.4069
264	69696	16.2481		304	92416	17.4356
265	70225	16.2788		305	93025	17.4642
266	70756	16.3095		306	93636	17.4929
267	71289	16.3401		307	94249	17.5214
268	71824	16.3707		308	94864	17.5499
269	72361	16.4012		309	95481	17.5784
270	72900	16.4317		310	96100	17.6068
271	73441	16.4621		311	96721	17.6352
272	73984	16.4924		312	97344	17.6635
273	74529	16.5227		313	97969	17.6918
274	75076	16.5529		314	98596	17.7200
275	75625	16.5831		315	99225	17.7482
276	76176	16.6132		316	99856	17.7764
277	76729	16.6433		317	100489	17.8045
278	77284	16.6733		318	101124	17.8326
279	77841	16.7033		319	101761	17.8606
280	78400	16.7332		320	102400	17.8885

Table **K** (continued)

N	N^2	$\sqrt{N}$	N	N^2	$\sqrt{N}$
321	103041	17.9165	361	130321	19.0000
322	103684	17.9444	362	131044	19.0263
323	104329	17.9722	363	131769	19.0526
324	104976	18.0000	364	132496	19.0788
325	105625	18.0278	365	133225	19.1050
326	106276	18.0555	366	133956	19.1311
327	106929	18.0831	367	134689	19.1572
328	107584	18.1108	368	135424	19.1833
329	108241	18.1384	369	136161	19.2094
330	108900	18.1659	370	136900	19.2354
331	109561	18.1934	371	137641	19.2614
332	110224	18.2209	372	138384	19.2873
333	110889	18.2483	373	139129	19.3132
334	111556	18.2757	374	139876	19.3391
335	112225	18.3030	375	140625	19.3649
336	112896	18.3303	376	141376	19.3907
337	113569	18.3576	377	142129	19.4165
338	114244	18.3848	378	142884	19.4422
339	114921	18.4120	379	143641	19.4679
340	115600	18.4391	380	144400	19.4936
341	116281	18.4662	381	145161	19.5192
342	116964	18.4932	382	145924	19.5448
343	117649	18.5203	383	146689	19.5704
344	118336	18.5472	384	147456	19.5959
345	119025	18.5742	385	148225	19.6214
346	119716	18.6011	386	148996	19.6469
347	120409	18.6279	387	149769	19.6723
348	121104	18.6548	388	150544	19.6977
349	121801	18.6815	389	151321	19.7231
350	122500	18.7083	390	152100	19.7484
351	123201	18.7350	391	152881	19.7737
352	123904	18.7617	392	153664	19.7990
353	124609	18.7883	393	154449	19.8242
354	125516	18.8149	394	155236	19.8494
355	126025	18.8414	395	156025	19.8746
356	126736	18.8680	396	156816	19.8997
357	127449	18.8944	397	157609	19.9249
358	128164	18.9209	398	158404	19.9499
359	128881	18.9473	399	159201	19.9750
360	129000	18.9737	400	160000	20.0000

Table **K** (continued)

N	N^2	$\sqrt{N}$	N	N^2	$\sqrt{N}$
401	160801	20.0250	441	194481	21.0000
402	161604	20.0499	442	195364	21.0238
403	162409	20.0749	443	196249	21.0476
404	163216	20.0998	444	197136	21.0713
405	164025	20.1246	445	198025	21.0950
406	164836	20.1494	446	198916	21.1187
407	165649	20.1742	447	199809	21.1424
408	166464	20.1990	448	200704	21.1660
409	167281	20.2237	449	201601	21.1896
410	168100	20.2485	450	202500	21.2132
411	168921	20.2731	451	203401	21.2368
412	169744	20.2978	452	204304	21.2603
413	170569	20.3224	453	205209	21.2838
414	171396	20.3470	454	206116	21.3073
415	172225	20.3715	455	207025	21.3307
416	173056	20.3961	456	207936	21.3542
417	173889	20.4206	457	208849	21.3776
418	174724	20.4450	458	209764	21.4009
419	175561	20.4695	459	210681	21.4243
420	176400	20.4939	460	211600	21.4476
421	177241	20.5183	461	212521	21.4709
422	178084	20.5426	462	213444	21.4942
423	178929	20.5670	463	214369	21.5174
424	179776	20.5913	464	215296	21.5407
425	180625	20.6155	465	216225	21.5639
426	181476	20.6398	466	217156	21.5870
427	182329	20.6640	467	218089	21.6102
428	183184	20.6882	468	219024	21.6333
429	184041	20.7123	469	219961	21.6564
430	184900	20.7364	470	220900	21.6795
431	185761	20.7605	471	221841	21.7025
432	186624	20.7846	472	222784	21.7256
433	187489	20.8087	473	223729	21.7486
434	188356	20.8327	474	224676	21.7715
435	189225	20.8567	475	225625	21.7945
436	190096	20.8806	476	226576	21.8174
437	190969	20.9045	477	227529	21.8403
438	191844	20.9284	478	228484	21.8632
439	192721	20.9523	479	229441	21.8861
440	193600	20.9762	480	230400	21.9089

Table **K** (continued)

N	N²	√N	N	N²	√N
481	231361	21.9317	521	271441	22.8254
482	232324	21.9545	522	272484	22.8473
483	233289	21.9773	523	273529	22.8692
484	234256	22.0000	524	274576	22.8910
485	235225	22.0227	525	275625	22.9129
486	236196	22.0454	526	276676	22.9347
487	237169	22.0681	527	277729	22.9565
488	238144	22.0907	528	278784	22.9783
489	239121	22.1133	529	279841	23.0000
490	240100	22.1359	530	280900	23.0217
491	241081	22.1585	531	281961	23.0434
492	242064	22.1811	532	283024	23.0651
493	243049	22.2036	533	284089	23.0868
494	244036	22.2261	534	285156	23.1084
495	245025	22.2486	535	286225	23.1301
496	246016	22.2711	536	287296	23.1517
497	247009	22.2935	537	288369	23.1733
498	248004	22.3159	538	289444	23.1948
499	249001	22.3383	539	290521	23.2164
500	250000	22.3607	540	291600	23.2379
501	251001	22.3830	541	292681	23.2594
502	252004	22.4054	542	293764	23.2809
503	253009	22.4277	543	294849	23.3024
504	254016	22.4499	544	295936	23.3238
505	255025	22.4722	545	297025	23.3452
506	256036	22.4944	546	298116	23.3666
507	257049	22.5167	547	299209	23.3880
508	258064	22.5389	548	300304	23.4094
509	259081	22.5610	549	301401	23.4307
510	260100	22.5832	550	302500	23.4521
511	261121	22.6053	551	303601	23.4734
512	262144	22.6274	552	304704	23.4947
513	263169	22.6495	553	305809	23.5160
514	264196	22.6716	554	306916	23.5372
515	265225	22.6936	555	308025	23.5584
516	266256	22.7156	556	309136	23.5797
517	267289	22.7376	557	310249	23.6008
518	268324	22.7596	558	311364	23.6220
519	269361	22.7816	559	312481	23.6432
520	270400	22.8035	560	313600	23.6643

Table **K** (continued)

N	N^2	$\sqrt{N}$	N	N^2	$\sqrt{N}$
561	314721	23.6854	601	361201	24.5153
562	315844	23.7065	602	362404	24.5357
563	316969	23.7276	603	363609	24.5561
564	318096	23.7487	604	364816	24.5764
565	319225	23.7697	605	366025	24.5967
566	320356	23.7908	606	367236	24.6171
567	321489	23.8118	607	368449	24.6374
568	322624	23.8328	608	369664	24.6577
569	323761	23.8537	609	370881	24.6779
570	324900	23.8747	610	372100	24.6982
571	326041	23.8956	611	373321	24.7184
572	327184	23.9165	612	374544	24.7386
573	328329	23.9374	613	375769	24.7588
574	329476	23.9583	614	376996	24.7790
575	330625	23.9792	615	378225	24.7992
576	331776	24.0000	616	379456	24.8193
577	332929	24.0208	617	380689	24.8395
578	334084	24.0416	618	381924	24.8596
579	335241	24.0624	619	383161	24.8797
580	336400	24.0832	620	384400	24.8998
581	337561	24.1039	621	385641	24.9199
582	338724	24.1247	622	386884	24.9399
583	339889	24.1454	623	388129	24.9600
584	341056	24.1661	624	389376	24.9800
585	342225	24.1868	625	390625	25.0000
586	343396	24.2074	626	391876	25.0200
587	344569	24.2281	627	393129	25.0400
588	345744	24.2487	628	394384	25.0599
589	346921	24.2693	629	395641	25.0799
590	348100	24.2899	630	396900	25.0998
591	349281	24.3105	631	398161	25.1197
592	350464	24.3311	632	399424	25.1396
593	351649	24.3516	633	400689	25.1595
594	352836	24.3721	634	401956	25.1794
595	354025	24.3926	635	403225	25.1992
596	355216	24.4131	636	404496	25.2190
597	356409	24.4336	637	405769	25.2389
598	357604	24.4540	638	407044	25.2587
599	358801	24.4745	639	408321	25.2784
600	360000	24.4949	640	409600	25.2982

Table **K** (continued)

N	N²	√N		N	N²	√N
641	410881	25.3180		681	463761	26.0960
642	412164	25.3377		682	465124	26.1151
643	413449	25.3574		683	466489	26.1343
644	414736	25.3772		684	467856	26.1534
645	416025	25.3969		685	469225	26.1725
646	417316	25.4165		686	470596	26.1916
647	418609	25.4362		687	471969	26.2107
648	419904	25.4558		688	473344	26.2298
649	421201	25.4755		689	474721	26.2488
650	422500	25.4951		690	476100	26.2679
651	423801	25.5147		691	477481	26.2869
652	425104	25.5343		692	478864	26.3059
653	426409	25.5539		693	480249	26.3249
654	427716	25.5734		694	481636	26.3439
655	429025	25.5930		695	483025	26.3629
656	430336	25.6125		696	484416	26.3818
657	431649	25.6320		697	485809	26.4008
658	432964	25.6515		698	487204	26.4197
659	434281	25.6710		699	488601	26.4386
660	435600	25.6905		700	490000	26.4575
661	436921	25.7099		701	491401	26.4764
662	438244	25.7294		702	492804	26.4953
663	439569	25.7488		703	494209	26.5141
664	440896	25.7682		704	495616	26.5330
665	442225	25.7876		705	497025	26.5518
666	443556	25.8070		706	498436	26.5707
667	444889	25.8263		707	499849	26.5895
668	446224	25.8457		708	501264	26.6083
669	447561	25.8650		709	502681	26.6271
670	448900	25.8844		710	504100	26.6458
671	450241	25.9037		711	505521	26.6646
672	451584	25.9230		712	506944	26.6833
673	452929	25.9422		713	508369	26.7021
674	454276	25.9615		714	509796	26.7208
675	455625	25.9808		715	511225	26.7395
676	456976	26.0000		716	512656	26.7582
677	458329	26.0192		717	514089	26.7769
678	459684	26.0384		718	515524	26.7955
679	461041	26.0576		719	516961	26.8142
680	462400	26.0768		720	518400	26.8328

Table **K** (continued)

N	N²	$\sqrt{N}$	N	N²	$\sqrt{N}$
721	519841	26.8514	761	579121	27.5862
722	521284	26.8701	762	580644	27.6043
723	522729	26.8887	763	582169	27.6225
724	524176	26.9072	764	583696	27.6405
725	525625	26.9258	765	585225	27.6586
726	527076	26.9444	766	586756	27.6767
727	528529	26.9629	767	588289	27.6948
728	529984	26.9815	768	589824	27.7128
729	531441	27.0000	769	591361	27.7308
730	532900	27.0185	770	592900	27.7489
731	534361	27.0370	771	594441	27.7669
732	535824	27.0555	772	595984	27.7849
733	537289	27.0740	773	597529	27.8029
734	538756	27.0924	774	599076	27.8209
735	540225	27.1109	775	600625	27.8388
736	541696	27.1293	776	602176	27.8568
737	543169	27.1477	777	603729	27.8747
738	544644	27.1662	778	605284	27.8927
739	546121	27.1846	779	606841	27.9106
740	547600	27.2029	780	608400	27.9285
741	549081	27.2213	781	609961	27.9464
742	550564	27.2397	782	611524	27.9643
743	552049	27.2580	783	613089	27.9821
744	553536	27.2764	784	614656	28.0000
745	555025	27.2947	785	616225	28.0179
746	556516	27.3130	786	617796	28.0357
747	558009	27.3313	787	619369	28.0535
748	559504	27.3496	788	620944	28.0713
749	561001	27.3679	789	622521	28.0891
750	562500	27.3861	790	624100	28.1069
751	564001	27.4044	791	625681	28.1247
752	565504	27.4226	792	627264	28.1425
753	567009	27.4408	793	628849	28.1603
754	568516	27.4591	794	630436	28.1780
755	570025	27.4773	795	632025	28.1957
756	571536	27.4955	796	633616	28.2135
757	573049	27.5136	797	635209	28.2312
758	574564	27.5318	798	636804	28.2489
759	576081	27.5500	799	638401	28.2666
760	577600	27.5681	800	640000	28.2843

Table **K** (continued)

N	N^2	$\sqrt{N}$		N	N^2	$\sqrt{N}$
801	641601	28.3019		841	707281	29.0000
802	643204	28.3196		842	708964	29.0172
803	644809	28.3373		843	710649	29.0345
804	646416	28.3549		844	712336	29.0517
805	648025	28.3725		845	714025	29.0689
806	649636	28.3901		846	715716	29.0861
807	651249	28.4077		847	717409	29.1033
808	652864	28.4253		848	719104	29.1204
809	654481	28.4429		849	720801	29.1376
810	656100	28.4605		850	722500	29.1548
811	657721	28.4781		851	724201	29.1719
812	659344	28.4956		852	725904	29.1890
813	660969	28.5132		853	727609	29.2062
814	662596	28.5307		854	729316	29.2233
815	664225	28.5482		855	731025	29.2404
816	665856	28.5657		856	732736	29.2575
817	667489	28.5832		857	734449	29.2746
818	669124	28.6007		858	736164	29.2916
819	670761	28.6182		859	737881	29.3087
820	672400	28.6356		860	739600	29.3258
821	674041	28.6531		861	741321	29.3428
822	675684	28.6705		862	743044	29.3598
823	677329	28.6880		863	744769	29.3769
824	678976	28.7054		864	746496	29.3939
825	680625	28.7228		865	748225	29.4109
826	682276	28.7402		866	749956	29.4279
827	683929	28.7576		867	751689	29.4449
828	685584	28.7750		868	753424	29.4618
829	687241	28.7924		869	755161	29.4788
830	688900	28.8097		870	756900	29.4958
831	690561	28.8271		871	758641	29.5127
832	692224	28.8444		872	760384	29.5296
833	693889	28.8617		873	762129	29.5466
834	695556	28.8791		874	763876	29.5635
835	697225	28.8964		875	765625	29.5804
836	698896	28.9137		876	767376	29.5973
837	700569	28.9310		877	769129	29.6142
838	702244	28.9482		878	770884	29.6311
839	703921	28.9655		879	772641	29.6479
840	705600	28.9828		880	774400	29.6648

Table **K** (continued)

N	N^2	$\sqrt{N}$	N	N^2	$\sqrt{N}$
881	776161	29.6816	921	848241	30.3480
882	777924	29.6985	922	850084	30.3645
883	779689	29.7153	923	851929	30.3809
884	781456	29.7321	924	853776	30.3974
885	783225	29.7489	925	855625	30.4138
886	784996	29.7658	926	857476	30.4302
887	786769	29.7825	927	859329	30.4467
888	788544	29.7993	928	861184	30.4631
889	790321	29.8161	929	863041	30.4795
890	792100	29.8329	930	864900	30.4959
891	793881	29.8496	931	866761	30.5123
892	795664	29.8664	932	868624	30.5287
893	797449	29.8831	933	870489	30.5450
894	799236	29.8998	934	872356	30.5614
895	801025	29.9166	935	874225	30.5778
896	802816	29.9333	936	876096	30.5941
897	804609	29.9500	937	877969	30.6105
898	806404	29.9666	938	879844	30.6268
899	808201	29.9833	939	881721	30.6431
900	810000	30.0000	940	883600	30.6594
901	811801	30.0167	941	885481	30.6757
902	813604	30.0333	942	887364	30.6920
903	815409	30.0500	943	889249	30.7083
904	817216	30.0666	944	891136	30.7246
905	819025	30.0832	945	893025	30.7409
906	820836	30.0998	946	894916	30.7571
907	822649	30.1164	947	896809	30.7734
908	824464	30.1330	948	898704	30.7896
909	826281	30.1496	949	900601	30.8058
910	828100	30.1662	950	902500	30.8221
911	829921	30.1828	951	904401	30.8383
912	831744	30.1993	952	906304	30.8545
913	833569	30.2159	953	908209	30.8707
914	835396	30.2324	954	910116	30.8869
915	837225	30.2490	955	912025	30.9031
916	839056	30.2655	956	913936	30.9192
917	840889	30.2820	957	915849	30.9354
918	842724	30.2985	958	917764	30.9516
919	844561	30.3150	959	919681	30.9677
920	846400	30.3315	960	921600	30.9839

Table **K** (continued)

N	N²	$\sqrt{N}$	N	N²	$\sqrt{N}$
961	923521	31.0000	981	962361	31.3209
962	925444	31.0161	982	964324	31.3369
963	927369	31.0322	983	966289	31.3528
964	929296	31.0483	984	968256	31.3688
965	931225	31.0644	985	970225	31.3847
966	933156	31.0805	986	972196	31.4006
967	935089	31.0966	987	974169	31.4166
968	937024	31.1127	988	976144	31.4325
969	938961	31.1288	989	978121	31.4484
970	940900	31.1448	990	980100	31.4643
971	942841	31.1609	991	982081	31.4802
972	944784	31.1769	992	984064	31.4960
973	946729	31.1929	993	986049	31.5119
974	948676	31.2090	994	988036	31.5278
975	950625	31.2250	995	990025	31.5436
976	952576	31.2410	996	992016	31.5595
977	954529	31.2570	997	994009	31.5753
978	956484	31.2730	998	996004	31.5911
979	958441	31.2890	999	998001	31.6070
980	960400	31.3050	1000	1000000	31.6228

ANSWERS
TO THE
EXERCISES

ANSWERS TO THE EXERCISES

chapter 1

pg. 16. **(1a)** ordinal; **(1b)** ratio; **(1c)** nominal; **(1d)** the difference centers on the fact that the centigrade scale is interval while the Kelvin is ratio. **(2)** Student f has a rank of 2 and Student e a rank of 3. Their ranks as well as their scores (24 and 25, respectively) differ by one point. In contrast, Student d also differs from Student e by a rank of one, but has 16 more score points. Thus, when scores are transformed to ranks, the equal interval property of the measurement scale will be lost. **(3a)** continuous; **(3b)** discrete; **(3c)** continuous; **(3d)** discrete. **(4a)** .5–1.5; **(4b)** 17.5–18.5; **(4c)** 76.5–77.5; **(4d)** 1.05–1.15; **(4e)** 24.25–24.35; **(4f)** 1002.35–1002.45; **(4g)** 3.835–3.845; **(4h)** 12.605–12.615; **(4i)** 129.795–129.805. **(5a)** 2.7; **(5b)** 9.5; **(5c)** 4.1; **(5d)** 8.6; **(5e)** 6.0. **(6a)** 21; **(6b)** 14; **(6c)** 16; **(6d)** 20; **(6e)** 41; **(6f)** 78; **(6g)** 111; **(6h)** 441; **(7a)** 105; **(7b)** 390; **(7c)** 205; **(7d)** 25; **(7e)** 26. **(8a)** $k + 1$; **(8b)** 1; **(8c)** $1 + \dfrac{\sum Z}{Nk(\sum Z + 1)}$.

chapter 2

pg. 37. **(1)**

Class Interval	Real Limits	Interval Size	Midpoint	f	Rel. f	Cum. f	Cum. Rel. f
88–95	87.5–95.5	8	91.5	3	.06	50	1.00
80–87	79.5–87.5	8	83.5	3	.06	47	.94
72–79	71.5–79.5	8	75.5	5	.10	44	.88
64–71	63.5–71.5	8	67.5	4	.08	39	.78
56–63	55.5–63.5	8	59.5	6	.12	35	.70
48–55	47.5–55.5	8	51.5	4	.08	29	.58
40–47	39.5–47.5	8	43.5	7	.14	25	.50
32–39	31.5–39.5	8	35.5	4	.08	18	.36
24–31	23.5–31.5	8	27.5	8	.16	14	.28
16–23	15.5–23.5	8	19.5	2	.04	6	.12
8–15	7.5–15.5	8	11.5	4	.08	4	.08
				$N = 50$			

Eleven intervals of size 8 were selected but 9 to 11 intervals might have been picked as long as they covered the range of scores and the lower stated limit of the first interval was evenly divisible by the interval size. See Table 2–7 in text, page 28. **(2)** See examples of graphs in text, paying close attention to the points mentioned in the text.

(3)

Class Interval	Real Limits	Interval Size	Midpoint	f	Rel. f	Cum. f	Cum. Rel. f
50–51	49.5–51.5	2	50.5	1	.02	60	1.00
48–49	47.5–49.5	2	48.5	0	.00	59	.98
46–47	45.5–47.5	2	46.5	2	.03	59	.98
44–45	43.5–45.5	2	44.5	4	.07	57	.95
42–43	41.5–43.5	2	42.5	5	.08	53	.88
40–41	39.5–41.5	2	40.5	8	.13	48	.80
38–39	37.5–39.5	2	38.5	12	.20	40	.67
36–37	35.5–37.5	2	36.5	10	.17	28	.47
34–35	33.5–35.5	2	34.5	9	.15	18	.30
32–33	31.5–33.5	2	32.5	4	.07	9	.15
30–31	29.5–31.5	2	30.5	4	.07	5	.08
28–29	27.5–29.5	2	28.5	1	.02	1	.02
				$N = 60$			

As in Problem 1, fewer or more than 12 intervals might have been used. See text for examples of graphs.

(4)

Class Interval	Real Limits	Interval Size	Midpoint	f	Rel. f	Cum. f	Cum. Rel. f
2.8–3.1	2.75–3.15	.4	2.95	2	.07	28	1.00
2.4–2.7	2.35–2.75	.4	2.55	3	.11	26	.93
2.0–2.3	1.95–2.35	.4	2.15	9	.32	23	.82
1.6–1.9	1.55–1.95	.4	1.75	4	.14	14	.50
1.2–1.5	1.15–1.55	.4	1.35	6	.21	10	.36
.8–1.1	.75–1.15	.4	.95	2	.07	4	.14
.4– .7	.35– .75	.4	.55	2	.07	2	.07
				$N = 28$			

Because of rounding, the rel. f columns of problems 3 and 4 do not sum to 1.00.

chapter 3

(1) means = 5.29, 6.40, 4.55, 7.22; medians = 6.00, 7.50, 5.00, 5.67; modes = 7, 9, **pg. 52.** 2 and 6, 6. **(2a)** mean or median because distribution is not highly skewed; **(2b)** median because distribution is skewed to the left; **(2c)** mean and median are acceptable since distribution is rather symmetrical but the modes should also be mentioned since distribution is bimodal; **(2d)** median because of the extreme score. **(3)** If a distribution is highly skewed, the median is often selected as the measure of central tendency. Why? **(4a)** 6; **(4b)** 5.5; **(4c)** 2.75; **(4d)** 2.875; **(4e)** 10.75; **(4f)** 3.325.

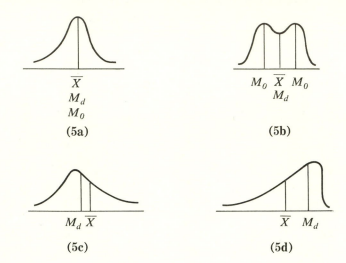

$$\overline{X}$$
$$M_d$$
$$M_0$$

(5a)

$$M_0 \; \overline{X} \; M_0$$
$$M_d$$

(5b)

$$M_d \; \overline{X}$$

(5c)

$$\overline{X} \; M_d$$

(5d)

(6) The sum of the deviations about the median (6) is -5, making the sum of the deviations about the median less than the deviations about the mean. Remember, it is the sum of the *squared* deviations (not unsquared) about the mean which is smaller than about any other value (the median included). **(7)** A sample is a subgroup of a population, but that population may in turn be a subgroup (i.e., a sample) of a larger group or population. Can you illustrate with an example? **(8)** Much effort will be made to determine estimates (statistics) of population values that we do not know (parameters). **(9)** See text p. 50.

pg. 62. **(1)** See text p. 53. **(2)** The range is based upon only the two most extreme scores, not all the scores, and the range is a statistic that itself is quite variable from one sample to another. **(3a)** $\overline{X} = 7.0$, $s^2 = .67$, $s = .82$; **(3b)** $\overline{X} = 7.00$, $s^2 = 8.67$, $s = 2.94$; **(3c)** $\overline{X} = 7.00$, $s^2 = 11.43$, $s = 3.38$. **(4)** The denominator $N - 1$ is used so that s^2 is an unbiased estimator of σ^2. What does unbiased mean? **(5)** See text p. 60 for a discussion of this issue.

chapter 4

pg. 68. **(1a)** 59.5; **(1b)** 78; **(1c)** 49.5 **(1d)** 85; **(1e)** 71.83; **(1f)** 72.17; **(1g)** 78.25; **(1h)** 72.5. **(2a)** $P_{.1125}$; **(2b)** $P_{.55}$; **(2c)** $P_{.7625}$; **(2d)** $P_{.65}$; **(2e)** $P_{.175}$; **(2f)** $P_{.3125}$; **(2g)** $P_{.85}$; **(2h)** $P_{.075}$

(1a) 60, 64, 8; (1b) 38, 64, 8; (1c) 500, 6400, 80; (1d) 10, 2.56, 1.60; (1e) −43.75, 1, 1. pg. 73.
(2a) 2, .25, .50; (2b) 40, 36, 6; (2c) 45, 225, 15.

(1) Percentiles only reflect ordinal position (i.e., the proportion of the group falling pg. 87.
below a given score) and do not indicate how far the other scores were from a given
percentile value. Standard scores take into account the variability of the distribution.
(2) See page 75 of text. (3) $\bar{X} = 8.00$, $s = 2.37$; $z_i = -1.27$, $-.42$, $-.42$, 0, .42,
1.69; $\bar{z} = 0$, $s_z = 1.00$; yes, because a distribution of standard scores has a mean of 0
and a standard deviation of 1. (4) Relative frequency or the proportion of cases falling between two specified values on the abscissa. (5) .50, .50, .1587, .8413. (6a) .6826;
(6b) .1359; (6c) .0668; (6d) .0500; (6e) .0100. (7a) $\pm 3\sigma$; (7b) 37, 49. (8a) .7734; (8b)
.1587; (8c) .3707. (9a) 63.16; (9b) 44.60 approximately; (9c) 31.39. (10a) .6524; (10b)
.2075; (10c) .0521; (11) Section (d), because a score of 90 in this distribution yields a z
of 2.5.

chapter 5

(1a) $b_{yx} = .21$, $a_{yx} = 4.64$; (1b) $b_{wx} = -.81$, $a_{wx} = 9.25$; (1c) $b_{wy} = -.008$, $a_{wy} =$ pg. 113.
4.71. (2a) 5.90; (2b) 6.82; (2c) 4.69; (2d) $X = 12$ not within the range of original
X values. (3a) $s_{y \cdot x} = 3.11$, $-.20$ to 12.00; (3b) $s_{w \cdot x} = 2.63$, -1.67 to 11.97; (3c)
$s_{w \cdot y} = 3.79$, -2.74 to 12.12. (4) See p. 100 of text. (5) $\tilde{Y} = .05X + 350$ in which
$\tilde{Y} = $ predicted income and $X = $ dollar value of sales. (6) Both are measures of variability, but one reflects variability about a mean and the other variability about a
regression line. (7) See p. 103 of text. (8) See p. 111 of text. (9a) Impossible, line intersects x-axis at -5; (9b) Possible; (9c) No, $s_{y \cdot x}$ must be $\leq s_y$.

chapter 6

(1) $r_{AB} = .14$, $r_{AC} = -.01$, $r_{BC} = -.26$; $r_{2(A+5)B} = .14$; Changing the unit and/or pg. 138.
origin of a scale (even for only one of the two scales) does not alter the correlation between the two variables. (2) $r_{xy} = .39$, $r_{x'y'} = .85$. The correlation changes because
the score pair (12, 8) deviates markedly from $(\bar{X}, \bar{Y})$. In a small sample such an extreme score can alter the correlation coefficient to a considerable degree. Adding the
points (12, −8) or (−12, 8) would shift r in the opposite direction. (3) See p. 131
of text. (4) $\sum(\tilde{Y}_i - \bar{Y})^2$, the total sum of squares of points about their mean can be
partitioned into the following components:

$$\sum(Y_i - \bar{Y})^2 = \sum(\tilde{Y}_i - \bar{Y})^2 + \sum(Y_i - \tilde{Y}_i)^2$$

The $\sum(Y_i - \tilde{Y}_i)^2$ represent the squared deviations of the points about the regression
line, that is, the error remaining after predicting Y from X. The $\sum(\tilde{Y}_i - \bar{Y})^2$ is that

portion of the total which is not error, that is, the variability in Y_i associated with X.
(5) The two regression lines result from the fact that minimizing the squared deviations between points and the line for Y_i does not minimize these deviations for the
X_i. However, the *degree* of linear relationship as reflected in r is the same regardless
of the direction of prediction. **(6)** Extreme points influence the regression constants
and r more than points near $(\overline{X}, \overline{Y})$ because their deviations from $(\overline{X}, \overline{Y})$, being large,
contribute disproportionately to the numerators of b and r when they are squared.
(7) Since $r = b_{yx}(s_x/s_y)$, when scores are standardized, $s_x = s_y = 1$, making $s_x/s_y = 1$.
The result is $r = b_{z_y z_x}$. **(8)** Since $r^2 = 1 - s_{y.x}^2/s_y^2$, the correlation becomes larger
as $s_{y.x}^2/s_y^2$ becomes smaller. **(9a)** Impossible, with an N of 2, both points would fall
precisely on the regression line and $s_{y.x}$ would be 0 not 2.5; **(9b)** Impossible, if $s_{y.x} = 0$,
r must be ± 1.00; **(9c)** Impossible, if b is negative, r must be negative; **(9d)** Possible;
(9e) Impossible, the means and standard deviations indicate that X and Y are in
standard score form and thus r must equal b; **(9f)** Possible.

chapter 7

pg. 164. **(1)** Only (a) is mutually exclusive. **(2)** (a), (b) (if drawing is with replacement), and (c)
are independent. **(3)** Events A and B are independent if and only if $P(B \mid A) = P(B)$ in
which $P(B \mid A)$ is the conditional probability of B given A. **(4a)** 2/3, 2/3; **(4b)** 5/6,
5/6; **(4c)** 1/36; **(4d)** 2/3, 4/7, 2/7, 2/7. **(5a)** 720; **(5b)** 60; **(5c)** 840. **(6)** 665, 280.
(7a) 1; **(7b)** 20, 15; **(7c)** 70. **(8)** 35, 840. **(9)** .0005, .002. **(10)** 1/56, 1/336, 1/6. **(11)**
$35 \left(\frac{1}{12}\right)^4 \left(\frac{11}{12}\right)^3 = .0013, .0024.$

chapter 8

pg. 182. **(1a)** An 8 A.M. class appeals to only some students. One might wonder if the sample
of students in an 8 A.M. class was typical of college students and whether it would be
composed of a different type of student than a 2 P.M. class; **(1b)** Although all students
must participate in an experiment, they can select which they want to do. Are those
who volunteer for a jury experiment, as opposed to some other type, typical of all
college students? **(1c)** Are those people who own color TV sets typical of shoppers in
general? **(2)** The values differ because they estimate a common parameter $(\sigma_{\overline{x}})$ on
the basis of a different set of scores. The larger the N the less error (variability) is in
the estimate. **(3a)** 3; **(3b)** 2; **(3c)** 1.33. **(4)** If the population distribution of raw scores is
normal or if the N is large, the sampling distribution of the mean will be normal.
(5) Two variables are independent if they are unrelated in such a way that the value of
one does not influence (or relate to) the value of the other. $\overline{X}$ and s_x^2 are independent if
the population distribution of X's is normal (symmetrical). **(6)** The theoretical relative
frequency of an event in an idealized experiment is the probability of that event.
(7a) .1587; **(7b)** .0139; **(7c)** .1841; **(7d)** .4060. **(8a)** .1151; **(8b)** .0548; **(8c)** .1056; **(8d)** .5788.

chapter 9

(1) If there is considerable evidence or a decisive theory which indicates that the result pg. 206.
of the experiment will be in a specified direction (e.g., mean A will be larger than mean
B), then a directional test can be performed. Otherwise, use a nondirectional test.
(2) α is the probability of a Type I Error. As α becomes smaller, the probability of a
Type II Error increases. **(3)** Assumptions are held true throughout the hypothesis
testing procedure whereas hypotheses consist of a set of mutually exclusive alternatives
one of which is being tested and will or will not be rejected by the procedures. **(4)**
"Chance" implies that the result is simply sampling error and that no differences exist
in the population. **(5)** This ratio is used to decide between rejecting or not rejecting H_0
(i.e., it is "critical" to this decision). **(6)** H_0 not H_1 is being tested. One can only find no
evidence to reject H_0 rather than evidence for its validity. **(7)** A Type I Error occurs
when H_0 is erroneously rejected while a Type II Error occurs when H_0 is erroneously
not rejected. **(8)** α and β are inversely related; **(9)** Power is the probability that the test
will correctly reject H_0. **(10)** Use z if σ_x is available, use t if σ_x is estimated with s_x.
(11a) *Assumptions.* The members of the sample are randomly and independently
selected and the population involved is normal with $\mu = 81$ and $\sigma = 10$. *Hypotheses.*
H_0: $\bar{X}$ is computed on a sample from a population with $\mu = 81$. H_1: $\bar{X}$ is computed on
a sample from a population with $\mu \neq 81$. *Formula.*

$$z = \frac{\bar{X} - \mu}{\sigma_{\bar{x}}} = \frac{\bar{X} - \mu}{\sigma_x/\sqrt{N}}$$

Significance level. Assume $\alpha = .05$. *Critical values.* -1.96 and $+1.96$ for a two-tailed
test. *Decision rules.* If z_{obs} is between -1.96 and $+1.96$, do not reject H_0; if z_{obs} is less
than or equal to -1.96 or more than or equal to $+1.96$, reject H_0. *Computation.* $z_{obs} = 1.50$. *Decision.* Do not reject H_0, the observed mean deviates from the population mean
by an amount that is within the range of sampling error. **(11b)** One would then use the
formula for t with $df = 24$ rather than the z distribution. The critical values of t
would be ± 2.064 for a two-tailed test at $\alpha = .05$, and the decision rules would be:
If t_{obs} is between -2.064 and $+2.064$, do not reject H_0. If t_{obs} is less than or equal to
-2.064 or more than or equal to $+2.064$, reject H_0. Because s_x is also 10, the observed
t would be calculated by

$$t_{obs} = \frac{\bar{X} - \mu}{s_x/\sqrt{N}} = \frac{84 - 81}{10/\sqrt{25}} = 1.50$$

This would result in the same decision (i.e., do not reject H_0) and interpretation as in
Problem 11a. **(11A)** *Assumptions.* The members of the sample are randomly and independently selected and the population of non-pierced males is normal with a mean of
62 inches. *Hypotheses.* H_0: $\bar{X}$ is computed on a sample from a population with $\mu = 62$.
H_1: $\bar{X}$ is computed on a sample from a population with $\mu > 62$. (Notice that this is a
directional alternative. Why?) *Formula.*

$$t = \frac{\bar{X} - \mu}{s_{\bar{x}}} = \frac{\bar{X} - \mu}{s_x/\sqrt{N}}$$

Significance level. Assume $\alpha = .05$. *Critical value.* From Table B with $df = N - 1 = 35$, one-tailed, $\alpha = .05$: $+1.691$ (approximately; obtained by interpolation). *Decision rules.* If t_{obs} is less than 1.691, do not reject H_0. If t_{obs} is greater than or equal to 1.691, reject H_0. *Computation.*

$$t_{obs} = \frac{\bar{X} - \mu}{s_x/\sqrt{N}} = \frac{64.5 - 62}{7/\sqrt{36}} = 2.14$$

Decision. Reject H_0, the observed mean of 64.5 is greater than would be expected to occur from errors of sampling from a population with $\mu = 62$. This result does not constitute proof that the piercing and molding causes increased height since factors that cause or are related to determining which cultures pierce and mold might also produce skeletally tall males (e.g., diet, genetic stock, amount of sunshine, etc.). **(11d)** *Assumptions.* The sample of applicants is randomly and independently selected and the mean of the current student population is 113. *Hypotheses.* H_0: $\bar{X}$ is computed on a sample from a population with $\mu = 113$. H_1: $\bar{X}$ is computed on a sample from a population with $\mu \neq 113$. *Formula.*

$$t = \frac{\bar{X} - \mu}{s_{\bar{x}}} = \frac{\bar{X} - \mu}{s_x/\sqrt{N}}$$

Significance level. Assume $\alpha = .05$. *Critical values.* Given a non-directional test, $df = N - 1 = 120$, $\alpha = .05$: $t_{crit} = \pm 1.98$. *Decision rules.* If t_{obs} is between -1.98 and $+1.98$, do not reject H_0. If t_{obs} is less than or equal to -1.98 or more than or equal to $+1.98$, reject H_0. *Computation.*

$$t_{obs} = \frac{\bar{X} - \mu}{s_x/\sqrt{N}} = \frac{117 - 113}{16/\sqrt{121}} = 2.76$$

Decision. Reject H_0, the observed mean is too deviant from $\mu = 113$ to be simply a function of sampling error. **(12a)** 19.82 to 36.18, 16.976 to 39.024; **(12b)** 126.428 to 177.572, 116.636 to 187.364; **(12c)** 32.5 to 42.5 approximately (no interpolation in Table B used), 30.85 to 44.15 approximately; **(12d)** 62.2 to 81.8, 59.12 to 84.88.

chapter 10

pg. 232.   **(1)** The assumption of normality is made so that the standard normal or the t distribution may be used to determine the required probability. This assumption can be made if the population distribution(s) are normal or if the sample size is sufficiently large. **(2)** When the same subjects produce both groups of scores, the individual differences that characterize those subjects influence the scores in both groups causing them to be correlated to some extent. This correlation affects the accuracy of the estimate of the standard error of the difference between means based upon independent groups, so another procedure must be used. **(3)** Test for the difference between independent means. *Hypotheses.* H_0: $\mu_1 = \mu_2$. H_1: $\mu_1 < \mu_2$. *Assumptions.* The subjects are randomly and independently sampled, the groups are independent, variances are homogeneous, and X is normally distributed. *Decision rules*. Given .05 level and $df = N_1 + N_2 - 2 = 18$, directional test. If $-1.734 \leq t_{obs}$, do not reject H_0. If $t_{obs} \leq -1.734$, reject H_0. *Computation*.

$$t_{obs} = (\bar{X}_1 - \bar{X}_2) \Big/ \sqrt{\left[\frac{(N_1 - 1)s_1{}^2 + (N_2 - 1)s_2{}^2}{N_1 + N_2 - 2}\right] \cdot \left[\frac{1}{N_1} + \frac{1}{N_2}\right]}$$

$$t_{obs} = (2.8 - 6.5) \Big/ \sqrt{\left[\frac{(10 - 1)3.07 + (10 - 1)5.39}{10 + 10 - 2}\right] \cdot \left[\frac{1}{10} + \frac{1}{10}\right]} = -4.02$$

Decision. Reject H_0, the observed difference in means is too great to be a simple result of sampling error. The dissonance theory is supported. **(4)** Test of the difference between two correlated means. *Hypotheses*. $H_0: \mu_1 = \mu_2$. $H_1: \mu_1 \neq \mu_2$. *Assumptions*. The data are in the form of pairs of scores which were randomly and independently sampled and the population of the D_i is normally distributed. *Decision rules*. Given .05 level, $df = N - 1 = 7$, directional test. If $-1.895 < t_{obs} < 1.895$, do not reject H_0. If $t_{obs} \leq -1.895$ or $t_{obs} \geq 1.895$, reject H_0. *Computation*.

$$t_{obs} = \frac{\sum D}{\sqrt{(N\sum D^2 - (\sum D)^2)/(N - 1)}} = \frac{9}{\sqrt{(8(35) - (9)^2)/7}} = 1.69$$

Do not reject H_0, the observed difference between means is too small to be due to sampling error. The mothers are not better at detecting hunger cries. **(5)** Test of difference between independent means. *Hypotheses*. $H_0: \mu_1 = \mu_2$. $H_1: \mu_1 \neq \mu_2$. *Assumptions*. The subjects are randomly and independently sampled, the groups are independent, variances are homogeneous, and X is normally distributed. *Decision rules*. Given .05 level, $df = N_1 + N_2 - 2 = 22$, non-directional test. If $-2.074 < t_{obs} < 2.074$, do not reject H_0. If $t_{obs} \leq -2.074$ or $t_{obs} \geq 2.074$, reject H_0. *Computation*.

$$t_{obs} = \frac{(19.75 - 11.75)}{\sqrt{\frac{(12 - 1)12.93 + (12 - 1)4.93}{12 + 12 - 2}\left[\frac{1}{12} + \frac{1}{12}\right]}} = 6.56$$

Reject H_0, the difference in observed means is too great to be simply a function of sampling error. There is a difference between the two therapeutic approaches. **(6)** Verify that the following set of numbers satisfies the conditions of this problem.

A	B
2	0
4	3
6	4
8	7
10	8
12	9
14	13
16	15

(7) *Hypotheses.* $H_0: \rho = 0$. $H_1: \rho \neq 0$. *Assumptions.* The subjects were randomly and independently sampled and the population distributions of the two variables are normal. *Decision rules.* Given .05, $df = N - 2 = 6$, non-directional test. If $-.7067 < r_{obs} < .7067$, do not reject H_0. If $r_{obs} \leq -.7067$ or $r_{obs} \geq .7067$, reject H_0. *Computation.* $r_{obs} = .34$. *Decision.* Do not reject H_0, the observed correlation is too small to be simply a function of sampling error. **(8)** *Hypotheses.* $H_0: \rho_1 \leq \rho_2$. $H_1: \rho_1 > \rho_2$. *Assumptions.* The subjects are randomly and independently sampled, the groups are independent, the population distributions of X and Y for each correlation are normal, and N_1 and N_2 are both greater than 20. *Decision rules.* Given .05, directional test. If $z_{obs} < 1.645$, do not reject H_0. If $z_{obs} \geq 1.645$, reject H_0. *Computation.*

$$z_{obs} = \frac{z_{r_1} - z_{r_2}}{\sqrt{1/(N_1 - 3) + 1/(N_2 - 3)}} = \frac{1.333 - .590}{\sqrt{1/(38 - 3) + 1/(27 - 3)}} = 2.80$$

Decision. Reject H_0, the difference between the correlations is too large to be a simple function of sampling error. The correlation between the IQs of identical twins is higher than between the IQs of fraternal twins. **(9a)** *t* test for correlated groups. Teacher A. $H_0: \mu_1 = \mu_2$. $H_1: \mu_1 \neq \mu_2$. Given .05 level, $df = N - 1 = 7$, nondirectional test. If $-2.365 < t_{obs} < 2.365$, do not reject H_0. If $t_{obs} \leq -2.365$ or $t_{obs} \geq 2.365$, reject H_0. $t_{obs} = 3.00$. Reject H_0, the children improved. Teacher B. $H_0: \mu_1 = \mu_2$. $H_1: \mu_1 \neq \mu_2$. Given .05 level, $df = N - 1 = 9$, nondirectional test. If $-2.262 < t_{obs} < 2.262$, do not reject H_0. If $t_{obs} \leq -2.262$ or $t_{obs} \geq 2.262$, reject H_0. $t_{obs} = 4.51$. Reject H_0, the children improved. **(9b)** *t* test for independent groups. $H_0: \mu_1 = \mu_2$. $H_1: \mu_1 \neq \mu_2$. If $-2.12 < t_{obs} < 2.12$, do not reject H_0. If $t_{obs} \leq -2.12$ or $t_{obs} \geq 2.12$, reject H_0. $t_{obs} = 1.61$. Do not reject H_0, the observed difference between teachers is within the realm of sampling error. **(9c)** Teacher A. $H_0: \rho_1 = 0$. $H_1: \rho_1 \neq 0$. Given .05 level, $df = 6$, non-directional test. If $-.7067 < r_{obs} < .7067$, do not reject H_0. If $r_{obs} \leq -.7067$ or $r_{obs} \geq .7067$, reject H_0. $r_{obs} = .83$. Reject H_0, the observed correlation could not have occurred by sampling error. Teacher B. $H_0: \rho_2 = 0$. $H_1: \rho_2 \neq 0$. Given .05 level, $df = 8$, non-directional test. If $-.6319 < r_{obs} < .6319$, do not reject H_0. If $r_{obs} \leq -.6319$ or $r_{obs} \geq .6319$, reject H_0. $r_{obs} = .96$. Reject H_0, the probability that $r_{obs} = .96$ could come from a population with $\rho = .00$ is too small. A correlation exists between pretest and posttest scores. Test for the difference between two *r*'s. $H_0: \rho_1 = \rho_2$. $H_1: \rho_1 \neq \rho_2$. Given .05 level, non-directional test. If $-1.96 < z_{obs} < 1.96$, do not reject H_0. If $z_{obs} \leq -1.96$ or $z_{obs} \geq 1.96$, reject H_0. $z_{obs} = 1.29$. Do not reject H_0, the difference between the two correlations is probably a function of sampling error. **(9d)** The data and analyses indicate that children in both classes improved over the period between pretest and posttest, and pupils in the two classes did not differ in the amount of this improvement. These data by themselves do not indicate that these pupils improved more than they would have under another teaching method or even without any special program of instruction. The fact that there was a correlation between pretest and posttest scores for both teachers and no evidence suggesting a difference in these *r*'s, indicates that the teaching program was relatively equal in its effectiveness across initial ability level. There was no obvious difference in variability of change scores between teachers.

chapter 11

(1a) *Hypotheses.* H_0: $\mu_1 = \mu_2 = \mu_3 = \mu$. H_1: Not H_0. *Assumptions.* Homogeneity   **pg. 263.**
and normality of population group variances, random sampling, and independent
groups. *Decision rules.* If $F_{obs} < 3.74$, do not reject H_0. If $F_{obs} \geq 3.74$, reject H_0.
Computation.

$$T_1 = 21 \qquad\qquad T_2 = 12 \qquad\qquad T_3 = 28 \qquad\qquad T_{total} = 61$$
$$n_1 = 5 \qquad\qquad n_2 = 5 \qquad\qquad n_3 = 7 \qquad\qquad N = 17$$
$$\bar{X}_1 = 4.2 \qquad\qquad \bar{X}_2 = 2.4 \qquad\qquad \bar{X}_3 = 4.0$$
$$\sum X_{i1}^2 = 123 \qquad \sum X_{i2}^2 = 50 \qquad \sum X_{i3}^2 = 164 \qquad \sum\sum X_{ij}^2 = 337$$
$$\frac{T_1^2}{n_1} = 88.2 \qquad \frac{T_2^2}{n_2} = 28.8 \qquad \frac{T_3^2}{n_3} = 112.0 \qquad \frac{\sum T_j^2}{n_j} = 229$$

(I) = 218.8824	(II) = 337.0000	(III) = 229.0000

$$SS_{between} = 10.1176 \qquad df_{between} = 2 \qquad MS_{between} = 5.0588$$
$$SS_{within} = 108.0000 \qquad df_{within} = 14 \qquad MS_{within} = 7.7143$$
$$SS_{total} = 118.1176 \qquad df_{total} = 16$$

Source	df	SS	MS	F
Between Groups	2	10.1176	5.0588	.66
Within Groups	14	108.0000	7.7143	
Total	16	118.1176		

Decision. Do not reject H_0, the observed means are similar enough so that their small
differences could be attributable to sampling error. **(1b)** Adding different constants
to the groups is analogous to introducing a treatment difference. Reanalyzing, MS_{within}
remains the same ($MS_{within} = 7.7143$) while $MS_{between}$ reflects the introduction of
mean differences ($MS_{between} = 57.4706$). $F_{obs} = 7.45$ which is greater than the critical
value of 3.74 and leads to rejecting H_0. **(1c)** Adding 20 to the last score in each group
will increase within-group variability ($MS_{within} = 81.9184$) but will influence between-
group variability very little ($MS_{between} = 4.4538$). $F_{obs} = .05$, do not reject H_0.
(2) $X_{ij} = \bar{X} + (\bar{X}_j - \bar{X}) + (X_{ij} - \bar{X}_j) = 14$.
(3) See p. 242 of text.

(4)

Source	df	SS	MS	F
Between Groups	2	582.5738	291.2869	14.74**
Within Groups	17	335.9762	19.7633	
Total	19	918.5500		

chapter 12

pg. 295. **(1)** See pp. 267–271 of text.

(2) No, for the same reason that $2 + 3 = 5$ and $1 + 4 = 5$ but $\frac{2}{1} + \frac{3}{4} \neq \frac{5}{5}$. Can you apply this numerical fact to explaining why?

(3a) *Hypotheses.* Factor A. H_0: $\alpha_1 = \alpha_2 = 0$. H_1: Not H_0. Factor B. H_0: $\beta_1 = \beta_2 = 0$. H_1: Not H_0. AB Interaction. H_0: $\alpha\beta_{11} = \alpha\beta_{12} = \alpha\beta_{21} = \alpha\beta_{22} = 0$. H_1: Not H_0. *Assumptions.* The groups are independent and randomly sampled with $n > 1$ from populations having normal distributions and homogeneous variances. The factors are fixed. *Decision rules.* For all tests $df = 1$, 12, and $\alpha = .05$. If $F_{\text{obs}} < 4.75$, do not reject H_0. If $F_{\text{obs}} \geq 4.75$, reject H_0. *Computation.* (I) = 370.5625, (II) = 469.0000, (III) = 372.1250, (IV) = 371.1250, (V) = 375.7500.

Source	df	SS	MS	F
A	1	1.5625	1.5625	.20
B	1	.5625	.5625	.07
AB	1	3.0625	3.0625	.39
Within	12	93.2500	7.7708	
Total	15	98.4375		

Decision. Do not reject H_0 for all tests.

(3b) *Computation.* (I) = 1540.5625, (II) = 2089.0000, (III) = 1992.1250, (IV) = 1541.1250, (V) = 1995.7500.

Source	df	SS	MS	F
A	1	451.5625	451.5625	58.11**
B	1	.5625	.5625	.07
AB	1	3.0625	3.0625	.39
Within	12	93.2500	7.7708	
Total	15	548.4375		

By increasing the scores in a single level of Factor A, only the total sum of squares and SS_A are increased. **(3c)** *Computation.* (I) = 855.5625, (II) = 1249.0000, (III) = 932.1250, (IV) = 941.1250, (V) = 1155.7500.

Source	df	SS	MS	F
A	1	76.5625	76.5625	9.85*
B	1	85.5625	85.5625	11.01*
AB	1	138.0625	138.0625	17.77**
Within	12	93.2500	7.7708	
Total	15	393.4375		

By increasing the scores in a single cell, the total sum of squares increases with most of the increment given to SS_{AB}, but SS_A and SS_B also become larger. SS_{within} does

not change because adding a constant to each score does not alter the variability of scores about their mean. The fact that SS_A and SS_B are increased as well as SS_{AB} is one reason why sometimes when a significant interaction exists, the presence of main effects are difficult to interpret. Discuss this issue with respect to the current problem.
(4) *Computation.* (I) = 48330.3750, (II) = 49643.0000, (III) = 48422.4167, (IV) = 48331.4167, (V) = 48445.5000.

Source	df	SS	MS	F
User	1	92.0417	92.0417	1.54
Drug	1	1.0417	1.0417	<1
User × Drug	1	22.0417	22.0417	<1
Within	20	1197.5000	59.8750	
Total	23	1312.6251		

Decision. None of the observed F's even approached the critical value (α = .05) of 4.35 indicating that there is no evidence that marijuana altered perceptual performance and that naive users were affected differently than regular users.
(5) *Computation.* (I) = 8400.8928, (II) = 9491.0000, (III) = 9071.2142, (IV) = 8479.7857, (V) = 9204.4286.

Source	df	MS	MS	F
User	1	670.3214	670.3214	56.14**
Drug	1	78.8929	78.8929	6.61*
User × Drug	1	54.3215	54.3215	4.55*
Within	24	286.5714	11.9405	
Total	27	1090.1072		

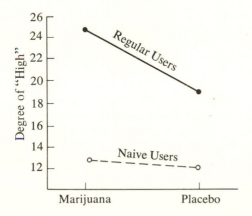

Decision. All F's exceeded the critical value of 4.26 and thus the three H_0 are rejected. From the graph and the fact that 60% of the variance was accounted for by differences between regular marijuana users and those naive to it, it is clear that users report better "highs" than non-users, even for the placebos (it would appear). Although the effect for marijuana verses placebo was significant, it seems that such a result is produced mainly by the regular users since the interaction is also significant. Thus, it would appear that regular users discriminate the difference between marijuana and a placebo better than non-users.

chapter 13

pg. 330. **(1)** A nonparametric test might be used if nominal or ordinal data are involved or if some of the assumptions of the parametric test (e.g., homogeneity of variance, normality) cannot be met. **(2)** Power-efficiency is the probability that the statistical test will correctly reject the null hypothesis. For a given N, parametric tests are more powerful than analogous nonparametric tests. **(3)** Chi Square 2 × 3 Table. $\chi_{obs}^2 = 20.67$ which exceeds the critical value of 5.99 ($df = 2$). Reject H_0. Children who showed increases in IQ over age were more likely to have had mothers who held high aspirations for their children than if an IQ decrease was observed. **(4a)** Mann-Whitney U Test. *Hypotheses.* H_0: The population distributions are identical. H_1: The population distributions are not identical. *Assumptions.* The observations are randomly and independently sampled, the groups are independent, and the measurement scale is continuous with ordinal properties. *Decision rules.* Given .05 level, $n_A = 8$, $n_B = 8$. If $13 < U_{obs} < 51$, do not reject H_0. If $U_{obs} \le 13$ or $U_{obs} \ge 51$, reject H_0. *Computation.* $U_{obs} = 47$. *Decision.* Do not reject H_0. For Groups A and C. *Computation.* $U_{obs} = 54.5$, reject H_0. For Groups B and C. *Computation.* $U_{obs} = 47$, do not reject H_0; **(4b)** Kruskal-Wallis Test for 3 Independent Samples. *Hypotheses.* H_0: The three population distributions are identical. H_1: The population distributions are not identical. *Assumptions.* Subjects are randomly and independently sampled, the groups are independent with $n_j > 5$, the measurement scale is continuous with ordinal properties. *Decision rules.* Given .05 level, $df = 2$ (Chi Square, Table F). If $H_{obs} < 5.99$, do not reject H_0. If $H_{obs} \ge 5.99$, reject H_0. *Computation.* $H_{obs} = 7.03$. *Decision.* Reject H_0; **(4c)** Exercise 4b asks whether three groups differ in the population, whereas Exercise 4a asks whether a specific pair of groups differ. They are different questions and different statistical tests must be used. The three tests on pairs are not an appropriate substitute for the test on all three groups considered simultaneously. Why? **(4d)** Wilcoxon Test. Groups A and B. *Hypotheses.* H_0: The population distributions are identical. H_1: The distributions are different. *Assumptions.* The subjects are randomly selected and ordinal measurement is available both within and between pairs of scores. *Decision rules.* Given .05 level, $N = 8$, and non-directional test. If $W_{obs} > 3$, do not reject H_0. If $W_{obs} \le 3$, reject H_0. *Computation.* $W_{obs} = 1$. *Decision.* Reject H_0. For Groups A and C. $W_{obs} = 0$, reject H_0. For Groups B and C, $W_{obs} = 2$, reject H_0; **(4e)** The difference between A and B is not significant when the scores are conceived to be from independent groups but (4a) is significant when the scores are conceived to be pairs of scores from the same 8 subjects. This is possible because in (a) the groups are compared relative to the variability within groups whereas in (d) the difference between scores is compared relative to the variability of such differences; **(4f)** Pearson correlation on raw data from Groups A and C equals .76. After ranking within each group, the r and r_S both equal .71. The correlations on the ranked data are equivalent because the Spearman formula is the Pearson coefficient applied to ranked data. The correlations on the raw and ranked data differ because the data are different; (4g) For Groups A and C. *Hypotheses.* $H_0: \rho_S = 0$. $H_1: \rho_S \neq 0$. *Assumptions.* The sample is randomly selected and has ordinal measurement. *Decision rules.* Given .05 and non-directional test with $N = 8$. If $-.715 < r_S < .715$, do not reject H_0. If $r_S \leq -.715$ or $r_S \geq .715$, reject H_0. *Computation.* $r_S = .708$. *Decision.* Do not reject H_0, but observe that the probability that such an r_S could be obtained by sampling error alone is $p < .06$. For Groups A and B. $r_S = .875$, reject H_0. For Groups B and C. $r_S = .548$, do not reject H_0. (5) Chi Square 2×3 Table. $\chi_{obs}^2 = 11.18$. $df = 2$, $\chi_{crit}^2 = 5.99$, reject H_0. If father is censored the child is more likely to remember the profane response of father. (6) Mann-Whitney U Test. $U_{obs} = 79$, $U_{crit} = 23$ and 76 for $n = 9, 11$, .05 level, nondirectional test. Reject H_0. (7) For Group A, $\bar{X} = 19.57$, $M_d = 13$; for Group B, $\bar{X} = 19.29$, $M_d = 19$. t test for the difference between independent groups, $t_{obs} = .04$, do not reject H_0. Mann-Whitney U test. $U_{obs} = 42$. $U_{crit} = 8, 41$. Reject H_0. The means of the groups are very similar but the medians are somewhat different. Because of the distributions (e.g., $X = 62$) the median is more appropriate. The $X = 62$ elevates the mean of Group A and makes its variance quite large. The t test is not significant. When the data are ranked, the 62 does not exert such an influence and the U test is significant. The median and U test both predominantly use the ordinal characteristics of the scale. (8) Kruskal-Wallis Test for three independent samples. $H_{obs} = 7.78$. $H_{crit} = 5.99$. Reject H_0. (9) Wilcoxon Test. $W_{obs} = 4.5$. $W_{crit} = 17$ for $N = 12$, .05 level, directional. Reject H_0. (10) $r_S = .27$. Critical value of $r_S = .504$ for $N = 12$, at .05 level, directional. Do not reject H_0. This result suggests that although the children generally improved during the year, this improvement was not particularly uniform among all children.

appendix I

(1a) $\frac{5}{7}$; (1b) $\frac{9}{10}$; (1c) $\frac{98}{99}$; (1d) $\frac{55}{14}$; (1e) $\frac{1}{6}$; (1f) $\frac{7}{9}$; (1g) $\frac{59}{180}$. (2a) $\frac{2}{9}$; (2b) $\frac{2}{7}$; (2c) 1; (2d) $\frac{8}{9}$; **pg. 348.**
(2e) $\frac{6}{5}$; (2f); $\frac{16}{5}$. (3a) 24; (3b) 20; (3c) 480. (4a) 27; (4b) 18; (4c) 24; (4d) 7; (4e) $2^7 = 128$; (4f) 144; (4g) 1; (4h) 4; (4i) $\frac{25}{9}$; (4j) $\frac{27}{125}$; (4k) $\frac{25}{54}$. (5a) $a^2 + 2ab + b^2$; (5b) $a^2 - 2ab + b^2$; (5c) $X^2 - 2X\bar{X} + \bar{X}^2$; (5d) $(cd)^2 - 2abcd + (ab)^2$ or $c^2d^2 - 2abcd + a^2b^2$; (5e) c; (5f) $\dfrac{ca - b}{c}$ or $a - \dfrac{b}{c}$. (5g) $\dfrac{(d + c)}{(d - c)}$. (6a) 38; (6b) 359; (6c) 69.3;
(6d) .75; (6e) 31.5; (6f) 10.9; (6g) 108.1.

GLOSSARY
OF SYMBOLS

GLOSSARY
OF SYMBOLS

Symbol	Meaning	Symbol	Meaning
a	Regression constant representing the y-intercept. It is also written with paired subscripts (a_{yx}, a_{xy}) which denote whether the regression is Y on X or X on Y.	e	The base of Napierian logarithms, $e = 2.7183\ldots$.
α	Greek alpha is the significance level in hypothesis testing, which is also the probability of a Type I error.	F	A test statistic, usually the ratio of two independent variances. It is sometimes subscripted to indicate if the value is an observed (F_{obs}) or a critical one (F_{crit}).
b	Regression constant indicating the slope of the regression line. It is also written with paired subscripts (b_{yx}, b_{xy}) which indicate whether the regression is Y on X or X on Y, and with multiple subscripts ($b_{z_y z_x}$) indicating the value is for standardized variables z_y and z_x.	f	Frequency.
		°F	Degrees Fahrenheit.
		H	Test statistic for the Kruskal-Wallis test.
		H_0	The null hypothesis.
β	Unsubscripted Greek beta represents the probability of a Type II Error.	H_1	The alternative hypothesis.
		i	The size of a class interval.
c	Often used to denote any non-zero constant.	k	Often used to denote any non-zero constant.
°C	Degrees centigrade.	L	The lower limit of the interval containing the median.
$_nC_r$	The number of combinations (order irrelevant) of n things taken r at a time.	$\log_e$	The logarithm to the base e; also the natural or Napierian logarithm. Sometimes written ln in other contexts.
χ^2	Greek chi squared, a test statistic used in several nonparametric tests. It is often subscripted to indicate if the value is an observed (χ_{obs}^2), or a critical one (χ_{crit}^2).	$\log_{10}$	The logarithm to the base 10. Most frequently written without subscript.
		μ	The population mean. It is also written with subscripts, for example, $\mu_{\bar{x}}$, indicating the population mean of the distribution of sample means.
Cum. f	Cumulative frequency.		
Cum. Rel. f	Cumulative relative frequency.	M_d	The median.
D_i	The difference between pairs of scores (e.g., in the t test for the difference between means for correlated groups).	M_o	The mode.
		MS	Mean square or variance estimate in the analysis of variance. It is often written with subscripts indicating the mean square for a particular source of variability (e.g., $MS_{between}$, MS_{AB}).
d_i	The difference between ranks of paired scores (e.g., in Spearman's rank-order correlation).		
		N	The total number of subjects, observations, or paired observations (check the precise definition for each application).
df	Degrees of freedom		
E_{jk}	The expected frequency for the jkth cell.	n	The number of subjects or observations within a specific subgroup of a larger sample.

Symbol	Meaning
n_b	The number of scores falling below the lower limit of the interval containing the median.
n_w	The number of scores within the interval containing the median.
O_{jk}	The observed frequency for the jkth cell.
$P(A)$	The probability of event A.
$P(B \mid A)$	The conditional probability of the event B, given that event A has already occurred.
p	The probability that the observed data could be obtained if the null hypothesis were true.
$P_{.n}$	The nth percentile point.
$_nP_r$	The number of permutations (order considered) of n things taken r at a time.
π	A constant equal to $3.1416\ldots$
r	The sample Pearson product-moment correlation coefficient.
r^2	The estimated proportion of variance in Y attributable to X (the square of the correlation coefficient).
ρ	The population correlation coefficient.
r_s	The sample Spearman rank-order correlation coefficient.
ρ_s	The population Spearman rank-order correlation.
Rel. f	Relative frequency.
S	The universal set or sample space.
s	The sample standard deviation. It is also written with subscripts indicating the variable or statistic for which the standard deviation applies (e.g., s_x, the standard deviation of the X's; $s_{\bar{x}}$, the standard error of the mean; $s_{\bar{x}_1-\bar{x}_2}$, the standard error of the difference between two means).
s^2	The sample variance. It is also written with subscripts (see s).
σ	Lower case Greek sigma, the population standard deviation. It is also written with subscripts (see s).
σ^2	Lower case Greek sigma squared, the population variance. It is also written with subscripts (see s).

Symbol	Meaning
$s_{y.x}$	The sample standard error of estimate in regression.
$\sigma_{y.x}$	The population standard error of estimate, read "sigma sub y dot x."
$s_{y \mid x=2}$	The sample standard deviation of the Y's at $X = 2$.
$\sigma_{y \mid x=2}$	The population standard deviation of the Y's at $X = 2$.
SS	Sum of squares. It is often written with subscripts indicating the mean square for a particular source of variability (e.g., SS_{between}, SS_{AB}, etc.).
$\sum\limits_{i=1}^{N} X_i$	Capital Greek sigma directs one to sum the X_i for $i = 1$ to N. It is also written without limits on the summation sign and subscripts, $\sum X$.
T	A total, sometimes written with subscripts indicating which scores are summed.
t	Student's t test statistic. It is also written with subscripts indicating the value is an observed (t_{obs}) or a critical one (t_{crit}), or indicating the value of t at $p = .05$ ($t_{.05}$), etc.
U	The test statistic for the Mann-Whitney U test. It is also written with subscripts indicating the value is an observed (U_{obs}) or a critical one (U_{crit}).
X_i	The ith score of a variable. Other letters (e.g., Y_i, W_i, etc.) are also used to denote variables.
$\bar{X}$	The sample mean. Any variable with a bar over it signifies the mean of that variable (e.g., $\bar{Y}$). It is also written with subscripts indicating the levels and factors involved (e.g. $\bar{X}_{j.}$, $\bar{X}_{.k}$, $\bar{X}_{..}$, etc.).
$\tilde{Y}$	The value of Y predicted on the basis of the regression line. One may also find $\tilde{X}$, when the regression is for X on Y.
W	The test statistic for the Wilcoxon test. It is also written with subscripts indicating if the value is an observed (W_{obs}) or a critical one (W_{crit}).
z	A standard normal deviate. It is also written with subscripts indicating if the value is an observed (z_{obs}) or a critical one (z_{crit}).

Symbol	Meaning	Symbol	Meaning
z_r	A transformed value of the correlation coefficient, r.	$\neq$	"is not equal to"
A'	The prime after a capital letter A (for example) indicates the set complement to A (i.e., all elements not in A).	$<$	"is less than"
		$\leq$	"is less than or equal to"
		$>$	"is greater than"
		$\geq$	"is greater than or equal to"
$\subseteq$	The sign $\subseteq$ in $A \subseteq B$ indicates that A is a subset of B.	$\pm$	"plus or minus"
		$\sqrt{}$	"square root of"
$\cup$	The sign $\cup$ in $A \cup B$ indicates union, the set of elements that are in either A, in B, or in both A and B.	$\lvert c \rvert$	"the absolute value of" c
		∞	Infinity
$\cap$	The sign $\cap$ in $A \cap B$ indicates intersection, the set of elements that are in A and in B.	$\varnothing$	The null or empty set.
$=$	"is equal to"	*,**,***	The stated observed value of the test statistic is significant at the .05(*), the .01(**), or the .001(***) level.

INDEX

INDEX

C   5
D   6
E   7
F   8
G   9
H   0
I   1
J   2
    3
    4